THIS BOOK IS THE PROPERTY OF:

STATE_____

PROVINCE _____

COUNTY _____

PARISH _____

SCHOOL DISTRICT_____

OTHER _____

Book No. _____

Enter information
in spaces
to the left as
instructed

ISSUED TO	Year Used	CONDITION	
		ISSUED	RETURNED
....	....		
....	....		
....	....		
....	....		
....	....		
....	....		
....	....		
....	....		

PUPILS to whom this textbook is issued must not write on any page
or mark any part of it in any way, consumable textbooks excepted.

1. Teachers should see that the pupil's name is clearly written in ink in the spaces above in every book issued.

2. The following terms should be used in recording the condition of the book: New; Good; Fair; Poor; Bad.

Foundations of Personal Fitness

Any
Body
Can...Be Fit!

Foundations of Personal Fitness

Any
Body
Can...Be Fit!

Don L. Rainey
Edward Marcus High School
Flower Mound, Texas

Tinker D. Murray
Southwest Texas State University
San Marcos, Texas

West Publishing Company
Minneapolis/St. Paul   New York   Los Angeles   San Francisco

Copyedit: Mary Berry, Naples Editing Service
Composition: Parkwood Composition Services, Inc.
Index: Terry Casey
Illustrations: Precision Graphics, Gary Carroll
Exercise & weightlifting images: David Hanover, Hanover
Photography (complete photo credits follow the index)
Cover image: David Hanover, Hanover Photography

WEST'S COMMITMENT TO THE ENVIRONMENT

In 1906, West Publishing Company began recycling materials left over from the production of books. This began a tradition of efficient and responsible use of resources. Today, 100% of our legal bound volumes are printed on acid-free, recycled paper consisting of 50% new paper pulp and 50% paper that has undergone a de-inking process. We also use vegetable-based inks to print all of our books. West recycles nearly 27,700,000 pounds of scrap paper annually—the equivalent of 229,300 trees. Since the 1960s, West has devised ways to capture and recycle waste inks, solvents, oils, and vapors created in the printing process. We also recycle plastics of all kinds, wood, glass, corrugated cardboard, and batteries, and have eliminated the use of polystyrene book packaging. We at West are proud of the longevity and the scope of our commitment to the environment.

West pocket parts and advance sheets are printed on recyclable paper and can be collected and recycled with newspapers. Staples do not have to be removed. Bound volumes can be recycled after removing the cover.

Production, Prepress, Printing and Binding by West Publishing Company.

British Library Cataloguing-in-Publication Data. A catalogue record for this book is available from the British Library.

COPYRIGHT © 1997   By WEST PUBLISHING COMPANY
                        610 Opperman Drive
                        P.O. Box 64526
                        St. Paul, MN 55164-0526

Library of Congress Cataloging–in–Publication Data

Murray, Tinker Dan, 1951–
    Foundations of Personal Fitness: Any Body Can Be Fit (student edition) ISBN #- 0-314-08465-7
    Foundations of Personal Fitness: Any Body Can Be Fit (Texas Teachers Wraparound edition)
        ISBN #- 0-314-08466-5
    Foundations of Personal Fitness: Any Body Can Be Fit (National Teachers Wraparound edition)
        ISBN #- 0-314-09622-1
    Includes index.
    Summary: Discusses the foundations of physical fitness, the benefits of regular exercise, and the advantages of weight training and proper nutrition.
    ISBN 0-314-08465-7 (Hard : alk paper)
1. Physical fitness—Health aspects—Juvenile literature. 2. Exercise—Physiological effect—
Juvenile literature. (1. Physical fitness. 2. Exercises. 3. Health.) I. Rainey, Don. II. Title.
RA781.M778 1997
613.7—dc20   96-4956
                                                                      CIP

About The Authors

Don L. Rainey

Don L. Rainey, M.S., is a physical educator and coordinator of health and physical education at Marcus High School in Flower Mound, Texas. He earned a bachelor of science degree in Health and Physical Education at Lamar University in 1971. He also earned a master of science degree in Health and Physical Education at Lamar in 1972, and has completed postgraduate studies at East Texas State University in Commerce, Texas. Don has taught the Foundations of Personal Fitness Course at Marcus High School for the past 12 years. He served as a national fitness consultant to the Boy's Clubs of America from 1983 to 1984. From 1985 to 1988 Don was a sub-committee member for the Governor's Commission on Physical Fitness that developed the Fit Youth Today Program. He served as Chair for the Texas Association for Health, Physical Education, Recreation, and Dance (TAHPERD) from 1985 to 1986. He was a founding member of the TAHPERD Foundations of Personal Fitness Course Committee in 1991, and continues to serve on that committee. He was named Teacher of the Year in Secondary Physical Education by TAHPERD in 1989 and was part of the Texas Teacher of the Year "Tour of Texas" in 1992. He was given the Honor Award from TAHPERD in 1994. He also was awarded a Physical Education Public Information (PEPI) Award in 1994. Don has conducted over forty workshops about the Foundations of Personal Fitness Course for physical educators. He has also presented and published numerous papers related to physical education and exercise science issues.

Tinker D. Murray

Tinker D. Murray, Ph.D., FACSM, is a professor and director of the human performance laboratory in the Health, Physical Education, and Recreation Department at Southwest Texas State University in San Marcos, Texas. He earned a bachelor of science degree in Physical Education and Biology from the University of Texas in 1973. He earned his master of education degree in Physical Education from Southwest Texas State University in 1976, and completed his Ph.D. in Physical Education from Texas A&M University in 1984. Tinker served as Director of Cardiac Rehabilitation at Brooke Army Medical Center from 1982 to 1984. Tinker has been a lecturer and examiner for the U.S.A. Track and Field Level II Coaching Certification Program since 1988. He served as the Vice Chair of the Governor's Commission for Physical Fitness in Texas from 1993-1994. Tinker was awarded a Physical Education Public Information (PEPI) Award in 1993 by the Texas Association for Health, Physical Education, Recreation, and Dance (TAHPERD) and was named TAHPERD Scholar for 1995. He also was given the Honor Award from TAHPERD in 1995. Tinker is a Fellow of the American College of Sports Medicine (ACSM) and certified as an ACSM Program Director. He served as the Chair of the TAHPERD Foundations of Personal Fitness Course Committee from 1991–1995 and is currently a member of the committee. He has conducted over twenty-five workshops about the Foundations of Personal Fitness Course for physical educators. Tinker has presented and published numerous papers related to physical education and exercise science issues.

Contents in Brief

Table of Contents

Any Body Can!

CONSUMER CORNER

Foreword

Health-related fitness programs are now clearly established to be important in the prevention of lifestyle generated diseases, including heart disease, diabetes, obesity, and even certain cancers.

The principles and concepts in *FOUNDATIONS OF PERSONAL FITNESS: Any Body Can Be Fit* are ones that will help with the understanding and development of health-related fitness programs for our students. These programs should be supported by all parents, teachers, physicians, and health care personnel. I strongly support them.

Steven P. Van Camp, M.D.
President,
American College of Sports Medicine,
1995–1996

Acknowledgements

To both of our wives, we appreciate you for helping make this book a reality and encouraging us to live up to what we said we ought to be able to do. A special thanks to all of our contributors who provided timely professional input and inspired us throughout this project. To Steven Van Camp, M.D. thanks for your medical advice and the foreword for this text. To Bill Squires, Ph.D. a special thanks for serving as our exercise science advisor for the text. We would also like to thank our editors, Bob Cassel, Mario Rodriguez, and Glenda Samples. We would like to thank all of our professional colleagues and friends from the Texas Association for Health, Physical Education, Recreation, and Dance (TAHPERD), the American Alliance of Health, Physical Education, Recreation, and Dance (AAHPERD), the American College of Sports Medicine (ACSM) and the Texas Regional Chapter of the American College of Sports Medicine (TACSM) for their support and guidance throughout our professional careers.

Reviewers

We would also like to acknowledge the following manuscript reviewers who made many valuable comments and suggestions during the early development stages of the project.

Jennifer Arant
Green County Technical Schools
Paragould, AR

Cinda Baer
Nimitz High School
Irving, TX

Dr. Robert Case
Sam Houston State University
Huntsville, TX

Dr. Paula Dohoney
Oklahoma State University
Stillwater, OK

Deanna Harris
Lake Highlands Junior High School
Dallas, TX

Dr. Mary McCabe
Hurst-Euless-Bedford ISD
Bedford, TX

Manuel Pacheco
J.M. Hanks High School
El Paso, TX

Sue Rehm
Byrd Middle School
Tulsa, OK

Marie Rossman
Trinity High School
Euless, TX

Thomas Schlarbaum
Hillsborough County Schools
Tampa, FL

Dr. Fred Wheeler
Pope High School
Marietta, GA

James Whitman
Charles Henderson Middle School
Troy, AL

Elly Zanin
Broward County Schools
Ft. Lauderdale, FL

Dedication

To my lovely wife, Julie — Thanks for all your love, patience, motivation, and professional expertise.
To my parents Louise and Bob — Thanks for your love and for encouraging me in my educational pursuits.
And, to my grandmother Rose — Thanks for your love and the great example of active living you provide at age 90.

Tinker

To my best and closest friend, my wife Reneé. Your support, encouragement, and assistance will be forever appreciated. To all of my family and friends, thank you for being a part of the successful completion of this book.

Don

Chapter 1

Foundations of Personal Fitness: Why Should It Be Important to You?

2

Introduction

Many research studies show the positive influence of physical fitness on physical and mental health, self-esteem, and learning. Physical fitness promotes self-confidence, enhances learning, and is society's wise investment in the future.

Emphasis on academic achievement produces knowledgeable individuals. However, an educated mind cannot repay society's investment when that mind resides in a body poorly prepared for a long, productive, and healthy life. All too often an individual's contribution to society is cut short by disability, sickness, or premature death. Society's investment in education yields maximum returns only when there is a sound mind in a healthy body.

This book has been designed to allow you to experience and become educated about the **ABCs** of a healthy, active, and fit lifestyle. It is our hope that in this course, you will develop positive health and fitness attitudes, skills, and behaviors that you will adopt and enjoy for the rest of your long and healthy life.

Don Rainey
Tinker D. Murray

Contents

Outcomes

After reading and studying this chapter, you will be able to:

1. Define and explain the terms related to personal fitness.
2. Explain how negative or positive attitudes and beliefs about personal fitness can influence your health and physical fitness.
3. Explain and identify modifiable and less modifiable risk factors and how they influence life expectancy.
4. Explain and identify the positive outcomes that physical activity, exercise, or both can have on your health and physical fitness level.
5. Explain and discuss the national goals and recommendations for physical activity, exercise, or both, for adolescents.
6. Define and explain the stages of your personal fitness continuum.

Key Terms

After reading and studying this chapter, you will be able to understand and provide practical definitions for the following terms:

personal fitness
health
wellness
functional health
physically active lifestyle
sedentary lifestyle
exercise
physical fitness
risk factor
hypokinetic
cardiovascular disease

hypertension
osteoporosis
obesity
cholesterol
triglyceride
heart attack
stroke
atherosclerosis
high-density lipoprotein (HDL)

low-density lipoprotein (LDL)
very low density lipoprotein (VLDL)
stress
stressor
distress
eustress
predisposition
life expectancy
longevity

INTRODUCTION

Welcome to your course on the foundations of personal fitness! This course is different from any of the physical education courses that you may have taken in elementary, junior high, or middle school. In those courses you primarily played games or participated in sports activities. In this course you will learn that Any Body Can develop a plan for a physically active lifestyle that you can use now and throughout your adult life. You are about to start a journey during which you will learn about and experience personal fitness in a positive and successful way. Personal fitness is both obtainable and enjoyable. It is as easy as A, B, C: Any Body Can be fit!

This book and course have been designed to challenge you to do these things:

- Become educated about your personal levels of physical activity and physical fitness.
- Successfully experience the benefits of physical activity and physical fitness conditioning.
- Assess your own level of physical fitness and progress in the course.
- Design a physical activity and physical fitness program that can meet your individual needs now and in the future.

Throughout this book, you will be asked to explain, demonstrate, and experience the concepts presented to you by completing the "Active Mind/Active Body" activities. These activities will help you become responsible for planning, developing, and maintaining your own healthy lifestyle. In the first "Active Mind/Active Body" activity, on page 6, you will examine your current knowledge about what a physically active lifestyle is and what it involves. Completing this activity will increase your knowledge and help you identify the areas of fitness requiring further study.

SECTION 1   Personal Fitness: What's It All About?

personal fitness

the result of a way of life that includes living an active lifestyle, maintaining good or better levels of physical fitness, consuming a healthy diet, and practicing good health behaviors throughout life.

health

a state of well-being that includes physical, mental, emotional, spiritual, and social aspects.

Personal fitness has many definitions because the term means many different things to different people. In this section you will learn about some of the key concepts that are common to any definition of personal fitness. After concluding this section, you might want to create your own definition of fitness.

Personal Fitness and Its Benefits

Personal fitness is the result of a way of life that includes living an active lifestyle, maintaining good or better levels of physical fitness, consuming a healthy diet, and practicing good health behaviors throughout life. **Health** is a state of well-being that includes physical, mental, emotional, spiritual, and social aspects. Good health is

• *You can participate in personal fitness activities in a number of different ways. With such a wide range of sports and exercises to choose from, you will be sure to find activities that match your interests and abilities.*

wellness

the attainment and maintenance of a moderate to high level of physical, mental, emotional, spiritual, and social health.

functional health

a person's physical ability to function independently in life, without assistance.

physically active lifestyle

a way of living that regularly includes physical activity such as walking, climbing stairs, or participating in recreational movements.

sedentary lifestyle

an inactive lifestyle.

important to teens and adults, regardless of their age. Good health is necessary for performing normal daily tasks.

Wellness is the attainment and maintenance of a moderate to high level of physical, mental, emotional, spiritual, and social health. Wellness is a goal that requires a lifetime of commitment, from young adulthood through the Golden Years. In striving for wellness, you are trying to reach your full potential in all the areas of your life.

Functional health is a term that describes a person's physical ability to function independently in life, without assistance. If your functional health status drops below minimal levels, you can lose your physical independence in daily living. Examples of the loss of physical independence include losing the ability to walk, to drive a car, or to feed yourself. A person may have functional health but may possess a low level of wellness. For example, a person may still be able to drive his or her car but have the signs and symptoms of cardiovascular disease.

A **physically active lifestyle** is a way of living that regularly includes physical activity such as walking from class to class, climbing stairs, or participating in recreational activities. Researchers have recently shown that people who live a physically active lifestyle are able to maintain their functional health status longer than people who lead an inactive lifestyle, or **sedentary lifestyle**. Inactive people are often referred to as "couch potatoes."

Active Mind! Active Body!

What Do You Know Now about Personal Fitness?

The following is a series of 50 statements about personal fitness. They are designed to evaluate your current knowledge about health and physical fitness. Some of the statements are true, and some are false. Try to be as honest as you possibly can with each of your answers. (Write your answers on a separate sheet of paper. **Do Not** write in this book.) If you are unsure about your answer, mark "unsure" for your response. There will be no grade assigned to this activity, so feel free to express your opinions. At the completion of the course, do this activity again to determine if your knowledge about physical fitness has increased.

	A I Am Certain It Is True	B I Think It Is True	C I Am Unsure	D I Think It Is False	E I Am Certain It Is False
1. People who have well-toned, fit muscles are automatically also cardiovascularly fit.	___	___	___	___	___
2. Regular exercise can reduce the heart rate at rest.	___	___	___	___	___
3. Many of the cardiovascular benefits that result from regular exercise are gradually lost if exercise is not continued.	___	___	___	___	___
4. A single exercise session will have little lasting effect on the cardiovascular system.	___	___	___	___	___
5. Unexercised muscles can turn to fat.	___	___	___	___	___
6. Regular exercise can help reduce a person's resting blood pressure.	___	___	___	___	___
7. Regular exercise can increase the strength of your bones.	___	___	___	___	___
8. Ballistic stretching is an unsafe method for improving flexibility.	___	___	___	___	___
9. Isometric exercises involve static muscle contractions with little or no movement.	___	___	___	___	___
10. Regular exercise has little effect on the body's ability to use fat.	___	___	___	___	___
11. Swimming is an excellent way to increase one's cardiorespiratory endurance capacity.	___	___	___	___	___

	A I Am Certain It Is True	B I Think It Is True	C I Am Unsure	D I Think It Is False	E I Am Certain It Is False
12. Muscular strength is the ability to move a heavy weight one time.	____	____	____	____	____
13. Playing soccer regularly can improve one's cardiorespiratory endurance capacity.	____	____	____	____	____
14. Weight training is a good way to improve one's cardiorespiratory endurance capacity.	____	____	____	____	____
15. Disorders such as obesity, high blood pressure, and back pain can be a result of no exercise.	____	____	____	____	____
16. A person with a high level of muscular strength has little danger of heart attack.	____	____	____	____	____
17. Skill-related components of fitness measure such things as balance, agility, coordination, and speed.	____	____	____	____	____
18. The overload principle involves three factors: intensity, duration, and frequency.	____	____	____	____	____
19. Jogging, swimming, cross-country skiing, and cycling are all examples of aerobic activity.	____	____	____	____	____
20. Cardiorespiratory endurance activities must be repeated at least five times per week in order to get any benefit.	____	____	____	____	____
21. Cardiorespiratory endurance refers to the body's ability to perform exercises for an extended period of time.	____	____	____	____	____
22. The target heart rate level for a healthy person building cardiorespiratory endurance is 60 to 80 percent of one's maximum heart rate.	____	____	____	____	____
23. Cool-down activities help prevent blood pooling.	____	____	____	____	____
24. Warm-up and stretching exercises will reduce the muscle soreness often felt when first starting an exercise program.	____	____	____	____	____
25. Cool-down periods are just as important as warm-up periods.	____	____	____	____	____
26. A weight training program is best used for building muscular endurance.	____	____	____	____	____

(Continued on next page)

What Do You Know Now about Personal Fitness? (continued)

	A I Am Certain It Is True	B I Think It Is True	C I Am Unsure	D I Think It Is False	E I Am Certain It Is False
27. The benefits gained from exercise depend in part on the number of days and the length of time that a person exercises.	___	___	___	___	___
28. The warm-up and stretching period of an exercise session need not be more than one or two minutes.	___	___	___	___	___
29. All individuals should have a complete physical exam before starting an exercise program.	___	___	___	___	___
30. Participating in an activity program where everyone exercises at the same intensity and frequency can be dangerous.	___	___	___	___	___
31. Participation in a regular exercise program can reduce one's ability to sleep soundly.	___	___	___	___	___
32. Exercise can provide an opportunity to reduce stress.	___	___	___	___	___
33. Experts believe there is very little relationship between physical fitness and academic performance.	___	___	___	___	___
34. Regular exercise can slow down the natural aging process.	___	___	___	___	___
35. Physically active individuals are less likely than inactive individuals to develop cardiovascular disease.	___	___	___	___	___
36. Regular exercise combined with dieting is a more effective way to reduce fat than just exercising.	___	___	___	___	___
37. The number of calories burned during exercise depends on the type and the intensity of the exercise.	___	___	___	___	___
38. An obese person uses the same number of calories as a light person during comparable exercise periods.	___	___	___	___	___
39. An individual's body fat can be determined by skinfold measurements.	___	___	___	___	___
40. Regular exercise increases the amount of oxygen the body can use while exercising.	___	___	___	___	___
41. A person's health-related fitness refers to how that person's body looks.	___	___	___	___	___
42. Exercising abdominal muscles may help prevent lower back muscle pain.	___	___	___	___	___
43. Hypokinetic diseases are a result of too much activity.	___	___	___	___	___

Foundations of Personal Fitness: Why Should It Be Important to You?

9

	A I Am Certain It Is True	B I Think It Is True	C I Am Unsure	D I Think It Is False	E I Am Certain It Is False
44. Static stretching is the recommended method for conducting flexibility exercises.	___	___	___	___	___
45. A well-balanced diet can provide you with all the vitamins and minerals you need.	___	___	___	___	___
46. High repetitions during an exercise will produce more strength benefits.	___	___	___	___	___
47. You can never have too much flexibility.	___	___	___	___	___
48. The principle of progression deals with exercise improvement.	___	___	___	___	___
49. Exercise workouts should be at least 30 minutes long to provide any benefit.	___	___	___	___	___
50. The benefits of regular exercise are reduced as you become older.	___	___	___	___	___

exercise

physical activity that is planned, structured, repetitive, and results in the improvement or maintenance of personal fitness.

physical fitness

a level of individual physical ability that allows a person to perform daily physical tasks effectively with enough energy reserves for recreational activities or unexpected physical challenges.

By engaging in regular physical activity or **exercise**, you can improve or maintain an acceptable level of physical fitness. Physically active people are more likely to live life to its fullest. They add more than just years to their life. They add life to their years, by feeling and looking better.

Physical fitness is defined as a level of individual physical ability that allows a person to perform normal daily physical tasks effectively with enough energy reserves for recreational activities or unexpected physical challenges. Physical fitness is an outcome of a physically active lifestyle or exercise program that is practiced over time. A more detailed explanation of the different types of physical fitness will be presented in Chapter 4.

Moderate to high levels of physical fitness are associated with good health and wellness. Physical fitness is also related to how efficiently the heart, lungs, circulation, bones, and muscles function. Young adults who maintain a physically active lifestyle now and remain physically fit throughout life can expect a higher quality of life. They also reduce their risks for developing chronic diseases (high blood pressure, heart disease, stroke, and so on). Sedentary living habits and low physical fitness levels have a negative impact on both health and daily living.

It is important for you to understand that you *do not* have to be an athlete to reach moderate to high levels of physical fitness. Remember, **A**ny **B**ody **C**an be fit! Will you?

RUBES   by Leigh Rubin

"... Therefore, after a 40-year case study, it is my contention that couch potatoes actually begin to develop early in life as tater tots."

Attitudes and Beliefs about Personal Fitness

Both young and old people often fail to realize the importance of being physically active or engaging in exercise to maintain good health. They have negative attitudes or beliefs about physical activity, exercise, and physical fitness programs for a variety of reasons. Some of these reasons follow:

- They lack time.
- They are in poor physical condition.
- They have a high percentage of body fat.
- They have unrealistic physical fitness goals or expectations.
- They lack accurate knowledge about physical fitness.
- They feel that they are not athletic.
- They are afraid of physically overstraining themselves.
- They have had negative experiences with physical activity, exercise, or both.
- They have concerns about negative peer pressure.

If you have many of these negative attitudes, the odds are that you will live a sedentary lifestyle as you get older. By learning more about your own personal fitness you can develop positive experiences leading to an active and more productive lifestyle.

At this point, we challenge you to explore your attitudes and beliefs about physical activity, exercise, and physical fitness programs. From the questionnaire in the "Active Mind/Active Body" activity on the next two pages, identify your current attitudes and beliefs. If you do not already have positive attitudes about physical activity, exercise, and physical fitness, we hope you will develop them through your experiences in this course. If you are inactive or do not exercise regularly, we challenge you to change your behaviors and improve your physical fitness. You can do it. In fact, **A**ny **B**ody **C**an!

- *Physical activity and exercise can promote positive mental attitudes.*

SECTION 1 REVIEW

Answer the following questions on a separate sheet of paper:

1. What is the difference between functional health and the absence of disease?
2. Why is it important for you to pursue wellness throughout your life?
3. List five negative attitudes and beliefs that are associated with becoming a "couch potato."

Active Mind! Active Body!

What Are Your Current Attitudes and Beliefs about Personal Fitness?

The following is a series of 25 statements of attitudes and beliefs about physical activity, exercise, and physical fitness. They are designed to evaluate your current attitudes and beliefs about physical activity, exercise, and physical fitness. Use the scale to rate how you feel about the statements presented. Try to be as honest as you possibly can with each of your answers. If you are unsure about your answer, mark "unsure" for your response. (Write your answers on a separate sheet of paper. **Do Not** write in this book.) There will be no grade assigned to this activity, so feel free to express your opinions. At the completion of the course do this activity again and determine if your attitudes and beliefs about physical activity, exercise, and physical fitness have changed.

	A I Agree Strongly	B I Agree	C I Am Unsure	D I Disagree	E I Disagree Strongly
1. I don't have time to exercise.	___	___	___	___	___
2. Regular physical activity and exercise make me feel better.	___	___	___	___	___
3. I am not very athletic.	___	___	___	___	___
4. I have always enjoyed participation in physical activities and exercise.	___	___	___	___	___
5. I enjoy physical education classes.	___	___	___	___	___
6. I have a moderate to high level of health and physical fitness.	___	___	___	___	___
7. I am happy with my physical appearance.	___	___	___	___	___
8. I like to walk and jog.	___	___	___	___	___
9. I like team games and sports.	___	___	___	___	___
10. I like to lift weights.	___	___	___	___	___
11. I like to engage in physical activities with friends.	___	___	___	___	___
12. Exercising twice a week is all I need to do to stay in shape.	___	___	___	___	___
13. Athletes, cheerleaders, and band members should be excused from taking physical education.	___	___	___	___	___

(Continued on next page)

What Are Your Current Attitudes and Beliefs about Personal Fitness? *(continued)*

	A I Agree Strongly	B I Agree	C I Am Unsure	D I Disagree	E I Disagree Strongly
14. Learning about personal fitness will be valuable to me later in life.	___	___	___	___	___
15. Physical education classes have always been boring to me.	___	___	___	___	___
16. Physical education should be a required class.	___	___	___	___	___
17 Engaging in physical activity or exercise helps me forget my problems and reduces my stress levels.	___	___	___	___	___
18. Grades should not be given in physical education.	___	___	___	___	___
19. I would take physical education as an elective class even if it were not a required course.	___	___	___	___	___
20. I know how to design my own personal fitness program.	___	___	___	___	___
21. Personal fitness teaches self-discipline.	___	___	___	___	___
22. Doing physical activity and exercise can improve your health.	___	___	___	___	___
23. After a day at school, I am too tired to exercise.	___	___	___	___	___
24. I would rather watch sports on television than actually participate in sports.	___	___	___	___	___
25. I feel guilty when I don't exercise everyday.					

SECTION 2 Risk Factors and Your Personal Fitness

In the United States today people can expect to live about seventy-five years. By the time you are seventy-five, however, the number of years a person can expect to live may be higher.

It may be difficult for you to think of yourself becoming older. Eventually you will age, though, just as your parents and grandparents have. Therefore, it is important for you to understand and develop healthy personal fitness habits now.

Risk Factors for Heart and Artery Disease

- Heredity (history of CVD prior to age 55 in family members).
- Gender (being male).
- Smoking.
- Hypertension.
- High blood cholesterol, high LDL, and/or low HDL.
- Glucose intolerance (diabetes).
- Lack of exercise.
- Obesity (30 percent or more overweight).
- Stress.

risk factor

a condition or trait that increases the likelihood that people will develop chronic diseases.

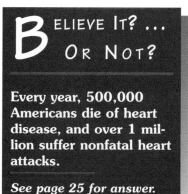

BELIEVE IT? ...
OR NOT?

Every year, 500,000 Americans die of heart disease, and over 1 million suffer nonfatal heart attacks.

See page 25 for answer.

Unfortunately, many adults die or become disabled prematurely (at age fifty or sixty, for example) because of chronic diseases for which they are at high risk. Chronic diseases are illnesses that usually develop over several years. They can cause disability and even death. Examples of chronic diseases include heart disease, cancer, hypertension, and osteoporosis. The good news is that you can reduce your chance for developing many chronic diseases.

Health **risk factors** are variables or conditions that increase the likelihood that people will develop chronic diseases. You can modify or influence many risk factors, at least in part, if you practice positive health behaviors. In fact, research has shown that the health behaviors that you establish as a young adult will most likely continue into your later adult life. The health behaviors you adopt now may either benefit or injure your health. Thus, it is important that you be able to recognize the risk factors that you currently have. You can then develop and practice a plan to reduce or eliminate your risk factors, if possible.

- *Are you a couch potato? It is okay to relax in front of the television from time to time, if you don't overdo it and you get plenty of exercise.*

Risk Factors You Can Modify

You can control many health risk factors. Others you can do little about, but your lifestyle can help you control their effects on your life.

A person who is **hypokinetic** throughout life is at an increased risk for problems such as **cardiovascular disease**, **hypertension**, low back pain, **osteoporosis**, **obesity**, negative emotional stress, colon cancer, and high blood **cholesterol** and **triglyceride** levels.

Research has shown that adults who are sedentary die from chronic diseases at a much higher rate than do more active individuals. Figure 1.1 shows that when adults move from low fitness levels (sedentary) to moderately active fitness levels, they significantly reduce their risk of dying from chronic disease. (An example of a moderate level is walking two miles in about thirty minutes, four days per week.) If adults obtain a higher fitness level (for example, jog two

hypokinetic
physically inactive, or sedentary.

cardiovascular disease
heart and blood vessel disease.

hypertension
high blood pressure.

osteoporosis
a condition in which the bones are porous and brittle.

obesity
excessive body fat; excessive weight (20% or more above appropriate weight).

cholesterol
a blood fat.

triglyceride
a blood fat.

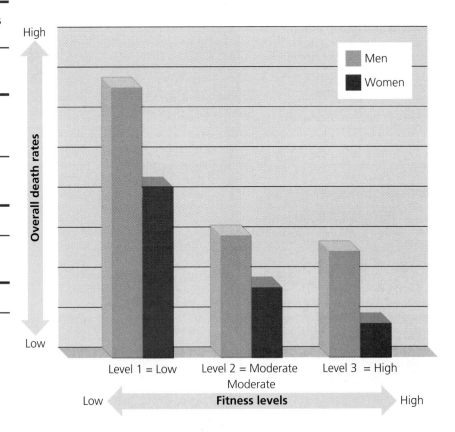

• **Figure 1.1** *The Relationship Between Levels of Physical Fitness and All Causes of Death.*
Source: Adapted with permission from Blair, S.N. "Exercise and Health," *Sports Science Exchange* (Gatorade Sports Science Institute, 1990), Vol. 3, no. 29: 1–6.

How Physically Active Are You Now?

On a separate sheet of paper, answer the questions below "yes" or "no." For each question answered yes, give yourself the number of points indicated. Add the points to determine your level of physical activity.

Occupation and Daily Activities

1. I usually walk to and from school and work (at least ½ mile each way). (1 point)
2. I usually take the stairs rather than use elevators or escalators. (1 point)
3. My typical daily physical activity is best described by the following statement:
   a. Most of my day is spent walking to class, sitting in class or at home, or in light activity. (0 points)
   b. Most of the day is spent in moderate activity such as fast walking. (4 points)
   c. My typical day includes several hours of heavy physical activity (football, volleyball, basketball, gym workout, or the like). (9 points)

Leisure Activities

4. I spend a few hours in light leisure activity each week (such as slow canoeing or slow cycling). (1 point)
5. I hike or bike (at a moderate pace) once a week or more on the average. (1 point)
6. At least once a week, I participate for an hour or more in vigorous dancing, such as aerobic or folk dancing. (1 point)
7. I play racquetball or tennis at least once a week. (2 points)
8. I often walk for exercise or recreation. (1 point)
9. When I feel bothered by pressures at school, work, or home, I use exercise as a way to relax. (1 point)
10. Two or more times a week, I perform calisthenic exercises (sit-ups, push-ups, etc.) for at least 10 minutes per session. (3 points)
11. I regularly participate in yoga or perform stretching exercises. (2 points)
12. Twice a week or more, I engage in weight training for at least 30 minutes. (4 points)
13. I participate in active recreational sports such as volleyball, baseball, or softball.

(Continued on next page)

How Physically Active Are You Now? *(continued)*

    a. about once a week. (2 points)

    b. about twice a week. (4 points)

    c. three times a week or more. (7 points)

14. At least once a week, I participate in vigorous fitness activities like jogging or swimming (at least 20 continuous minutes per session).

    a. about once a week. (3 points)

    b. about twice a week. (5 points)

    c. three times a week or more. (10 points)

Total Points Earned _____

Scoring:

0–5 points—inactive.   This amount of physical activity leads to a steady decline in fitness.

6–11 points—moderately active.   This amount of physical activity slows fitness loss but will not maintain fitness.

12–20 points—active.   This amount of physical activity will build or maintain an acceptable level of physical fitness.

21 points or over—very active.   This amount of physical activity will maintain a high level of fitness.

Source: Reprinted with permission from F. S. Sizer, E. N. Whitney, L. K. DeBruyne, *Making Life Choices: Health Skills and Concepts* (St. Paul: West, 1994), 240. Activity adapted from Russell Pate (University of South Carolina, Department of Exercise Science).

miles in about twenty minutes, four days per week), they reduce their risk even further. The most important point, however, is that people should increase their physical activity enough to get out of the low fitness category.

To figure out how your current level of physical fitness would rate health-wise, please do the "Active Mind/Active Body" activity that begins on the preceding page.

Smoking.   Chronic smokers (people who have smoked consistently for ten, twenty, or even thirty years) have an increased risk for heart and lung disease compared with nonsmokers. For example, smokers are two times as likely as nonsmokers to have a **heart attack**. Smokers tend to be less active than nonsmokers, which increases their risk of premature chronic disease.

heart attack

the blockage of vessels feeding the heart, causing the death of heart tissue.

• *Smoking increases your risk for chronic heart and lung diseases.*

stroke

blockage of blood flow to the brain.

Smokers who stop smoking and choose an active lifestyle can reduce their heart attack risk level to that of nonsmokers in two to three years. Although it is very difficult to stop smoking, it is never too late to quit smoking and begin a more active lifestyle. (Obviously, it is best never to start.)

Hypertension.   A person with high blood pressure (hypertension) is at increased risk for **stroke** and heart attack. There are few symptoms of hypertension, which is one reason why it can be so dangerous. Hypertension is associated with genetic makeup, aging, a high salt or sodium intake, obesity, and also by excessive alcohol consumption.

Blood pressure is easy to measure. Do you know what yours is? Everyone should know what it is (see Chapter 5).

When physicians diagnose people as having hypertension, they usually recommend weight loss (if appropriate). People are also told to modify their diets (for example, consume less sodium) and to become more physically active.

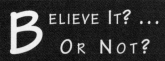

A healthy, active lifestyle practiced over time can add 2.5 years to your life. This is important for maintaining physical independence later in life.

See page 25 for answer.

• *Many foods that we eat are high in fat and cholesterol.*

atherosclerosis

a disease process that causes substances to build up inside arteries, blocking blood flow.

high-density lipoprotein (HDL)

"good cholesterol"; the type of cholesterol that is associated with a lower atherosclerosis risk.

low-density lipoprotein (LDL)

"bad cholesterol"; a type of cholesterol that is associated with higher atherosclerosis risk.

very low density lipoprotein (VLDL)

"bad cholesterol"; a type of cholesterol that is associated with higher atherosclerosis risk.

High Levels of Cholesterol and Triglycerides.   A person with an elevated level of cholesterol is at an increased risk for the development of **atherosclerosis**. The total amount of cholesterol in the blood is determined by the combination of the fats we eat, as well as the fats produced by our bodies.

Cholesterol is usually classified as either "good cholesterol" or "bad cholesterol." **High-density lipoprotein (HDL)** is "good cholesterol" and is associated with a lower atherosclerosis risk. **Low-density lipoprotein (LDL)** and **very low density lipoprotein (VLDL)** are types of "bad cholesterol" and are associated with higher atherosclerosis risk.

Triglycerides are another type of blood fat. Triglycerides are also usually associated with a higher atherosclerosis risk. Therefore, it is important to control and limit fat intake in the diet. In that way we can help lower our cholesterol and triglyceride levels or maintain acceptable levels. Maintaining appropriate levels of personal fitness can also help control normal cholesterol and triglyceride levels.

Body Composition.   The amount of water, bone, muscle, and fat in your body determines your body composition. A person who carries too much body fat is at an increased risk for problems such as hypertension, heart disease, and diabetes mellitus (high blood sugar disease). Obesity (excessive body fat) often begins in childhood

REMEMBER This!

Smoking, reducing stress, eating right, and being physically active are all behaviors that you decide to include or exclude in your lifestyle. A wise and healthy person recognizes the importance of this point. Make *your* lifestyle choices wisely.

---

stress

the physical and psychological responses of your body as you try to adapt to stressors.

---

stressor

anything that requires you to adapt and cope with either positive or negative situations.

---

distress

excess negative stress, such as fear, anger, or confusion.

---

eustress

positive stress; an enjoyable type of stress.

and usually persists into adulthood, unless an obese person alters his or her diet and adopts an active lifestyle.

A person with too little body fat (excessive leanness), in contrast, is at risk for problems such as osteoporosis and certain forms of cancer. Excessive leanness is usually associated with abnormal eating and psychological or addictive behaviors that require professional attention.

Stress. **Stress** is defined as the physical and psychological responses of your body as you try to adapt to stressors. A **stressor** is anything that requires you to adapt and cope with either positive or negative situations.

Distress is excess negative stress, such as fear, anger, confusion, or other similar mood states in your life. Distress can increase your risk for chronic disease (such as heart attack) or can make a disease process worse. Distress can produce negative physical responses (increased heart rate, increased hormone levels, headaches, and so on). It can also have negative emotional effects (anxiety, sleeplessness, depression, and so on).

Eustress is positive stress. It is an enjoyable type of stress, such as what you might feel in being elected class president, scoring well on an exam, or obtaining your driver's license.

A few ways to cope positively with stress include changing your diet (eating breakfast regularly and reducing caffeine intake), meditation (reflecting about a pleasant event in your life), or physical activity (brisk walking or weight lifting). Dealing with stress in a positive way is something that will challenge you daily for the rest of your life. Therefore, future chapters in this text will present discussions and activities that focus on teaching you to cope with stress in positive ways. Look for the "Stress Break" strategies in the margins throughout the remainder of the book.

Less Modifiable Risk Factors

Three health risk factors related to death or disability due to chronic disease are age, gender (sex), and heredity (genetics). You cannot change or even completely modify these risks. You can, however, live an active lifestyle that minimizes the consequences of these factors on your good health.

Age. An older person tends to be at increased risk for diseases such as high blood pressure, heart disease, and cancer as compared with younger individuals. This makes sense when you realize that most people who die in old age (at ages seventy, eighty, ninety, and beyond) die as the result of chronic disease processes. You cannot change your age. However, you can optimize your functional health as you age and live a higher-quality lifestyle by being physically active and by eating a healthy diet throughout your life.

REMEMBER This!

You cannot change your age, your gender, or your heredity. However, you can choose to be physically active and to eat wisely. These behaviors will help you maximize your functional health for years to come and reduce your health risks as much as possible.

---

predisposition

---

susceptibility to increased health risk due to genetic makeup.

Gender (Sex).   Some health risk factors are influenced by gender. For example, men between the ages of forty and fifty have a higher risk for heart disease than do women of the same age range. The risk for heart disease for women increases dramatically after age fifty and then matches that of men. Women have a higher risk than men for osteoporosis beginning at ages forty-five to fifty. The risk for osteoporosis for men increases dramatically after age seventy and then matches that of women.

It is important that you recognize the health risk factors associated with your gender. Even if you have an increased health risk due to your gender, there are behaviors that can help you modify and minimize that risk. For example, a woman is at an increased risk for osteoporosis. However, she can take calcium and hormone supplements and exercise regularly to modify and reduce that risk (see Chapters 7 and 10).

Heredity (Genetics).   A person may be born with a **predisposition** to increased health risk for various disease processes. For example, some individuals are born with extremely high blood cholesterol levels. They develop atherosclerosis at an early age (in their

• *Heredity can influence your health risks.*

Stress Break

Have you ever noticed what happens to your heart rate and rate of breathing when you get angry or frightened? Both your heart rate and your breathing speed up very quickly, which is a normal response of your body to stress. This response is caused by a chemical that is released into your bloodstream. The chemical, called *adrenaline,* can be very helpful in times of emergency. Other reactions to adrenaline include muscle tension, pupil dilation, increased blood nutrients, and raised blood pressure.

Frequent and prolonged sessions of stress or high levels of adrenaline can be dangerous. Problems such as high blood pressure, ulcers, and diabetes can result. However, a good fitness program can help use up or metabolize excess adrenaline. Be active!

twenties or thirties), which can cause them to have heart attacks and die prematurely.

Fortunately, even if your family has a history of a disease, you can often modify your behaviors or lifestyle to minimize your own risks. For example, if your father or grandfather had a heart attack before age sixty, you have most likely inherited some heart disease risk. However, by controlling such health risk factors as cholesterol intake, obesity, physical inactivity, and so on, you can significantly reduce your overall risk for a heart attack.

Now you know about the modifiable and less modifiable risk factors associated with chronic diseases or disease processes. Next, it is important for you to identify the risk factors you already have. Take a moment and check off the risks that you have in the "Active Mind/Active Body" activity on the next page. It is not unusual for young adults to have at least one or more risk factors. However, it is important that you develop a personal risk factor modification plan to minimize the risks that you do have.

SECTION 2 REVIEW

Answer the following questions on a separate sheet of paper:

1. How can you eliminate each of the six modifiable health risk factors?
2. What is the significance of moving from a low level of fitness to a moderate level of fitness? (See Figure 1.1.)
3. Identify two positive and two negative behaviors you might use to deal with the stress in your life. Give examples and explain them.

SECTION 3   Personal Fitness and Positive Outcomes

Numerous health benefits of physical activity and exercise have been documented for adults. National organizations have recommended physical activity and exercise programs as ways to provide health benefits to young adults as well. People who are physically active and have a personal fitness program can expect many benefits. Section 3 will discuss the benefits of personal fitness.

Improvements in Physical Appearance

> " Health and intellect are the two blessings of life.
>
> Menander
> c. 342–292 BC "

Almost everyone is concerned, to some degree, about physical appearance. Young adults are particularly preoccupied with their appearance. Often people base much of their feelings of self-esteem and self-worth on how they look. Physical size and shape, to some degree, can determine if a person is to be an athlete or a nonathlete, or if a person is accepted in certain social settings.

During your young adult years, you may experience periods of growth that are governed by your genetic makeup. By engaging in regular physical activity or exercise, combined with a sound nutrition plan, you can help bring about some of your desired physical growth changes. These include increased strength, muscle tone, and body size, along with weight control and reduced levels of body fat. Your personal fitness behaviors will have an influence on your physical appearance both now and in the future.

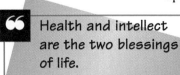

Active Mind! Active Body!

What Are Your Health Risk Factors?

Identify the health risk factors that you have from the list below. Then determine which ones you can modify. Mark your answers on a separate sheet of paper.

	Yes	No	Don't Know	Can Modify	Cannot Modify
1. Sedentary lifestyle					
2. Smoking					
3. Hypertension					
4. High level of blood fats					
5. Obesity					
6. Excessive stress					
7. Age					
8. Gender					
9. Heredity					

Enhancement of Self-Esteem

Most people agree that self-esteem is a powerful force within each individual. It enables people to cope better with the basic challenges of life. A healthy, fit person is more likely to experience the feelings of happiness, self-worth, and a sense of enjoying their accomplishments. Simply put, people who are fit, healthy, and feel good about their health and physical appearance are more likely to live an enjoyable, productive life. Look at Figure 1.2 to see some of the more important factors affecting your self-esteem, and especially your *physical* self-concept.

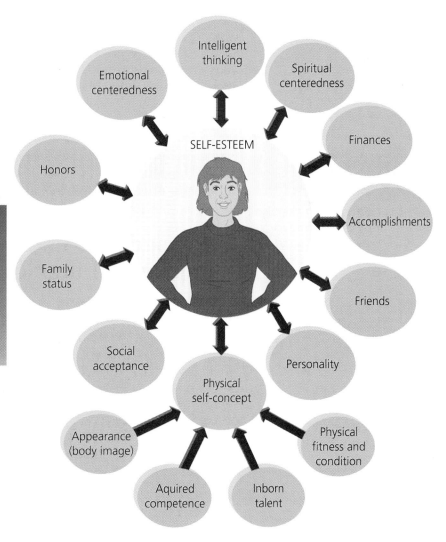

• ***Figure 1.2***   *Factors Influencing Self-Esteem.*

• *Physical activity and exercise can have a positive influence on your academic and physical performance.*

life expectancy

the number of years a person can expect to live.

longevity

the actual length of a person's life.

Stress Reduction

As mentioned earlier, there are two kinds of stress: positive and negative. As a young adult, you can't escape being bombarded every day with stressors that lead to both types of stress. How you deal with stressors, however, can and will have a large impact on your life. Will you respond in positive, productive ways, or will you respond in negative, possibly unhealthy ways? You will need to consider and develop coping strategies that work for you. Regular physical activity or exercise combined with a sound nutrition plan can be a good step in the right direction.

Improvements in Academic and Physical Performance

Regular participation in physical activity, exercise, or both has been shown to enhance student academic performance, as well as to speed up the rate at which we learn physical skills. These observations are based on the fact that active students often have greater attention spans, have higher energy levels, and miss fewer days of school. Similarly, workers in business and industry settings who participate in wellness programs have higher physical working capacities and are absent fewer days than workers who do not participate. Furthermore, active employees have enhanced social interactions, reduced boredom, and improved mental attitudes. Therefore, adopting a physically active lifestyle can improve your academic success, as well as your job and physical performance.

Increased Life Expectancy and Improved Functional Health

Physical activity and exercise increase muscular strength and endurance and cause people to burn or expend energy. Researchers have shown that an active lifestyle improves blood cholesterol and triglyceride levels. Physical activity, exercise, or both help people feel better and help them cope with emotional stress. Physically active people are also less likely to smoke or begin smoking. For these reasons, physical activity and exercise not only have positive influences on cardiovascular disease risks, hypertension, preventable cancers, obesity, osteoporosis, and low back pain but also can increase **life expectancy** and **longevity**.

Figure 1.3 shows two different ways in which fifteen-year-old students might age and influence their functional health. It is important to note that in theory, the physically inactive person (life expectancy = seventy-five) would not live as long as the physically active person (life expectancy = eighty-six). The graph also illustrates that the inactive person would most likely lose functional health at age sixty-

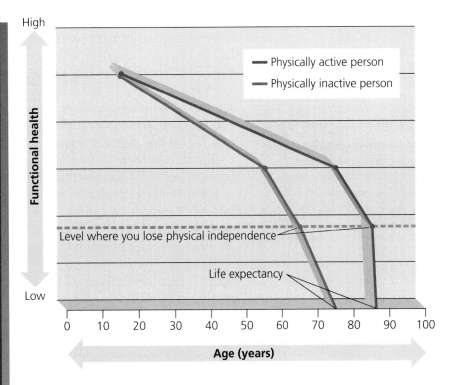

• **Figure 1.3** *The Influence of a Physically Active Lifestyle on Functional Health.*

Source: Theory adapted from S. N. Blair (Cooper Institute for Aerobics Research, 1996).

two—earlier than the active person, who probably would lose it at age eighty-five. The physically active person not only would live longer but would probably have a higher quality of life. Furthermore, the active person would minimize the time that he or she was physically dependent on others.

As you have probably heard, government leaders are very concerned about controlling the costs of health care in the United States. One of the least expensive and most productive methods for reducing health-care costs is to encourage people to develop and maintain healthy, physically active lifestyles. It is estimated that 60 percent of all current U.S. health-care costs can be attributed to unhealthy lifestyles. As an adult, wouldn't you rather spend your hard-earned money on new cars and vacations than on doctor and hospital bills? An active lifestyle can make the difference.

As you can see in Figure 1.4 on the next page, functional health changes with age in different ways, depending on the changes in a person's physical activity patterns and percentage of body fat. For example, let's imagine a thirty-year-old male who is moderately active (4, for example, on a Personal Activity Rating (PAR) scale of 0 to 7, with 0 = inactive and 7 = highly active).

Let's further imagine that this moderately active male has 20 percent body fat. Now let's look at how our imaginary 30-year-old might age in several different ways. Suppose that the person moves to a high physical activity level (PAR = 7) and, as he ages, reduces his body fat by five percent. He will maintain a high level of functional health. If, however, the person increases his physical activity level slightly (PAR = 5) and maintains his present percentage of body fat, he will still have a moderate level of functional health at age seventy. But, more importantly, if the person becomes sedentary (like many adults) and increases his body fat to 30 percent, he will most likely lose his functional health by age seventy (which is premature).

Remember, health-care costs are lower for people who maintain higher levels of functional health. In other words, the greatest amount of health-care dollars are spent on people who have lost their functional health.

• *You have a choice—Be Active!*

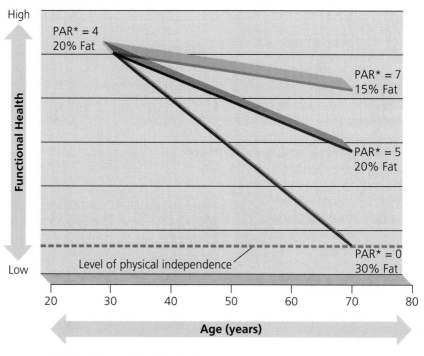

* PAR = Personal Activity Rating

• ***Figure 1.4***   *Projected Changes in Functional Health with Regard to Age, Changes in Physical Activity Patterns, and Percentage of Body Fat.*

Source: Adapted with permission from A. S. Jackson, et al. "Changes in Aerobic Power of Men, Ages 25–70 Years," *Medicine and Science in Sports and Exercise,* Vol. 27, no. 1 (1995): 113–120.

Any Body Can!

Jack LaLanne

Jack LaLanne, the godfather of physical fitness, opened the nation's first health club in 1936. He was one of the first people to promote active lifestyles, and at eighty-one, he still vigorously works out for two hours a day.

In the late 1950s he began the first televised aerobic exercise program. The Jack LaLanne Show, promoting nutrition and fitness, lasted 34 years. During the early shows, LaLanne encouraged women to exercise, to take charge of their appearance and their health. At the time, the idea that women should work out was an unusual philosophy, and LaLanne was one of the first to proclaim that exercising is both healthy and sensible.

Jack was among the first individuals to recommend that athletes use weights to develop strength. In the 1940s and 1950s he invented and built some of the first exercise machines for his gym, including a cable-pulley machine, a leg-extension machine, and a safety system for doing squats (a weightlifting technique explained in Chapter 8).

Jack was not always as physically fit as he is today. As a teenager, Jack was skinny and shy. When he was a young man, his mother took him to hear a nutritionist lecture. He was so motivated by the talk that he began to exercise and learn all he could about nutrition.

Jack is known for his Herculean feats of muscular strength and endurance. For example, he has done 100 handstand push-ups in 6 minutes and over 1,000 push-ups in 23 minutes. He swam across the San Francisco Bay while handcuffed. He also towed a 2000 pound boat the length of the Golden Gate Bridge (about 2 miles) while swimming underwater with air tanks but no swim fins. At the age of 70, he towed 70 friends in 70 different boats across Long Beach Harbor, near Los Angeles, California.

At an age when most people are quietly reflecting back on their lives, Jack is as busy as ever. He lectures regularly about the benefits of an active lifestyle and about false advertising in health and fitness issues. Currently he is in training for a 20 mile swim underwater from Catalina Island to Los Angeles.

Not everyone can be a fitness expert like Jack LaLanne, but **A**ny **B**ody **C**an lead an active lifestyle, exercise regularly, and make physical fitness an important part of their everyday life. That's right, you can do it!

REMEMBER This!

Personal fitness is not something that you can develop and automatically keep for the rest of your life. You must continually practice personal fitness to maintain it. Make personal fitness as much a part of your lifestyle as brushing your teeth is. Participate in it daily.

Throughout future chapters in this text, discussions and activities will teach you about various consumer issues (such as health-care costs) related to your personal fitness. Look for the "Consumer Corner" boxes throughout the book.

SECTION 3 REVIEW

Answer the following question on a separate sheet of paper:

1. Explain how obtaining or maintaining physical fitness can benefit each of the following:

   a. Physical appearance.

   b. Self-esteem.

   c. Stress.

   d. Academic performance.

   e. Life expectancy.

   f. Health-care costs.

CONSUMER CORNER

Stay Active and Save Money

Health-care costs in the United States have been rising dramatically over the past several years. You've probably heard your parents and other adults talk about how much they have had to pay for a trip to the doctor's office, a tiny bottle of medicine, or a short stay in the hospital. People who suffer from chronic diseases and ailments that require surgery or constant medication often find themselves overloaded with medical bills they can never seem to overcome.

The federal government and many state governments are searching for ways to hold the line on escalating health-care costs and to provide quality health care to everyone at affordable prices. Until a solution is found, however, we all must be prepared to deal with these high costs. Even if you are fortunate enough to be healthy for most of your life, health insurance costs will take a significant part of your income.

Although the situation doesn't look promising, you should realize that you can do something about health-care costs. You can get started now on a plan for lifetime fitness and good health by developing and sticking with a personal physical fitness plan, which will greatly increase your chances of avoiding illnesses and injuries that result in doctor and hospital bills. Of course there are no guarantees. As you know from reading this chapter, many health risks are beyond your control. There is no doubt, however, that you can prevent or reduce many health risks by staying active.

SECTION 4   Personal Fitness: How Much Is Enough?

Regular physical activity and exercise have been recommended by the U.S. Public Health Service for children, adolescents, and adults as part of the *Healthy People 2000* health promotion and disease prevention objectives for the nation. The *Healthy People 2000* objectives are designed to encourage all Americans to develop and maintain healthy, active lifestyles. Experts have found that by becoming more active, Americans can improve both their health and their physical fitness levels.

Your Health versus Your Physical Fitness Level

Figure 1.5 on the next page shows that improvements in health versus physical fitness come about at different levels of physical activity or exercise. Health benefits can be obtained from minimal levels of physical activity or exercise. In contrast, higher levels of activity or exercise are required to stimulate moderate to high physical fitness benefits. This means that sedentary people can improve their health immediately just by raising their level of physical activity or exercise from low to moderate. However, to achieve higher personal fitness goals (for example, preparing for sports participation, running a 5K road race, or increasing your bench press maximum by 25 pounds), you will need to engage in higher levels of physical activity, exercise, or both. (See Chapter 3 for more details.)

Recently, researchers developed general physical activity and exercise guidelines for adolescents (ages eleven to twenty-one years). These guidelines were designed to help you develop and maintain your health and physical fitness. No one knows for sure the amount of physical activity or exercise needed for optimal health and physical fitness for young adults. However, the following guidelines were designed to provide you with target goals now, as well as to encourage you to continue to be active throughout your life:

- *Guideline 1.* All adolescents should be physically active daily or nearly every day, as part of play, games, sports, work, transportation, recreation, physical education, or planned exercise, in the context of family, school, or community activities.

- *Guideline 2.* Adolescents should engage in three or more sessions per week of activities that last twenty minutes or more at a time and that require moderate to vigorous levels of exertion.

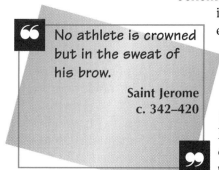

> *No athlete is crowned but in the sweat of his brow.*
>
> **Saint Jerome**
> c. 342–420

• *You can make personal fitness a pleasurable social experience with others.*

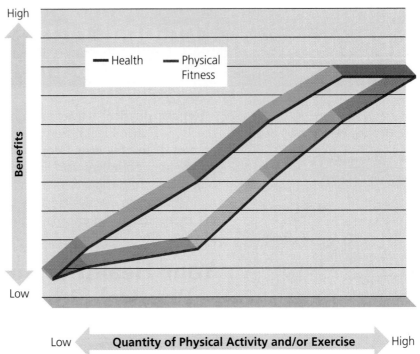

• **Figure 1.5** *Comparing Health Benefits and Physical Fitness Benefits of Physical Activity, Exercise, or Both.*

• *Being physically active can positively influence your health and physical fitness.*

As you learn to design your personal fitness program during the rest of this course, keep these guidelines in mind, and use them as you develop your program.

The personal fitness continuum in Figure 1.6 is designed to help you visualize how you can achieve and maintain personal fitness (level 5 in Figure 1.6). Initially, (1), when someone has low fitness, he needs to learn about the concepts of how to achieve physical fitness by participating safely in physical activity, exercise, or both. Once the person begins to (2) experience physical activity and exercise successfully, he will begin to have improved fitness levels. At that point, the individual should explore his activity options (3) and become actively and safely involved in a variety of physical activities. Then he can decide which activities are the most enjoyable and beneficial personally. By evaluating (4) the level of physical fitness, the individual can then modify his personal fitness program to meet individual needs for ongoing success (5).

Now that you understand the process of moving from low fitness levels to moderate or high fitness levels, it is important for you to motivate yourself to begin experiencing physical activity, exercise, or both. Remember, **A**ny **B**ody **C**an be fit! Will you?

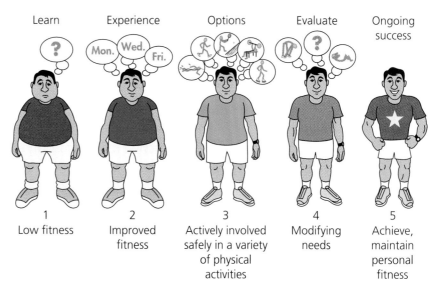

Learn	Experience	Options	Evaluate	Ongoing success
1	2	3	4	5
Low fitness	Improved fitness	Actively involved safely in a variety of physical activities	Modifying needs	Achieve, maintain personal fitness

• **Figure 1.6** *Your Personal Fitness Continuum.*

REMEMBER **This!**

The knowledge and activity experiences from this course will prepare you to solve your fitness problems for the future. What is important to your personal fitness is not just what you do today. It's what you do today, tomorrow, and in the extended future that is important.

Let's Get Started!

In this course you will participate in a conditioning program that will allow you to experience the benefits of physical activity and regular exercise in a positive way. The conditioning program can be designed by you and your instructor and should consist of a cardiovascular component (such as walking, jogging, or aerobic dance), a flexibility component (for example, stretching or range-of-motion activities), and a muscular strength and endurance component (weight lifting, calisthenics, and so on). You'll learn more about each of these components of fitness as you read this text.

It is important for you to get started *now* on your personal conditioning program so that later (starting in Chapter 4) you will be able to assess your fitness levels accurately and safely. It is also important that you follow the personal conditioning program for *several weeks* prior to your physical evaluations. Doing so will help you improve your levels of physical fitness.

Begin your conditioning program at a low to moderate level. Gradually increase this level over a period of *several weeks* to reduce injury risk. When you first start your program, it will be difficult to include all the fitness components at one time. It is best to start with the cardiovascular and flexibility components and add the muscular strength and endurance components later.

BELIEVE IT? ... OR NOT?

If you have enough money, you do not have to worry about your personal fitness level.

See page 25 for answer.

SECTION 4 REVIEW

Answer the following questions on a separate sheet of paper:

1. How do the first two physical activity guidelines for adolescents differ from one another?
2. Describe the process and stages in moving from low fitness levels to moderate or high fitness levels.

SUMMARY

Numerous scientific studies have documented the beneficial effects of physical activity, exercise, or both, in groups of men and women across the entire adult age range. Research has also shown that physical activity patterns and fitness levels established during childhood and adolescence are likely to carry over into adult life. Sound physical activity and nutrition habits developed in these early years provide the foundation for a lifetime of physical fitness.

Many scientific studies over the past twenty years support the value of regular exercise as part of a healthy lifestyle. Studies have documented a sedentary lifestyle as a risk factor for major chronic diseases. In many cases of fatigue, the cause is a lack of regular physical exercise. National health studies indicate that a high percentage of visits to physicians are for vague complaints such as chronic fatigue.

Regular, vigorous physical activity throughout life significantly reduces the risk of disability and premature death from stroke and heart disease. It can also effectively alter many of the important risk factors for cardiovascular disease by lowering body weight and blood cholesterol levels, raising HDL ("good cholesterol"), and promoting the maintenance of normal blood pressure. Regular exercise also has several potential benefits for people with diabetes. In addition, preliminary evidence indicates that active individuals may have a lower risk of dying of cancer.

The benefits of regular exercise on psychological health have also been clearly documented. People with anxiety and depression do better if exercise training is combined with other treatments. In fact, the vast majority of individuals who take up regular physical activity, exercise, or both, report an improved sense of general well-being and an enhanced self-image.

The health benefits of lifelong exercise habits and a high level of physical fitness are clear. This course and text are designed to help you develop the skills and behaviors you need to establish healthy, active lifestyle habits now and in the future.

Chapter 1 Review

True/False

On a separate piece of paper, mark each question below either T for True or F for False.

1. Moderate to high levels of physical fitness are associated with good health and wellness.
2. The best way to develop fitness is to become an athlete.
3. A lack of accurate physical fitness knowledge can contribute to a negative attitude about physical activity, exercise, or both.
4. The fitness behaviors that you develop as a young adult will have little effect on you and your health as an adult.
5. A sedentary lifestyle is one of the major risk factors for early death.
6. To significantly reduce your chances of early death from chronic disease, you will need to maintain a *high level* of fitness.
7. Eustress is the positive stress we all must deal with in our lives.
8. Men between the ages of fifty and sixty are more likely to die of heart disease than women of the same age.
9. Physical fitness is associated with enhanced self-esteem.
10. The *Healthy People 2000* objectives are designed to encourage all Americans to develop and maintain healthy, active lifestyles.

Multiple Choice

1. Health is a state of well-being that includes which of the following?

   a. physical aspects
   b. social aspects
   c. mental-emotional aspects
   d. spiritual aspects
   e. all of the above

2. The ability to maintain physical independence throughout your life is called

   a. sedentary health.
   b. functional health.
   c. physical fitness.
   d. less modifiable risk.

3. People who lead sedentary lifestyles are often referred to as

   a. couch potatoes.
   b. athletes.
   c. physically fit.
   d. low-health-risk people.

4. Smokers who stop smoking and adopt an active lifestyle can reduce their heart attack risk level to that of nonsmokers in ____ year(s).

   a. one-half
   b. one
   c. one to two
   d. two to three

5. The average life expectancy for adults in the United States today is about ___ years.

   a. seventy-five
   b. seventy
   c. sixty-five
   d. sixty

6. Which of the following is the most easily modified risk factor?

   a. age
   b. gender
   c. genetics
   d. stress

7. People who are physically active throughout their lives may add about ___ year(s) to their life expectancy.

   a. 1
   b. 1.5
   c. 2
   d. 2.5

8. Cholesterol is usually classified as "good" or "bad." Which of the following refers to the "good" cholesterol?

   a. LDL
   b. HDL
   c. VLDL
   d. Triglycerides

9. Which of the following is *not* a positive outcome of personal fitness?

   a. improved physical appearance
   b. enhanced self-esteem
   c. hypertension
   d. stress reduction

10. Which of the following is the correct order for designing your personal fitness continuum?

    a. learn, experience, options, evaluate, and ongoing success
    b. experience, learn, evaluate, options, and ongoing success
    c. evaluate, experience, learn, ongoing success, and options
    d. options, ongoing success, evaluate, learn, and experience

Discussion

1. Explain how two seventy-five-year-old adults could both have their functional health but at the same time differ in relation to their wellness levels. Give examples.

2. Explain how you can adjust your lifestyle and behaviors to reduce your risk for premature death due to inherited genes.

3. In your opinion, which positive outcome of physical fitness is the most important, and why?

Vocabulary Experience

Match the correct term in Column A to the definition in Column B by writing the appropriate number in each blank.

Column A

_____ wellness

_____ physical fitness

Column B

1. Variables or conditions that increase the likelihood that you will develop chronic diseases.

2. The attainment and maintenance of a moderate to high level of physical, mental, emotional, spiritual, and social health.

_____ risk factors

_____ predisposition

_____ sedentary lifestyle

_____ hypokinetic

3. Physically inactive.

4. Susceptibility to increased health risk due to genetic makeup.

5. Individual physical abilities that allow you to perform normal daily physical tasks effectively.

6. Inactive lifestyle.

Critical Thinking

1. Evaluate your self-esteem. Do you think that living a physically active lifestyle can have a positive influence on your self-esteem? Why or why not?

2. What advantages does a physically fit person have over a person with a low level of physical

fitness on a day-to-day basis? Explain your answer.

3. How can living a physically active lifestyle improve your academic performance? Explain your answer.

Case Study — Raul Cuts Class

Raul is a seventeen-year-old junior who has become an expert at avoiding physical education classes. Since his first days in middle school, he has managed to develop a bag of tricks that allow him to sit out more days than he participates, and in some cases, avoid the physical education course entirely.

His problems with physical education classes began years ago. It seemed that he was always being required to take physical fitness tests that he was not prepared for. Later he would be sore and uncomfortable. He also hates sweating and messing up his hair. He spends the better part of his morning before school getting his hair just right, and then, after just five minutes of P.E., his hair is a mess and all that careful styling has been wasted.

What Raul doesn't mention is that he is also overweight and out of shape. He doesn't like to admit it, but he is embarrassed by his physical appearance when he has to wear anything other than his loose-fitting clothes, and it only takes about half a lap around the football field before he is totally winded.

There is a history of heart trouble in his family, and Raul thinks he heard somewhere that there is a connection between heart attacks and working out, but he is not sure. He thinks that there is probably nothing to this—it's just another trick to get you to come to class.

Here is your assignment:

Assume that you are Raul's friend. Write a letter to Raul trying to convince him not only to enroll in a P.E. class this semester, but to work hard during this class to get himself into shape. Use the information that you have read in this chapter to support your case.

KEYS TO HELP YOU

- Consider Raul's self-esteem
- Be sure you mention health risks

Chapter 2

Making Physical Activity and Exercise Safe for You

Contents

Outcomes

After reading and studying this chapter, you will be able to:

1. Define and explain the terms related to physical activity participation and safe exercise.

2. Explain the importance of having a medical evaluation prior to beginning a personal fitness program.

3. Tell how you can determine whether or not you need to undergo medical screening.

4. Discuss how weather conditions can influence the safety of your personal fitness program.

5. Explain how the outdoor environment can be hazardous. Identify specific situations that would cause you to modify your physical activity or exercise plans.

6. Explain the importance of choosing appropriate clothing and safety equipment for your personal fitness program. Identify specific items you will need.

7. Describe the proper way to walk and jog, based on the principles of biomechanics.

8. Identify and describe the injuries commonly experienced in personal fitness programs and how you might prevent and treat them.

9. Explain the importance of adherence to your personal fitness program, and how you can improve your adherence.

Key Terms

After reading and studying this chapter, you will be able to understand and provide practical definitions for the following terms:

medical screening	rehydration	strain
medical examination	diuretic	tendon
hyperthermia	heat stress index	stitch
dehydration	hypothermia	ligament
heat cramps	frostbite	cartilage
heat exhaustion	supination	stress fracture
heat stroke	pronation	adherence
acclimatization	biomechanics	

INTRODUCTION

*T*he previous chapter clearly established the benefits of participating in regular physical activity and exercise throughout your life. This new knowledge, it is hoped, has motivated you to start or upgrade your personal fitness program. Should you jump right in and get going with the program that you have been putting off for so long? No, you should consider many things before you start or revise a personal fitness program.

The first step is to learn how to plan a safe and reasonable program that will not only be productive for you but also will increase the likelihood of your adherence to your personal fitness program. Many people start personal fitness programs with the best intentions. However, a 40 to 50 percent dropout rate is typical due to poor planning, unrealistic goals, and unsafe practices.

A journey of 1,000 miles starts with the first step. The material in Chapter 2 can help make this first step not only a safe one but also one that can be continued throughout your journey so that you can obtain your goals. Personal fitness is a journey that should have no end. A major goal of your long personal fitness journey is to make it enjoyable.

SECTION 1 Medical Evaluations

We generally think of physical activity and exercise as being good for us. However, safety risks can be involved. If you consider important medical guidelines, you can minimize these risks. Some questions you should consider are whether or not you should have a medical evaluation, how often you should be evaluated, and what should be included in the evaluation.

Who Needs an Evaluation?

Many people should have medical evaluations before beginning physical activity or exercise programs. Some people increase their risks for injury and other health problems if they start a program without medical clearance. If you have any known chronic disease, it is strongly recommended that you get medical clearance before beginning any formal exercise program, regardless of your age. Examples of chronic diseases could include any of the following:

• Heart disease or cardiovascular disorders.

• Severe obesity.

• *Everyone needs regular medical evaluations. As you age, you will need to be evaluated more frequently.*

---

medical screening

a basic evaluation of the eyes, ears, nose, throat, blood pressure, height, weight, and a check for possible hernia.

---

medical examination

a more extensive evaluation than is done in a medical screening, assessing any or all of the following: exercise stress test, blood test, urinary analysis, or family health-risk history.

• High blood pressure.
• Kidney disease.
• Diabetes.

Men forty years old and above and women fifty and above who have not exercised vigorously for a number of years, and who have not had a medical examination in the past two to three years, are also encouraged to see a physician. A young adult with no medical history of heart problems in the family and no more than one risk factor (see Chapter 1) may begin an exercise program without a medical evaluation.

How Often Is the Evaluation Recommended?

There are no absolute guidelines for how often a person needs a medical evaluation. Some general guidelines for healthy people would include the following:

• Between the ages of six and fifteen: once every three years.
• Between the ages of fifteen and thirty-four: once every two years.
• Between the ages of thirty-five and fifty-nine: once a year.
• Sixty years old and older: twice a year.

What Should the Evaluation Include?

Most healthy young adults will be evaluated with a **medical screening**. During a medical screening any or all of the following will be assessed: eyes, ears, nose, throat, blood pressure, hernia, height, weight, and a check of how the heart and lungs sound. If a more serious **medical examination** is needed, the physician may examine the heart with an exercise stress test. In this test, the heart is monitored very closely as the patient walks or runs on a treadmill. Other parts of a medical examination may include a blood test, a urinary analysis, and a study of the family health-risk history.

The Physical Activity Readiness Questionnaire on the next page is an example of a simple health screening questionnaire. This type of questionnaire is often used by adults to determine whether or not they may safely begin an exercise program without a medical evaluation. Complete the questionnaire carefully. Then determine whether it may or may not be safe for you to begin a physical activity and exercise program.

PAR - Q & YOU

(Physical Activity Readiness–Questionnaire)

(A Questionnaire for People Aged 15 to 69)

Regular physical activity is fun and healthy, and increasingly more people are starting to become more active every day. Being more active is very safe for most people. However, some people should check with their doctor before they start becoming much more physically active.

If you are planning to become much more physically active than you are now, start by answering the seven questions in the box below. If you are between the ages of 15 and 69, the PAR-Q will tell you if you should check with your doctor before you start. Common sense is your best guide when you answer these questions. Please read the questions carefully and answer each one honestly: check YES or NO.

YES	NO	
☐	☐	1. Has your doctor ever said that you have a heart condition *and* that you should only do physical activity recommended by a doctor?
☐	☐	2. Do you feel pain in your chest when you do physical activity?
☐	☐	3. In the past month, have you had chest pain when you were not doing physical activity?
☐	☐	4. Do you lose your balance because of dizziness or do you ever lose consciousness?
☐	☐	5. Do you have a bone or joint problem that could be made worse by a change in your physical activity?
☐	☐	6. Is your doctor currently prescribing drugs (for example, water pills) for your blood pressure or heart condition?
☐	☐	7. Do you know of *any other reason* why you should not do physical activity?

NOTE: If the PAR-Q is being given to a person before he or she participates in a physical activity program or a fitness appraisal, this section may be used for legal or administrative purposes.

I have read, understood and completed this questionnaire. Any questions I had were answered to my full satisfaction.

NAME _____ DATE _____

SIGNATURE _____ WITNESS _____

SIGNATURE OF PARENT _____
or GUARDIAN (for minors)

If you answered

YES to one or more questions

Talk with your doctor by phone or in person BEFORE you start becoming much more physically active or BEFORE you have a fitness appraisal. Tell your doctor about the PAR-Q and which questions you answered YES to.

- You may be able to do any activity you want—as long as your start slowly and build up gradually. Or, you may need to restrict your activities to those which are safe for you. Talk with your doctor about the kinds of activities you wish to participate in and follow his/her advice.
- Find out which community programs are safe and helpful for you.

DELAY BECOMING MUCH MORE ACTIVE:

- if you are not feeling well because of a temporary illness such as a cold or a fever—wait until you feel better; or
- if you are or may be pregnant—talk to your doctor before you start becoming more active.

Please note: If your health changes so that you then answer YES to any of the above questions, tell your fitness or health professional. Ask whether you should change your physical activity plan.

NO to all questions

If you answered NO honestly to all PAR-Q questions, you can be reasonably sure that you can:

- start becoming much more physically active—begin slowly and build up gradually. This is the safest and easiest way to go.
- take part in a fitness appraisal—this is an excellent way to determine your basic fitness so that you can plan the best way for you to live actively.

- *The Physical Activity Readiness Questionnaire will help you determine whether or not you can safely participate in physical activity.*

Source: Reprinted with permission from S. Thomas, J. Reading, R. J. Shephard: Revision of the Physical Activity Readiness Questionnaire (PAR-Q), *Canadian Journal of Sports Science* 17 (1992): 338–345 (based on the British Columbia Department of Health, PAR-Q Validation Report, 1975).

SECTION 2   Weather Conditions

hyperthermia

overheating; body temperature above 98.6 degrees Fahrenheit.

dehydration

excess fluid loss from the body; symptoms include weakness and fatigue.

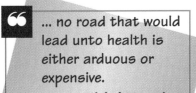

> ... no road that would lead unto health is either arduous or expensive.
>
> **Michel Montaigne**

Another important safety consideration for your exercise program is weather conditions. If the environment is too hot, or too humid, or too cold, you will significantly increase your risk for injuries.

The Dangers of Physical Activity in Heat and Humidity

During physical activity or exercise, your body produces heat and raises your body temperature above what is normal at rest (98.6 degrees Fahrenheit). To control overheating (**hyperthermia**), your body sweats. The sweat evaporates on your skin to cool your body. When the weather is hot and humid, you sweat excessively and lose excess fluids (**dehydration**), which can produce weakness and fatigue. In hot, humid weather it can be difficult for you to maintain a normal body temperature during physical activity. This can put you at a higher risk for developing heat injuries, including heat cramps, heat exhaustion, and heat stroke.

Heat Cramps.   **Heat cramps** are painful contractions of the muscles used during physical activity or exercise due, at least in part, to dehydration. Heat cramps are the mildest form of heat injury and can be minimized by drinking plenty of fluids and maintaining a normal body fluid balance. Normal body fluid balance refers to your ability to balance the amount of water you consume with the amount that you lose or excrete daily (see Chapter 10 for more details).

REMEMBER This!

It is important to continue the rehydration process after an exercise session has been completed. It may take up to twelve hours to achieve complete fluid replacement after strenuous exercise in the heat. An easy way to monitor whether fluids are being adequately replaced, from day to day, is by weighing yourself. If you have weight loss on a daily basis that exceeds 3 percent of your total body weight, the rehydration process is probably not complete. For example, if you weigh 120 pounds, a 3 percent weight loss would be 3.6 pounds. If this happens to you, you should not participate in heavy physical activity until your body weight is back to normal.

Heat Exhaustion.   **Heat exhaustion** is an overheating condition that includes feelings of weakness; headache; rapid pulse; stomach discomfort; dizziness; heavy sweating; muscle cramps; and cool, clammy skin. If you have the symptoms of heat exhaustion, you should stop physical activity or exercise immediately. You should then get to a cool, dry environment and drink plenty of fluids. You should not return to your normal personal fitness program again until you have had a chance (usually a day or two) to replace your normal fluid balance.

Heat Stroke.   **Heat stroke** can be life threatening. Its symptoms include fainting or nearly fainting; a lack of sweating; hot, dry skin; and a very high body temperature. Heat stroke requires immediate medical treatment.

• *Learn to recognize the symptoms of heat stress during physical activity and exercise.*

Any Body Can!

The Tarahumara Indians

The Tarahumara Indians from Mexico's Copper Canyon are known as the "Raramuri," or foot runners. They live at high altitudes and are famous for their 50- to 200-mile foot races. Known for their Spartan-like lifestyle, they consume a diet that is very low in fat and total calories.

For decades, the Tarahumara have had competitions between villages where runners wearing sandals kick wooden balls along trails. Contests can last for several days, and runners often cover more than 100 miles before they give up due to fatigue. Legends about their long distance running capabilities include stories of their running up to 70 miles a day, 170 miles without stopping, and 500 miles a week carrying 40 pounds of mail.

The unusual endurance capabilities of the Tarahumara have been recognized by outsiders ever since the 1920s, and they have been encouraged to compete nationally and internationally in long distance running events. However, with the exception of the 1928 and 1968 Olympic Games, few Indians have left their native land to compete. This has been due in part to the differences in cultural habits of the Indians and the outside world.

In 1992, a group of five Tarahumara were coaxed out of Copper Canyon to compete in the Leadville, Colorado, 100-mile Race (run over mountainous trails) by a wilderness guide who had befriended them and had become their sponsor and coach. The Indians were expected to do very well in the race because it was at high altitudes (9,000 to over 12,000 feet), similar to their native environment. However, after leading the race for 40 miles, the five Tarahumara dropped out because they were unfamiliar with the course and with racing strategies needed for success.

In the 1993 Leadville 100-miler, three better prepared Tarahumara Indians placed first, second, and fifth. And, in the 1994 race, two of the Tarahumara placed first and third. The Tarahumara Indians are gaining international fame as endurance running champions.

Not everyone can conquer fierce environmental challenges during exercise like the Tarahumara Indians, but **A**ny **B**ody **C**an live a healthy lifestyle and make physical fitness an important part of their everyday life. That's right, you can do it!

How to Avoid Heat Injury.   You may have noticed that activities that are easily accomplished in cool weather become much more difficult to accomplish, and are more physically demanding, in hot, humid weather. If exercising in the heat is unavoidable, try to allow your body to adapt slowly to the heat—a process called **acclimatization**. It has been shown that you can become acclimatized to working out in the heat after five to ten days. The first few physical activity or exercise sessions in the heat should be light and last for only about twenty minutes. After you get acclimatized to the heat, you can increase your exercise gradually in both duration and intensity.

It is important to drink plenty of fluids prior to and during physical activity in the heat. Your body needs fluids to maintain sweating for body cooling. Inadequate fluid intake can lead to dehydration. Dehydration leads to a reduction in sweating and, ultimately, a significant rise in body temperature. A balance of water loss and water intake must be maintained.

Water loss through sweating during vigorous physical activity or exercise can reach as much as 3 liters per hour (see Figure 2.1). To maintain water balance, you should consume between 1.5 and 2.5 cups (1 cup = 8 ounces) of cold water ten to twenty minutes *before* exercising in the heat. During physical activity in the heat, attempt to match fluid loss with fluid intake. A rule of thumb would be approximately 1 cup of water *every* ten to fifteen minutes.

The body's thirst mechanism may lag behind the body's actual need for fluid. Therefore, to prevent heat injuries, you must continue to replace fluids despite the fact that you may not feel thirsty. Water is an excellent fluid to consume when you exercise in the heat. For most situations, water works as well as anything for preventing dehydration. However, numerous sports drinks are also on the market, and you may want to try some of them.

The following are some guidelines for consuming fluids when exercising in hot weather:

- Look for fluids that have an appealing taste during heavy exercise.
- A sports drink that provides an optimal fluid replacement has a 5 to 8 percent carbohydrate (sugar) content. You can find the contents of these drinks by reading the container labels or nutrition facts (more about this in Chapter 10).
- Replacement fluids containing carbonation, fruit juices, and fruit drinks are not the best choices because they may upset your stomach. They also are absorbed at a much slower rate than plain water or specially made sports drinks.
- Drinks containing caffeine may slow **rehydration** attempts, because caffeine acts as a **diuretic**.

Clothing is also important for safe exercise in the heat. Choose clothing that is loose and light in color to promote optimal heat loss

---

acclimatization

the process of allowing the body to adapt slowly to new conditions.

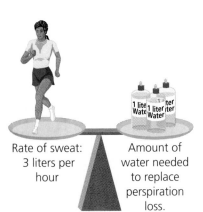

Rate of sweat: 3 liters per hour

Amount of water needed to replace perspiration loss.

• **Figure 2.1** *Maintaining Water Balance. Think about how much soda there is in a 3-liter soda bottle. That's how much water your body can sweat in an hour-long workout.*

rehydration

the process of replacing fluids that have been lost or excreted from the body.

diuretic

a substance that promotes water loss through urination.

Relative Humidity	Air Temperature (°F)										
	70°	75°	80°	85°	90°	95°	100°	105°	110°	115°	120°
0%	64	69	73	78	83	87	91	95	99	103	107
10%	65	70	75	80	85	90	95	100	105	111	116
20%	66	72	77	82	87	93	99	105	112	120	130
30%	67	73	78	84	90	96	104	113	123	135	148
40%	68	74	79	86	93	101	110	123	137	151	
50%	69	75	81	88	96	107	120	135	150		
60%	70	76	82	90	100	114	132	149			
70%	70	77	85	93	106	124	144				
80%	71	78	86	97	113	136					
90%	72	80	91	108							

Low Risk 90 or Less	Medium Risk 90 – 105	Higher Risk 105 to 130	Probable Injury 130 or More

RISK OF HEAT INJURY

• **Figure 2.2** *Heat Stress Index. Use this chart to calculate the heat stress index when you exercise if you know the temperature and humidity. For example, if it were 90 degrees Fahrenheit and the humidity was 70 percent, the heat stress index would be 106, which places you at higher risk for heat injury.*

heat stress index

a number that reflects a combination of high temperatures and high humidity.

hypothermia

a condition in which the body temperature drops below normal (98.6 degrees Fahrenheit).

frostbite

damage to the body tissues due to freezing.

as you sweat. Tight clothes do not allow air to circulate between the skin and the clothing. Dark clothing absorbs heat, whereas light clothing reflects heat rays. Cotton fabrics are best, as they absorb moisture rapidly and promote evaporation and cooling. Never wear sweatshirts or rubber suits, which limit your ability to have excessive sweat evaporate and cool your body.

You can reduce your risk for heat injury by limiting your activity when the **heat stress index** reaches or exceeds 105 (see Figure 2.2). You can also reduce your risk for heat injuries by exercising during the cooler parts of the day, either in the early morning or the evening.

The Dangers of Physical Activity in Cold Weather

When you are physically active or exercise in cold weather, your body temperature can drop below normal (a condition called **hypothermia**). In extremely cold conditions you significantly increase your risk for tissue damage from freezing (**frostbite**). It is important to consider the combined influences of wind and temper-

Wind Speed (mph)	Air Temperature (°F)														
Calm	40	35	30	25	20	15	10	5	0	−5	−10	−15	−20	−25	−30
5	37	33	27	21	16	12	6	1	−5	−11	−15	−20	−26	−31	−35
10	28	21	16	9	4	−2	−9	−15	−21	−27	−33	−38	−46	−52	−58
15	22	16	11	1	−5	−11	−18	−25	−36	−40	−45	−51	−58	−65	−70
20	18	12	3	−4	−10	−17	−25	−32	−39	−46	−53	−60	−67	−76	−81
25	16	7	0	−7	−15	−22	−29	−37	−44	−52	−59	−67	−74	−83	−89
30	13	5	−2	−11	−18	−26	−33	−41	−48	−56	−63	−70	−79	−87	−94
35	11	3	−4	−13	−20	−27	−35	−43	−49	−60	−67	−72	−82	−90	−96
40	10	1	−6	−15	−21	−29	−37	−45	−53	−62	−69	−76	−85	−94	−101

Low Risk Warmer than −21	Increasing Risk −22 to −67	High Risk Colder than −67

RISK OF FROSTBITE

• **Figure 2.3** *Wind Chill Index. Use the chart to calculate the wind chill if you know air temperature and wind speed. If it were 15 degrees Fahrenheit and the wind was blowing at 30 mph, the wind chill would be −26, which places you at a higher risk for injury.*

ature, or the wind chill factor, before you decide to be active on a cold and windy day (see Figure 2.3).

When you exercise in cold weather, wear warm, loose-fitting clothing in layers. Pay attention to media weather forecasts. Finally, be sure to protect your extremities (hands, feet, head, ears, and so on) from extreme cold.

BELIEVE IT? ... OR NOT?

Death during vigorous exercise is rare. It is estimated that there is one death per year in a population of 15,000 to 20,000 adult exercisers.

See page 57 for answer.

SECTION 2 REVIEW

Answer the following questions on a separate piece of paper:

1. Describe the differences between heat cramps and heat exhaustion.
2. When the outside temperature is 20 degrees Fahrenheit and the wind is blowing at 15 miles per hour, what is the wind chill factor?

Danger under
-22 degrees

- *When you exercise in cold weather, dress appropriately for the challenge.*

CONSUMER CORNER

Beware of the "Quick Fix"

Many people still believe they can speed up the loss of fat by wearing a plastic or rubber suit during exercise sessions. This is a false belief, as well as a dangerous one. Most of the weight you lose is fluid, not fat, and will quickly be replaced when you drink fluids following your activity. Using this type of suit places you at risk for dehydration.

You should always be aware of the fact that there are many false advertisements about health and fitness "quick fixes." Be sure you thoroughly investigate any quick-weight-loss or fitness gimmicks before you buy or use them.

Some of the claims that should alert you to gimmicks and unreliable products are:

- ads that rely solely upon identification of a product with a famous person, such as a movie star or sports hero

- weight-loss promises that say you will lose large amounts of weight in a short period of time

- solutions to weight loss that involve products other than regular foods. Try not to get yourself into a position in which you are dependent upon special products. These products are often expensive, and they usually do not contain the variety of nutrients that you consume with natural foods.

Remember, nothing worthwhile comes easy. If you want to lose weight, you will need to work at it. You will learn more about the sensible way to lose weight in Chapters 9 and 10.

SECTION 3

The Outdoor Environment: It Can Be Hazardous

Your medical evaluation came up with no problems. Now you are ready to head outdoors to begin your exercise program. It sounds safe enough, but first you should be aware of some serious environmental concerns. Your community may have any or all of these safety hazards. Take some time to determine if any of these hazards are present in your physical activity and exercise environment.

Air Pollution: Industrial and Automobile Emissions

Industrial pollutants and carbon monoxide (a gas created by combustion engines, including those in cars and trucks) have created potentially dangerous exercise environments in many cities. Many of the industrial pollutants can restrict our breathing passages making it difficult to breathe, especially when large amounts of air are needed during exercise. You might compare the difficulty caused by these pollutants to the difficulty you'd experience if you had to do all your breathing through a long, narrow straw.

In addition, harmful materials can collect in our lungs. Carbon monoxide is dangerous because it is more readily absorbed by the

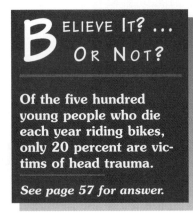

BELIEVE IT? ... OR NOT?

Of the five hundred young people who die each year riding bikes, only 20 percent are victims of head trauma.

See page 57 for answer.

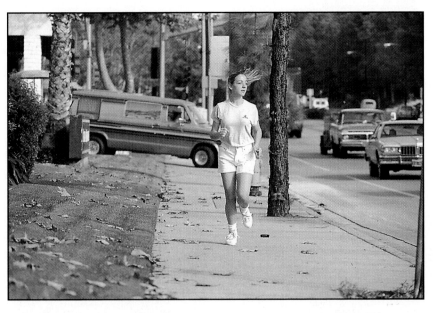

• *Air pollution can make physical activity and exercise hazardous.*

Stress Break

. . . .

One of the reasons why millions of people participate in regular physical activity is to reduce the stress in their lives. A regular walk through the park, a bike ride around the neighborhood, or even a vigorous game of tennis can help you relax. It may be the only time of the day that you get to do something just for yourself. Find a place and a time of day that insures the experience will be a positive one. If you are concerned about traffic, dogs, potential violence, or time constraints, you may find that your workouts are more stress producing than stress reducing. Plan your workout to make it positive and enjoyable. You need opportunities to deal with stress in positive ways.

bloodstream than is the needed oxygen. If you exercise regularly in an environment with polluted air, you will increase your risk for respiratory problems.

You can take several steps to minimize your risks from air pollution. First, pay attention to media reports of high pollution levels. Next, identify the areas and the times of day that have less traffic. During peak traffic or high-pollution periods, limit or eliminate completely your exercise, especially if you have respiratory problems. Finally, find suitable indoor physical activity and exercise opportunities if you cannot avoid peak traffic or high-pollution periods.

Altitude

High altitude (starting at about 5,000 feet above sea level) can reduce your ability to exercise or perform work, especially if you have been living at lower altitudes. Moving from lower to higher altitudes will reduce the ability of your heart and lungs to deliver and utilize oxygen. This causes you to get tired more quickly than you would at sea level. It can also cause high altitude sickness (upset stomach, headache, dehydration, and so on). A person who moves from a low to a high altitude and then lives and trains in the high altitude over a period of time can increase the work capacity of the heart and lungs. However, this person's capacity will never be as high as it would be at sea level.

When you move from a low altitude to a high altitude, gradually increase the amount you exercise over a period of days. If possible, change altitude slowly over several hours. This can help prevent altitude sickness. Drink plenty of fluids. This can also help prevent altitude sickness. Individuals with heart or lung problems, of course, should consult a doctor before attempting vigorous exercise at any altitude.

Bad Dogs

Even if the air quality is good and the weather is great, you may encounter other outdoor hazards. For example, the exercise environment may have loose dogs. Nothing is worse than having a pleasant jog, walk, or bike ride interrupted by an unfriendly canine.

As you exercise outdoors, be alert for dogs. If you encounter a dog, do not unnecessarily frighten or threaten it. If confronted by a dog, it may be best to face it and yell, "***Bad dog! Stop!***" Then walk slowly away—never run.

Crime

It is a sad fact, but a necessary consideration, that crime is commonplace in our society. Women should be especially concerned

• *Being aware of potential hazards in your exercise environment will enable you to minimize injuries.*

about when and where they exercise. Take some time to examine and plan your outdoor exercise routes and routines to avoid crime.

The following guidelines can help you avoid crime or threatening situations:

• Exercise in well-lighted areas.

• Exercise with friends.

• Avoid high-crime neighborhoods.

• Avoid verbal confrontations, if possible.

• Let someone know where you are going and when you expect to return.

SECTION 3 REVIEW

Answer the following questions on a separate sheet of paper:

1. Explain the hazards associated with physical activity or exercise in environments with polluted air.

2. List precautions you can take to avoid bad dogs and crime in your exercise environment.

SECTION 4 — Dressing for Safety and Enjoyment

If you dress properly for physical activity and exercise, you will be more comfortable. You will also reduce your risk for injury. An understanding of clothing and safety needs for specific physical activities can enhance your adherence to, and enjoyment of, your personal fitness program.

Clothing

On mild to warm days, wear loose, comfortable clothes (shorts, T-shirts, tank tops, socks, and the like). Avoid clothes that restrict your movements or that cause you to overheat (see Section 2, earlier in the chapter). When it is cold, wear sweatshirts and pants, tights, windbreakers, and gloves or mittens. Wear different layers of clothing when it is cold. That way, you can remove a layer or two if you get too warm.

Clothing does not need to be expensive to be effective for physical activity and exercise. However, you should be a wise consumer when selecting clothing. For example, consider the temperature of your exercise environment, safety factors (reflective clothing might be useful), price, quality of material, and type of cleaning required before you decide to buy anything.

Some considerations in selecting your physical activity and exercise clothing are specific to your gender. For example, to provide additional exercise safety and comfort, women may want to purchase a sports bra. For the same reasons, men may want to purchase sport briefs or an athletic supporter.

REMEMBER This!

Your safety and successful participation in your personal fitness program may depend upon your choice, purchase, and proper care of exercise clothing and equipment. Therefore, when you decide to buy personal fitness gear, make informed consumer choices as you shop.

Safety Equipment

If you participate in an activity such as bicycling, skateboarding, or in-line skating, you should always wear protective equipment. For example, you should always wear a helmet. Statistics show that the likelihood of head injury is reduced 85 percent by using a bike helmet. When skateboarding or in-line skating, wear elbow pads, knee pads, and wrist guards.

A protective helmet should have a foam liner inside to absorb blows to the head in case of a fall. Choose a helmet that meets the standards set by either the American National Standards Institute (ANSI) or the Shell Memorial Foundation. Make sure the helmet has a snug but comfortable fit. Finally, check the helmet for a chin strap and buckle, so it will stay securely fastened.

Footwear

Shoes are essential for your personal fitness program. You should select the right shoe based on your activities and type of exercise. Numerous types of shoes are specifically designed for particular activities and sports. You can significantly reduce your risk for skeletal and muscular injuries by making wise footwear choices.

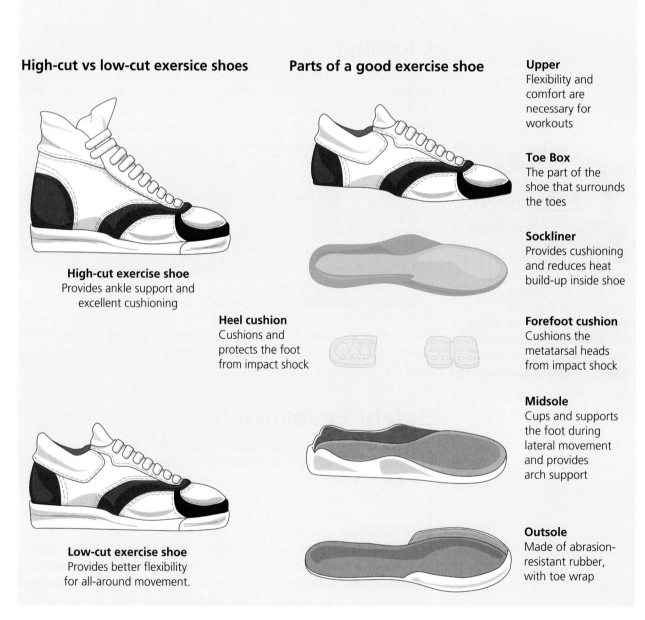

High-cut vs low-cut exersice shoes

High-cut exercise shoe
Provides ankle support and excellent cushioning

Low-cut exercise shoe
Provides better flexibility for all-around movement.

Parts of a good exercise shoe

Heel cushion
Cushions and protects the foot from impact shock

Upper
Flexibility and comfort are necessary for workouts

Toe Box
The part of the shoe that surrounds the toes

Sockliner
Provides cushioning and reduces heat build-up inside shoe

Forefoot cushion
Cushions the metatarsal heads from impact shock

Midsole
Cups and supports the foot during lateral movement and provides arch support

Outsole
Made of abrasion-resistant rubber, with toe wrap

• ***Figure 2.4*** *Features of an Exercise Shoe.*

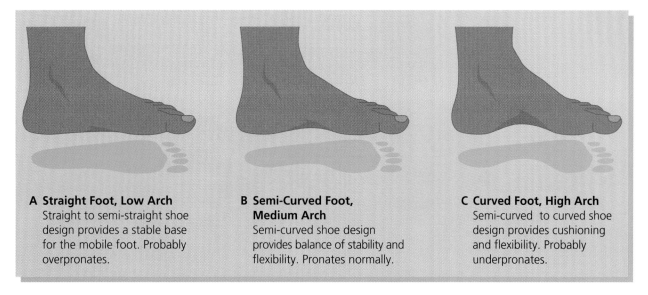

A Straight Foot, Low Arch
Straight to semi-straight shoe design provides a stable base for the mobile foot. Probably overpronates.

B Semi-Curved Foot, Medium Arch
Semi-curved shoe design provides balance of stability and flexibility. Pronates normally.

C Curved Foot, High Arch
Semi-curved to curved shoe design provides cushioning and flexibility. Probably underpronates.

• *Figure 2.5* *Matching Feet and Shoes.*

supination

a movement of the foot when walking or jogging in which the foot strikes the ground on the outside of the heel.

pronation

an inward rolling of the foot in walking or jogging.

Select a style of shoe that will meet your specific needs. For example, if you are going to engage primarily in a walking program, you need to buy a "walking shoe." If you are going to play basketball, you need to buy a shoe specifically designed for basketball. Of course, if you are going to do a variety of activities, you may want to buy an all-purpose (cross-training) pair of shoes. Figure 2.4 shows the features you should look for in a physical activity or exercise shoe.

It is a good idea to visit a local sporting goods store to seek out advice before you buy shoes for physical activity or exercise. If you cannot find a knowledgeable salesperson to help you when you shop for shoes, ask your physical education instructor for advice.

The shape of your shoe should match the shape of your foot (see Figure 2.5). If you have a normal foot shape (Type B), your foot will strike the ground on the outside of the heel when you walk, a movement called **supination**. Your foot will then roll inward (a movement referred to as **pronation** as you walk or jog. Pronation and supination are normal foot movements. However, too much pronation causes excessive wear on the inside of the heels of shoes. Too much supination causes excessive wear on the outside of the heels of shoes. In addition, too much pronation or supination can increase the risk for leg and knee injuries.

If you have a normal foot shape, with normal amounts of pronation and supination (Type B in Figure 2.5), a shoe without special motion control features should work for you. If you have a foot that has too much pronation (Type A), you have a more mobile foot when you walk or jog. You may need a shoe that provides stability and reduces the overpronation. If your foot has too little pronation when you walk or jog (Type C), you have a less mobile foot. You

• *Before you buy a new pair of athletic shoes, find a store that has knowledgeable salespeople.*

REMEMBER This!

Try on shoes before you buy them. Walk around in the store to make sure the shoes are comfortable. Be sure to try on shoes when you're wearing the same type of socks that you intend to wear during physical activity or exercise.

CONSUMER CORNER

Smart Shoe Shopping

You can spend anywhere from $25 to $200 for a pair of athletic shoes. If you plan to be physically active—and hopefully you do—you need to purchase a pair of quality shoes. Unless you feel you must have the latest, "hottest" shoe from companies such as Nike and Reebok, you will be able to find a fine shoe for around $50. The features to look for are comfort, cushioning, flexibility, stability, and ventilation.

Buy your shoes at a store that has knowledgeable clerks who can help you find the shoes that are right for your feet and your needs.

The kind of shoes you wear are important, but it is just as important to know when to replace your shoes. Once a fitness shoe starts to lose its support and cushion, it should no longer be used for fitness activities. This shoe could do more harm than good to your feet and joints. If it is financially possible, you should have two pairs of fitness shoes and alternate their use. This will give the shoes time to dry out and regain their cushioning effect. This strategy will provide you with the support you need and can extend the life of your shoes significantly.

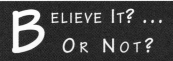

probably need a shoe that has greater cushioning and flexibility features. Once you determine your foot type, a knowledgeable salesperson or your physical education teacher can advise you about the type of shoe that will be best for your foot type and personal fitness needs. To analyze your foot shape, see the "Active Mind/Active Body" activity on this page.

Determine your foot size as well. The size of your physical activity and exercise shoes will probably differ from the size of your dress shoes. Physical activity and exercise shoes should have a snug heel and a space of about a half-inch between your longest toe and the end of the shoe. A roomy toe box (the part of the shoe that surrounds the toes) will allow your foot to swell during activity. (Refer back to Figure 2.4 on page 52.)

SECTION 4 REVIEW

Answer the following questions on a separate sheet of paper:

1. Explain why exercising in hot, humid environments requires special clothing.

2. It is especially important to select and wear proper footwear for physical activity and exercise. Give some reasons to support this statement.

Wet Foot Test

Lay a piece of paper (colored paper, if possible) on a hard floor. Get your foot wet. Then stand on the paper. Straight feet (Type A) leave an imprint that is oval shaped. Semi-curved feet (Type B) show the forefoot and the heel connected by a band about 2 inches wide or more. Curved feet (Type C) have a narrow band connecting the forefoot and heel. (See Figure 2.5.)

SECTION 5   How to Put Your Best Foot Forward

Now that you know how to choose the right size, shape, and kind of footwear, you need to learn about the proper techniques for walking and jogging. The movements used in walking and jogging are often used in other activities that you might participate in, such as in-line skating, tennis, and other recreational sports. As you learn new skills and participate in new activities, you should be aware that biomechanical factors can influence how well you perform in terms of both efficiency and safety.

Biomechanics is the study of the principles of physics applied to human motion. For example, when you jog slowly, your foot strikes the ground with a force that is three to five times your body weight. This activity places tremendous force and stress on the feet, lower legs, knees, upper legs, hips, and back. By understanding the biomechanics of walking and jogging, you can minimize these forces and stresses. You then can avoid injuries and reduce excessive wear and tear on your footwear.

The following suggestions will help you walk and jog safely and efficiently from a biomechanical standpoint:

- Start slowly. Follow the recommendations for efficient, gentle walking and jogging in Figure 2.6.
- Breathe deeply through your nose and mouth, rather than through your nose only.
- Relax your fingers, hands, arms, shoulders, neck, and jaw.
- Bend your arms at the elbows at about 90 degrees. Swing your arms straight forward and back instead of across your body.
- Stand nearly erect. Hold your head up, and minimize your head motion.
- Develop a smooth, even stride that feels natural and comfortable to you.
- When your foot strikes the ground, it should land on the heel. Try to point your toes straight ahead as your heel strikes the ground. You should push off on the ball of your foot.
- Do not pound noisily as you walk or jog. Avoid slapping your feet and excessive bouncing.
- Try to walk or jog on a soft surface, such as a dirt road, track, or grassy area, as opposed to a concrete or asphalt surface. Avoid hilly surfaces, because they can place unusual stress on your muscles and joints.

biomechanics

the study of the principles of physics applied to human motion.

A sound mind in a sound body, is a short but full description of a happy state in this world.

John Locke
1632–1704, from *Some Thoughts Concerning Education*, 1693.

Use the "Active Mind/Active Body" activity on page 59 to evaluate your walking and jogging form. This information will help you prevent injuries and may improve your form.

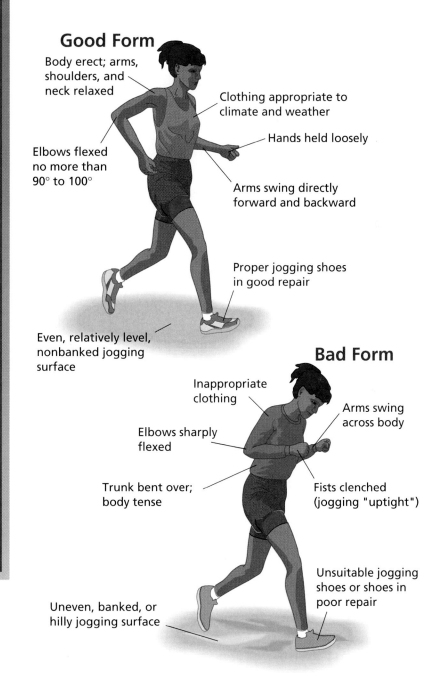

Good Form

Body erect; arms, shoulders, and neck relaxed

Clothing appropriate to climate and weather

Hands held loosely

Elbows flexed no more than 90° to 100°

Arms swing directly forward and backward

Proper jogging shoes in good repair

Even, relatively level, nonbanked jogging surface

Bad Form

Inappropriate clothing

Arms swing across body

Elbows sharply flexed

Trunk bent over; body tense

Fists clenched (jogging "uptight")

Unsuitable jogging shoes or shoes in poor repair

Uneven, banked, or hilly jogging surface

• **Figure 2.6** *Good and Bad Jogging Form. Start Slow and Follow the Illustrated Mechanics for Efficient Gentle Jogging.*

SECTION 5 REVIEW

Answer the following questions on a separate sheet of paper:

1. What is biomechanics?
2. List and compare correct and incorrect biomechanical walking and jogging techniques.

SECTION 6   Injury Prevention and Care

REMEMBER This!

A little thought and planning can help you avoid many injuries. However, if you do get injured, take care of even the most minor cases. You can then prevent injuries from getting worse. For example, you can avoid letting a cut get infected.

Injuries often occur in personal fitness programs. The best way to prevent injuries is by recognizing the common types of injuries. You also need to care for injuries properly and, when necessary, have them evaluated by medical professionals.

The most common types of fitness injuries are to the skin, muscles, connective tissue, and bones. Most of the injuries you encounter will probably be minor. However, you should always pay close attention to any injury, and seek out medical attention if the injury continues to interfere with your personal fitness program for more than a week or two. Discuss injuries that might happen to you with your physical education instructor, the school nurse, your parents, and your personal doctor.

Injuries to the Skin

Common skin injuries include cuts, scrapes, bruises, and blisters. Minor cuts and scrapes usually heal in a few days if you keep them clean, apply antiseptic medicine to the injured area, and cover the injury site with a bandage. Most minor bruises will not need treatment and will disappear in a week or so.

Blisters are usually caused by excessive friction between the skin and another surface. Foot blisters are common when you first start conditioning. They can be prevented by gradually breaking your shoes in and wearing socks that fit well. If you get a blister, treat it like a cut or scrape, and do not let it dry out.

Muscle Injuries

Muscle injuries usually involve **strains** or muscle cramps. A strain can be a pull, tear, or rip in a muscle or tendon. (**Tendons** are bands

strain

a pull, tear, or rip in a muscle or tendon.

tendon

a band of tissue that connects muscle to bone.

Biomechanically Correct Walking and Jogging Checklist

Use the questions below to analyze your walking and jogging form. Be sure to mark your answers on a separate sheet of paper, not in your book.

	I'm Doing Fine!	Improvement Needed!
1. Is my breathing relaxed and rhythmical?	_____	_____
2. Are my hands, arms, shoulders, neck, and jaw relaxed?	_____	_____
3. Are my arms at about 90 degrees and swinging straight forward, not across my body?	_____	_____
4. Is my upper body erect, with minimal head motion?	_____	_____
5. Is my stride length not too long, not too short?	_____	_____
6. Is my foot stride heel to toe, with toes pointed straight ahead?	_____	_____
7. Is there excessive bouncing or slapping of my feet?	_____	_____

BELIEVE IT? ... OR NOT?

Sport shoes can easily last for two to three years and still have plenty of cushioning for walking or jogging.

See page 57 for answer.

of tissue that connect muscles to bones.) Strains may result from insufficient warm-up, lack of flexibility, overtraining, or other situations. Strains often cause the injured area to swell. You should seek medical attention for any swelling. Proper first aid for a strain that has swelling includes rest (*R*), ice (*I*), compression (*C*), and elevation (*E*), or *RICE*. For example, if you get a strain, stop activity. Apply ice to the area. (Do not apply ice directly to the skin. Use an ice pack or ice in a towel.) Wrap the area in an elastic bandage. Finally, raise the body part. Never immediately apply heat to a strain because this can cause additional swelling and slow the recovery process.

Muscle cramps are painful spasms that can occur during physical activity or exercise. Muscle cramps are usually associated with dehydration or an imbalance in minerals in the body. You can avoid most muscle cramps by making sure you are not dehydrated. One com-

stitch

a sharp pain on the side or sides of the abdomen; a common form of muscle cramp most commonly caused by improperly conditioned breathing muscles.

ligament

a band of tissue that connects bone to bone and limits the movement of a joint.

cartilage

a soft, cushioned material that surrounds the ends of bones at a joint to prevent the bones from rubbing against each other.

stress fracture

a bone injury caused by overuse; also called *fatigue fracture.*

BELIEVE IT? ... OR NOT?

If your best time in the mile at sea level is ten minutes, you will be able to run the mile in about eleven minutes at an altitude of 7,000 feet.

See page 57 for answer.

mon form of a muscle cramp is a **stitch**, a sharp pain on the side or sides of your upper abdomen. The most common cause for stitches is a lack of proper conditioning for the breathing muscles. Stitches often occur when you are not used to breathing deeply for several minutes at a time. Side stitches usually disappear as you become conditioned and improve your personal fitness level.

Connective Tissue Injuries

Connective tissue can be injured by overuse. The kinds of connective tissue (soft tissue material that helps hold bones and joints in place) usually involved are tendons, ligaments, and cartilage. **Ligaments** are bands of tissue that connect bone to bone and limit the movement of joints. **Cartilage** surrounds the ends of bones at a joint to prevent the bones from rubbing against each other (see Figure 2.7).

Two of the most common connective tissue injuries you may see are shinsplints and sprains. *A shinsplint* is an inflammation of a tendon or muscle, which causes several types of pain in the front or side of the lower leg. Shinsplints can have a variety of causes. They can usually be treated by wearing proper footwear and using RICE. Sometimes shinsplints can get severe and require care by a doctor. Sprains usually involve a partial tear of a ligament. (A familiar cause is twisting your ankle.) Sprains can be minor or severe and are often treated with RICE. Always have a doctor evaluate a sprain immediately for proper care.

Injuries to Bones

Injuries to bones are serious and require medical care. Some bone injuries, such as **stress fractures**, are caused by overuse. Your doctor may not be able to diagnose such an injury until several weeks after it occurs. Stress fractures start as a small crack in a bone. There is usually pain above and below the crack in the bone, and it is very tender to touch. Over time (four to six weeks), the stress fracture will get worse. At that time it can often be noticed by your doctor upon X-ray examination.

Preventing Injuries

You may be asking yourself, "Why should I be active if I am going to get injured?" In terms of your health, it is far more hazardous to be inactive than to face the risks of injury by being active. To prevent or safely treat common injuries, follow these guidelines:

- Pay attention to your body. If you feel unusually sore or fatigued, postpone activity or exercise until you feel better.

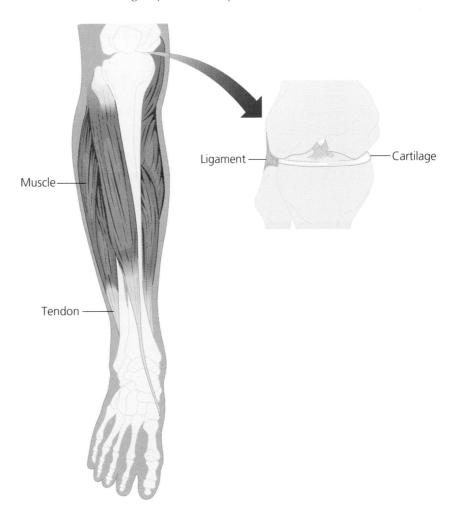

Muscle

Tendon

Ligament

Cartilage

• *Figure 2.7* *A Joint and Its Connective Tissue.*

- Include a proper warm-up and cool-down in your personal fitness program. You'll learn about warm-ups and cool-downs in the next chapter.
- Monitor the frequency, intensity, and time/duration of your exercise closely, and make your progression slow and steady (more about this in Chapter 3).
- If you run or walk in traffic, always face the oncoming traffic.
- Wear reflective clothing during night physical activities or exercise (walking, jogging, and so on).
- Use proper safety equipment for activities with a higher injury risk (skateboarding, in-line skating, cycling, and the like).
- Always seek out proper medical advice when you have an injury.

SECTION 6 REVIEW

Answer the following questions on a separate sheet of paper:

1. What is RICE?
2. For treatment of a strain, why should heat not be applied to the injured area?

SECTION 7 — Adherence to a Personal Fitness Program

adherence

the ability to continue something, such as your chosen personal fitness program, over a period of time.

Adherence refers to your ability to continue, or stick to, your personal fitness program. If you adhere to it, your program is a success. Unfortunately, many people stop participating in their personal fitness programs. Many of the factors with a negative impact on adherence were listed in Chapter 1's discussion of attitudes and beliefs about personal fitness. These factors are repeated here:

- Lack of time.
- Poor physical condition.
- High percentage of body fat.
- Unrealistic personal fitness goals or expectations.
- Lack of accurate knowledge about physical fitness.
- Feelings of being unathletic.

BELIEVE IT? ... OR NOT?

Ten to fifteen high school athletes die every year from heat injuries that are preventable.

See page 57 for answer.

- *Working out with a friend can help you improve your adherence.*

Stress Break

Don't let your workouts become a source of stress in your life. Instead, let your workouts fit into your life. If you have a tight schedule, and other priorities sometimes interfere with your workout time, don't get too worried. Deal with your priorities and, as soon as possible, get back on your routine. This way you won't resent your working out. In fact, often you will notice that the lay-off was good for your mental attitude. You may find that after a break you are more relaxed and enjoying your workout time even more.

- Fear of physical overstrain.
- Past negative experiences with physical activity, exercise, or both.
- Concerns about negative peer pressure.

By understanding some of the factors that might interfere with your adherence, you can increase your odds for achieving a successful personal fitness program. Remember, it is your right and your duty to yourself to develop personal fitness. Figure 2.8 highlights several factors that can help you improve your adherence.

What can you do to improve your adherence to your program? First, make a contract with yourself to participate regularly in personal fitness.

Second, set reasonable, achievable, and specific goals. Develop realistic expectations. For example, you may want to be able to swim one mile continuously, in thirty minutes. You will need to start with a program that helps you work up to that level—for example, swimming steadily for five minutes, then ten minutes, and so on up to thirty minutes. It may be several weeks before you can achieve your goal. This is normal.

Third, be patient. The positive changes and benefits of your personal fitness program will occur gradually. Control your initial enthusiasm. Listen to your body for any signs that you are working too hard, too soon (see the previous discussion on preventing injuries).

Fourth, develop a schedule for your regular participation in physical activity and exercise. If a conflict interferes with your schedule, get back to your personal fitness program as soon as you can. Remember, do not dwell on feelings of guilt if you occasionally have to skip your physical activity or exercise. Focus on the positive aspects of your personal fitness program, and recognize that it is what you do over the long haul that is important.

Fifth, participate with friends or family members when you can. Make physical activity or exercise a social experience as well as a physical one.

- Choose activities of moderate intensity
- Choose low-impact weight-bearing activities
- Start slowly
- Progress gradually
- Emphasize activities you prefer
- Avoid injuries
- Participate in cross-training
- Make your program convenient
- Expand your total time up to thirty to sixty minutes

- *Figure 2.8* *How to Improve Your Adherence.*

Sixth, develop a progress chart to plot your improvements. Occasionally assess your physical fitness level to determine if you are maintaining reasonable levels of personal fitness. (Chapters 4, 5, 6, 8, and 9 will discuss this further.)

Finally, engage in physical activities and exercises that you like to do. Vary your routine with a variety of activities. Adherence levels are usually higher if you choose activities of low impact (low stress on the joints) and do them at a moderately intense level.

SECTION 7 REVIEW

Answer the following questions on a separate sheet of paper:

1. Give three reasons why people drop out of personal fitness programs.
2. What are some things you could do to improve your adherence to your personal fitness program?

SUMMARY

Participation in physical activity and exercise programs can benefit your health and well-being. However, to maximize the benefits of participation, you need to make sure that your physical activity and exercise are safe for you.

You should recognize the factors (heart disease, severe obesity, high blood pressure, kidney disease, and diabetes) that determine whether you need to have a medical evaluation prior to beginning your personal fitness program. You should be able to identify the dangers (heat injuries or frostbite) of participating in physical activity or exercise when it is very hot or very cold, as well as be able to minimize your injury risks. Various outdoor environmental problems (including air pollution, dogs, and crime) can also be hazardous to you. Investigate your environment before you begin your program.

Choosing the right clothing and footwear for physical activity and exercise will help you be more comfortable and safe. Proper safety equipment (helmets, elbow pads, knee pads, and so on) will significantly reduce your risks for muscle and skeletal injuries. If you apply an understanding of biomechanics to activities such as walking and jogging, you will avoid injuries and minimize excessive wear and tear on your footwear.

You can significantly reduce the risk of injuries in your personal fitness program by safely and slowly changing the frequency, intensity, and time/duration of your exercise. Finally, you can improve your personal fitness adherence by paying attention to conflicts that will interfere with your success and by developing a realistic plan to enhance your opportunities to be physically active.

Chapter 2 Review

True/False

On a separate sheet of paper, mark each question below either T for True or F for False.

1. Healthy young adults with no history of heart problems are unlikely to need a medical examination before starting an exercise program.

2. Healthy young adults should be encouraged to have a medical evaluation every two to three years.

3. In cold weather, exercise clothing should be made of a heavy material and be tight fitting. This will help prevent heat loss.

4. Carbon monoxide, a dangerous gas, is associated with streets and highways that have high volumes of traffic.

5. Exercising at low or high altitudes has little effect on your performance.

6. A good pair of basketball shoes, a T-shirt, and a pair of shorts are all the things you need to get started with a jogging program.

7. It is always a good idea to try on exercise shoes with socks before you purchase them.

8. Statistics show that wearing a helmet when skateboarding is really not necessary.

9. It is a good idea to match the shape of your foot with the shape of the shoe you buy.

10. *RICE* stands for rest, ice, compression, and elevation.

Multiple Choice

1. A medical examination would include tests to study which of the following?
   a. blood pressure, hernia, and lung sounds
   b. exercise stress test, urine, and blood
   c. medical history, eyes, and ears
   d. nose, throat, and heart sounds

2. Which of the following is not an example of a chronic disease?
   a. heart disease
   b. kidney disease
   c. diabetes
   d. two or three colds per year

3. Which of the following should be considered when purchasing a new pair of shoes?
   a. the shape of the shoe
   b. pronation support
   c. supination support
   d. flexible sole
   e. all of the above

4. When the weather is hot and humid, you will sweat excessively and lose large amounts of fluids. What is this condition called?
   a. hyperthermia
   b. dehydration
   c. heat cramps
   d. heat stroke

5. Anyone exercising in warm and humid environments should pay attention to which of the following?
   a. drinking plenty of fluids
   b. proper clothing
   c. heat injury symptoms
   d. all of the above

6. If you decide to drink a commercially made sports drink when you exercise in the heat, what percentage of carbohydrates should you look for in the drink?
   a. 1 percent
   b. 2 to 3 percent
   c. 5 to 8 percent
   d. 9 to 10 percent
   e. greater than 15 percent

7. When exercising in extreme cold conditions, it is possible for your body temperature to drop below normal (98.6 degrees Fahrenheit). What is this condition called?

   a. frostbite
   b. hyperthermia
   c. hypothermia
   d. none of the above

8. Which of the following is *not* a guideline for exercising in high altitudes?

   a. Drink plenty of fluids.
   b. Gradually change altitude.
   c. Eat meals more often to prevent altitude sickness.
   d. Gradually increase exercise over a period of time.

9. If you were going to exercise in a potentially dangerous area, which of the following guidelines would you *not* use?

   a. avoid verbal confrontation
   b. exercise in well-lit areas
   c. exercise alone, when possible
   d. let someone know where you have gone

10. Which of the following will not improve your adherence to your personal fitness program?

   a. working at moderate intensities
   b. starting slowly
   c. engaging in high-impact, weight-bearing activities
   d. making your program convenient
   e. participating in cross-training

Discussion

1. Explain why it is important to know the air temperature and the amount of humidity in the air. How can this affect exercise?

2. Identify and explain the main differences between symptoms of heat exhaustion and heat stroke. What are the treatments for each condition?

3. Tell what you should consider and do before you ever buy a pair of physical activity or exercise shoes.

Vocabulary Experience

Match the correct term in Column A to the definition in Column B by writing the appropriate number in each blank.

Column A

_____ medical screening

_____ hypothermia

_____ heat exhaustion

_____ pronation

_____ adherence

_____ biomechanics

Column B

1. An inward roll of the foot during jogging.

2. An evaluation of the eyes, ears, nose, throat, blood pressure, and so on.

3. Continued success with a personal fitness program.

4. The study of the principles of physics applied to human motion.

5. A drop in body temperature to below normal.

6. A condition with symptoms that include weakness; headache; stomach discomfort; and cool, clammy skin.

Critical Thinking

1. What kinds of physical activities that you like to do require protective safety equipment? List the safety equipment you feel you would need to perform these activities. Explain how the equipment would help you prevent injuries.

2. What is your level of adherence to physical activity and exercise? Why?

3. Explain the importance of using replacement fluids following vigorous exercise in the heat. Which fluids do you use? Why?

Case Study—David's Fitness Program

David is an unfit, overweight fifteen-year-old who has lived all his life in Anchorage, Alaska. His father recently made a career change that required the family to move to central Texas. David has never been very athletic or physically active, and he has not paid much attention to his health or personal fitness.

Now that he has moved to a much warmer climate and the different weather conditions of Texas, he would like to make some improvements in his fitness habits (behaviors). He feels he should take advantage of his new environment by starting a physical activity and exercise program. His goals are to lose 20 pounds and to improve his cardiovascular fitness level.

David has no experience with personal fitness programs and knows little about them. He does realize that he needs the help of someone knowledgeable about designing and implementing fitness programs—someone like you!

Here is your assignment: David—Part I

Assume you are David's neighbor, and he has asked you to help him plan his new physically active lifestyle. Organize a list of things David should consider and do before beginning a moderate to vigorous personal fitness program.

KEYS TO HELP YOU

- Consider David's current medical status.
- List the concerns David must deal with as he changes from his previous environment to his new environment.
- Consider David's needs and desires.

Chapter 3

Designing Physical Activity and Exercise Programs

Contents

Outcomes

After reading and studying this chapter, you will be able to:

1. Define and explain the terms related to designing physical activity and exercise programs.
2. Explain the importance of understanding exercise science principles and how they apply to the workout component of your personal fitness program.
3. Explain the purpose of proper warm-up, and describe the different types of warm-up.
4. Describe how you would design your personal fitness prescription for working out.
5. Explain the purpose of proper cool-down, and describe the different types of cool-down.

Key Terms

After reading and studying this chapter, you will be able to understand and provide practical definitions for the following terms:

dose	conditioning	warm-up
overload principle	mode	active warm-up
FIT	progression principle	muscle/skeletal warm-up
personal fitness	overuse injury	static body stretches
prescription	trainability	cardiovascular warm-up
frequency	plateau effect	specific active warm-up
intensity	detraining	general active warm-up
heart rate	cross-train	passive warm-up
maximum heart rate	overtraining	blood pooling
perceived exertion	physical activity zealot;	cardiovascular cool-down
talk test	exercise zealot	stretching cool-down
time/duration	acute	
specificity principle	chronic	

INTRODUCTION

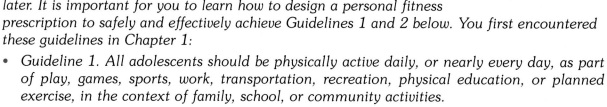

*P*hysical activity and exercise can be prescribed much like medication because the benefits of physical activity or exercise are dose related. In other words, amount and frequency of physical activity and exercise in your life will determine the benefits that you can gain by participating in your personal fitness program. For example, the dose of physical activity or exercise necessary for health benefits (reduced risk of chronic disease) is often less than the dose needed for physical fitness benefits (such as higher personal fitness goals). After taking this course, you will not have to go to the doctor to get a prescription for physical activity or exercise. You will be highly qualified to write your own personal fitness prescription.

A personal fitness prescription includes several factors: how often you work, how hard you work, length of time you work, the type of activity or exercise you do, and other factors that will be discussed later. It is important for you to learn how to design a personal fitness prescription to safely and effectively achieve Guidelines 1 and 2 below. You first encountered these guidelines in Chapter 1:

- *Guideline 1. All adolescents should be physically active daily, or nearly every day, as part of play, games, sports, work, transportation, recreation, physical education, or planned exercise, in the context of family, school, or community activities.*

- *Guideline 2. Adolescents should engage in three or more sessions per week of activities that last twenty minutes or more at a time and that require moderate to vigorous levels of exertion.*

To meet the objective of Guideline 1, it is important for you to adopt an active lifestyle that encourages you to spend time in physical activity or exercise every day. A simple personal fitness plan is all that is necessary to achieve Guideline 1. Include physical activity as part of your daily lifestyle. Make it a simple and common occurrence, like brushing your teeth.

To meet the objective of Guideline 2, you will find it helpful to develop a more detailed personal fitness prescription that will meet your individual goals and interests. To carry out Guideline 2, you will need to set reasonable goals, engage in moderate to vigorous physical activity or exercise, and keep records of your progress.

Before you can design your personal fitness prescription, you must understand the scientific principles of physical activity and exercise. You must also learn about the art of applying these scientific principles to insure that your program is safe and effective. The material in the first two sections of this chapter is based on recommendations from the leading exercise science organization in the world, the American College of Sports Medicine (ACSM). Let's begin by exploring some of the primary scientific principles you'll need.

REMEMBER This!

Get off the couch and move! Find ways to be active. Take the stairs, not the elevator. Walk to school when possible, instead of riding in a car. Engage in recreational activities regularly.

* Reprinted with permission from "A Consensus on Physical Activity Guidelines for Adolescents" by J. F. Sallis and Kevin Patrick, *Pediatric Exercise Science*, Vol. 6, no. 4 (1994): 302–314.

SECTION 1   The Scientific Principle of Overload (Do More!)

dose

the amount and frequency of an activity or substance.

overload principle

the principle that says to improve your level of physical fitness, you must increase the amount of activity or exercise that you normally do.

FIT

the three components of the overload principle: Frequency, Intensity, and Time/Duration; a level of physical conditioning that is desirable and obtainable by everyone.

personal fitness prescription

an exercise or physical activity plan that includes frequency, intensity, time/duration, mode, and other factors.

frequency

in a personal fitness prescription, how often you work.

To improve your level of physical fitness, you must increase the **dose** (amount) of activity or exercise that you normally do. This is called the **overload principle**. The amount of overload can be increased in three different ways, as shown in Figure 3.1. The three parts of the overload principle—frequency, intensity, and time/duration—can be remembered by using the first letter of each word to form the word **FIT**. The word *FIT* describes a level or dose of physical conditioning that is desirable and obtainable by everyone.

Any **B**ody **C**an be FIT! The beginning exerciser, as well as the high-performance athlete, should incorporate the use of FIT into daily and weekly **personal fitness prescriptions** and records.

Frequency

Frequency refers to how often you engage in regular physical activity or exercise. Exercise that is too infrequent results in limited progress. Too frequent exercise can increase the possibility of injury. If you are just beginning your personal fitness program, your frequency for cardiovascular conditioning should be three to five days per week. Cardiovascular conditioning consists of specific activities that improve the efficiency of your heart, lungs, blood, and blood vessels. The frequency for a beginning weight trainer should be two to three days per week (Figure 3.2 on the next page).

Individuals of average to high fitness levels will need to consider their specific goals before they determine how frequently they will

Frequency	Intensity	Time/Duration
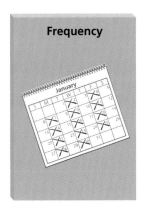		

• **Figure 3.1**   *The FIT Formula Includes Three Ways to Increase Overload.*

Activity	Frequency for Beginners	Frequency for Those of Average to High Fitness Levels
Cardiovascular conditioning	3–5 days per week	4–6 days per week
Weight training	2–3 days per week	3–5 days per week

• **Figure 3.2**   *Activity Frequency for Exercisers of Varying Fitness Levels.*

need to be active (Figure 3.2). For example, a competitive cyclist interested in competition will need to work four to six days per week. The cyclist may even occasionally want to work out multiple times per day.

The frequency of your workout sessions should be determined by the following considerations:

- What is your level of fitness?
- What are your specific goals (health or performance)?
- How hard are you working (intensity)?
- How long does each session last (time/duration)?
- How much time does your lifestyle allow you for exercise (determined by how much time you devote to jobs, schoolwork, and other commitments)?

Intensity

intensity

in a personal fitness prescription, how hard you work.

heart rate

the number of times your heart beats per minute.

maximum heart rate

the maximum number of times your heart can beat in a minute.

Intensity refers to the difficulty of your physical activity or exercise. If the intensity is too low, progress is limited. If you work too hard, you fatigue quickly and increase your risk for injury.

Suggested Heart Rate and Weight Lifting Intensities. **Heart rate** is the number of times your heart beats per minute. It is recommended that the beginning exerciser work at an intensity that is 60 to 70 percent of his or her maximum heart rate for cardiovascular conditioning. **Maximum heart rate** is the maximum number of times your heart can beat per minute. Maximum heart rate is determined, to a great extent, by age. It will be discussed in greater detail in Chapter 5. Figure 3.3 shows the range of predicted maximum heart rates for students fourteen to eighteen years of age.

A beginning heart rate level for cardiovascular fitness would be about 120 to 145 beats per minute. If you are of an average to high fitness level, you can and should work at moderate to higher intensities, or heart rates of about 145 to 185 beats per minute.

The beginning weight trainer should determine intensity of exercise differently. He or she should use as a guide 60 to 70 percent of the maximum amount of weight he or she can lift one time for any exercise. For example, say your maximum lift for the bench press is

• *These water polo players are working at high intensity.*

Age	Predicted Maximum Heart Rate
14	206
15	205
16	204
17	203
18	202

• **Figure 3.3** *Your Predicted Maximum Heart Rate.*

100 pounds. You would then bench press 60 or 70 pounds eight to twelve times. The weight trainer of average to high fitness levels can work at moderate to higher intensities, or 70 to 85 percent of the maximum amount of weight he or she can lift one time for any exercise. These recommendations are summarized in Figure 3.4.

The intensity of your workout sessions should be determined by the following considerations:

• What is your level of fitness?

• What are your specific goals (health or performance)?

Activity	Intensity for Beginners	Intensity for Those of Average to High Fitness Levels
Cardiovascular conditioning	120–145 beats/min.	145–185 beats/min.
Weight training	60–70% of max. lift	70–85% of max. lift

• **Figure 3.4** *Activity Intensity for Exercises of Varying Fitness Levels.*

perceived exertion

how hard a person feels he or she is working during physical activity or exercise.

talk test

a test that uses a person's ease or difficulty in carrying on a conversation while engaged in physical activity or exercise to measure exercise intensity.

time/duration

in a personal fitness prescription, the length of time you work.

6	No exertion at all
7	Extremely light
8	
9	Very light
10	
11	Light
12	
13	Somewhat hard (moderate)
14	
15	Hard/heavy
16	Vigorous
17	Very hard
18	
19	Extremely hard
20	Maximal exertion

• **Figure 3.5** *Perceived Exertion Scale. How hard a person feels he/she has worked during physical activity or exercise.*

Source: Adapted with permission from G. Borg, "Psychophysical Bases of Perceived Exertion," *Medicine and Science in Sports and Exercise,* Vol. 14, no. 5 (1982), 377.

- How often do you engage in physical activities or exercise (frequency)?
- How long does each session last (time/duration)?

You have learned that an important way to determine your target physical activity or exercise intensity is by measuring your heart rate. The "Active Mind/Active Body" activities on pages 75 and 76 will give you experience in measuring your resting and exercising heart rates.

Perceived Exertion.   Another simple method of determining intensity is based on Figure 3.5. Use the figure to rate how hard overall you feel you are working during physical activity or exercise (**perceived exertion**). The perceived exertion scale in Figure 3.5 ranges in value from 6 to 20. If you were sitting at rest, your rating of perceived exertion would probably be 6 and would represent "no exertion at all." If you were cycling, you would monitor your feelings of how hard you were breathing, your heart rate, your body temperature, and any muscle or skeletal discomfort to get your overall perceived exertion. You then might rate the intensity of your cycling as 13 if you were working moderately hard, or 16 if you were working vigorously. The perceived exertion method of determining intensity is easy to use once you have gained experience with physical activity and exercise in your personal fitness program.

Talk Test.   Another way to use perceived exertion to monitor your intensity is with the **talk test**. The talk test determines how easily you are able to carry on a conversation while you are engaged in physical activity or exercise. For example, if you rate your intensity between 11 and 16 (light to vigorous), you should be able to carry on a conversation with an exercising partner. This is an appropriate intensity level for your fitness program. However, if you and your partner are struggling to talk to each other, you are probably working harder than the *vigorous* level, which is harder than you need to work for basic personal fitness goals.

Time/Duration

Time/duration refers to how long in minutes, hours, or days you engage in physical activities or exercise sessions. A time/duration that is too short may result in limited progress. A time/duration that is too long will increase your risk for overuse injuries.

Beginning exercisers should accumulate twenty to thirty minutes of cardiovascular activity or exercise three to five days a week. You may accumulate your twenty to thirty minutes in one continuous workout session, or you may choose to collect your thirty minutes in three separate, ten-minute activity or exercise sessions. For example, you might take a brisk walk for ten minutes in the morning, another at noon, and another in the evening.

Active Mind! Active Body!

Taking Your Resting Pulse

The photographs below show you how to locate and take your pulse at two sites (the carotid artery, located at your throat, and the radial artery, located on the thumb side of your wrist). Use your index and middle fingers together on your dominant hand (preferred writing hand) to locate your pulse at either your neck or wrist. To measure your carotid pulse, put your fingers on the side of your throat by your Adam's apple, and press lightly. (Do not use both hands, as you may cut off the circulation of blood to your head.) Use a clock or watch to count for six seconds. Record the number of beats you get in six seconds. Then multiply that number by 10 to get your heart rate for one minute.

What did you get? Try it again on yourself. Then get a partner, and measure each other. To get your true resting pulse, you will need to take your pulse immediately when you wake up in the morning. Measure your resting pulse the next two mornings. What did you get?

Now that you know how to get your resting pulse, let's explore how different levels of work (intensities) influence your physical activity or exercise heart rate. Do the "Active Mind/Active Body" activity on the next page.

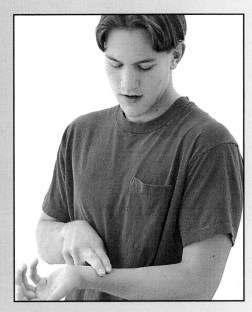

Active **Mind!**
Active **Body!**

The Effect of Intensity on Heart Rate

Carefully record your pulse rate on a separate sheet of paper after each of the following activities:

1. Lie down for five minutes. Be as still and quiet as possible. Record your pulse rate. (This is not a true resting rate, because you have been up and active for some time. To measure your true resting heart rate, you would need to take it just when you woke up in the morning, before you got out of bed.)

2. Stand up, and record your pulse rate.

3. Walk around the gym for one minute, and record your pulse rate.

4. Jog slowly around the gym for one minute, and record your pulse rate.

5. Bound, jump, or hop around the gym for forty seconds, and record your pulse rate.

6. Do thirty jumping jacks, and record your pulse rate.

7. Do an all-out sprint for forty seconds, and record your pulse rate. Be sure to keep good spacing between you and your classmates. Take your pulse at the completion of your run, but remember to continue to walk for an additional three minutes after you take your pulse.

8. After you do a three-minute walk, sit down and do static stretching for an additional two minutes, then record your pulse. Keep stretching for another two minutes, and record your pulse rate again. These pulse readings will be used as recovery pulse rates.

REMEMBER This!

A quick and easy way to estimate your exercise heart rate is to count your pulse rate for six seconds immediately after activity. Then add a 0 to the number of beats you counted, and you will automatically have your estimated exercise heart rate. The number you get should be in your intensity zone (for example, beginner, or average to high fitness level).

Look at the sample graph on the next page. In this graph the nine pulse rates you just recorded have been plotted for an imaginary person. After studying this sample, plot your pulse rates to create your own personal graph. Then answer the questions below the graph.

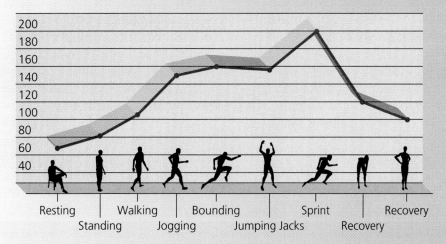

Sample Effects of Different Exercises on Your Heart Rate

1. Which activity generated the highest pulse rate?
2. Which activity generated the lowest pulse rate?
3. Which activity was the easiest and which was the most difficult?
4. What is the relationship between your pulse rate and the intensity of the physical activity (work load)?
5. If two people start and finish a 1-mile run at the same time, making sure to remain side by side during the entire activity, how could you determine which person worked the hardest?
6. Which of these activities would be the best choice for a daily 20-minute aerobic activity and why?

• **Figure 3.6** *Use the graph above as a reference to plot all nine of your pulse recordings. On a separate sheet of paper, draw a graph similar to the one shown above. Make a small circle to indicate the beats per minute. Then connect the circles with a thin line. Be sure to discuss the questions below the graph.*

CONSUMER CORNER

High Tech vs. Low Tech Heart Monitors

Many exercisers are using technology to monitor their heart rates. There are a variety of shapes, styles, and prices in the heart rate monitoring business. One type of heart rate monitor is the pulse bar, which you hold in your hand. Another type can fit on your ear or on your finger to give you a pulse readout. The most accurate type fits around your chest right over the heart and transmits a signal of your pulse to a wristwatch. You may want to experiment with one of these heart rate monitors when you work out.

Heart rate monitors provide a simple, accurate way to measure your heart rate, and thereby, the intensity of your workout.

Do not think, however, that heart rate monitors are necessary for a safe, effective personal fitness program.

You will find directions and photos that will help you learn to take your own pulse with nothing more than a watch on page 75 of this text. You will probably feel uncertain and clumsy the first few times you try to take your pulse. With a little practice, however, you will become very skilled at measuring your heart rate accurately.

Remember, you do not need a lot of expensive equipment to make yourself physically fit. With a pair of exercise shoes and the desire to be fit, you can be successful at obtaining and maintaining personal fitness.

BELIEVE IT? ... OR NOT?

The Centers for Disease Control in Atlanta, Georgia, has found that 13 percent of all male runners and 17 percent of all female runners seek medical attention for running-related injuries during any given year.

See page 96 for answer.

Continue these beginning cardiovascular workout sessions for the first two to three weeks, which will allow you to improve slowly and safely. As you become more fit, increase the length of time for each session anywhere from 35 minutes to 1 hour. The American College of Sports Medicine recommends 20 to 60 minutes of continuous or noncontinuous activity per physical activity or exercise session. Your specific goals will determine the time/duration for your prescription. For example, your goal may be to lose weight. Longer workout sessions of lower intensity, in your case, will result in a greater loss of weight.

If you are already of an average to high fitness level, you may find that the length of your daily workouts needs to be longer based on your personal goals. One way you can adjust your time/duration is by alternating harder days (45 minutes to 1 hour) with easier days (20 to 40 minutes).

If you are doing weight training, the time/duration will be determined by the number of exercises you perform. The beginning weight trainer will spend twenty to thirty minutes, whereas the individual of average to high fitness level will spend forty-five minutes to one hour. These recommendations are summarized in Figure 3.7.

Activity	Time/Duration for Beginners	Time/Duration for Those of Average to High Fitness Levels
Cardiovascular conditioning	20–30 minutes	35 minutes to 1 hour
Weight training	20–30 minutes	45 minutes to 1 hour

• **Figure 3.7** *Activity, Time/Duration for Exercisers of Varying Fitness Levels.*

REMEMBER This!

Intensity and time/duration for physical activity or exercise are difficult to determine separately. The higher the intensity of your activity, the shorter your activity time/duration will typically be. The lower the intensity of your activity, the longer your activity time/duration can be.

The time/duration of your workout sessions should be determined by the following considerations:

- What is your level of fitness?
- What are your specific goals (health or performance)?
- How hard are you working (intensity)?
- How often are you working (frequency)?
- How much time does your lifestyle allow you for exercise (determined by how much time you devote to jobs, schoolwork, and other commitments)?

SECTION 1 REVIEW

Answer the following questions on a separate sheet of paper:

1. What is the overload principle, and why is it important to your personal fitness program?
2. What are the relationships between FIT and your personal fitness program?
3. What is the talk test, and how and when should you use it?

SECTION 2 The Scientific Principle of Specificity (Be Specific!)

Improvements in your personal fitness will occur in the particular muscles that you overload during physical activity or exercise. This is called the **specificity principle**. You will see personal fitness adaptations your body makes according to your involvement in different

specificity principle

the principle that says improvements in your personal fitness will occur in the particular muscles that you overload during physical activity or exercise.

conditioning

engaging in regular physical activity or exercise that results in an improved state of physical fitness.

mode

in a personal fitness prescription, the type of activity or exercise you do.

BELIEVE IT? ...
OR NOT?

"No train, no gain!" is a good way to describe physical activity or exercise; if you do not engage in physical activity or exercise on a regular basis, you will not acquire the positive benefits of a personal fitness program.

See page 96 for answer.

activities. For example, if you lift weights, the muscles that you move to lift the weights will get stronger as you overload them. Muscles that are not required to help move the weights will not change in terms of strength.

The specific changes that you see following a period of **conditioning** occur in different ways, depending on the activities or exercise you engage in. For example, if your goal is to become a better in-line skater, you will get the best results by focusing on improving your skills and conditioning while in-line skating. You may see some improvements in your in-line skating if you perform other activities, such as cycling on a regular basis, but the changes will not be as great as they would be if you were more specific in your conditioning. Also, if you condition yourself specifically to improve your strength, you will see minimal changes in your cardiovascular endurance.

To apply the specificity principle effectively, you need to evaluate your personal fitness goals and determine the realistic improvements you want to achieve. You can then choose specific activities or exercises to help yourself achieve your goals.

Mode of Activity

You do have a choice in the type of physical activity in which you participate. **Mode** refers to the type of physical activity or exercise you choose to do. For example, modes of cardiovascular conditioning include walking, jogging, swimming, and cycling. The mode of physical activities and exercises you do should be determined by the following considerations:

- What are your specific goals?
- How much time do you have?
- What do you like to do for fun?
- How much money do you have to spend on equipment?
- How do you plan to achieve Guidelines 1 and 2 (discussed previously) in your personal fitness plan?

Special Situations

In certain situations, such as those in which you are injured, sick, or on medication, you will need to adjust your personal fitness plan. For example, if you suffer a leg injury during a jogging program, you may have to stop jogging and engage in other cross-training activities (cycling, swimming, and so on) until your leg heals. If you get sick for several days, you should modify your personal fitness plan so you can gradually return to your previous conditioning level over a few weeks. Your personal fitness program should be designed to optimize your health and well-being. Thus, you should adjust your program to accommodate situations that might negatively influence your benefits.

• The variety of physical activities that you can choose to include in your personal fitness program is almost limitless. Try to find new activities that you enjoy.

Record Keeping

Record keeping is just as important to the beginning exerciser as it is to the high-performance athlete. Anyone involved in physical activity or exercise should have specific goals and a plan to reach those goals. A physical activity and exercise record book can help you safely and successfully reach your goals. Your record-keeping book should consider any or all of the following items:

- Your goals (for example, to lose weight, get stronger, reduce stress, or run a marathon).
- How many and which days you exercise (try not to miss more than one day between exercise sessions).
- Time, distance, and intensity (heart rate, amount of weight lifted on hard and easy days).
- Weather conditions (temperature, smog, or humidity).
- Different routes you may have taken; places you exercised.
- Specific activities or exercises you did (weight training, swimming, backpacking, in-line skating, lawn mowing, etc.).
- Injuries.
- Foods and liquids consumed.
- Weight loss or gain.
- Progress.

Any Body Can!

David B. ("D. B.") Dill

David B. "D. B." Dill (1891–1986) was a pioneer in the area of exercise science and the development of scientific principles that apply to physical activity and exercise programs. He did extensive research on the body's responses to working in different environments, and on the effects of aging.

Orphaned at a young age, Dill moved to California with his uncle in 1905. He attended Santa Ana High School in California, where he was a member of the track team. Following high school, he spent a year working as a ranch foreman in Santa Fe, New Mexico.

In 1913 he earned a Bachelor of Science degree in Chemistry from Occidental College in California. The next year he earned a Master of Science degree in Chemistry from Stanford University. Following college, he taught high school chemistry in Salt Lake City, Utah, where he also coached and served as principal.

During World War I, D. B. Dill began work on his Doctor of Philosophy degree in Physiology at Harvard University. He was particularly interested in physiology related to physical activity and exercise. In 1927 he became a professor at Harvard and Director of the Harvard Fatigue Laboratory. From 1927 to 1947, Dr. Dill and his colleagues conducted some of the first research projects related to physical activity and exercise.

One of Dr. Dill's most important contributions to personal fitness and exercise science was the research he conducted on himself. He began testing himself regularly, in his early 30s, by running on a treadmill until he was totally exhausted. He also monitored the changes in his functional health as he aged, continuing this process until he was 94. Much of what we know today about the way that functional health decreases with age is a result of Dr. Dill's work.

Dr. Dill continued to conduct research until he died at the age of 95. He wrote three books and more than 325 research papers. He served as president of the American Physiological Society from 1950–1951 and president of the American College of Sports Medicine from 1960–1961. He continued to be physically active throughout his life. Dr. Dill is perhaps best known for putting the results of scientific research into practice.

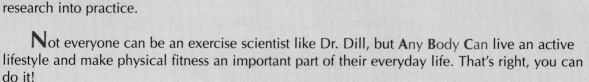

Not everyone can be an exercise scientist like Dr. Dill, but **Any Body Can** live an active lifestyle and make physical fitness an important part of their everyday life. That's right, you can do it!

SECTION 3   The Scientific Principle of Progression (Improve!)

progression principle

the rate at which you change the frequency, intensity, and time/duration (FIT) of your personal fitness prescription.

overuse injury

an injury caused by doing too much, too soon, too often in an exercise program.

BELIEVE IT? ... OR NOT?

Physical activity and exercise are panaceas (cure-alls).

See page 96 for answer.

The **progression principle** refers to the rate at which you change the FIT (frequency, intensity, and time/duration) of your personal fitness prescription. Your FIT should be gradually increased over time. The rate of progression should be based on your listening to your body and analyzing how you feel as you adapt to physical activity and exercise. You should never increase all the factors in your program (frequency, intensity, and time/duration) at the same time or increase any one factor too fast or too soon. This would probably overload your body too much and increase your risk for an **overuse injury** such as straining a muscle.

Stages of Progression

Progression in your personal fitness program should occur in stages, including an initial stage, an improvement stage, and a maintenance stage. Figure 3.8 on the next page shows how a person might move through the progression stages. The initial stage in the figure takes about eight weeks. Note the quick improvements in the fitness level of the person charted. This indicates that the person probably was very inactive at the start. (Remember, each person will adapt differently.)

From nine to thirty weeks the figure shows the improvement stage of conditioning. During this stage more gradual improvements in fitness are usually observed as FIT increases. The line extending from thirty-one weeks to one year illustrates the maintenance stage of conditioning. During this stage your FIT levels off, but don't forget that you must continue your program to keep your FIT at this level.

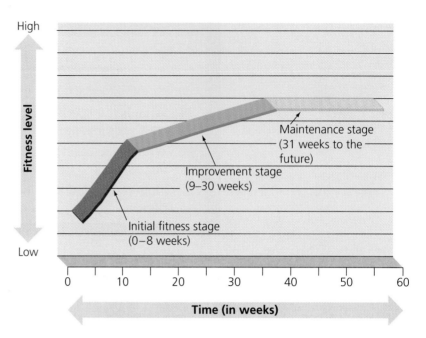

High

Fitness level

Low

Maintenance stage
(31 weeks to the
future)

Improvement stage
(9–30 weeks)

Initial fitness stage
(0–8 weeks)

0   10   20   30   40   50   60

Time (in weeks)

• **Figure 3.8** *Example of the Progression Principle. Improvement usually occurs in stages.*

> "Those who think they have not time for bodily exercise will sooner or later have to find time for illness" (Edward Stanley, Earl of Derby, in an 1873 speech).

Remember, the body can have a variety of responses to progressive overload from physical activity and exercise. Your own improvement response will depend on the following factors:

• Your initial fitness level (the lower you start, the more quickly you usually improve).

• Your genetic makeup and trainability (to be discussed shortly).

• The rate at which you overload your body or change FIT.

• Your specific goals (health or performance).

You will become better at designing and changing the progression of your personal fitness program as you gain experience with a variety of physical activities and exercise.

Trainability

trainability

the rate at which a person improves personal fitness following physical activity or exercise conditioning. Trainability is determined, to a large extent, by genetic makeup.

Trainability refers to the rate at which a person improves personal fitness following physical activity or exercise conditioning. Trainability is determined, to a large extent, by genetic makeup. For example, athletes have unusual physical abilities due, at least in part, to inherited traits. These traits allow athletes to work out at higher levels than the average person and to improve more quickly. The concept of trainability is illustrated in Figure 3.9.

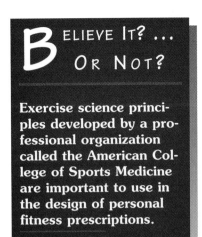

BELIEVE **I**T? ...
OR **N**OT?

Exercise science principles developed by a professional organization called the American College of Sports Medicine are important to use in the design of personal fitness prescriptions.

See page 96 for answer.

REMEMBER
This!

Not everyone can reach certain goals, such as running a mile in six minutes or becoming a champion body builder. However, given enough time and proper conditioning *Any Body* Can achieve Guidelines 1 and 2 and have positive influences on their health and well-being.

plateau effect

the leveling off of physical fitness improvement in a personal fitness program.

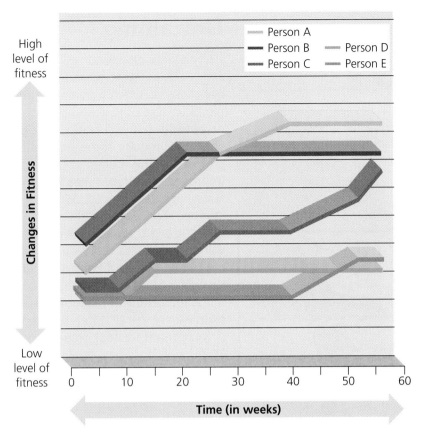

• *Figure 3.9* *Differences in Trainability Among Individuals.*

Figure 3.9 shows that Person A has a moderate initial fitness level and improves steadily during one year of conditioning to a high level of fitness. Individual B has a moderately high initial fitness level, improves rapidly in fitness for about twenty weeks, and then experiences a **plateau effect**. *Plateau effect* refers to the fact that there is a period of time when little, if any, fitness improvement occurs.

Individual C begins with an average initial fitness level and improves significantly during one year of conditioning. Individual D begins with a below-average level of fitness and does not improve to average levels until after a half-year of conditioning. Individual E begins at about the same fitness level as Individual D and experiences early modest improvements in fitness with a later plateau effect in fitness.

Individuals D and E were not able to improve as much as A, B, and C. However, both D and E were able to improve over time with conditioning. These differences could have occurred, even if all five people used exactly the same fitness program, due to inherited differences in trainability.

Detraining

Chapter 1 discussed some of the benefits of engaging in physical activity or exercise. **Detraining** is the loss of health or physical fitness benefits when a personal fitness program is stopped. For example, if you become ill and have to remain in bed for several days with no activity, you will notice that you are weak and have less fitness, which will require some time to regain.

Most of the benefits of a physical fitness program (such as improved functional health, enhanced self-esteem, and reduced stress) are lost, at least to some extent, over time if the program is stopped. For example, if you are able to walk or jog 2 miles in twenty minutes and then stop all conditioning for two to three weeks, you will probably find that you are unable to do 2 miles in twenty minutes when you start back on your program. It may take you three to six weeks of new conditioning to get back to the same level of fitness.

It is important to recognize that the benefits of physical activity or exercise are lost at different rates following detraining. For example, if you detrain for four weeks, you may notice that your cardiovascular fitness level has dropped significantly, whereas your levels of strength have not decreased as much. You should also realize that you cannot lose your personal fitness benefits in a day, or two, or even three. In fact, it is always a good idea to take off a day or two if you are unusually tired, you are sick, or you have a significant schedule conflict. However, it is important not to discontinue your program for too long (one to two weeks), or you will detrain.

You may also find that it is to your advantage to **cross-train** to prevent detraining, particularly if you are injured. In that way you can rest your injury while maintaining the most fitness benefits. For example, if you like to lift weights and you hurt your shoulder, you may still be able to ride a stationary cycle and lift leg weights to maintain some fitness.

A knowledge of detraining will help you *maintain* a reasonable level of personal fitness—which is much easier than *obtaining* the level in the first place. You should also realize that just about everyone has to start and stop his or her personal fitness program several times in adult life. To maximize your personal fitness benefits, simply minimize your periods of detraining.

Overtraining

Overtraining is being too active or exercising too much. Overtraining can produce abnormal physical and mental stress and is associated with increased overuse injuries (muscle and skeletal problems caused by overexercising). Overtraining is also characterized by behaviors characteristic of addiction (for example, believing you will lose fitness if you miss just one day of conditioning).

• Working hard is good, but be careful not to overtrain. An injury resulting from overtraining can bring a quick halt to your fitness program, which could mean starting from the beginning once your injury heals.

Believe It? ... Or Not?

Less than 50 percent of adults say they feel better after physical activity or exercise.

See page 96 for answer.

physical activity zealot; exercise zealot

a person who is addicted to a physical activity or exercise program.

It is very important that you be able to recognize the symptoms of overtraining. You may have chronic fatigue, for example. You feel tired all the time, especially after starting a personal fitness program or after overloading your body. You may have constant muscle soreness.

Another sign of overtraining is insomnia. You may not be able to sleep at night, particularly after a day or two of vigorous activity or exercise. You may have a rapid weight loss because your physical activity or exercise program leaves you so tired that you do not feel like eating. Your morning resting pulse rate may be elevated since overtraining is often associated with an elevated pulse rate of about 10 beats above normal.

Other signs of overtraining include mental stress or "burnout". You are not only tired physically, but you are also mentally stressed or feel burned out. The physical activities and exercises you usually like to do are just not fun anymore.

If you are becoming a physical activity or exercise zealot, you are overtraining. A **physical activity zealot**, or **exercise zealot**, is a person who believes that if a little bit of activity or exercise is good, then more is better. Zealots can become addicted to their physical activity or exercise programs and do serious harm to themselves by overloading themselves too much.

acute

occurring over a short time.

chronic

occurring over an extended time.

REMEMBER This!

Some rest may be just what you need if you are physically and mentally stressed out, are sick, or have other significant schedule conflicts.

Overtraining can be **acute** (occur over a short period of time), or it can be **chronic** (occur over an extended time). An example of acute overtraining is the two-a-day or three-a-day practices that an athlete might do for two or three weeks before the football or volleyball season. In this case, the acute overtraining is planned to be an intense learning and practice time for sports preparation. This type of overtraining can only last two or three weeks. Most athletes would burn out and increase their overuse injury rate if they continued to overload themselves at these high levels. If you ever feel like you are suffering from acute overtraining, you will usually recover rapidly by taking a few days off from your physical activity or exercise program.

Chronic overtraining is more serious than acute overtraining. Chronic overtraining occurs over several weeks or months and often leads to serious mental distress. It is important to avoid chronic overtraining by recognizing the symptoms of overdoing your personal fitness program. Most people will not recover from chronic overtraining by just taking a few days off from their personal fitness program. Several weeks or months can be required to recover from chronic overtraining. Physical activity or exercise zealots may even require special counseling in order to recover.

SECTION 3 REVIEW

Answer the following questions on a separate sheet of paper:

1. What is the progression principle, and why is it important to your personal fitness program?

2. Why do some individuals realize more improvement and improve at faster rates than others?

3. Explain the differences between overtraining and detraining. How can these concepts affect your personal fitness?

SECTION 4   Warm It Up, First!

warm-up

a variety of low-intensity activities that are designed to prepare your body for moderate to vigorous activities.

The **warm-up** portion of a personal fitness program should always be done before any moderate or vigorous physical activities are performed. Unfortunately, many people do their warm-up too quickly, or not at all. A well-designed warm-up will help you participate in a safe, successful, and enjoyable workout.

• *Be sure to warm up before starting the workout phase of your personal fitness program or before engaging in any sports activities. By warming up you reduce your chance of injury and increase the effectiveness of your workout.*

Purpose of the Warm-up

The warm-up should raise your heart rate gradually before physical activity or exercise. This gradual increase causes a slight rise in muscle temperature, which enables your muscles to work safely and more efficiently. In fact, your whole body benefits. Muscles, bones, and nerves seem to perform better when the body temperature is slightly increased. Evidence suggests that warm-up helps minimize physical activity and exercise injuries and may help reduce some of the symptoms of muscle soreness.

Active Warm-up

Warm-up may be active or passive. In **active warm-up**, you attempt to raise your body temperature by actively involving the muscular, skeletal, and cardiovascular (heart and circulation) systems. The **muscle/skeletal warm-up** is usually performed by doing a series of static body stretches. (This will be covered in detail in Chapter 6.) Body stretches can loosen up muscles and better prepare them for working out. **Static body stretches** are stretches that are done slowly, smoothly, and in a sustained fashion.

active warm-up

a warm-up that attempts to raise the body temperature by actively involving the muscular, skeletal, and cardiovascular systems.

muscle/skeletal warm-up

a warm-up that usually involves a series of static body stretches.

static body stretches

stretches that are done slowly, smoothly, and in a sustained fashion.

cardiovascular warm-up

a warm-up that gradually increases the heart rate and internal body temperature.

specific active warm-up

a warm-up structured primarily for a specific skill or game activity.

general active warm-up

a warm-up tailored to individual physical activities. It is less structured than a specific active warm-up.

passive warm-up

a warm-up that raises the body temperature using outside heat sources such as blankets, and hot baths.

• *Safety reminder—wear proper exercise shoes during all phases of your workout.*

In addition to stretching, it is necessary to do a cardiovascular warm-up. The **cardiovascular warm-up** gradually increases your heart rate and your internal body temperature. Both the muscle/skeletal and cardiovascular warm-ups should be done prior to moderate or vigorous physical activity or exercise.

There are two types of active warm-up: general and specific. A **specific active warm-up** is structured primarily for skill or game activities (football, volleyball, basketball). A **general active warm-up** is less structured and is usually used for individual physical activities. For example, a specific warm-up designed to be performed before a game of basketball might include layups, jump shots, and upper and lower leg stretches. A general warm-up designed for swimming or jogging might include running in place, calisthenics, and various stretches.

Passive Warm-up

The **passive warm-up** raises body temperature through the use of outside heat sources such as covering oneself with blankets, taking hot baths or saunas, or applying skin creams. This process is not very effective because it does not involve adequate muscle/skeletal or heart activity.

Warm-up Guidelines

Follow these guidelines for a safe warm-up:

- Do both heart and muscle/skeletal warm-ups.
- Start slowly, and gradually increase intensity.
- Warm-up for five to fifteen minutes (colder weather may require more time).
- Design a specific warm-up intended for your exercises or physical activities.
- Make your warm-up intensity high enough to produce an increase in heart and breathing rates and a light sweat.

The "Active Mind/Active Body" activities on pages 91 and 95 will give you practice in designing your own warm-up program.

SECTION 4 REVIEW

Answer the following questions on a separate sheet of paper:

1. Why is it important to warm up prior to exercise?
2. What is the static stretching technique?
3. What is the difference between active and passive warm-up?

Learning to Stretch Correctly

As you begin a walking/jogging program, it is important that you use appropriate warm-up stretches. Practice performing each of the warm-up stretches shown in Figure 3.10 correctly and safely. The exercises can be used to stretch the whole body. For best results, you should do these after a light cardiovascular warm-up. Start slowly, and hold static positions.

The numbers in the following list refer to the exercises in Figure 3.10 on the next page.

1. Single knee press—stretches lower back and gluteals:
   - Lie on your back, and bring your left leg toward your chest by placing both hands under the left knee and slowly pulling.
   - Exhale while pulling your leg.
   - Hold this position for eight to twelve seconds; then change legs and repeat.

2. Side stretcher—stretches obliques:
   - From a standing position with feet a shoulders' width apart, put your right hand on the back of your neck.
   - Place your left hand near the side of your left knee, and bend sideways (to the left) as far as possible.
   - Do not lean forward or backward.
   - Hold the position for eight to twelve seconds, and then repeat on the other side.

3. Thigh stretcher—stretches quadriceps:
   - From a standing position, bend your right knee backward and up.
   - With your left hand, grasp your right foot, and gently pull upward toward the gluteals.
   - Avoid leaning forward.
   - It may be helpful to hold onto a wall or chair with the other hand.
   - Hold this position for eight to twelve seconds, and then change legs and repeat.

4. Chest and arm stretch—stretches pectoralis and deltoids:
   - From a standing or sitting position, raise your arms and hands to a shoulder-high position.
   - Straighten your arms, and place your hands palm down.
   - Try to touch your hands behind your back.
   - Hold this position for eight to twelve seconds.

(Continued on next page)

• **Figure 3.10**   *Recommended Warm-up Stretches. These stretches can help you meet flexibility goals safely.*

Learning to Stretch Correctly *(continued)*

5. Trunk twist—stretches back and hips:
    -   Sit on the floor with both legs straight in front of you.
    -   Bend the left knee far enough to place the left foot flat on the floor next to the right knee.
    -   Now cross the left leg over the right leg, and place the left foot flat on the floor next to the right knee.
    -   Place your right elbow on the left side of your left leg.
    -   Place your left arm and hand on the floor behind you.
    -   While pressing with your right arm, try to twist your body and head as far to the left as possible.
    -   Hold this position for eight to twelve seconds. Then change your leg and arm position and repeat.

6. Single leg toe touch—stretches hamstrings and lower back:
    -   Sit on the floor, with both legs straight in front of you.
    -   Bend your right knee far enough to place your right foot flat on the floor next to the left knee.
    -   Reach for your left ankle with both hands.
    -   Gently pull your body forward while trying to touch your head to your knee.
    -   Hold this position for eight to twelve seconds. Then change your leg and arm position and repeat.

7. "Yes," "no," "maybe"—stretches head and neck:
    -   Slowly tilt your head backward as far as possible. Then bring your head forward and touch your chin to your chest. This is the "yes" stretch.
    -   Slowly turn your head as far to the right as possible, then back to the left as far as possible. This is the "no" stretch.
    -   Now pull both of your shoulders up toward your ears. This is the "maybe" stretch.
    -   Avoid rotating your head and neck in a complete circle.
    -   Hold each position for eight to twelve seconds.

8. Side lunge—stretches inner thigh and groin:
    -   From a standing position, step to the right with your right foot and leg.
    -   Bend your left knee, and balance most of your weight on your left leg.
    -   Keep your right leg straight out to the side.
    -   Balance yourself with one or both hands touching the floor.
    -   Hold this position for eight to twelve seconds. Then change legs and repeat.

(Continued on next page)

Learning to Stretch Correctly

9. Forward lunge—stretches hip flexors:
   - From a standing position, step directly to the front with your right leg.
   - Bend your right knee to a 90-degree angle while keeping your left leg back and straight. Your left foot should be on its toes.
   - Be sure not to let your right knee extend past your right foot.
   - Balance yourself with one or both hands on the floor.
   - Hold this position for eight to twelve seconds. Then change legs and repeat.

10. Reverse hurdle—stretches hamstrings and lower back:
    - Sit on the floor, with both legs straight in front of you.
    - Bend your left knee far enough to place the bottom of your left foot against the side of your right knee.
    - Reach for your right ankle with both hands.
    - Gently pull your body forward while trying to touch your head to your knee.
    - Hold this position for eight to twelve seconds. Then change your leg and arm position and repeat.

11. Butterfly—stretches groin:
    - From a sitting position, bend both knees, and place the bottoms of both feet against each other.
    - Lean forward, and place both hands on your feet.
    - Slowly pull the heels of your feet toward your body.
    - You may slightly lean forward.
    - Try to keep your knees out and down.
    - Hold this position for eight to twelve seconds.

12. Calf stretch—stretches gastrocnemius:
    - From a standing position, face a wall. Place your feet 3 feet from the wall.
    - Step forward with your left foot, and support your weight by placing your hands on the wall.
    - Your right foot should remain in its position and should stay flat on the floor as you lean forward.
    - There should be no weight on your left foot.
    - Hold this position for eight to twelve seconds. Then change legs and repeat.

Active Mind! Active Body!

Designing a Sample Warm-up

Design a specific active warm-up program for softball. (*Hint:* What body parts are most often used by a softball player?) Then design a general active warm-up program for cycling.

SECTION 5   Work It Out!

The workout phase of your personal fitness program is the period of time that you should spend daily, or almost daily, in physical activity or exercise. A well-designed workout phase should be based on scientific exercise principles. Your workout phase should also be tailored to your personal fitness goals and experiences with physical activity and exercise.

BELIEVE IT? ... OR NOT?

"No pain, no gain!" is a good way to describe physical activity or exercise.

See page 96 for answer.

• *Girls, as well as boys, benefit greatly from a well-designed weight training program.*

Answers to Believe It? ... Or Not?

Pg. 72 False. Physical activity and exercise are dose (amount) related. For example, if you engage in physical activity or exercise very infrequently, you will not be able to develop or maintain adequate levels of personal fitness. If you do too much physical activity or exercise, you can increase your risk of injuries caused by overuse.

Pg. 78 True.

Pg. 80 True.

Pg. 83 False. Physical activity or exercise will not solve all health problems. However, physical activity or exercise may be a valuable part of the treatment for various physical and mental disorders.

Pg. 85 True.

Pg. 87 False. Ninety percent of adults say they feel better after they participate in physical activity or exercise.

Pg. 95 False. You can achieve an acceptable level of personal fitness by engaging in moderate physical activities or exercise. Physical activity or exercise does not have to be painful to help you achieve many personal fitness goals.

Designing a Workout

Figure 3.12 on the next page gives an example of a personal fitness prescription. You might want to use this prescription in designing your workout. The figure shows you how to combine the modes of your conditioning with FIT.

Figure 3.11 below provides an example of a six-week walking/jogging conditioning program designed to help you walk/jog 1.6 to 2.0 miles (for boys) or 1.4 to 1.8 miles (for girls) in twenty minutes. These standards are consistent with good to better levels of cardio-

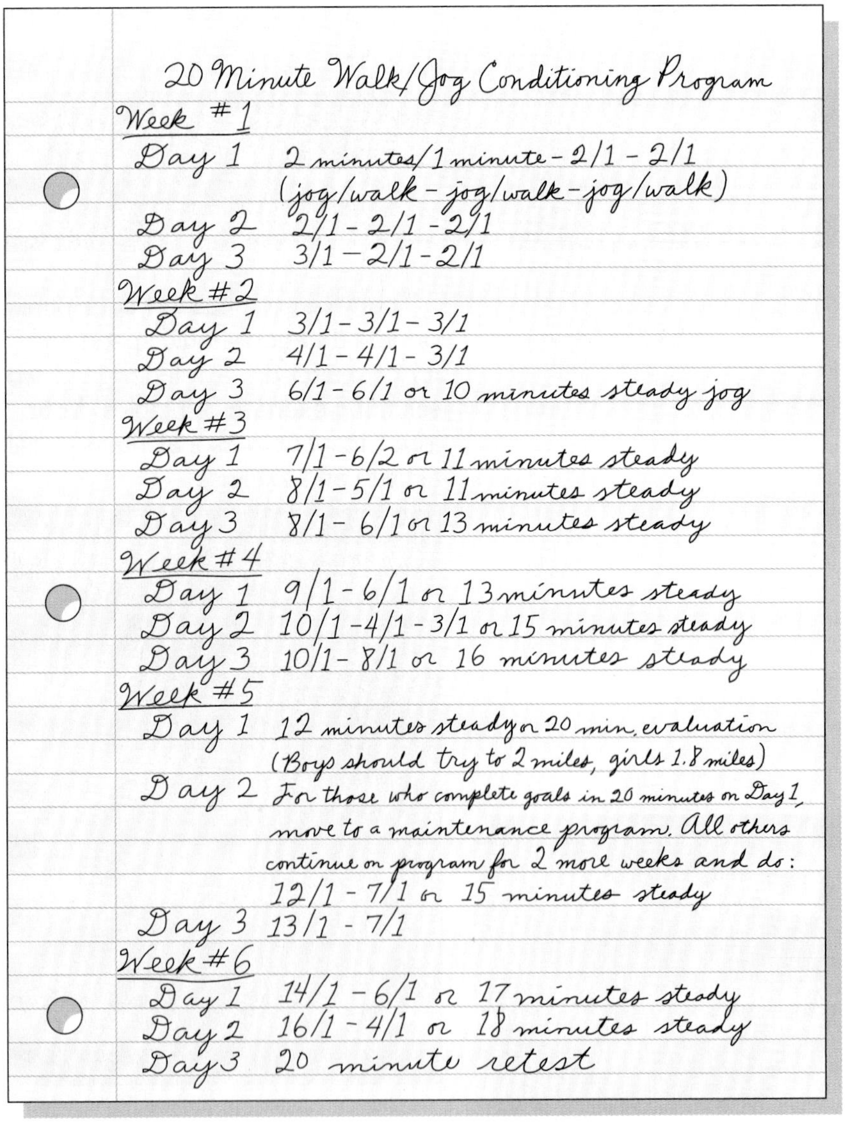
20 Minute Walk/Jog Conditioning Program

Week #1
Day 1 2 minutes/1 minute - 2/1 - 2/1
(jog/walk - jog/walk - jog/walk)
Day 2 2/1 - 2/1 - 2/1
Day 3 3/1 - 2/1 - 2/1

Week #2
Day 1 3/1 - 3/1 - 3/1
Day 2 4/1 - 4/1 - 3/1
Day 3 6/1 - 6/1 or 10 minutes steady jog

Week #3
Day 1 7/1 - 6/2 or 11 minutes steady
Day 2 8/1 - 5/1 or 11 minutes steady
Day 3 8/1 - 6/1 or 13 minutes steady

Week #4
Day 1 9/1 - 6/1 or 13 minutes steady
Day 2 10/1 - 4/1 - 3/1 or 15 minutes steady
Day 3 10/1 - 8/1 or 16 minutes steady

Week #5
Day 1 12 minutes steady or 20 min. evaluation
(Boys should try to 2 miles, girls 1.8 miles)
Day 2 For those who complete goals in 20 minutes on Day 1, move to a maintenance program. All others continue on program for 2 more weeks and do:
12/1 - 7/1 or 15 minutes steady
Day 3 13/1 - 7/1

Week #6
Day 1 14/1 - 6/1 or 17 minutes steady
Day 2 16/1 - 4/1 or 18 minutes steady
Day 3 20 minute retest

• ***Figure 3.11*** *20-Minute Walk/Jog Conditioning Program.*

Frequency	3–5 days per week
Intensity	Moderate to vigorous and continuous, if possible
Time/Duration	Accumulate 20–60 minutes each session
Modes	Walk–hike, run–jog, bike, cross-country ski, dance, skip rope, row, stair climb swim, skate, in-line skating, endurance games
Resistance-Weight Training	8–10 exercises, 2–3 times per week
Flexibility	Include warm-up and cool-down stretches

• **Figure 3.12**   *Example of a Personal Fitness Prescription for Fitness in Young Adults.*

REMEMBER This!

Workout sessions with lower intensity (60 percent) and longer duration (fifty to sixty minutes) will usually cause you to expend more energy than workout sessions of higher intensity (80 percent) and shorter duration (twenty minutes).

Stress Break

How we feel about ourselves, and what we believe others think about us, can influence the amount of positive and negative stress in our lives. By organizing our daily routines, improving our self-esteem, or improving our fitness levels, we can greatly improve our ability to deal with stress. Stress is always going to be in our lives, so how we deal with and avoid stress is important.

Here are some ways to deal positively with exercise, improve adherence, and consequently reduce stress:

• Plan your days ahead of time. Don't put things off to the last minute. Decide on the most important things that must get done. Planning ahead can save you a lot of confusion, frustration, and stress.

• Remember that fitness does not happen overnight. It takes time and patience. A consistent, well-organized fitness plan will improve your fitness level. With this kind of plan, reasonable gains are made quickly, and you obtain all the benefits that go along with being fit.

• Eat a sensible diet and follow a consistent workout schedule to reduce body fat and stress.

• Don't set your goals too high. Set short-term goals that will keep you motivated. Don't be in a hurry. You have the rest of your life to be fit!

• Start slowly, and have reasonable goals. You will then be less likely to overtrain. In fact, by progressing slowly, you are more likely to find out that you are capable of many things you didn't believe you could do.

• Remember that being fit is a personal choice. Your choice to be fit should not be determined by others. However, working out can be a pleasant experience to share with a partner who values fitness as much as you do. It is also a great way to meet new friends.

vascular fitness. This walking/jogging program is designed to increase your FIT over time and to provide you with the choice of combining walking and jogging or doing continuous jogging. If you prefer a continuous walking program, you can follow the sample walking conditioning program explained later in Chapter 5. It is hoped, as recommended in Chapter 1, that you are already involved in a cardiovascular conditioning program similar to the one shown in Figure 3.11.

SECTION 5 REVIEW

Answer the following questions on a separate sheet of paper:

1. How do you combine your mode of physical activity with FIT?
2. List a variety of physical activities that are modes of cardiovascular conditioning.

SECTION 6 Cool It Down, Afterward!

blood pooling

a condition, following exercise, in which blood collects in the large veins of the legs and lower body, especially when the exercise is stopped abruptly.

cardiovascular cool-down

a period after exercise in which you try to prevent blood pooling by moving about slowly and continuously for about three to five minutes.

The cool-down portion of a personal fitness program should always be done after any moderate or vigorous physical activities or exercises are performed. Like the warm-up, the cool-down is often done too quickly or not at all. A well-designed cool-down will help you recover from physical activity or exercise safely and more effectively.

It is important to lower your heart rate gradually following physical activity or exercise. This gradual decrease in heart rate will help you prevent blood pooling in the lower body. **Blood pooling** is a condition, following exercise, in which blood collects in the large veins of the legs and lower body (Figure 3.13). It can cause you to become dizzy and feel like you are going to faint because less blood is pumped to your brain. Blood pooling typically follows moderate or vigorous physical activity or exercise, especially if you stop abruptly and just sit or lie down. You can prevent blood pooling by moving about slowly and continuously (walking, standing in place and moving your feet up and down, and jogging slowly) for about three to five minutes following physical activity or exercise. This is called **cardiovascular cool-down**.

stretching cool-down

a period after cardiovascular cool-down in which you perform stretching exercises for three to five minutes to minimize stiffness and muscle soreness.

Following your three- to five-minute cardiovascular cool-down recovery period, it is important for you to stretch for another three to five minutes to minimize stiffness and muscle soreness. This is called your **stretching cool-down**. Cool-down stretches should use the same static stretching exercises that were discussed for warming up prior to exercise (see the discussion on warm-up). Try designing your own cool-down program in the "Active Mind/Active Body" activity on this page.

• *Cool-down is just as important as warm-up. Be sure to always include a cool-down in each workout session.*

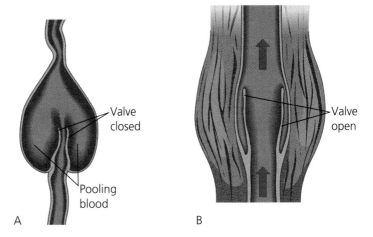

• **Figure 3.13** *Blood Pooling. [A] Valves in the large veins (like the legs) close and cause blood to pool while the body is at rest or when there is no muscle contraction. [B] During a proper cool-down the muscles contract against the leg veins and squeeze blood back towards the heart.*

Active Mind! *Active* Body!   **Your Cool-Down Program**

Design a cool-down program for a physical activity or exercise that you like to do. Include both a cardiovascular and a stretching component.

REMEMBER This!

A complete workout includes several components. Figure 3.14 shows an example of the necessary workout considerations you can use to design your personal fitness program.

Component	Activity	Duration (min)
Warm-up	Stretch, low-level calisthenics, walking	10
Muscular Conditioning	Calisthenics, weight training	15-30
Cardiovascular Conditioning	Walk, jog/run, swim, bike, cross-country ski, dance, stair step, in-line skating	20-50
Cool-down	Walk, stretch	5-10

• **Figure 3.14**   *Necessary Workout Considerations.*

SECTION 6 REVIEW

Answer the following questions on a separate sheet of paper:

1. Why and how can you prevent blood pooling?
2. How do warm-up and cool-down activities differ?

SUMMARY

An understanding of exercise principles can help you successfully design your personal fitness prescription to achieve Guidelines 1 and 2 in Chapter 1. It is important for you to accumulate time daily or nearly every day in physical activity or exercise to improve and maintain your good health and to achieve Guideline 1.

To achieve Guideline 2, you will need to apply the scientific conditioning principles of overload, specificity, and progression when you plan your workout. To reduce significantly your risk of injuries in your personal fitness program, apply the concepts of FIT:

frequency, intensity, and time/duration. As you gain more experience in the art of applying other scientific principles, such as trainability, detraining, and overtraining, you will be better at modifying your personal fitness program to meet special situations.

When you do a proper warm-up, you will be better prepared to work out safely. Your workout will vary from day to day.

Following your workout, it is very important for you to cool down. A proper cool-down can help you prevent blood pooling and minimize stiffness and muscle soreness.

Chapter 3 Review

True/False

On a separate sheet of paper, mark each question below either T for True or F for False.

1. The three parts of the overload principle are frequency, intensity, and type.

2. Young adults just beginning an aerobic exercise program should maintain a heart rate of 130 to 150 beats per minute.

3. The workout frequency is the length of time your workout takes each day.

4. Beginning exercisers can prevent injury if their intensity stays between 70 and 90 percent of their maximum heart rate.

5. If the workload on the heart increases, the pulse rate will decrease.

6. A primary purpose of a warm-up is to increase the heart rate gradually prior to exercise.

7. An active warm-up can be either specific or general.

8. Moderate to vigorous exercise sessions should always include a warm-up phase and a cool-down phase.

9. The warm-up phase and cool-down phase can help prevent injury and soreness.

10. Blood pooling can be prevented by sitting down and relaxing after vigorous exercise.

Multiple Choice

1. The overload principle involves which of the following?
   a. an increase in physical activity or exercise above what you normally do
   b. an increase in the improvement you would normally expect
   c. an increase in the changes that occur in your body
   d. an increase in the negative effects that occur in your body

2. Your exercise intensity is affected by which of the following?
   a. level of fitness
   b. fitness goals
   c. length of each workout session
   d. number of workout sessions per week
   e. all of the above

3. Which of the following would be recorded in an exercise record book?
   a. food eaten
   b. FIT
   c. goals
   d. all of the above

4. Potential differences in physical fitness improvement between two people training the same way for the same length of time is due to which of the following?
   a. overload
   b. specificity
   c. progression
   d. trainability

5. Which principle refers to the rate at which you change your personal fitness prescription?
   a. specificity
   b. progression
   c. overload
   d. mode

6. Which of the following is not a symptom of overtraining?
   a. constant muscle soreness
   b. mental burnout
   c. high performance
   d. chronic fatigue

7. Which of the following is an example of a passive warm-up?

    a. toe touch
    b. walk around the gym
    c. basketball layups
    d. whirlpool bath

8. Which of the following is a static stretching technique?

    a. slowly stretching
    b. smoothly stretching
    c. sustained stretching
    d. none of the above
    e. a, b, and c

9. Which of the following would *not* be a specific warm-up for basketball?

    a. jumping jacks
    b. layups
    c. passing drills
    d. free throw shooting

10. Which cool-down procedure is best for preventing blood pooling?

    a. leg stretches
    b. slow walk
    c. arm stretches
    d. deep breathing techniques

Discussion

1. Explain how the perceived exertion scale and your heart rate can be used to determine your exercise intensity. How are they similar?

2. Identify and explain the common signs of detraining.

3. Explain how each of the components of the overload principle (FIT) are related to one another.

Vocabulary Experience

Match the correct term in Column A to the definition in Column B by writing the appropriate number in each blank.

Column A	Column B
_____ blood pooling	**1.** Frequency, intensity, and time/duration.
_____ static body stretch	**2.** The need to increase the amount of activity or exercise above what you normally do to improve your fitness level.
_____ overload principle	**3.** The type of activity or exercise you do.
_____ FIT	**4.** A slow, smooth, sustained stretch.
_____ mode	**5.** How often you engage in physical activity or exercise.
_____ frequency	**6.** A condition in which blood collects in the large veins of the legs and lower body.

Critical Thinking

1. How can you influence your personal fitness progression by changing your FIT? Explain your answer.

2. If a friend tells you that she started an exercise program to improve her physical fitness but quit after two weeks because she didn't see any improvements, what would you tell her? Why wasn't she successful? How can she improve her chances for personal fitness success?

3. What advice can you give someone you know who has the symptoms of being an exercise zealot? He is concerned that if he misses a workout for one or two days, he will get out of shape. Explain your answer.

Case Study — David—Part 2

Do you remember David from Chapter 2? He is an overweight fifteen-year-old who has lived all his life in Anchorage, Alaska. His father recently made a career change that required the family to move to central Texas. David has never been very athletic or physically active, and he has not paid much attention to his health or personal fitness.

Now that he has moved to a much warmer climate and the different weather conditions of Texas, he would like to make some improvements in his fitness habits (behaviors). He feels he should take advantage of his new environment by starting a physical activity and exercise program. His goals are to lose 20 pounds and to improve his cardiovascular fitness levels. David needs your personal fitness expertise again.

Design a beginning physical activity and exercise plan for David. Prepare a detailed two-week warm-up, workout, and cool-down program for David. Try to be as specific as possible when choosing activities and exercises. It is possible to design many programs that would benefit David. Use your knowledge and imagination to create a safe and effective personal fitness program.

KEYS TO HELP YOU

The following tips may help you design David's program:

- Consider his history of personal activity and exercise.
- Consider his current fitness level.
- Consider his needs and goals.
- Determine a reasonable intensity, duration, and frequency for a beginning program.

Chapter 4

Skill-related and Health-related Fitness

104

Contents

Outcomes

After reading and studying this chapter, you will be able to:

1. Explain how health-related fitness and skill-related fitness are related to physical fitness.
2. Explain the differences between health-related fitness and skill-related fitness.
3. Identify and explain examples of skill-related fitness.
4. Identify and explain examples of health-related fitness.
5. Identify and explain examples of skill-related fitness evaluations.
6. Identify and explain examples of health-related fitness evaluations.
7. Describe your personal fitness profile.

Key Terms

After reading and studying this chapter, you will be able to understand and provide practical definitions for the following terms:

skill-related fitness	power	energy cost
agility	reaction time	muscular endurance
balance	health-related fitness	body composition
center of gravity	cardiovascular fitness	percentage of body fat
coordination	flexibility	kilocalorie
speed	muscular strength	energy expenditure

INTRODUCTION

*B*y now you understand the need for regular physical activity or exercise and, it is hoped, value that need. Chapter 4 will guide you through a variety of physical activities and physical evaluations that can help you determine your path to developing and maintaining moderate to high levels of physical fitness.

What is physical fitness? Is it the high cardiovascular capacity of a marathoner, or is it the sculptured body of Arnold Schwarzenegger? Maybe your picture of a physically fit person is an Olympic gymnast or a highly skilled soccer player. The truth is that you do not need to be an athlete to be physically fit.

Many components contribute to the state of being physically fit. These components can be categorized as skill-related fitness or health-related fitness (Figure 4.1). Skill-related fitness, or performance fitness, has six parts, which are primarily associated with the ability to perform successfully during games and sports. Health-related fitness has five parts, which are primarily associated with disease prevention and functional health. You need both skill- and health-related fitness, because both types of fitness can contribute to your ability to do everyday life activities. Activities such as walking, climbing stairs, bending over, lifting things, or any of the recreational activities that many of us do daily require some degree of physical fitness. This means that our bodies will perform and function more efficiently and effectively if we maintain acceptable levels of physical fitness.

This course places a greater emphasis on the health-related aspects of physical fitness than on the skill-related aspects. Knowing how to correctly perform health-related physical activities and evaluations can help you prepare for a long, happy, productive, and fit life. Health-related fitness is an obtainable goal that *A*ny *B*ody *C*an reach.

REMEMBER This!

Physical fitness depends on physical abilities that allow you to perform daily physical tasks effectively, with enough energy reserves to engage in recreational activities or to meet unexpected physical challenges. Physical fitness is an outcome of a physically active lifestyle or exercise program that occurs over time.

SECTION 1   Whats and Whys of Skill-related Fitness

skill-related fitness

the ability to perform successfully during games and sports; also called *performance fitness.* Skill-related fitness has six components: agility, balance, coordination, power, speed, and reaction time.

Skill-related fitness, or performance fitness, includes the six components of physical fitness that are often associated with games and sports. Also, many of the chores and jobs we do daily require the use of one or more of these six physical abilities. The six skill-related components of fitness are agility, balance, coordination, speed, power, and reaction time (Figure 4.2).

The highly skilled athlete will possess a high level of ability in most, if not all, of the six components. The weekend athlete, often referred to as the "weekend warrior," will also possess a certain level of pro-

Skill-related Fitness

Agility
Balance
Coordination
Speed
Power
Reaction Time

Health-related Fitness

Cardiovascular Fitness
Muscular Endurance
Flexibility
Muscular Strength
Body Composition

• *Figure 4.1*
Components of Fitness.

• *Prior to his movie career, Arnold Schwarzenegger was a body-builder. Do you think he is exhibiting health-related or skill-related fitness in this photo?*

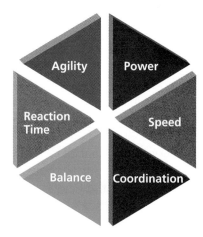

• *Figure 4.2* *Skill-related Fitness.*

agility

the ability to change and control the direction and position of your body while maintaining a constant, rapid motion.

ficiency in many of the skill-related components. This supports the belief that people tend to be involved in activities and games they do well. Unfortunately, too many adults do not participate in either skill- or health-related activities.

Being actively involved in leisure activities, such as sports and games, can contribute to the maintenance or improvement of physical fitness, a reduction in stress, and an enhancement of self-esteem. In fact, one of the main goals of the *Healthy People 2000* national health objectives is to get more people participating in physical activities during their leisure time.

Even though the skill-related fitness components can contribute greatly to your success in sports and games, they will not necessarily contribute to your health or to the reduction of health risk factors. However, a more complete understanding of each of the skill-related components can positively contribute to your personal fitness. Let's explore each of the skill-related fitness components in more detail.

Agility

The ability to change and control the direction and position of your body while maintaining a constant, rapid motion is **agility**. The soccer player, football running back, basketball player, and tennis player will all require agility. Other skill-related components of fitness, such as speed and coordination, may influence your level of agility.

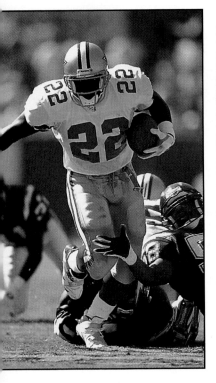

• *Most people will never obtain the levels of skill-related fitness demonstrated by these athletes. Any Body Can, however, obtain good to better levels of health-related fitness.*

Balance

The ability to control or stabilize your body while moving or staying still is **balance**. A simple act such as walking requires a great deal of balance. The gymnast, golfer, or ice skater all require well-developed balance.

Your **center of gravity** is the area of your body that determines how your weight is distributed. Your center of gravity is probably near your pelvic region (hips) and should stay over the base of support, which is your feet. You can improve your balance and biomechanics in many physical activities or exercises by shifting your center of gravity. For example, shifting your body weight while swinging a golf club would change your center of gravity and improve your golf shot.

Coordination

The ability to use your eyes and ears to determine and direct the smooth movement of your body (hands, feet, arms, head, and so on) is **coordination**. The jogger, soccer player, basketball player, and volleyball player, for example, all require coordination. Coordination requires using a combination of different muscle groups at once. Combining more than one set of muscle movements takes practice.

balance

the ability to control or stabilize your equilibrium while moving or staying still.

center of gravity

the area of your body that determines how your weight is distributed.

coordination

the ability to use your eyes and ears to determine and direct the smooth movement of your body.

speed

the ability to move your body or parts of your body swiftly.

power

the ability to move your body parts swiftly while at the same time applying the maximum force of your muscles.

Other components of fitness, such as speed, reaction time, and agility, may influence your level of coordination.

Speed

The ability to move your body or parts of your body swiftly is **speed**. Foot speed is usually measured over a short and straight distance, usually less than 200 meters. Other speed evaluations might include hand or arm speed. The baseball pitcher, boxer, sprinter, and volleyball spiker all require specific kinds of speed. Certain types of muscle fibers (muscle cells), which are determined by hereditary factors, can influence your speed. Reaction time and muscular strength may also influence your speed.

Power

The ability to move your body parts swiftly (speed) while at the same time applying the maximum force of your muscles (strength) is **power**. The shot-putter, long jumper, power lifter, and swimmer all require high levels of power. Some degree of power is also important for everyday activities, such as lifting heavy items or making quick or sudden body movements. Strength is a fitness component that can be improved over time. As you increase your strength, you can increase your power. Biomechanical movement techniques can also affect your power, which means you can gain power by practicing your technique.

Stress Break

Many Americans regularly participate in games and sports in an effort to reduce their stress levels. However, you may find that the challenges of being a part of a competitive team, the intensity of competition, and the pressures of peer criticism often create stress instead of relieve it.

Competitive activities may be part of your personal fitness today, but you will find that as you age, health-related activities will become a bigger part of your personal fitness routine. Learn how to use your health-related fitness activities to help control daily stress. You will learn that these activities not only can help you get through today's problems but also can help you live a healthier, happier, and longer life.

• *These athletes possess extraordinary levels of speed and power.*

Reaction Time

The ability to react or respond quickly to what you hear, see, or feel is **reaction time**. The more quickly you respond, the better your reaction time. Good reaction time is required for sprinters and swimmers, who must react to starts. The tennis player, boxer, and hockey goalie all require quick reaction times. Factors such as motivation, fatigue, and practice can influence reaction time.

Figure 4.3 lists the degree of benefits for skill-related fitness associated with different physical activities and sports. You can survey the figure and determine which of the physical activities you can participate in to improve or maintain your skill-related fitness.

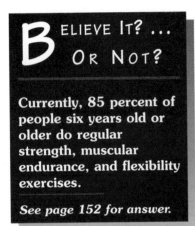

BELIEVE IT? ...
OR NOT?

Currently, 85 percent of people six years old or older do regular strength, muscular endurance, and flexibility exercises.

See page 152 for answer.

Factors That Can Influence Skill-related Performance

Why are some individuals capable of outstanding physical performance? How can the marathoner run nonstop for 26 miles and average under five minutes per mile? What enables the Olympic weight lifter to lift incredible amounts of weight? Why aren't we all capable of such superhuman physical talents? Are there certain factors that determine these talents? Yes, there are!

Pick Your Parents Well.   Heredity is a major factor in determining performance potential. Your physical characteristics, such as height, weight, and body type, are generally similar to those of your parents. Your physical capabilities, such as speed and reaction time, are also inherited from your parents. Once you are fully grown, it is unlikely that you will ever see a drastic improvement in either of these components.

Practice, Practice, Practice.   Even if you have inherited a potential for great physical abilities, you still need to practice specific skills over and over to reach the level of performance exhibited by top athletes. Practice is important to anyone who wants to improve skills in a specific game or sport. Agility, coordination, power, and balance are skill-related components that can be improved through practice. How often and how specifically you practice will determine, to a great extent, how successful you will become. Later in the chapter you will conduct self-evaluations for skill-related fitness. You will notice that often one skill-related ability will also require the use of other skill-related components.

• *Heredity is a major factor in determining your performance skills.*

You can learn how to survey your skill-related fitness levels by completing the "Active Mind/Active Body" activities (pages 112 and 113) for each of the six skill-related fitness components. These activities are designed to introduce you to the skill-related fitness concepts.

• *Soccer players must have high levels of both skill- and health-related fitness.*

Activity/Sport and Primary Emphasis*	Agility	Balance	Reaction Time	Power	Speed	Coordination
Archery S	*	***	*	*	*	****
Backpacking H	**	**	*	**	*	**
Badminton S	***	**	***	**	***	****
Ballet B	****	****	**	***	*	****
Baseball S	***	***	****	****	***	****
Basketball B	****	***	****	****	***	****
Bicycling H	*	****	**	*	**	**
Bowling S	**	***	*	**	**	****
Canoeing B	*	***	**	***	*	***
Circuit training H	**	**	*	***	**	**
Dance, aerobic H	***	**	**	*	*	****
Dance, line S	***	**	**	*	**	***
Dance, social H	***	**	**	*	**	***
Fitness calisthenics H	***	**	*	**	*	**
Football S	****	***	****	****	****	***
Golf (walking) B	**	**	*	***	*	****
Gymnastics B	****	****	***	****	**	****
Handball H	****	**	***	***	***	****
Hiking H	**	**	*	**	*	**
Horseback riding S	***	***	**	*	*	***
Interval training H	*	**	*	*	**	**
Jogging H	*	**	*	*	*	**
Judo S	****	***	****	****	****	****
Karate S	****	***	****	****	****	****
Mountain climbing H	***	****	**	***	*	****
Pool; billiards S	**	**	*	**	*	***
Racquetball; paddleball B	****	**	***	**	***	****
Rope jumping H	***	**	**	**	*	***
Rowing H	***	**	*	****	**	****
Sailing S	***	***	***	**	*	***
Skating, ice B	***	****	**	**	***	***
Skating, in-line B	***	****	*	**	***	***
Skiing, cross-country B	***	**	*	****	**	****
Skiing, downhill B	****	****	***	***	*	****
Soccer B	****	**	***	***	***	****
Softball (fast pitch) S	***	**	****	***	***	****
Softball (slow pitch) S	**	**	***	***	***	****
Surfing B	****	****	***	***	*	****
Swimming H	***	**	*	**	*	***
Table tennis S	**	**	***	**	**	***
Tennis B	***	**	***	***	***	****
Volleyball B	***	**	***	**	**	****
Walking H	*	**	*	*	*	**
Waterskiing S	***	***	*	**	*	***
Weight training H	*	**	*	**	*	**

*Primary Emphasis
S = Skill-related Fitness.
H = Health-related Fitness.
B = Both Skill- and Health-related Fitness.

Better – ****
Good – ***
Fair – **
Low – *

• **Figure 4.3** *Skill-related Benefits.*

Active Mind!
Active Body!

Exploring Skill-related Fitness

Picking Up Lines

One test of agility is an activity called *picking up lines.* Mark off two parallel lines 5 feet apart. Start at one line. Run to the other line and bend over to touch the line with your hand. Reverse your direction and return to the start, again bending over to touch the line. Go to the other line and back twice without stopping (Figure 4.4). Try to accomplish this in five seconds or less.

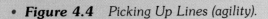

• **Figure 4.4**   *Picking Up Lines (agility).*

Blind One-Leg Stand

To test your balance, do the blind one-leg stand. Stand on one foot. Pull your other leg up and back. Close your eyes (Figure 4.5). Do not wobble or hop. Try to hold this position for ten seconds.

• **Figure 4.5**   *Blind One-Leg Stand (balance).*

• **Figure 4.6**   *Foot and Ball Volley (coordination).*

Foot and Ball Volley

Try the foot and ball volley to test your coordination (Figure 4.6). Drop a round ball (tennis ball size or bigger) over your dominant foot or the one you usually kick with. Try to bounce the ball off your foot three consecutive times. Now try it with your nondominant foot.

Standing Broad Jump

You can test your power with the standing broad jump (Figure 4.7). Lie on the floor. Mark off two lines, one at the top of your head and one at your feet. Now stand up and start at either end. Jump out toward the other line as far as possible. Try to jump past your height.

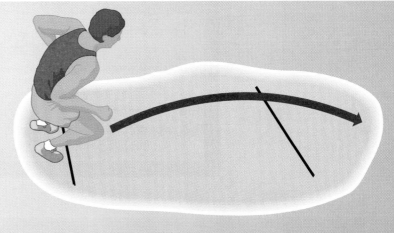

• *Figure 4.7* *Standing Broad Jump (power).*

 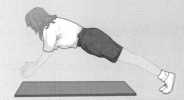 

• *Figure 4.8* *Push and Clap (speed).*

Push and Clap

To test your speed, do the push and clap (Figure 4.8). Lie face down on the floor in a push-up position. Place your hands to the sides of your chest. Push your body up in the air, and try to clap your hands twice before returning to the floor. Use a mat if one is available.

Hand Slap

Test your reaction time with the hand slap (Figure 4.9). Stand facing a partner. Have your partner place his or her hands palms up. Place your hands palms down over your partner's hands. Allow 4 inches of space between your hands and your partner's. Your partner will quickly attempt to touch the top of your hands. Try to remove your hands before being touched.

• *Figure 4.9* *Hand Slap (reaction time).*

SECTION 2   Whats and Whys of Health-related Fitness

health-related fitness

physical fitness primarily associated with disease prevention and functional health. Health-related fitness has five components: cardiovascular fitness, body composition, flexibility, muscular strength, and muscular endurance.

cardiovascular fitness

the ability to work continuously for extended periods of time.

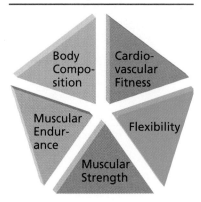

• *Figure 4.10*
Health-related Fitness.

Health-related fitness is a type of physical fitness that emphasizes physical activities and exercise that will improve or help you maintain your functional health. The five components of health-related fitness are cardiovascular fitness, flexibility, muscular strength, muscular endurance, and body composition (Figure 4.10). Let's explore each of the health-related components of physical fitness in more detail.

Cardiovascular Fitness

Cardiovascular fitness refers to your ability to work continuously for extended periods of time (for example, walking briskly for twenty to forty minutes, cycling 5 to 10 miles, or in-line skating for thirty minutes to an hour). Your level of cardiovascular fitness depends on the ability of your heart to pump large amounts of blood to the muscles and organs of your body. It also is related to how well your lungs function and how well your blood vessels can deliver blood (oxygen) to your body. Examples of cardiovascular fitness activities might include walking, hiking, jogging, dancing, skipping rope, rowing, swimming, skating, and endurance games or sports.

Moderate to high levels of cardiovascular fitness are associated with increased longevity and reduced risk for cardiovascular disease and other hypokinetic conditions (see Chapter 1). Moderate to high levels of cardiovascular fitness are also associated with improved functional health.

Cardiovascular fitness can be improved simply by accumulating several minutes per day of activity in play, games, sports, work, getting to school, recreation, or planned exercise. Your cardiovascular fitness level is also determined to some extent by other factors, such

flexibility

the range of motion that your joints have during movement.

• *Maintaining high levels of flexibility will help you prevent injuries.*

as age, heredity, gender, activity level, and body composition. You will learn more about cardiovascular fitness in Chapter 5.

Flexibility

Flexibility refers to the range of motion that your joints have during movement. Skin and connective tissue (such as tendons and ligaments) can restrict normal flexibility if not used regularly. Injured joints and excessive body fat can also restrict normal flexibility. Adults often lose their normal levels of flexibility because of the aging process and decreased participation in physical activities and exercise. Poor flexibility is associated with the development of many types of injuries, including lower back problems, muscle pulls, and muscle strains.

Good functional health depends on your improving or maintaining the range of motion (varying degrees of motion allowed) of your joints. You can do this by engaging in stretching activities that increase your muscular strength and muscular endurance, as well as improve your flexibility.

A moderate to high level of flexibility is important to you for efficient daily physical movements and can help reduce your risks for muscle and bone injuries. Moderate to high levels of flexibility can improve performance fitness and reduce some types of muscle sore-

• *Not all of us can become as flexible as this diver, but we can all strive for our own maximum flexibility.*

ness following physical activity or exercise. You will learn more about flexibility in Chapter 6.

Muscular Strength

muscular strength

the maximal force that you can exert when you contract your muscles.

energy cost

the amount of energy required for you to perform different physical activities or exercises.

Muscular strength refers to the maximal force that you can exert when you contract your muscles. Your muscular strength will vary according to several factors, such as your age, gender, genetic makeup, and conditioning level. A moderate to high level of muscular strength helps reduce your risk for muscle, bone, and joint injuries.

You can develop and maintain muscular strength in a variety of ways, such as doing weight training, calisthenics, or work that requires heavy lifting. Gains in muscular strength can occur rapidly, particularly if you have been very sedentary.

Muscular strength is also important to help you move efficiently and reduce your energy cost. **Energy cost** refers to the amount of

• *All people benefit in many ways from increased muscular strength.*

• *Cross country skiing is an excellent activity for increasing your muscular endurance.*

energy required for you to perform different physical activities or exercise. You have heard the saying "If you don't use it, you lose it!" This saying especially applies to the elderly, who become sedentary and lose their muscular strength. When you lose muscular strength, it has negative effects on your functional health level. You will learn more about muscular strength in Chapters 7 and 8.

Muscular Endurance

muscular endurance

the ability to contract your muscles several times without excessive fatigue.

Muscular endurance refers to your ability to contract your muscles several times without excessive fatigue. Moderate to high levels of muscular endurance enhance your muscular strength and allow you to do more work without getting tired than you could if you led a sedentary lifestyle. Like muscular strength, muscular endurance is important to help you move efficiently and reduce your energy cost for physical activities or exercises. Physical activities such as doing sit-ups, push-ups, or work that requires repetitive heavy lifting can help increase your muscular endurance. You will learn more about muscular endurance in Chapters 7 and 8.

Body Composition

body composition

the ratio of water, bone, muscle, and fat in the body.

percentage of body fat

the percentage of your body weight that is fat.

The ratio of water, bone, muscle, and fat in your body is what determines your **body composition** (see Chapter 1). Your **percentage of body fat** in relation to your percentage of water, bone, and muscle is important to your functional health and risks for chronic disease. You should have a reasonable amount of body fat

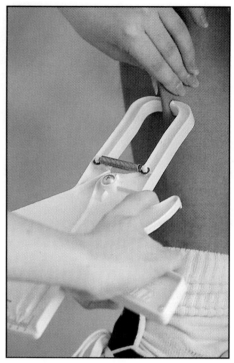

• One of the many methods of determining your body composition is to measure a skinfold with skinfold calipers. Males should carry 7 to 19 percent body fat, females 12 to 24 percent. If your percentages are higher than these, you need to begin a program to reduce your body fat.

kilocalorie

a unit used to measure energy; also called a *calorie.*

energy expenditure

the number of calories you burn each minute.

for good health (in other words, you should not be too fat or too lean).

By adopting a physically active lifestyle, you can help control your percentage of body fat. When you engage in physical activities or exercise, you burn or expend energy. When you expend energy, you are burning **kilocalories**. To control your weight, you need to balance the amount of calories you consume in your diet with the amount of calories you expend in daily living and physical activity. When you adopt an active lifestyle, your **energy expenditure** will be higher than if you are sedentary. You will learn more about body composition in Chapter 9.

Improving Your Personal Fitness Level

You can develop a moderate to high level of personal fitness without possessing an abundance of skill-related talents. Most adults who are active do not choose to participate in sports and games as their lifetime physical activities. Instead, they are more likely to choose health-related activities such as swimming, cycling, stair stepping,

Believe It? ... Or Not?

A basketball player who plays a full four-quarter game runs approximately 3 to 5 miles.

See page 152 for answer.

Rank	Activity
1	Swimming*
2	Fishing
3	Bicycling*
4	Bowling
5	Camping
6	Hiking*
7	Pool/billiards
8	Running/jogging*
9	Weight training*
10	Race cycling*
11	Softball
12	Volleyball
13	Motorboating
14	Dance exercising*
15	Golf
16	Basketball
17	Table tennis
18	Calisthenics*
19	Hunting
20	Baseball

*Denotes health-related activity or exercise

• ***Figure 4.11*** *Rankings of the Most Popular Lifetime Activities for Adults.*
Source: Data from *Gallup Poll,* George Gallup, Jr. (Wilmington, DE: Scholarly Resources Inc., 1991), 43.

Believe It? ... Or Not?

The typical young adult (fourteen to seventeen years old) is about 5 to 7 pounds heavier today than the typical young adult in 1980.

See page 152 for answer.

jogging, or weight training. Figure 4.11 lists, in order of popularity, the lifetime activities that adults participate in the most. Notice that the majority of the top ten activities listed are not team sports or game related. In fact, six of the top ten are health-related activities (swimming, bicycling, hiking, running/jogging, weight training, and race cycling).

• *You need not train at high intensities and compete with others to achieve and maintain satisfactory levels of health-related fitness.*

Figure 4.12 shows the health-related benefits associated with different physical activities and sports. From the figure you can determine which of the physical activities can improve or maintain your health-related fitness.

You can learn how to survey your health-related fitness levels by completing the "Active Mind/Active Body" activities—one for each of the health-related fitness components—on the next few pages. These activities are designed to introduce you to the health-related fitness concepts.

BELIEVE IT? ... OR NOT?

Surveys in 1992 showed that less than 40 percent of high school students engaged in adequate amounts of vigorous exercise each week.

See page 152 for answer.

SECTION 2 REVIEW

Answer the following questions on a separate sheet of paper:

1. List and define each of the five health-related fitness components.

2. Why are the health-related fitness components more important to your functional health than the skill-related fitness components?

Activity/Sport and Primary Emphasis	Cardio-vascular fitness	Flexi-bility	Muscular strength	Muscular endurance	Body com-position
Archery S	*	*	**	*	*
Backpacking H	***	**	**	****	***
Badminton S	**	**	*	**	**
Ballet B	***	****	***	***	***
Baseball S	*	*	*	*	*
Basketball B	***	*	*	**	**
Bicycling H	****	**	**	****	***
Bowling S	*	*	*	*	*
Canoeing B	**	*	*	**	**
Circuit training H	**	***	***	****	**
Dance, aerobic H	****	***	**	***	****
Dance, line S	**	*	**	**	**
Dance, social H	**	*	**	**	**
Fitness calisthenics H	*	****	**	***	**
Football S	**	*	***	**	**
Golf (walking) B	**	**	*	*	**
Gymnastics B	**	****	****	****	**
Handball H	****	*	*	***	***
Hiking H	***	**	**	****	***
Horseback riding S	*	*	*	*	*
Interval training H	****	*	**	***	****
Jogging H	****	*	**	***	****
Judo S	*	**	**	**	*
Karate S	*	**	**	**	*
Mountain climbing H	****	**	****	****	****
Pool; billiards S	*	*	*	*	*
Racquetball; paddleball B	****	*	*	***	***
Rope jumping H	***	*	**	***	***
Rowing H	****	**	**	****	****
Sailing S	*	*	*	*	*
Skating, ice B	***	*	*	***	***
Skating, in-line B	***	**	*	***	***
Skiing, cross-country B	****	**	**	***	****
Skiing, downhill B	**	**	**	**	**
Soccer B	****	**	**	***	****
Softball (fast pitch) S	*	*	*	*	*
Softball (slow pitch) S	*	*	*	*	*
Surfing B	**	**	**	***	**
Swimming laps H	****	**	**	***	****
Table tennis S	*	*	*	*	*
Tennis B	***	*	*	**	**
Volleyball B	**	*	**	*	**
Walking H	***	*	*	**	***
Waterskiing S	**	**	**	**	**
Weight training H	*	**	****	***	***

Primary Emphasis   Better – ****
S = Skill-related fitness.   Good – ***
H = Health-related fitness.   Fair – **
B = Both Skill- and Health-related fitness.   Low – *

• **Figure 4.12**   *Health-related Benefits.*

Active Mind!
Active Body!

Exploring Health-related Fitness

Jumping Jacks

You can assess your cardiovascular fitness level in a variety of ways. One simple way is to do thirty jumping jacks in thirty seconds, and then rest, standing in place, for thirty seconds (see Figure 4.13). After resting thirty seconds, take your pulse rate for thirty seconds. If your pulse rate is less than 60 beats in thirty seconds, you pass. If not, you may need to improve your cardiovascular fitness level.

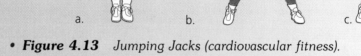

a.   b.   c.

• **Figure 4.13**   *Jumping Jacks (cardiovascular fitness).*

Zipper Stretch

There is no single method to determine your flexibility level. Tests of flexibility usually focus on determining the range of motion of one or two joints. For example, one way to assess your shoulder flexibility is the arm stretch, or zipper stretch (see Figure 4.14). To begin this evaluation, raise your right arm, bend your elbow, and reach down behind your back as far as possible. Then, at the same time, bend your left elbow and reach around your back and try to clasp your right hand. Your goal is to touch or overlap your right hand. Now switch arms and repeat the test. You may find that you do better on one side than the other. This is common because many individuals are more flexible on one side than the other. If you touched your fingers or had some overlap, then you pass and are in the healthy zone for flexibility on this test. If you were unable to touch your fingers on one or both sides, you may need to work on improving your shoulder flexibility.

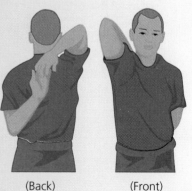

(Back)   (Front)

• **Figure 4.14**   *Zipper Stretch (flexibility).*

Push-Ups

A simple way to determine your muscular strength is to see if you can do a few push-ups (see Figure 4.15). Lie down so that you face the floor and put your hands under your shoulders. Keep your legs straight, and push off the floor until your arms are fully extended. To pass, boys should repeat this five times, and girls should complete three push-ups. If you cannot complete the appropriate number of push-ups, you may need to work on improving your muscular strength.

• **Figure 4.15**   *Push-ups (muscular strength).*

Wall Sit

You can survey your muscular endurance level by doing a wall sit (see Figure 4.16). Find a wall that you can lean back against comfortably and safely. Place your feet shoulders' width apart, and stand 1 to 1½ feet from the wall. Lean back against the wall so that your back is straight and your shoulder blades touch the wall. Now squat down until your knees are at a 90-degree angle. Try to hold this position for fifteen seconds. If you made fifteen seconds, you passed. If not, you may need to work on improving your muscular endurance.

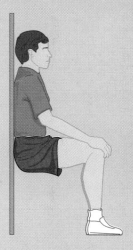

• **Figure 4.16**   *Wall Sit (muscular endurance).*

Finger Pinch Test

To analyze your body composition, pinch a fold of skin on your thigh (see Figure 4.17). Place the end of your little finger on your kneecap. Spread out your hand, and extend your thumb on the same hand as far as possible up your thigh. With your other hand, pinch a fold of skin at the end of your thumb. If your skin pinch is wider than your thumb, you may need to work on improving your body composition.

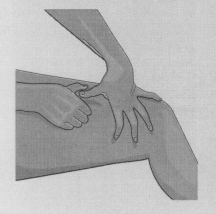

• **Figure 4.17**   *Finger Pinch Test (body composition).*

SECTION 3 Skill-related Fitness Evaluations

In this section you will learn how to evaluate, record, and interpret your skill-related fitness levels by performing one or more evaluations for each of the skill-related fitness components. These evaluations are designed to assess skill-related fitness levels more accurately than the activities you did earlier in the chapter. The skill-related self-evaluations in this section can be administered with the help of a partner. Give your best effort on each skill-related component. If necessary, you may make additional attempts.

Score each skill-related evaluation as low, fair, average, or good to better. Record your best scores on a personal fitness profile chart like the one provided in the "Active Mind/Active Body" activity at the end of the chapter.

As you conduct these self-evaluations, concentrate on how each activity relates to each of the specific skill components of fitness. Remember, practice can improve your scores. However, high skill scores are not necessary for good fitness.

Be sure to consider the following safety tips before attempting any of the self-evaluations:

• Adequate stretching and warm-up should precede all evaluations.

• Correct instructions and demonstrations should precede all evaluations.

> 66 Whenever the urge to exercise comes upon me, I lie down for a while and it passes.
>
> —Robert Maynard Hutchins, quoted in Harry S. Ashmore, *The Life of Robert Maynard Hutchins* [Hutchins, who headed the University of Chicago from 1929 to 1951, enjoyed good health throughout his life; he died at age 78.] 99

BELIEVE IT? ... OR NOT?

At least 250,000 deaths per year in the United States are linked to a lack of regular physical activity.

See page 152 for answer.

SECTION 3 REVIEW

Answer the following questions on a separate sheet of paper:

1. After you have done the "Fitness Check" that begins on the next page, identify the skill-related fitness evaluations you completed. Explain their importance to your overall personal fitness level.

2. How can scores of "good to better" on your skill-related fitness evaluations influence your sports performance levels?

Fitness Check ✓

Evaluating Skill-related Fitness

Agility

Side Step Shuffle.   *To evaluate your agility level, you can choose to use the side step shuffle, the agility run, or both. To do the side step shuffle, you'll need the following equipment: tape, chalk, or pens; a stopwatch; a smooth, flat surface 12 feet long; and a partner (to be a timer and counter). Use the following procedures:*

1. Make five parallel lines on the floor, each 2½ to 3 feet long. The lines should be three feet apart. (See Figure 4.18.)

2. Start the evaluation by standing astride the center line with one foot on the left and one on the right.

3. On the starting command of your partner, move to the right as quickly as possible. You must slide your feet. Do not allow them to cross over one another (any crossovers should be counted by your partner). Keep your center of gravity low by bending your knees.

4. Continue to the right until your right foot crosses the last line. You need only put one foot over the line. Then quickly change directions, and slide back to the left.

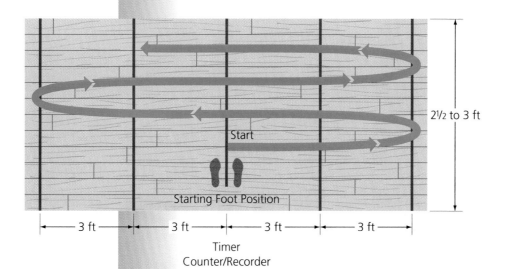

Start

2½ to 3 ft

Starting Foot Position

|← 3 ft →|← 3 ft →|← 3 ft →|← 3 ft →|

Timer
Counter/Recorder

• ***Figure 4.18*** *Side Step Shuffle (agility evaluation).*
Source: From *Essentials of Strength, Training, and Conditioning,* ed. T. R. Baechle (Champaign, IL: Human Kinetics Publishers, 1994), 269.

Skill Level	Males	Females
Good to better	More than 31	More than 28
Average	26 – 30	24 – 27
Fair	19 – 25	16 – 23
Low	Below 19	Below 16

• **Figure 4.19** *Agility Scores (number of lines crossed minus crossovers in side step shuffle).*
Source: From *Essentials of Strength, Training, and Conditioning*, ed. T. R. Baechle (Champaign, IL: Human Kinetics Publishers, 1994), 269.

5. Continue this procedure for ten seconds, at which time your partner will tell you to stop.

6. The objective is to cross as many lines as possible in ten seconds. Count your lines (include the starting line), and subtract one point for each time you crossed your feet. See Figure 4.19 to interpret your score. Record the score on your personal fitness profile chart like the one in the "Active Mind/Active Body" activity at the end of the chapter.

Agility Run.   *Equipment needed for the agility run includes four chairs, boxes, or cones; measuring tape; a stopwatch; a smooth, flat surface 30 feet long; and a partner (timer). Follow these steps:*

1. Place four chairs (or boxes or cones) in a straight line, ten feet apart from each other (see Figure 4.20).

2. Lie on your back with your arms across your chest. Your head should be on the starting line and the rest of your body behind the line.

• **Figure 4.20** *Agility Run (agility evaluation).*

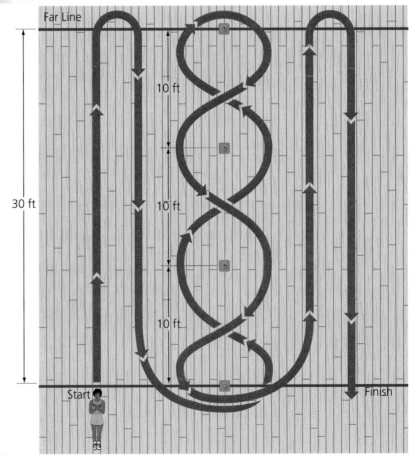

(Continued on next page)

Skill Level	Males	Females
Good to better	16.7 or less	18.4 or less
Average	16.8 – 18.6	18.5 – 22.3
Fair	18.7 – 18.8	23.4 – 22.4
Low	18.9 or Slower	23.5 or Slower

• **Figure 4.21** *Agility Scores (time in seconds in agility run).*
Source: Thomas K. Cureton, *Physical Fitness of Champion Athletes* (Urbana, IL: University of Illinois Press, 1951), 68.

• **Figure 4.22** *One-Foot Stand (balance evaluation).*

continued

3. On the starting command of your partner, stand up, and run through the course as quickly as possible (see Figure 4.20). Keep your turns close, and keep your center of gravity low.

4. Continue through the finish line, at which time your partner will record your time. Score your time to the nearest tenth of a second. See Figure 4.21 to evaluate your time. Record the score on your personal fitness profile chart like the one in the "Active Mind/Active Body" activity at the end of the chapter.

Balance

One-Foot Stand. *Now evaluate your balance skills. You can choose the one-foot stand, the squat-stand, or both. To do the one-foot stand, gather the following equipment: a stopwatch, a flat surface, and a partner (timer). Here's the procedure:*

1. Start by removing your shoes and socks. Stand on your dominant foot (the one you typically kick with). Place the other foot flat on the inside of the supporting knee.

2. Place your hands on your waist. When your partner says "Start," raise the heel of your dominant foot off the floor. Hold this position for as long as possible (see Figure 4.22).

3. The evaluation is over when one of the following takes place: the support foot twists, hops, or shuffles; the heel contacts the floor; your hands lose contact from your waist; or sixty seconds expires.

4. The objective is to hold the position for a maximum of sixty seconds. Have your partner count your time out loud. Score your time to the nearest tenth of a second. See Figure 4.23 on the next page to evaluate your time. Record your score on your personal fitness profile chart like the one in the "Active Mind/Active Body" activity at the end of the chapter.

Squat-Stand. *For the squat-stand, you'll need mats, a stopwatch, and a partner (timer). Follow these guidelines:*

1. Start by placing your feet shoulders' width apart. Bend your knees and back into a squat position. Go low enough to touch your hands on the floor. (It may be helpful to have mats *around* you, but it is not recommended to be *on* mats during this evaluation.)

2. Place your hands flat on the floor 8 to 12 inches in front of your feet. Spread your fingers. Your hands will require some adjusting.

Skill Level	Males	Females
Good to better	37 or longer	23 or longer
Average	15 – 36	8 – 22
Fair	5 – 14	3 – 7
Low	0 – 4	0 – 2

• **Figure 4.23** *Balance Scores (time in seconds in one-foot stand).*
Source: Adapted with permission from Johnson and Nelson, *Practical Measurements for Evaluation in Physical Education,* 4th ed. (Edina, MN: Burgess Publishing, 1986), 238.

Skill Level	Males	Females
Good to better	50 or longer	40 or longer
Average	25 – 49	21 – 39
Fair	14 – 24	8 – 20
Low	0 – 13	0 – 7

• **Figure 4.25** *Balance Scores (time in seconds in squat-stand).*
Source: Adapted with permission from Barrow, *A Practical Approach to Measurement in Physical Education,* 2nd ed. (Philadelphia: Lea and Febiger, 1971), 237.

• **Figure 4.24**   *Squat-Stand (balance evaluation).*

3. Lean forward slowly while placing the inside of your knees on the outside of your elbows (see Figure 4.24). Continue to lean forward until all of your weight is supported on your hands and elbows. Time starts when both feet are off the ground.

4. Hold this position for sixty seconds, at which time your partner will stop you. Time also stops if any part of your body other than your hands touches the floor.

5. The objective is to stay balanced for as many seconds as possible up to sixty seconds. See Figure 4.25 to evaluate your time. Record the score on your personal fitness profile chart like the one in the "Active Mind/Active Body" activity at the end of the chapter.

Coordination

Scarf Juggle (Eye-Hand Coordination).   *The next two skill-related fitness evaluations test your coordination. The scarf juggle tests your eye-hand coordination. The soccer ball kick evaluates your eye-foot coordination. To do the scarf juggle, get two scarves, two plastic bags, or two pieces of tissue paper (12 to 18 inches square), and a partner to count for you. Follow these steps:*

1. Place both scarves into your dominant (writing) hand (see Figure 4.26 on the next page).

2. Raise your hand up swiftly, and release one of the scarves. Then quickly repeat the same movement with the other scarf.

3. As soon as you have released the second scarf, quickly *grab and toss* the first scarf again, immediately followed by a grab and toss of the second scarf. Try to keep the toss *up*, not out.

(Continued on next page)

continued

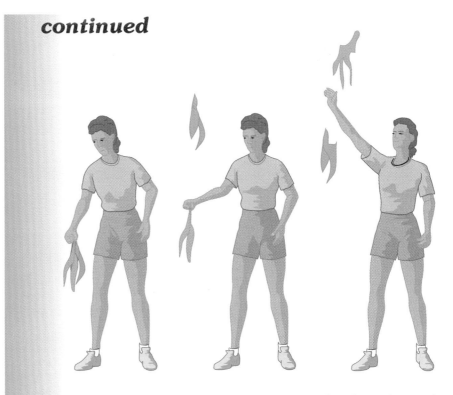

• **Figure 4.26**   *Scarf Juggle (evaluation of eye-hand coordination).*

Skill Level	Males and Females
Good to better	more than 13
Average	7 – 12
Fair	4 – 6
Low	0 – 3

• **Figure 4.27**   *Coordination Scores (number of caught tosses in scarf juggle).*

4. Keep both scarves in the air as long as you can by continuing to alternate tosses. Your partner should count each correct *grab and toss* as 1 point. (Do not count the first two tosses. Begin counting with your first grab.)

5. Repeat the process with your nondominant hand. Total the scores for both hands. See Figure 4.27 to evaluate your score. Record it on your personal fitness profile chart like the one in the "Active Mind/Active Body" activity at the end of the chapter.

Soccer Ball Kick (Eye-Foot Coordination).   *The soccer ball kick will assess your eye-foot coordination. You will need this equipment: three soccer balls or utility balls of similar size and weight, a standard gym wall (about 30 feet wide and 10 feet high), tape, a tape measure, a stopwatch, and a partner (timer and counter). Do the following:*

1. Place a piece of tape 9 feet from the wall. Place one ball on this line. The two spare balls are placed 9 feet behind the line.

2. Start the evaluation by standing behind the 9-foot line with one ball in front of you.

• **Figure 4.28** *Soccer Ball Kick (test of eye-foot coordination).*

Skill Level	Males	Females
Good to better	20 and above	15 and above
Average	11 – 19	7 – 14
Fair	8 – 10	2 – 6
Low	0 – 7	0 – 1

• **Figure 4.29** *Coordination Scores (number of kicks in soccer ball kick). Source:* Adapted with permission from McDonald soccer test in Johnson and Nelson, *Practical Measurements for Evaluation in Physical Education,* 4th ed. (Burgess Publishing, 1986), 298.

3. On the starting command of your partner, begin kicking the ball against the wall as many times as possible in a thirty-second period. Note that how well you control the ball is more important than how hard you strike the ball. (See Figure 4.28.)

4. You may only kick the ball from behind the 9-foot line. If necessary, you may retrieve the ball with your hands and place it at the 9-foot line. If the ball is out of control, you may choose to retrieve one of the spare balls.

5. Continue to kick for thirty seconds. Your partner will stop you when your time is up. Record the highest number of legal kicks. See Figure 4.29 to evaluate your score, and record it on your personal fitness profile chart like the one in the "Active Mind/Active Body" activity at the end of the chapter.

Power

Vertical Jump. *To assess your power level, use the vertical jump, standing broad jump, or both. The vertical jump test requires chalk, a wall 11 feet high or higher, measuring tape, and a partner to make measurements. Perform this test as follows:*

(Continued on next page)

continued

1. Start the evaluation by standing with your dominant arm next to the wall. Place the chalk in your dominant hand. Start with both feet together and your body sideways to the wall. Raise your dominant hand, and mark the wall with the chalk (see Figure 4.30).

2. Step one step back from the start, and place both feet back together. In a smooth, quick motion, step forward, bend your knees and back, and then push upward with both feet. Raise your arm, and make a chalk mark on the wall at the highest point you can reach (see Figure 4.30). Be sure to stay as close to the wall as possible.

3. Your partner will measure the distance between the two marks and record the distance to the closest inch.

Skill Level	Males	Females
Good to better	22 and above	15 and above
Average	20 – 21	13 – 14
Fair	12 – 19	8 – 12
Low	0 – 11	0 – 7

• **Figure 4.31** *Power Scores (inches in vertical jump). Source: Data from Johnson and Nelson, Practical Measurements for Evaluation in Physical Education, 4th ed. (1986) and Frierwood, Annual Official Rules and Reference Guide of U.S. Volleyball Association (U.S. Volleyball Association, 1967), 211.*

11' or higher

Step 1   Step 2

• **Figure 4.30** *Vertical Jump (power evaluation).*

4. The objective is to jump as high as possible above your standing reach mark. See Figure 4.31 to evaluate your score. Record it on your personal fitness profile chart like the one in the "Active Mind/Active Body" activity at the end of the chapter.

Standing Broad Jump.   *You can also test your power by performing the standing broad jump. You'll need chalk; measuring tape; and a smooth, flat area 10 feet long. Here's how to perform this evaluation:*

1. Mark a starting line. Then measure a distance of 9 feet from that line. The distance should be marked in 1-inch intervals.

2. Stand with both feet behind the starting line with your toes on the line (see Figure 4.32).

3. By combining the bending of your knees and the swinging of your arms, jump outward as far as possible. This movement must be done quickly. Be sure not to fall backward when landing, because measurements are taken from the closest point to the starting line.

4. Your partner will measure from the starting line to the closest point of your landing.

10 feet

• **Figure 4.32**   *Standing Broad Jump (power evaluation).*

(Continued on next page)

continued

5. The objective is to jump as far from the start as possible. See Figure 4.33 to evaluate your score. Record it on your personal fitness profile chart like the one in the "Active Mind/Active Body" activity at the end of the chapter.

Skill Level	Males (by age)				Females (by age)			
	14 yrs.	15 yrs.	16 yrs.	17+ yrs.	14 yrs.	15 yrs.	16 yrs.	17+ yrs.
Good to better	80 – 90	84 – 96	90 – 98	93 – 101	71 – 80	71 – 80	71 – 80	72 – 81
Average	74 – 79	80 – 83	84 – 89	86 – 92	64 – 70	65 – 70	65 – 70	65 – 71
Fair	66 – 73	73 – 79	78 – 83	78 – 85	58 – 63	59 – 64	59 – 64	59 – 64
Low	56 – 65	62 – 72	65 – 77	67 – 77	48 – 57	50 – 58	50 – 58	50 – 58

• **Figure 4.33** *Power Scores (inches in standing broad jump).* Source: Data from Johnson and Nelson, *Practical Measurements for Evaluation in Physical Education,* 4th ed. (1986) and *AAHPERD Youth Fitness Test Manual* (1976), 213.

Speed

Four-Second Dash. *You can evaluate your speed using the four-second dash or the 50-yard dash. Equipment for the four-second dash includes markers or tape, measuring tape, a whistle, a stopwatch, a flat running area 30 to 40 yards long, and a partner (starter and timer). To perform the four-second dash:*

1. Mark a starting line. Then mark a line 10 yards from the start. Mark nine additional lines that are each 2 yards apart (see Figure 4.34).

2. Where you begin is your choice. You may begin at the start line, or you may start 2 yards behind the start line. Regardless

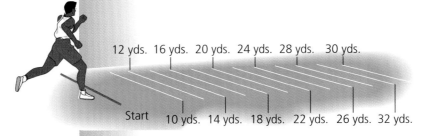

• **Figure 4.34** *Four-Second Dash (speed evaluation).*

Skill Level	Males	Females
Good to better	31 and above	27 and above
Average	29–30	25–26
Fair	27–28	23–24
Low	Below 27	Below 23

• **Figure 4.35** *Speed Scores (yards in four-second dash).*
Source: Adapted with permission from Johnson and Nelson, *Practical Measurements for Evaluation in Physical Education,* 4th ed. (1986), 258.

of where you start, your partner will begin your time as you cross the starting line. Four seconds from the beginning of your time, your partner will blow the whistle.

3. Continue to sprint until you hear the four-second whistle. Then slowly come to a stop.

4. Your partner will record the distance in (yards) that you reached at the four-second whistle.

5. The objective is to obtain the greatest distance in four seconds. See Figure 4.35 to evaluate your time. Record the score on your personal fitness profile chart like the one in the "Active Mind/ Active Body" activity at the end of the chapter.

50-Yard Dash.   *The 50-yard dash is a second way you can assess your speed. You'll need the following equipment: measuring tape; a smooth, flat surface 70 yards or longer; a stopwatch; and a partner (starter and timer). Here is how to perform the 50-yard dash (see Figure 4.36):*

1. Mark off a safe course 50 yards long. Be sure to allow additional distance for a safe stopping zone.

2. Have the starter positioned at the finish line with a stopwatch. The starter/timer will raise an arm, shout the instruction "Ready," and then simultaneously drop his or her arm and shout the instruction "Go."

3. You will sprint as quickly as possible to the finish line. Be sure to stay on the balls of your feet, pump your arms, and lean forward slightly.

4. Continue to the finish line, and record your score to the nearest tenth of a second. See Figure 4.37 to evaluate your time. Record the score on your personal fitness profile chart like the one in the "Active Mind/Active Body" activity at the end of the chapter.

Start

50 yrds finish

• **Figure 4.36**   *50-Yard Dash (speed evaluation).*

(Continued on next page)

continued

	Males (by age)			
Skill Level	**14 yrs.**	**15 yrs.**	**16 yrs.**	**17+ yrs.**
Good to better	6.3–7.0	6.1–6.8	6.0–6.6	6.0–6.5
Average	7.1–7.5	6.9–7.1	6.7–6.9	6.6–6.9
Fair	7.6–8.5	7.2–8.0	7.0–7.7	7.0–7.6
Low	>8.5	>8.0	>7.7	>7.6

	Females (by age)			
Skill Level	**14 yrs.**	**15 yrs.**	**16 yrs.**	**17+ yrs.**
Good to better	7.0–7.9	7.1–8.0	7.1–8.1	7.1–8.1
Average	8.0–8.7	8.1–8.7	8.2–8.9	8.2–8.9
Fair	8.8–10.3	8.8–10.3	9.0–10.4	9.0–10.4
Low	>10.3	>10.3	>10.4	>10.4

• ***Figure 4.37*** *Speed Scores (seconds in 50-yard dash).*
Source: Data from Johnson and Nelson, *Practical Measurements for Evaluation in Physical Education,* 4th ed. (1986) and *AAHPERD Youth Fitness Test Manual* (1976), 260.

Reaction Time

Yardstick Drop. *You can assess your reaction time with a test called the* yardstick drop. *You'll need a yardstick, a table and chair, and a partner. Follow these steps:*

1. Start by sitting in a chair and resting your arm on a table. You may use another chair as a table, if necessary (see Figure 4.38).

2. Extend your fingers over the edge of the table 3 inches. Rest the heel of your hand on the table.

3. Have your partner place the yardstick over your fingers. The placement of the 0 point of the stick should be even with the top of your thumb. Your thumb and index finger should be 2 inches apart with the end of the yardstick centered between them. Your hand must remain still (see Figure 4.38).

4. You should look only at the bottom of the stick. Do not look at your partner's hand.

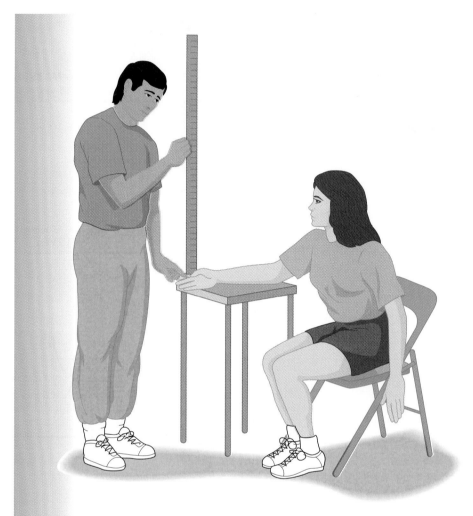

• **Figure 4.38**   *Yardstick Drop (evaluation of reaction time).*
Source: Data from Johnson and Nelson, *Practical Measurements for Evaluation in Physical Education,* 4th ed. (1986).

Skill Level	Males and Females
Good to better	1–2"
Average	3–4"
Fair	5–6"
Low	7" or more

• **Figure 4.39**   *Reaction Time Scores (average inches in yardstick drop).*

5. As your partner drops the stick at random times, try to catch it with your fingers as quickly as possible. Your partner will then record the measurement at the point on the yardstick that you caught it with your fingers. Each attempt is scored to the nearest half-inch. The reading is taken just above the thumb.

6. Do five trials. Your score is determined by discarding the best and worst scores. Add the remaining three scores, and divide by 3. See Figure 4.39 to evaluate your score. Record the score on your personal fitness profile chart like the one in the "Active Mind/Active Body" activity at the end of the chapter.

SECTION 4   Health-related Fitness Evaluations

You can evaluate, record, and interpret your own health-related fitness levels just as you did for the skill-related components. Many of the health-related tests in this section are based on the Prudential *Fitnessgram*.

To determine how you scored on an evaluation, refer to the figures for each health-related fitness evaluation. The figures show the healthy zone of fitness—scores that represent levels of personal fitness that are good to better. Scores that fall below the healthy fitness zone are considered to be lower than required for a reasonable level of personal fitness.

The following health-related self-evaluations can be administered with the help of a partner and your instructor. Give your best effort for each evaluation. If necessary, you may make additional attempts. Record your best scores on your personal fitness profile chart, like the sample provided in the "Active Mind/Active Body" activity at the end of the chapter. As you conduct these self-evaluations, concentrate on how each particular activity relates to each of the specific health-related components. Practice can improve your scores and your own level of personal fitness. Consider the following safety tips before attempting any of the self-evaluations:

- Adequate stretching and warm-up should precede all evaluations.

- Correct instructions and demonstrations should precede all evaluations.

It is important for you to learn to monitor your levels of both skill-related and health-related fitness throughout the rest of your life. This will help you gauge your personal fitness progress and allow you to make changes in your personal fitness goals.

BELIEVE IT? ... OR NOT?

Currently, all people six years old or older engage in leisure-time physical activity.

See page 152 for answer.

SECTION 4 REVIEW

Answer the following questions on a separate sheet of paper:

1. After you have done the "Fitness Check" that begins on the next page, identify health-related fitness evaluations you completed, and explain their importance to your overall personal fitness level.

2. List and explain the three health-related evaluations for flexibility.

Fitness Check ✓

Evaluating Health-related Fitness

Cardiovascular Fitness

One way to evaluate your cardiovascular fitness level is by taking the three-minute step test. The other way is to complete the PACER 20-meter shuttle run. Choose one or both evaluations.

Three-Minute Step Test.   In the three-minute step test, you step up and down on a 12-inch step at 24 steps per minute. (See Figure 4.40.) You then measure your recovery pulse for one minute immediately upon stopping to determine your cardiovascular fitness level. If your recovery pulse rate is low (less than 85 beats per minute), you are in the high fitness zone. If your recovery pulse is between 85 and 95 beats per minute, you are in the healthy fitness zone (in other words, you have good to better levels of cardiovascular fitness). If your recovery pulse is high (120 beats per minute or higher), you have a low level of cardiovascular fitness.

• **Figure 4.40**   *Three-Minute Step Test (cardiovascular fitness evaluation).*

(Continued on next page)

continued

PACER (Progressive Aerobic Cardiovascular Endurance Run) 20-Meter Shuttle Run.   To perform the PACER 20-meter shuttle run, begin walking or jogging when you hear the beep on the PACER cassette tape. You need to get to the line that is 20 meters away before the next beep (Figure 4.41). Then turn around and return to the starting line, trying to beat the next beep. If you don't reach the line before the beep, join the observers on the sideline. You (or a partner on the sidelines) will count the number of times you make it to each line before the beep. (From start

• *Figure 4.41*
Schematic Diagram of the PACER Test (cardiovascular fitness evaluation).
Source: With permission from The Cooper Institute for Aerobics Research, *The Prudential Fitnessgram Test Administration Manual* (Dallas, TX: 1992).

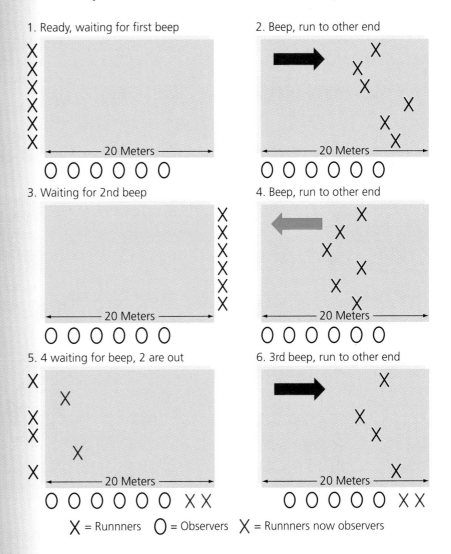

(Continued on next page)

| Males | PACER Scores |
Age	# of laps
13	35–74
14	41–80
15	46–85
16	52–90
17+	57–94

| Females | PACER Scores |
Age	# of laps
13	15–42
14	18–44
15	23–50
16	28–56
17+	34–61

• *Figure 4.42* *PACER Test Scores (healthy zone).* Note: Scores below the healthy fitness zone are considered low. *Source:* With permission from The Cooper Institute for Aerobics Research, *The Prudential Fitnessgram Test Administration Manual* (Dallas, TX: 1992), 12.

to the 20-meter mark equals 1, back to start equals 2, and so on.) The test is stopped if you don't make it to the line before the beep. The beeps on the tape are spaced to start you off at a slow pace, like a warm-up, and then gradually begin occurring more frequently to speed you up.

After you total the number of laps you complete during the PACER test, use Figure 4.42 to determine your results. For example, if Maureen, a sixteen-year-old female, completed 32 laps for the PACER test, she would be in the healthy fitness zone for cardiovascular fitness.

Once you have completed the step test or PACER test, evaluate your scores, and record them on your personal fitness profile chart like the one in the "Active Mind/Active Body" activity at the end of the chapter. If you did not score in the healthy fitness zone, you should try to improve your cardiovascular fitness levels. If you did score in the health fitness zone, be sure to maintain your cardiovascular fitness.

Flexibility

To evaluate your flexibility level, choose any or all of the following evaluations: trunk lift, arm lift, or back saver sit and reach.

Trunk Lift.   The Prudential *Fitnessgram* trunk lift evaluation can be used to assess your upper back and trunk flexibility (see Figure 4.43). Begin by lying face down on the floor. Point your toes, and place your hands under your thighs. A partner should hold your legs as you lift your chin slowly up as high as possible and hold this position for about three seconds. Another partner should use a yardstick to measure how many inches your chin is above the

Starting position for the trunk lift.

Student in the "up" position for the trunk lift test.

Measurement of trunk lift.

• *Figure 4.43*   *Trunk Lift (flexibility evaluation).* *Source:* With permission from The Cooper Institute for Aerobics Research, *The Prudential Fitnessgram Test Administration Manual* (Dallas, TX: 1992), 21.

(Continued on next page)

floor. Repeat this exercise twice. Then record your best score. To reach the healthy fitness zone for this test, you should be able to lift your chin 9 to 12 inches off the floor (see Figure 4.44). Record your score on your personal fitness profile chart like the one in the "Active Mind/Active Body" activity at the end of the chapter.

Healthy Zone

9–12 inches
Scores below the healthy zone are considered low.

• **Figure 4.44** *Trunk Lift Scores.*
Source: With permission from The Cooper Institute for Aerobics Research (Dallas, TX: 1992).

Healthy Zone

11–14 inches
Scores below the healthy zone are considered low.

Figure 4.46 *Arm Lift Scores (healthy zone).*
Source: Data from Johnson and Nelson, *Practical Measurements for Evaluation in Physical Education,* 4th ed. (1986).

Starting Position

Reach Position

• **Figure 4.47** *Back Saver Sit and Reach Exercise (flexibility evaluation).*
Source: With permission from The Cooper Institute for Aerobics Research (Dallas, TX: 1992).

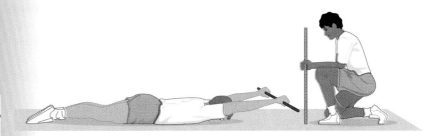

• **Figure 4.45** *Arm Lift (flexibility evaluation).*

Arm Lift.   The arm lift can be used to evaluate the flexibility of the front of the muscles in your shoulders (see Figure 4.45). Again, begin by lying face down on the floor. Hold a stick or other light rod out in front of you with your arms spread shoulders' width apart. Your palms should be face down, with your arms and wrists straight. As you keep your chin on the floor, raise your arms and the rod as high as possible. Hold the position for three seconds. Have your partner use a yardstick to measure how many inches the rod is above the floor. Repeat twice, and then record your best score. The healthy fitness zone for this test is 11 to 14 inches off the floor (see Figure 4.46). Record your score on your personal fitness profile chart like the one in the "Active Mind/Active Body" activity at the end of the chapter.

Back Saver Sit and Reach.   To evaluate your low back and hamstring flexibility level, complete the Prudential *Fitnessgram* back saver sit and reach exercise (see Figure 4.47). To perform this evaluation you will need a box 12 inches high. Tape a yardstick on top of the box so that it extends 9 inches toward you. The 0 end of the yardstick should be nearest you. Remove your shoes, and sit down with the back of the box against a wall. Extend one of your legs so that your foot is flat against the end of the box. Bend your other knee, with the sole of your foot flat on the floor 2 to 3 inches to the side of the straight knee. Extend your arms over the yardstick, with your hands placed one on top of the other, palms down. Reach forward in this manner four times, holding the position of the fourth reach for at least one second while a partner records how far you can reach. After you measure one side, switch the position of your legs, and measure your other side. You may find that you can do better on one side than the other, which is common.

(Continued on next page)

Healthy Zone	
Males	**Females**
8 inches	10 inches (ages 13-14)
	12 inches (ages 15+)

Scores below the healthy zone are considered low.

• **Figure 4.48** *Back Saver Sit and Reach Scores.*
Source: With permission from The Cooper Institute for Aerobics Research, *The Prudential Fitnessgram Test Administration Manual* (Dallas, TX: 1992), 46–47.

(continued)

To reach the healthy fitness zone for this test, males should be able to reach 8 inches. Females should be able to reach 10 inches (ages thirteen to fourteen) or 12 inches (ages fifteen and above; see Figure 4.48). Females, on average, are more flexible than males in this evaluation. Once you evaluate your back saver sit and reach flexibility, record your score on your personal fitness profile chart like the one in the "Active Mind/Active Body" activity at the end of the chapter.

Muscular Strength

To evaluate your muscular strength, choose any or all of these evaluations: push-up test, pull-up test, or flexed arm hang test.

Push-up Test.   The Prudential *Fitnessgram* push-up test can be used to help you determine your level of muscular strength. This test works best with a partner. To start this test, lie down on your stomach on a mat. Place your hands under your shoulders. Your fingers should be stretched out; your legs straight, parallel, and slightly apart; and your toes tucked under (see Figure 4.49). Push up off the mat with your arms until your arms are straight, keeping your legs and back straight. Now lower your body with your arms until your elbows bend at a 90-degree angle and your upper arms are parallel to the floor. Then return to the starting straight-arm position. Try to do as many push-ups as you can at a rhythm of about twenty push-ups per minute, or one every three seconds. Have your partner count and record your results. Then use Figure 4.50 on the next page to determine how well you did. For example, if Troy, a sixteen-year-old male, completed twenty push-ups, he would be in the healthy fitness zone for muscular strength.

Starting position   "Down" position

• **Figure 4.49**   *Push-up Test (muscular strength evaluation).*
Source: With permission from The Cooper Institute for Aerobics Research, *The Prudential Fitnessgram Test Administration Manual* (Dallas, TX: 1992), 23.

Pull-up Test. The Prudential *Fitnessgram* pull-up test can also be used to assess your muscular strength. Some people are not able to do pull-ups. If you are one of these people, choose another option (such as the Prudential *Fitnessgram* flexed arm hang test) to assess your muscular strength.

To start the pull-up evaluation, assume a hanging position on a horizontal bar with an overhand grip, palms facing away from the body (see Figure 4.51). Use your arms to pull your body up until your chin is above the bar. Then lower your body back to the hanging position. Repeat this as many times as you can. Then record your results. Use Figure 4.50 to determine how well you did. For example, if Mary, a fourteen-year-old female, completed two pull-ups, she would be in the healthy fitness zone for muscular strength.

Age	Push-ups	Pull-ups	Flexed Arm Hang
		Males	
13	12–25	1–4	12–17
14	14–30	2–5	15–20
15	16–35	3–7	15–20
16+	18–35	5–8	15–20
		Females	
13–16+	7–15	1–2	8–12

Scores below the healthy zone are considered low.

• **Figure 4.50** *Push-up, Pull-up, and Flexed Arm Hang Test Scores (healthy zone).* Source: With permission from The Cooper Institute for Aerobics Research, *The Prudential Fitnessgram Test Administration Manual* (Dallas, TX: 1992), 46–47.

Starting Position for the
Pull-up Test

Student in the "Up" Position
for the Pull-up Test

• **Figure 4.51** *Pull-up Test (muscular strength evaluation).* Source: With permission from The Cooper Institute for Aerobics Research, *The Prudential Fitnessgram Test Administration Manual* (Dallas, TX: 1992), 26.

(Continued on next page)

(continued)

• **Figure 4.52**   *Flexed Arm Hang Test (muscular strength evaluation).*
Source: With permission from The Cooper Institute for Aerobics Research, *The Prudential Fitnessgram Test Administration Manual* (Dallas, TX: 1992), 52.

Flexed Arm Hang Test.   A third way you can assess your muscular strength is by performing the Prudential *Fitnessgram* flexed arm hang test. This test is similar to the pull-up test but does not require you to lift your body up and down. To begin this test, grasp a horizontal bar with an overhand grip, palms facing away from the body (see Figure 4.52). Then, with the assistance of a partner or two, raise your body off the ground so that your chin is above the bar and your arms are flexed. As soon as you reach this position, your partner should start a stopwatch and time how many seconds you can hang in this position. If you touch the bar with your chin or your chin falls below the level of the bar, the stopwatch should be stopped.

Record your results, and use Figure 4.50 to determine how well you did. For example, if Gary, a seventeen-year-old male, was able to hang for eighteen seconds, he would be in the healthy fitness zone for muscular strength. Once you have completed one or more of the muscular strength evaluations, record your scores on your personal fitness profile chart like the one in the "Active Mind/ Active Body" activity at the end of the chapter.

Muscular Endurance

Curl-up Test.   *The curl-up evaluation can be used to assess your abdominal muscular endurance.* To begin this test you need two partners, a mat, and a measuring strip (such as a yardstick or tape measure) that is 30 inches long and 4.5 inches wide. Lie on your back on the mat with your knees bent at an angle of 140 degrees, feet flat on the floor, legs slightly apart, arms straight and parallel to your trunk, and palms resting on the mat. One partner

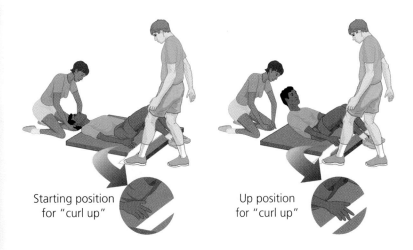

Starting position
for "curl up"

Up position
for "curl up"

• **Figure 4.53**   *Curl-up Test (muscular endurance evaluation).*
Source: With permission from The Cooper Institute for Aerobics
Research, *The Prudential Fitnessgram Test Administration Manual* (Dallas, TX: 1992), 19.

Age	Number of Curl-ups
	Males
13	21–40
14	24–45
15+	24–47
	Females
13	18–32
14	18–32
15+	18–35

Scores below the healthy zone are considered low.

• **Figure 4.54**   *Curl-up Scores (healthy zone).*
Source: With permission from The Cooper Institute for Aerobics Research, *The Prudential Fitnessgram Test Administration Manual* (Dallas, TX: 1992), 46–47.

should use his or her hands to make a resting place for your head. After you have assumed the correct position on the mat, have one of your partners place the measuring strip under your knees on the mat so that your fingertips are just resting on the edge of the measuring strip (see Figure 4.53). You may need a partner to secure the ends of the measuring strip. Start to curl up until your fingers reach the other side of the measuring strip, and keep your heels in contact with the mat. Then curl back down until your head touches your partner's hand. Do as many curl-ups as you can to a maximum of seventy-five. Pace yourself at a controlled rate of twenty curl-ups per minute, or about one curl-up every three seconds.

Record your results, and use Figure 4.54 to determine how well you did. For example, if Polly, a fourteen-year-old female, was able to do twenty-six curl-ups, she would be in the healthy fitness zone for muscular endurance. Once you have completed the muscular endurance evaluation, record your score on your personal fitness profile chart like the one in the "Active Mind/Active Body" activity at the end of the chapter.

Body Composition

You can use a body mass index to evaluate your body composition.

Body Mass Index (BMI).   The Prudential *Fitnessgram* Body Mass Index (BMI) evaluation gives you a description of your weight

(Continued on next page)

(continued)

Body Mass Index

Weight (pounds)	Height (inches)															
	48	49	50	51	52	53	54	55	56	57	58	59	60	61	62	63
80	24.5	23.5	22.5	21.7	20.8	20.1	19.3	18.6	18.0	17.3	16.8	16.2	15.7	15.1	14.7	14.2
85	26.0	24.9	24.0	23.0	22.1	21.3	20.5	19.8	19.1	18.4	17.8	17.2	16.6	16.1	15.6	15.1
90	27.5	26.4	25.4	24.4	23.5	22.6	21.7	21.0	20.2	19.5	18.8	18.2	17.6	17.0	16.5	16.0
95	29.1	27.9	26.8	25.7	24.8	23.8	23.0	22.1	21.3	20.6	19.9	19.2	18.6	18.0	17.4	16.9
100	30.6	29.3	28.2	27.1	26.1	25.1	24.2	23.3	22.5	21.7	20.9	20.2	19.6	18.9	18.3	17.8
105	32.1	30.8	29.6	28.4	27.4	26.3	25.4	24.5	23.6	22.8	22.0	21.3	20.5	19.9	19.2	18.6
110	33.6	32.3	31.0	29.8	28.7	27.6	26.6	25.6	24.7	23.9	23.0	22.3	21.5	20.8	20.2	19.5
115	35.2	33.7	32.4	31.2	30.0	28.8	27.8	26.8	25.8	24.9	24.1	23.3	22.5	21.8	21.1	20.4
120	36.7	35.2	33.8	32.5	31.3	30.1	29.0	27.9	27.0	26.0	25.1	24.3	23.5	22.7	22.0	21.3
125	38.2	36.7	35.2	33.9	32.6	31.4	30.2	29.1	28.1	27.1	26.2	25.3	24.5	23.7	22.9	22.2
130	39.8	38.1	36.6	35.2	33.9	32.6	31.4	30.3	29.2	28.2	27.2	26.3	25.4	24.6	23.8	23.1
135	41.3	39.6	38.0	36.6	35.2	33.9	32.6	31.4	30.3	29.3	28.3	27.3	26.4	25.6	24.7	24.0
140	42.8	41.1	39.5	37.9	36.5	35.1	33.8	32.6	31.5	30.4	29.3	28.3	27.4	26.5	25.7	24.9
145	44.3	42.5	40.9	39.3	37.8	36.4	35.0	33.8	32.6	31.4	30.4	29.3	28.4	27.5	26.6	25.7
150	45.9	44.0	42.3	40.6	39.1	37.6	36.2	34.9	33.7	32.5	31.4	30.4	29.4	28.4	27.5	26.6
155	47.4	45.5	43.7	42.0	40.4	38.9	37.5	36.1	34.8	33.6	32.5	31.4	30.3	29.3	28.4	27.5
160	48.9	47.0	45.1	43.3	41.7	40.1	38.7	37.3	35.9	34.7	33.5	32.4	31.3	30.3	29.3	28.4
165	50.5	48.4	46.5	44.7	43.0	41.4	39.9	38.4	37.1	35.8	34.6	33.4	32.3	31.2	30.2	29.3
170	52.0	49.9	47.9	46.6	44.3	42.6	41.1	39.6	38.2	36.9	35.6	34.4	33.3	32.2	31.2	30.2
175	53.5	51.4	49.3	47.4	45.6	43.9	42.3	40.8	39.3	37.9	36.7	35.4	34.2	33.1	32.1	31.1
180	55.0	52.8	50.7	48.8	46.9	45.1	43.5	41.9	40.4	39.0	37.7	36.4	35.2	34.1	33.0	32.0
185	56.6	54.3	52.1	50.1	48.2	46.4	44.7	43.1	41.6	40.1	38.7	37.4	36.2	35.0	33.9	32.8
190	58.1	55.8	53.5	51.5	49.5	47.7	45.9	44.3	42.7	41.2	39.8	38.5	37.2	36.0	34.8	33.7
195	59.6	57.2	55.0	52.8	50.8	48.9	47.1	45.4	43.8	42.3	40.8	39.5	38.2	36.9	35.7	34.6
200	61.2	58.7	56.4	54.2	52.1	50.2	48.3	46.6	44.9	43.4	41.9	40.5	39.1	37.9	36.7	35.5
205	62.7	60.2	57.8	55.5	53.4	51.4	49.5	47.7	46.1	44.5	42.9	41.5	40.1	38.8	37.6	36.4
210	64.2	61.6	59.2	56.9	54.7	52.7	50.7	48.9	47.2	45.5	44.0	42.5	41.1	39.8	38.5	37.3
215	65.7	63.1	60.6	58.2	56.0	53.9	51.9	50.1	48.3	46.6	45.0	43.5	42.1	40.7	39.4	38.2
220	67.3	64.6	62.0	59.6	57.3	55.2	53.2	51.2	49.4	47.7	46.1	44.5	43.1	41.7	40.3	39.1
225	68.8	66.0	63.4	60.9	58.6	56.4	54.4	52.4	50.5	48.8	47.1	45.5	44.0	42.6	41.2	39.9
230	70.3	67.5	64.8	62.3	59.9	57.7	55.6	53.6	51.7	49.9	48.2	46.6	45.0	43.5	42.2	40.8
235	71.9	69.0	66.2	63.7	61.2	58.9	56.8	54.7	52.8	51.0	49.2	47.6	46.0	44.5	43.1	41.7
240	73.4	70.4	67.6	65.0	62.5	60.2	58.0	55.9	53.9	52.0	50.3	48.6	47.0	45.4	44.0	42.6
245	74.9	71.9	69.0	66.4	63.8	61.5	59.2	57.1	55.0	53.1	51.3	49.6	47.9	46.4	44.9	43.5
250	76.4	73.4	70.5	67.7	65.1	62.7	60.4	58.2	56.2	54.2	52.4	50.6	48.9	47.3	45.8	44.4

• **Figure 4.55** *BMI Chart.*

relative to your height. You can use Figure 4.55 to find your BMI. For example, if John, a fifteen-year-old male, weighed 125 pounds and were 68 inches tall, his BMI in Figure 4.55 would be 19. This would place John in the healthy fitness zone for body composition based on the values in Figure 4.56.

To determine your BMI, look up your weight and height in Figure 4.55. When you have completed the body composition evaluation, record your score on your personal fitness profile chart like the one in the "Active Mind/Active Body" activity at the end of the chapter.

Body Mass Index

Weight (pounds)	Height (inches)														
	64	65	66	67	68	69	70	71	72	73	74	75	76	77	78
80	13.8	13.3	12.9	12.6	12.2	11.8	11.5	11.2	10.9	10.6	10.3	10.0	9.8	9.5	9.3
85	14.6	14.2	13.7	13.3	13.0	12.6	12.2	11.9	11.6	11.2	10.9	10.6	10.4	10.1	9.8
90	15.5	15.0	14.6	14.1	13.7	13.3	12.9	12.6	12.2	11.9	11.6	11.3	11.0	10.7	10.4
95	16.3	15.8	15.4	14.9	14.5	14.1	13.7	13.3	12.9	12.6	12.2	11.9	11.6	11.3	11.0
100	17.2	16.7	16.2	15.7	15.2	14.8	14.4	14.0	13.6	13.2	12.9	12.5	12.2	11.9	11.6
105	18.1	17.5	17.0	16.5	16.0	15.5	15.1	14.7	14.3	13.9	13.5	13.2	12.8	12.5	12.2
110	18.9	18.3	17.8	17.3	16.8	16.3	15.8	15.4	14.9	14.5	14.2	13.8	13.4	13.1	12.7
115	19.8	19.2	18.6	18.0	17.5	17.0	16.5	16.1	15.6	15.2	14.8	14.4	14.0	13.7	13.3
120	20.6	20.0	19.4	18.8	18.3	17.8	17.3	16.8	16.3	15.9	15.4	15.0	14.6	14.3	13.9
125	21.5	20.8	20.2	19.6	19.0	18.5	18.0	17.5	17.0	16.5	16.1	15.7	15.2	14.9	14.5
130	22.4	21.7	21.0	20.4	19.8	19.2	18.7	18.2	17.7	17.2	16.7	16.3	15.9	15.4	15.1
135	23.2	22.5	21.8	21.2	20.6	20.0	19.4	18.9	18.3	17.8	17.4	16.9	16.5	16.0	15.6
140	24.1	23.3	22.6	22.0	21.3	20.7	20.1	19.6	19.0	18.5	18.0	17.5	17.1	16.6	16.2
145	24.9	24.2	23.5	22.8	22.1	21.5	20.8	20.3	19.7	19.2	18.7	18.2	17.7	17.2	16.8
150	25.8	25.0	24.3	23.5	22.9	22.2	21.6	21.0	20.4	19.8	19.3	18.8	18.3	17.8	17.4
155	26.7	25.8	25.1	24.3	23.6	22.9	22.3	21.7	21.1	20.5	19.9	19.4	18.9	18.4	17.9
160	27.5	26.7	25.9	25.1	24.4	23.7	23.0	22.4	21.7	21.2	20.6	20.0	19.5	19.0	18.5
165	28.4	27.5	26.7	25.9	25.1	24.4	23.7	23.1	22.4	21.8	21.2	20.7	20.1	19.6	19.1
170	29.2	28.3	27.5	26.7	25.9	25.2	24.4	23.8	23.1	22.5	21.9	21.3	20.7	20.2	19.7
175	30.1	29.2	28.3	27.5	26.7	25.9	25.2	24.5	23.8	23.1	22.5	21.9	21.3	20.8	20.3
180	31.0	30.0	29.1	28.3	27.4	26.6	25.9	25.2	24.5	23.8	23.2	22.5	22.0	21.4	20.8
185	31.8	30.8	29.9	29.0	28.2	27.4	26.6	25.9	25.1	24.5	23.8	23.2	22.6	22.0	21.4
190	32.7	31.7	30.7	29.8	28.9	28.1	27.3	26.6	25.8	25.1	24.4	23.8	23.2	22.6	22.0
195	33.5	32.5	31.5	30.6	29.7	28.9	28.0	27.3	26.5	25.8	25.1	24.4	23.8	23.2	22.6
200	34.4	33.4	32.3	31.4	30.5	29.6	28.8	28.0	27.2	26.4	25.7	25.1	24.4	23.8	23.2
205	35.3	34.2	33.2	32.2	31.2	30.3	29.5	28.7	27.9	27.1	26.4	25.7	25.0	24.4	23.7
210	36.1	35.0	34.0	33.0	32.0	31.1	30.2	29.4	28.5	27.8	27.0	26.3	25.6	25.0	24.3
215	37.0	35.9	34.8	33.7	32.8	31.3	30.9	30.0	29.2	28.4	27.7	26.9	26.2	25.5	24.9
220	37.8	36.7	35.6	34.5	33.5	32.6	31.6	30.7	29.9	29.1	28.3	27.6	26.8	26.1	25.5
225	38.7	37.5	36.4	35.3	34.3	33.3	32.4	31.4	30.6	29.7	28.9	28.2	27.4	26.7	26.1
230	39.6	38.4	37.2	36.1	35.0	34.0	33.1	32.1	31.3	30.4	29.6	28.8	28.1	27.3	26.6
235	40.4	39.2	38.0	36.9	35.8	34.8	33.8	32.8	31.9	31.1	30.2	29.4	28.7	27.9	27.2
240	41.3	40.0	38.8	37.7	36.6	35.5	34.5	33.5	32.6	31.7	30.9	30.1	29.3	28.5	27.8
245	42.1	40.9	39.6	38.5	37.3	36.3	35.2	34.2	33.3	32.4	31.5	30.7	29.9	29.1	28.4
250	43.0	41.7	40.4	39.2	38.1	37.0	35.9	34.9	34.0	33.1	32.2	31.3	30.5	29.7	29.0

Age	BMI	Age	BMI
	Males		Females
13	23.0–16.6	13	24.5–17.5
14	24.5–17.5	14	25.0–17.5
15	25.0–18.1	15	25.0–17.5
16	26.5–18.5	16	25.0–17.5
17	27.0–18.8	17	26.0–17.5
17+	27.8–19.0	17+	27.3–18.0

Scores below the healthy zone are considered low.

• *Figure 4.56*   *BMI Evaluation (healthy zone).*
Source: With permission from The Cooper Institute for Aerobics Research, *The Prudential Fitnessgram Test Administration Manual* (Dallas, TX: 1992), 46–47.

Any Body Can!

"Babe" Didrikson Zaharias

Mildred "Babe" Didrikson Zaharias (1911–1956) was perhaps the greatest all-around woman athlete in American history. She had tremendous skills and, despite an early death, used them to maintain her health and fitness level.

Zaharias grew up in Port Arthur, Texas and earned the nickname "Babe" after baseball hero Babe Ruth because she could throw and hit baseballs harder than any boy in her neighborhood. In high school she played on every girls' team: volleyball, basketball, baseball, tennis, swimming, and golf. In one high school basketball game she scored 104 points.

While still in her teens, Babe became a two-time member of the All-American Women's basketball team. She helped her team win a national championship in 1931. At the 1932 Amateur Athletic Union National Track and Field Championships she won the shot put, baseball throw, long jump, 80-meter hurdles, and javelin throw. At the 1932 Olympics in Los Angeles, Babe won gold medals in the javelin throw and the hurdles, and finished second in the high jump.

After the Olympics, Babe became a national celebrity. She took up the game of golf in

earnest and won 17 amateur golf tournaments in a row, including both the U.S. and British National Championships. Babe joined the women's professional golf circuit in 1947 and won 31 Ladies Professional Golf Association (LPGA) victories.

At the height of her career, she was diagnosed with colon cancer. She underwent treatment, and returned to golf and won the 1954 U.S. Women's Open Golf Championship. After her victory, she told reporters, "This should show people not to be afraid of cancer."

Babe's commitment to her personal fitness made her the nation's leading female sports star for more than 30 years. The Associated Press named her Female Athlete of the year six times (1932, 1945, 1946, 1947, 1950, and 1954). She was elected to the LPGA Hall of Fame in 1951, the National Track and Field Hall of Fame in 1974, the International Women's Sports Hall of Fame in 1980, and the U.S. Olympic Hall of Fame in 1983. In 1950, the Associated Press named her the female Athlete of the Half Century.

Not everyone can be a world champion athlete like Babe Didrikson Zaharias, but Any Body Can learn to develop and maintain their skill- and health-related fitness. That's right, you can do it!

CONSUMER CORNER

Who Is the Expert?

At times you may need to seek out professional personal fitness advice. Where should you go for advice? Many people claim to be experts in the area of personal fitness. Unfortunately, many of these so-called experts are not really experts at all. How can you tell whether or not you're getting good advice?

Perhaps the smartest first step is to ask people you know—your parents, teachers, and friends—to make a recommendation. The physical education teachers at your school will be able to answer many of your questions. If they can't answer a particular question, they can probably recommend someone in your community who has developed a reputation for providing good, sound advice.

If someone has been recommended to you, ask about the person's education and training background. Does the person have a degree in physical fitness? What sort of training has the person had? Be sure that the person's education and training are directly related to your fitness questions. A medical doctor, for example, would be very knowledgeable about your cardiovascular system, but unless the doctor has had special training, he or she would probably not be the best person to offer advice about a weight-training program to rehabilitate your injured knee.

Being a wise fitness consumer can help you protect your health, as well as save you time and money. A wise fitness consumer has a wealth of knowledge about fitness-related evaluations in order to be able to assess the advice of the professionals.

Most of the time, however, you should be able to solve your own personal fitness problems. Correctly administering self-evaluations can help you understand your own fitness needs and solve your own problems.

Active Mind! Active Body!   Evaluating Fitness Levels

This "Active Mind/Active Body" activity is designed to help you learn to profile your personal fitness.

Use Figure 4.57 on page 150 as a sample to see how well you performed on the various skill-related fitness evaluations by checking off your score category on each test. Your personal fitness profile chart can be used to help you plot and identify your strengths and weaknesses on skill-related and health-related fitness components.

(Continued on next page)

Evaluating Fitness Levels (continued)

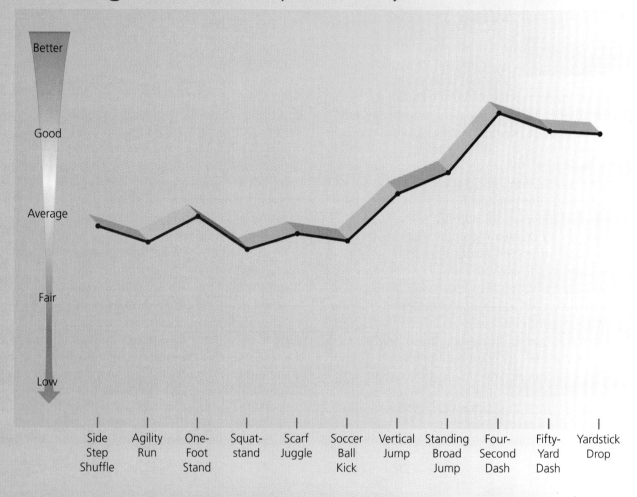

• **Figure 4.57** *Sample Skill-related Personal Fitness Profile Sheet.*

If you scored in the good to better zone on most of the skill-related evaluations, try to maintain your levels by practicing these skills in your personal fitness program. This is especially important if you are interested in performance fitness, which is primarily associated with your ability to perform successfully skills that are applied during games and sports. If your skill-related fitness scores were mostly low, you need to improve your skills so that you can engage in a variety of physical activities and influence your health-related fitness in a positive way. Even if you score low on every skill-related evaluation, you can still develop a personal fitness plan that can help you achieve a good to better level of health-related fitness.

Use Figure 4.58 on page 151 as a sample to rate yourself on the various health-related fitness evaluations you completed earlier in the chapter.

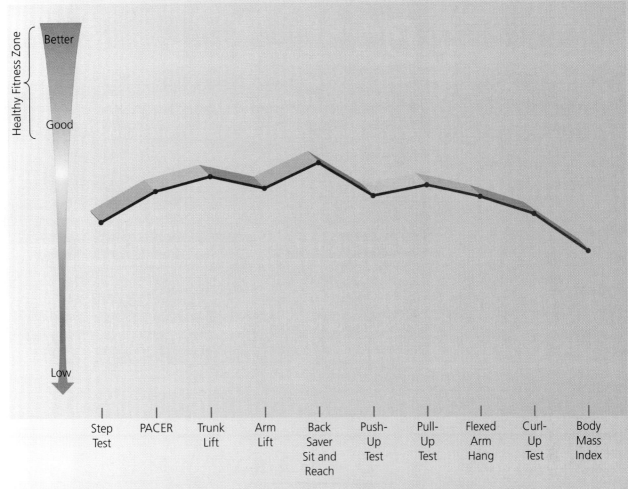

Healthy Fitness Zone

Better

Good

Low

| Step Test | PACER | Trunk Lift | Arm Lift | Back Saver Sit and Reach | Push-Up Test | Pull-Up Test | Flexed Arm Hang | Curl-Up Test | Body Mass Index |

• **Figure 4.58**   *Sample Health-related Personal Fitness Profile Sheet.*

REMEMBER This!

Your levels of health-related fitness determine your functional health. Therefore, you should do your best to develop and maintain good to better levels of health-related fitness throughout your life.

If you scored in the good to better zone on most of the health-related evaluations, try to maintain these levels by participating regularly in your personal fitness program. If you scored below the good to better zone on many or most of the health-related evaluations, try to improve these levels by developing and maintaining a personal fitness program. Be patient and recognize that participating in the process of living a physically active lifestyle is more important than the outcome of any one or two health-fitness evaluations.

Answers to

B ELIEVE IT? ...
OR NOT?

Pg. 110 False. The number of people six or older who regularly engage in these activities is unknown, but the goal of *Healthy People 2000* is 40 percent participation.
Pg. 115 True.
Pg. 119 True.
Pg. 119 True.
Pg. 120 True.
Pg. 121 False. It has been estimated that society could save $1,900 annually for each sedentary individual who begins a regular physical activity or exercise program. Savings would show up in such ways as fewer medical bills and less lost time at work.
Pg. 124 True.
Pg. 137 False. Of all people six years old or older, 24 percent do not participate in regular leisure-time physical activity. The goal of *Healthy People 2000* is to reduce this number to only 15 percent.

SUMMARY

Skill-related fitness, or performance fitness, has six parts. These parts are primarily associated with your ability to perform successfully skills that are applied during games and sports. Skill-related fitness includes agility, balance, coordination, speed, power, and reaction time. Health-related fitness has five parts, which are primarily associated with disease prevention and functional health. Health-related fitness includes cardiovascular fitness, flexibility, muscular strength, muscular endurance, and body composition. You need some degree of proficiency in both health-related and skill-related fitness because both kinds of fitness contribute to your performance in everyday life activities.

You can evaluate your skill-related and health-related fitness to determine your own levels of personal fitness. You can identify your strengths and weaknesses in skill-related and health-related fitness. You then can plot your results on a personal fitness profile chart and develop a method to monitor your personal fitness progress.

It is important for you to monitor your levels of both skill-related and health-related fitness throughout the rest of your life. By monitoring your personal fitness progress, you will be able to change your personal fitness goals as necessary and fine tune your personal fitness plan over time.

Chapter 4 Review

True/False

On a separate sheet of paper, mark each question below either T for True or F for False.

1. Health-related fitness is primarily associated with disease prevention and functional health.

2. Both skill-related and health-related fitness can contribute to how we perform *everyday* life activities.

3. Power is a combination of speed and agility.

4. Improving your muscular endurance can improve your power.

5. The two factors that affect skill-related fitness components the most are heredity and practice.

6. *Cardiovascular fitness* refers to your ability to exercise at high intensity for short periods of time.

7. Poor flexibility can be associated with many injuries, including low back problems.

8. The ability to repeat the same task over and over is muscular endurance.

9. The amount of water, muscle, bone, and fat contained by our bodies is referred to as *body composition.*

10. The highly skilled athlete will have minimal needs for health-related fitness components.

Multiple Choice

1. Which of the following fitness components is not skill-related?

   a. power
   b. speed
   c. muscular strength
   d. balance

2. If you had to cross a bridge that was 10 feet long and 6 inches wide, which skill-related component would you most need?

   a. coordination
   b. power
   c agility
   d. balance

3. Which of the following are associated with power?

   a. speed and reaction time
   b. strength and coordination
   c. speed and strength
   d. strength and reaction time

4. Which of the following has little or no influence on determining your foot speed?

   a. strength
   b. weight
   c. power
   d. heredity

5. Reaction time is best described by which of the following?

   a. the amount of time it takes you to respond to what you hear, see, or feel
   b. the amount of time it takes to cover a short distance
   c. the amount of time it takes to change the direction of your body
   d. none of the above

6. Which fitness component requires a great deal of oxygen over an extended period of time?

 a. agility
 b. coordination
 c. muscular endurance
 d. cardiovascular fitness

7. Which of the following statements is not true about flexibility?

 a. it can improve your performance fitness
 b. it can reduce your risk for injury
 c. it can reduce muscle soreness
 d. it can improve body composition

8. Your muscular strength is not influenced by which of the following?

 a. age
 b. gender
 c. heredity
 d. height

9. The vertical jump and standing broad jump are evaluations for which of the following?

 a. strength
 b. power
 c. agility
 d. coordination

10. Which of the following can be used as measures of flexibility?

 a. back saver sit and reach
 b. trunk lift
 c. arm lift
 d. all of the above

Discussion

1. List and explain three major differences between health-related fitness and skill-related fitness.

2. Explain how involvement in skill-related activities can contribute to the improvement or maintenance of health-related fitness.

3. Identify three of the health-related evaluations you used in this chapter, and explain how each can be of value to your fitness now and in the future.

Vocabulary Experience

Match the correct term in Column A to the definition in Column B by writing the appropriate number in each blank.

Column A

_____ health-related fitness

_____ muscular endurance

_____ balance

_____ skill-related fitness

_____ body composition

_____ reaction time

Column B

1. Your ability to contract your muscles several times without excessive fatigue.

2. Contains five components and is associated with disease prevention.

3. The ratio of water, bone, muscle, and fat in your body.

4. Your ability to control or stabilize your equilibrium while moving or staying still.

5. Your ability to react or respond quickly to what you hear, see, or feel.

6. Contains six components and is associated with performance fitness.

Critical Thinking

1. What criteria would you use to evaluate someone's skill-related and health-related fitness profile? Explain.

2. Compare muscular strength and muscular endurance. How can you evaluate each of them?

3. Discuss the accuracy of this statement: Health-related fitness is better for you than skill-related fitness.

Chapter 5

Cardiovascular Fitness and You

Contents

Outcomes

After reading and studying this chapter, you will be able to:

1. Explain how the heart, lungs, and blood vessels contribute to moderate to high levels of personal fitness.

2. Explain how moderate to high levels of cardiovascular fitness can reduce your risk for cardiovascular disease.

3. Identify examples of aerobic and anaerobic physical activities and exercises.

4. Describe the benefits of engaging in regular cardiovascular physical activity and exercise.

5. Identify and explain cardiovascular fitness evaluations that you could use to assess your cardiovascular fitness levels now and in the future.

6. Explain how you can develop moderate to high levels of cardiovascular fitness.

Key Terms

After reading and studying this chapter, you will be able to understand and provide practical definitions for the following terms:

recovery heart rate	vein	aerobic fitness level
diaphragm	muscle pump	interval training
intercostal	blood pressure	slow-twitch muscle fiber
abdominal	systolic blood pressure	fast-twitch muscle fiber
asthma	diastolic blood pressure	percentage of maximum heart rate
hemoglobin	atherosclerosis	target heart rate zone
circulatory system	myocardial infarction (MI)	
artery	aerobic	
capillary	anaerobic	

INTRODUCTION

O *f all the skill-related and health-related fitness components, cardiovascular fitness is the most important for maintaining your functional health throughout life. Cardio-vascular fitness is the ability of the body to work continuously for extended periods of time. If you develop moderate to high levels of cardiovascular fitness, you can reduce your risks for cardiovascular disease, increase your predicted longevity, and help maintain your physical independence in living. Moderate to high levels of cardiovascular fitness will also increase your energy levels, make you look and feel better, reduce your stress levels, and help you control your weight and body composition. In this chapter, you will learn about the components that influence cardiovascular fitness, facts about cardiovascular disease, the specific benefits of cardiovascular fitness, and how you can develop moderate to high levels of cardiovascular fitness.*

SECTION 1   Pump, Circulate, and Deliver

Cardiovascular fitness depends on a strong heart, an ability to deliver large amounts of blood to the muscles and organs of the body, and good lung function. In this section you will learn more about your heart, lungs, blood, blood vessels, and blood pressure.

Your Heart

Your heart is a muscle about the size and shape of your fist. It beats at the rate of about 50 to 80 (72, on average) beats per minute when your body is at rest, pumping about 5 liters of blood per minute (think of five 1-liter bottles of cola). See Figure 5.1. The heart is really two pumps in one. The right side of the heart pumps blood to the lungs, and the left side pumps blood to the upper and lower body (see Figure 5.2). During physical activity or exercise, your heart rate (pulse) increases (see Figure 5.3 on page 160) in response to your body's need for more blood. Your working muscles, tissues, and organs need blood to supply them with oxygen and other nutrients.

Your heart's ability to supply oxygen to your working muscles and organs is the major factor that determines your level of cardiovascular fitness. Oxygen, which is delivered by the blood, helps your cells produce the energy necessary for you to meet the demands of physical activities or exercise. As the demand for oxygen, and therefore blood, increases with increasing physical work, your heart must be able to meet this demand, or you quickly tire.

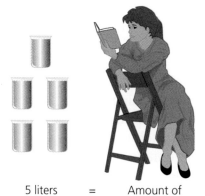

5 liters = Amount of
of blood   blood pumped
            by heart per
            minute while
            body is at rest

• **Figure 5.1** *Your heart pumps about 5 liters of blood every minute when your body is at rest.*

B ELIEVE IT? ...
OR NOT?

Your heart beats over
100,000 times a day
and more than 40 mil-
lion times a year.

See page 183 for answer.

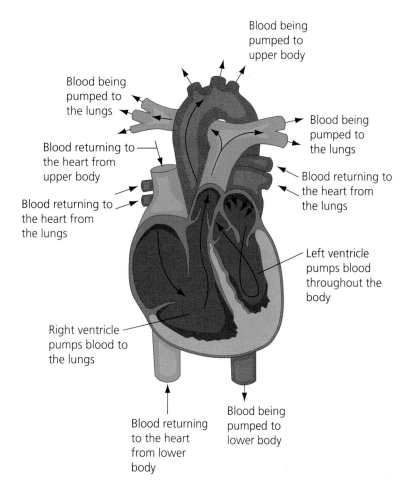

Blood being
pumped to
upper body

Blood being
pumped to
the lungs

Blood being
pumped to
the lungs

Blood returning to
the heart from
upper body

Blood returning to
the heart from
the lungs

Blood returning to
the heart from
the lungs

Left ventricle
pumps blood
throughout the
body

Right ventricle
pumps blood to
the lungs

Blood returning
to the heart
from lower
body

Blood being
pumped to
lower body

• **Figure 5.2** *The heart acts as a pump, pumping blood to the lungs and throughout the body.*

recovery heart rate

the gradual return of the heart
rate to resting levels within 5 to
10 minutes of a session of normal cardiovascular physical
activity or exercise.

At maximal or exhaustive levels of exercise, your heart can beat at a rate that can be estimated by subtracting your age from 220. For example, if you are fifteen years old, your maximum heart rate is approximately 220 – 15, or 205, beats per minute. (See the "Active Mind/Active Body" activity on page 161.) Also, as you reach maximal levels of exercise, your heart beats more strongly. Therefore, you can pump even more blood per minute (about 20 liters per minute).

Following a session of normal cardiovascular physical activity or exercise, your heart rate gradually returns to resting levels. This is called your **recovery heart rate** (see Figure 5.3). Your recovery heart rate should drop back toward normal levels within 5 to 10 minutes of finishing the exercise session. A general rule of thumb is that your heart rate should be 120 beats per minute or lower within ten minutes of cardiovascular conditioning. If it's higher than 120 beats, either you are working too hard or your cardiovascular fitness level is low.

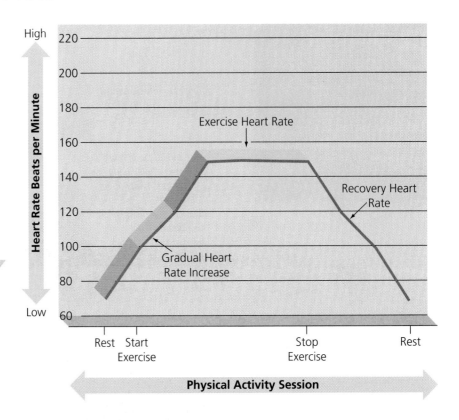

REMEMBER This!

Someone who is usually sedentary often gets a side stitch during cardiovascular activity. This type of problem usually goes away after a few weeks of regular physical activity or exercise as the muscles that control breathing become conditioned.

• *Figure 5.3*   *Normal Heart Rate Response to a Session of Cardiovascular Physical Activity.*

By engaging in regular physical activity or exercise, you can condition your heart to become more efficient at rest, as well as during exercise. After 8 to 30 weeks of conditioning, your resting heart rate will be much lower than it was before conditioning. It could drop from 72 beats to 60 beats per minute. The extra conditioning causes the nerves that control your heart rate to adapt to make your heart more efficient. Your heart will also beat with greater force if you begin and maintain a conditioning program. Your heart will be able to pump with greater force both while you are at rest and during maximal exercise. This means that you can pump even more blood (oxygen) to your muscles and tissues—possibly as much as 5 liters more than your maximum before you began conditioning.

Your Lungs

Your lungs exchange oxygen and carbon dioxide during rest, as well as during physical activity and exercise. If your lungs are healthy, you can breathe about 6 liters of air per minute at rest and up to 100 liters of air per minute during vigorous exercise (see Figure 5.5).

What is Your Maximum Heart Rate?

Age	Estimated Maximum Heart Rate
14	206
15	205
16	204
17	203
18	202

Figure 5.4 lists estimated maximum heart rates for both boys and girls, ages 14 to 18 years. You can calculate this rate for yourself by subtracting your age from 220.

• *Figure 5.4* *Estimated Maximum Heart Rate.*

When you move more air through your lungs, you can get more oxygen into your blood and to your body. You can also remove carbon dioxide from your body more effectively. (See Figure 5–5 again.) If you are a chronic smoker, you will probably damage your lungs, reducing your ability to breathe large amounts of air. That is one rea-

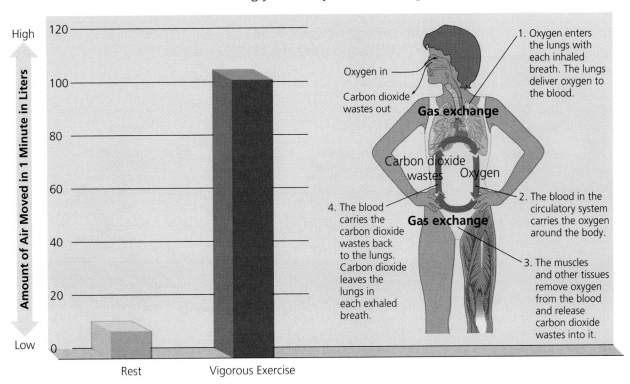

• *Figure 5.5* *The Circulatory System and a Comparison of Amount of Air You Breathe at Rest and During Vigorous Exercise.*

diaphragm

a muscle in the middle chest area that is used in breathing.

intercostal

a muscle around the ribs that is used in breathing.

abdominal

a muscle in the lower stomach area that is used in breathing.

asthma

restriction of the breathing passages due to dust, allergies, pollution, or even vigorous exercise.

son why chronic smokers usually have lower cardiovascular fitness levels than nonsmokers.

With cardiovascular conditioning, you improve your ability to breathe large amounts of air. Following several weeks of cardiovascular conditioning, the muscles that you use to breathe—such as the **diaphragm**, the **intercostals**, and the **abdominals**—do not fatigue as easily as they did when you were sedentary. (See Figure 5.6.)

During physical activity and exercise, the air passages in your lungs relax and open up so that you can move more air to meet the demands for oxygen in your muscles and tissues (Figure 5.7). When some people engage in physical activity or exercise, their air passages constrict instead of relax. These people often have trouble moving large amounts of air and may even get very short of breath.

Asthma is the most common condition causing the air passages to become restricted during physical activity or exercise. Several things can bring on asthma attacks, including dust, allergies, pollution, and even vigorous exercise. People with asthma should seek medical advice about their condition. They can usually engage in physical activity and exercise. However, they may need to spend more time warming up and need to work at more moderate levels of intensity to reduce the chances of an asthma attack. A doctor may also prescribe a "puffer," or inhaler, to use during workouts. Many people who have trouble with asthma when they are young have fewer problems with it as they age. Therefore, even if you have asthma, you can and should develop regular physical activity and exercise patterns that will help you later in life.

• *If you have asthma, you might benefit from the use of an inhaler, which will help you breathe during your workouts.*

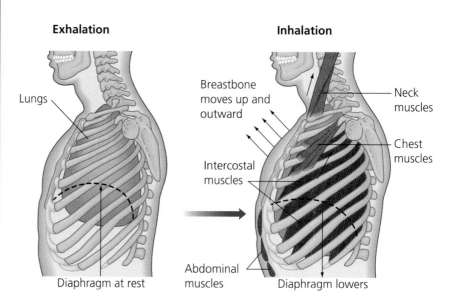

• **Figure 5.6**   *Muscles Used in Breathing.*

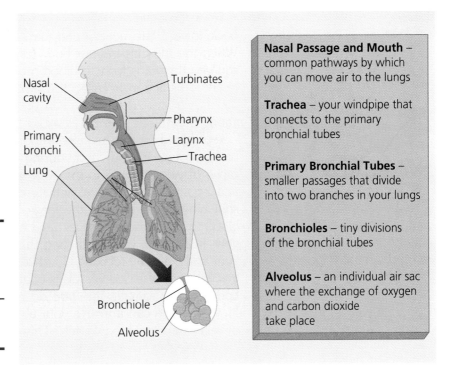

hemoglobin

an iron-rich compound in the blood that helps carry oxygen from the lungs to the muscles, tissues, and organs.

circulatory system

the heart and the system of blood vessels in the body, including the arteries, capillaries, and veins.

artery

a blood vessel that carries blood away from the heart and branches out to supply oxygen and other nutrients to the muscles, tissues, and organs of the body.

capillary

a small blood vessel that delivers oxygen and other nutrients to the individual muscle, tissue, and organ cells.

vein

a blood vessel that collects blood from the capillaries and carries it back to the heart.

• *Figure 5.7*   *Your Air Passageways.*

Your Blood and Blood Vessels

Your blood and blood vessels are important to your cardiovascular fitness. **Hemoglobin** is an iron-rich compound in your blood that helps carry oxygen from your lungs to your muscles, tissues, and organs. Hemoglobin levels can increase with cardiovascular training, which results in more effective delivery of oxygen to your body. Your blood also carries carbon dioxide from the cells of your muscles, tissues, and organs back to the lungs so the carbon dioxide can be removed from your body. Your blood contains additional substances needed for good cardiovascular health (for example, the substances that help keep your blood from clotting inside your blood vessels). These substances are more efficient with good to better levels of cardiovascular fitness.

The arteries, capillaries, and veins are blood vessels that, along with the heart, make up the **circulatory system**. **Arteries** carry blood away from the heart (see Figure 5.2 again) and branch out to supply the muscles, tissues, and organs of the body with oxygen and other nutrients. Blood moves through the arteries to the **capillaries**, which are near the cells of the body. The small capillaries deliver oxygen and other nutrients to the individual muscle, tissue, and organ cells. The blood from the capillaries is then collected in the **veins** and carried back to the heart. (See Figure 5.8.)

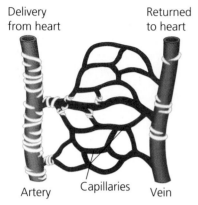

Delivery from heart   Returned to heart

Artery   Capillaries   Vein

• **Figure 5.8** *The blood travels from arteries, through the capillaries to deliver oxygen and nutrients, and then back to the heart through the veins.*

muscle pump

the contraction of the muscles in the body (especially the legs) as the muscles squeeze the veins to help blood move back to the right side of the heart.

blood pressure

the force by which blood is pushed against the walls of the arteries.

systolic blood pressure

the pressure on the arteries when the heart contracts.

diastolic blood pressure

the pressure on the arteries when the heart relaxes after contraction.

The veins have a series of one-way valves that cause blood to move back toward the heart (refer back to Figure 3.13 in Chapter 3). When the muscles in your body (especially your legs) contract, they squeeze the veins to help blood move back to the right side of your heart. This action is called the **muscle pump**. By doing your cardiovascular cool-down, you can prevent blood from pooling by activating the muscle pump.

Your blood vessels are also important because they help you shift blood around in your body during exercise. When you are at rest, much of your blood is in the large veins of your lower stomach area and legs. During physical activity or exercise, you must be able to shift blood quickly from the large veins to the arteries that deliver blood to the muscles, tissues, and organs. You do this by increasing your heart rate, by constricting the blood vessels in some areas of your body, and by relaxing blood vessels elsewhere. This constricting and relaxing of blood vessels is controlled by nerve activity that your body does automatically—you do not even need to think about it. However, you can improve your ability to shift blood by constricting or relaxing your blood vessels. This ability comes with good to better cardiovascular fitness levels.

Blood Pressure

Blood pressure is defined as the force by which blood is pushed against the walls of your arteries. Blood pressure consists of two parts. Your **systolic blood pressure** is the pressure on your arteries when your heart contracts. Your **diastolic blood pressure** is

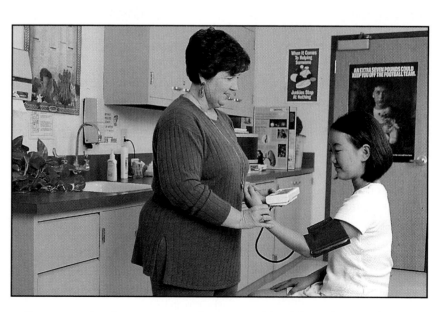

• *See your school nurse or another trained health professional to determine your blood pressure.*

Stress Break

Regular exercise can reduce or prevent high blood pressure. Exercise alone is not the answer, however. Two other parts of the puzzle are good nutrition and sound stress management strategies.

How you deal with your parents, teachers, and peers during irritating or emotional situations can raise your blood pressure. Therefore, having the ability to recognize stressful situations and then to deal with them in a positive way is vital to your health. Abilities that help you deal with stressful situations are called *coping strategies.*

You could use negative strategies such as drinking, smoking, yelling, screaming, or suppressing your emotions. However, positive coping strategies, such as eating well, exercising regularly, relaxing when possible, and learning to talk about your problems, are better for your health.

associated with the pressure on your arteries when your heart relaxes after contraction. Blood pressure is reported as two numbers, such as 120 over 80, which is written 120/80. Your systolic blood pressure is the top number. Your diastolic blood pressure is the bottom number. Normal blood pressure should fall below values of 140/90 on average, when measured on a regular basis. Blood pressure is easy to measure, but it should be determined by trained health professionals (see Figure 5.9). What is your blood pressure? See the "Active Mind/Active Body" activity on page 166 to find out.

Individuals with blood pressure above 140/90 may have hypertension (high blood pressure). Those with hypertension are at a higher risk for stroke and heart attack.

Individuals with hypertension may be told by their doctors to modify their diet and engage in regular physical activity or exercise. After several weeks of dieting and regular physical activity or exercise, a person can expect to reduce his or her blood pressure by about 10 units (for example, from 140/90 to maybe 130/80). This reduction is probably due to a lower resting heart rate and better nerve control of the blood vessels. If diet and regular physical activ-

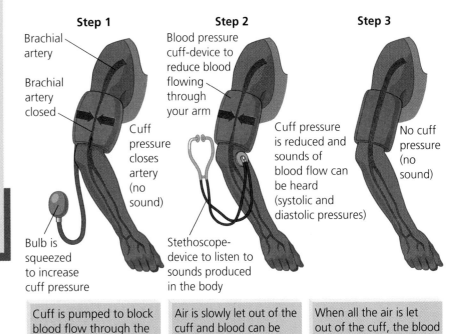

Step 1

Brachial artery

Brachial artery closed

Cuff pressure closes artery (no sound)

Bulb is squeezed to increase cuff pressure

Cuff is pumped to block blood flow through the brachial artery (the major artery in your upper arm).

Step 2

Blood pressure cuff-device to reduce blood flowing through your arm

Cuff pressure is reduced and sounds of blood flow can be heard (systolic and diastolic pressures)

Stethoscope-device to listen to sounds produced in the body

Air is slowly let out of the cuff and blood can be heard being pumped back into your forearm. This is called your systolic (or top) blood pressure.

Step 3

No cuff pressure (no sound)

When all the air is let out of the cuff, the blood flow is returned to normal in your arm and the sounds that can be heard disappear. This is called your diastolic blood pressure.

• **Figure 5.9**   *Measuring Your Blood Pressure with a Blood Pressure Cuff.*

What is Your Blood Pressure?

Have the school nurse measure your blood pressure. If the school nurse cannot measure your blood pressure, have it measured by your physician at your next medical checkup or at a health fair.

REMEMBER This!

Even if a person is on medication to control hypertension, regular physical activity or exercise habits usually allow the person to take less medication than if he or she were inactive. Taking a lower amount of medication is desirable, because it usually means fewer negative side effects from the medication.

ity or exercise do not return blood pressure to normal, the doctor may prescribe medication.

There is no such thing as low blood pressure unless a person has symptoms such as dizziness, feels tired all the time, or has had an accident that caused a substantial loss of blood. A person with any of these symptoms, along with low blood pressure, should consult a physician and get a checkup.

Some people experience dizziness or "see stars" if they change their posture rapidly. Have you ever jumped up quickly from the couch, perhaps when the doorbell rang? If so, you may have felt dizzy for a few seconds. This is because your heart rate and blood pressure levels were low while you were at rest, and it took a few seconds for your body to respond by pumping more blood to your brain when you jumped up. This kind of response is normal and happens at one time or another to everyone. If you ever have what seem to be abnormal symptoms involving your heart, lungs, blood, blood vessels, or blood pressure, however, see your physician immediately.

SECTION 1 REVIEW

Answer the following questions on a separate sheet of paper:

1. How does your heart change with cardiovascular conditioning to make it more efficient at rest, as well as during exercise?

2. What muscles do you use when you breathe?

3. What is blood pressure, and what numbers for it are considered normal?

Any Body Can!

Flora "Flo" Hyman

Flora "Flo" Hyman (1954–1986) has been called the best female volleyball player the U.S. has ever produced. She helped the U.S. women's volleyball team move from obscurity to international prominence (fame).

Flo began playing volleyball in high school and immediately became one of the nation's top players. She went on to become a three-time All-American at Houston, and was named to the U.S. national volleyball team in 1974. In 1976, she was named the nation's outstanding collegiate volleyball player.

The U.S. national volleyball team did not qualify for the 1976 Olympics, but by 1978 the U.S. team ranked fifth in the world, and moved to second place in 1979. Much of the improved success was due to Flo Hyman's contributions. She had grown to 6 feet, 5 inches tall and became one of the best "hitters" in the world.

Flo became the leader of the U.S. national volleyball team, which gained international recognition between 1979 and 1984. She stayed with the team through the 1980 Moscow Olympics boycott. Then, in the 1984 Los Angeles Olympics, thirty-year-old Flo Hyman helped lead her teammates to a silver medal finish behind the first place Chinese women.

Following the 1984 Olympics, Flo joined a professional volleyball circuit in Japan. On January 24, 1986, she collapsed during a match and died suddenly from a ruptured aorta (artery carrying blood from the heart to the rest of the body). Her death was due to a genetic disorder called *Marfan's syndrome* that can cause the aortic wall to become weak and to burst. Although Marfan's syndrome is very difficult to diagnose, Flo Hyman's tragic sudden death stimulated medical study in the diagnosis and treatment of this cardiovascular disorder. Today physicians are much more aware of the need to screen for and treat Marfan's syndrome. Flo Hyman's accomplishments on the volleyball court helped make volleyball the most popular high school sport today for girls in the U.S. Her aggressive, dominating style of play also helped stimulate the promotion of women's professional outdoor beach volleyball. In 1987, the Women's Sports Foundation honored her memory by establishing the "Flo Hyman Award" for women who capture Flo's dignity, spirit, and commitment to excellence.

Not everone can be as good at volleyball as Flo Hyman, but Any Body Can learn to identify and control cardiovascular disease risks while developing and maintaining their cardiovascular fitness. That's right, you can do it!

SECTION 2   Preventing Cardiovascular Disease

1	Heart attacks
2	Strokes
3	Hypertension
4	Peripheral vascular disease (such as atherosclerosis)

• **Figure 5.10**   *Major Cardiovascular Diseases.*

Cardiovascular disease affects the heart and blood vessels of the body. There are a variety of cardiovascular diseases, such as heart attacks, strokes, hypertension, and peripheral vascular diseases (diseases of the arteries and veins of the extremities). See Figure 5.10. Cardiovascular diseases continue to be the leading cause of death in the United States. Most forms of cardiovascular disease are preventable. Whether or not you get them usually depends on how well you can modify or lower your health risk factors. You may want to go back to the "Active Mind/Active Body" activity on page 22 to review your risk factors.

Atherosclerosis

atherosclerosis

a disease process that causes substances to build up inside arteries, reducing or blocking blood flow.

The most common cause of cardiovascular disease can be traced to the development of **atherosclerosis**, a disease process that makes substances build up inside arteries, reducing or blocking blood flow. The cause of atherosclerosis is not known for sure. Experts believe that atherosclerosis probably occurs because the walls of arteries become damaged from hypertension, substances in cigarette smoke, or other causes. When the artery walls are damaged, cholesterol and other blood fats attach to the artery walls as the arteries try to repair themselves. (This process is more likely to occur when the blood fat levels are too high.) The process usually begins in childhood or young adulthood and continues for many years before cardiovascular disease is recognized. In Figure 5.11 you can see the process of atherosclerosis beginning and eventually almost blocking an artery.

Although atherosclerosis is treatable, it is much easier, safer, and less costly for you to try to prevent the process by developing a healthy lifestyle and controlling all the risk factors you can. For example, you have learned that HDL cholesterol is "good cholesterol," and higher levels of HDL in the blood help lower the risk of developing atherosclerosis. Regular cardiovascular physical activity and exercise have been shown to raise HDL cholesterol levels and to reduce the risk of developing cardiovascular diseases. Also, regular cardiovascular physical activity and exercise lower LDL cholesterol (or "bad cholesterol") levels and thereby lower cardiovascular disease risk. You will learn more about cholesterol in Chapter 10.

BELIEVE IT? ... OR NOT?

People who die suddenly while exercising always have advanced cases of atherosclerosis.

See page 183 for answer.

BELIEVE IT? ...
OR NOT?

Of the 1 million people who have heart attacks in the United States each year, one-half die. For these people, this heart attack is their last symptom of cardiovascular disease.

See page 183 for answer.

Normal vessel

Atherosclerosis developing

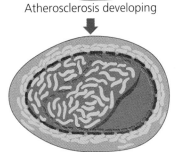

Partially blocked vessel

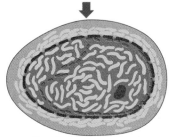

Totally blocked vessel

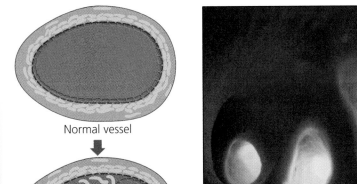

A healthy artery provides an open passageway for the flow of blood

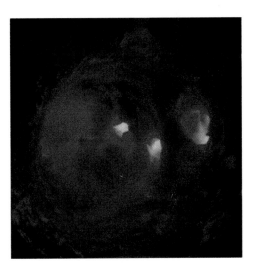

Plaques along an artery narrow its diameter and interfere with blood flow. Clots can form, making the problem worse.

• **Figure 5.11** *The Stages in Atherosclerosis.*

Heart Attacks

myocardial infarction (MI)

a heart attack; a blockage of a vessel that feeds the heart muscle.

Myocardial infarction (MI) is the medical term for *heart attack*. A heart attack is a blockage of a vessel that feeds the heart muscle (see Figure 5.12). People having a heart attack may have tightness in the chest, sweating, nausea, and shortness of breath. Anyone with these symptoms should get to a doctor or hospital quickly.

Myocardial infarctions can be minor or major, depending on which artery or arteries become blocked. A person who has a heart attack

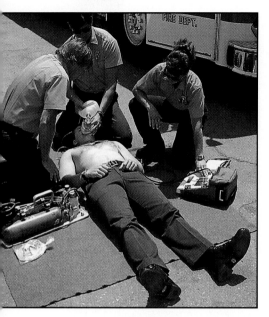

• *Participating in a regular cardiovascular fitness program will significantly decrease your risks for having a heart attack.*

and lives can often resume a normal lifestyle, particularly if the person modifies his or her health risks and follows medical advice. Many fatal heart attacks could have been prevented. If you perform regular cardiovascular physical activity or exercise, your risk for having a heart attack will be reduced. Regular exercise will also reduce your risk of dying from a heart attack if you do have one.

Strokes

Strokes occur when there is a blockage or partial blockage of an artery supplying blood to the brain. Strokes, like heart attacks, can be minor or more major, depending upon which artery or arteries become narrowed or blocked. Strokes usually damage the brain and can leave a person partially or almost totally paralyzed. Sometimes when the damage from a stroke is minor, a person may only be paralyzed temporarily. However, a major stroke often results in death. If you perform regular cardiovascular physical activity or exercise, you will significantly reduce your risk for strokes. Figure 5.13 shows the affected sites of cardiovascular disease, along with the complications that result.

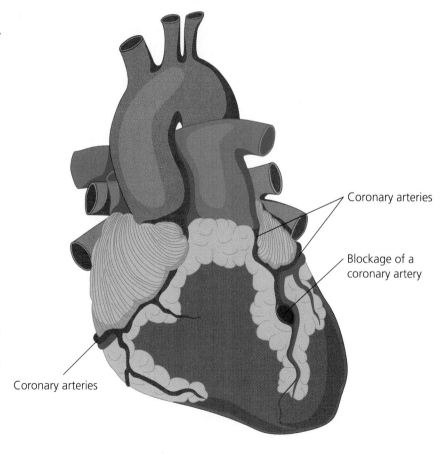

Coronary arteries

Blockage of a coronary artery

Coronary arteries

• *Figure 5.12   Artery Blockage on the Heart.*

B ELIEVE IT? ... OR NOT?

On average, someone in the United States experiences a stroke every minute.

See page 183 for answer.

People are usually classified as having Type A or Type B behavior. Type A individuals have been described as aggressive, concerned with time, tense, and competitive. Type B individuals are relaxed and generally do not get overstressed about things that would upset a Type A person.

Until recently, experts thought that all Type A individuals were at a higher risk for cardiovascular disease than Type B individuals. The experts reasoned that distress can cause increases in heart rate, blood pressure, and other important cardiovascular functions over time. However, most experts now agree that Type A individuals who can lower their stress levels with physical activity, exercise, or other methods are at no more risk for cardiovascular disease than Type B individuals. Type A individuals who do not reduce their stress levels effectively, however, have a higher than normal risk for developing cardiovascular disease.

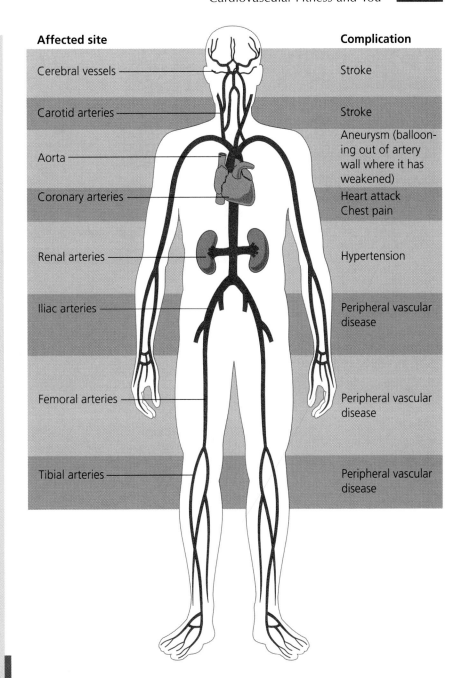

Affected site	Complication
Cerebral vessels	Stroke
Carotid arteries	Stroke
Aorta	Aneurysm (ballooning out of artery wall where it has weakened)
Coronary arteries	Heart attack Chest pain
Renal arteries	Hypertension
Iliac arteries	Peripheral vascular disease
Femoral arteries	Peripheral vascular disease
Tibial arteries	Peripheral vascular disease

• **Figure 5.13**   *Sites Where Atherosclerosis Can Occur.*

Hypertension

Hypertension is the number-one risk factor increasing the likelihood of strokes. Hypertension is also a major risk factor in heart attacks. As you have learned, we all can and should know what our blood pressure is. If you have hypertension or develop it in the future, you can treat it effectively and safely under a doctor's super-

vision. Your commitment to regular cardiovascular physical activity or exercise will reduce your risk for developing hypertension or help you manage it.

SECTION 2 REVIEW

Answer the following questions on a separate sheet of paper:

1. What is atherosclerosis and how does it occur?
2. What is a heart attack and what causes it?
3. What is a stroke and what causes it?

SECTION 3

Aerobic and Anaerobic Physical Activity and Exercise

aerobic

with oxygen.

anaerobic

without oxygen.

aerobic fitness level

cardiovascular fitness level.

Cardiovascular fitness is developed by engaging in aerobic activities. **Aerobic** means "with oxygen." Aerobic activities require you to work in a rhythmic, continuous manner using the large muscle groups of your body for several minutes at a time. **Anaerobic** means "without oxygen." Anaerobic activities require high levels of energy, are done at high intensity, and last only a few seconds or minutes.

Aerobic Work

When you work aerobically, you can supply large amounts of blood (and oxygen) to your muscles, tissues, and organs to meet their demands. Regular participation in aerobic activities is essential for good to better levels of health-related fitness. The term **aerobic fitness level** is often used to mean *cardiovascular fitness level.* Examples of aerobic activities include walking, hiking, jogging/running, swimming, cycling, cross-country skiing, dancing, skipping rope, rowing, stair climbing, in-line skating, and endurance games.

Anaerobic Work

Anaerobic activities are often, but not always, associated with developing skill-related fitness. Participation in anaerobic activities leads to moderate to high levels of muscular strength, muscular endurance, and flexibility. Examples of anaerobic activities include running up two flights of stairs, sprinting 40 yards, doing a fast break

• *Jumping rope continuously for several minutes is an example of aerobic activity. Sprinting over hurdles is an example of anaerobic activity.*

BELIEVE IT? ... OR NOT?

When you engage in physical activity or exercise, it is best to breathe in through your nose and out through your mouth.

See page 183 for answer.

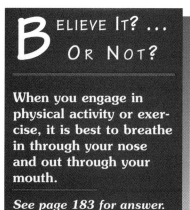

Aerobic Activity
Supply of Oxygen = Body's Demand for Oxygen

Anaerobic Activity
Body's Demand for Oxygen Exceeds Body's Ability to Supply Oxygen

• *Figure 5.14* *Aerobic versus Anaerobic Activities.*

in basketball, or swimming 100 meters as fast as you can. These activities require large amounts of energy—a requirement that your body cannot meet for very long, because you cannot supply enough blood (oxygen) to your muscles, tissues, and organs to meet the high demand. Therefore, your ability to work anaerobically depends on the ability of your muscles, tissues, and organs to work with limited amounts of oxygen.

Aerobic versus Anaerobic Work

When you can meet your energy needs by supplying large amounts of oxygen to your body, you are working primarily in an aerobic mode (see Figure 5.14). If you cannot meet the oxygen demands of a high-intensity physical activity, you are working in a more anaerobic mode. You learned about the talk test in Chapter 3. If you can pass the talk test by carrying on a conversation while working steadily, you are working aerobically. If you can't pass the talk test because you are breathless at a high work intensity, you are working more anaerobically.

Many of the physical activities you enjoy may be part aerobic and part anaerobic. For example, in tennis you might play for one full hour (aerobic component). You might also do quick sprinting and hit the ball hard (anaerobic components), then take short rest periods. If you sprinted the straightaways on a track and walked/jogged the curves for several laps, you would be working both aerobically and anaerobically. The short sprints would be anaerobic, but because you

BELIEVE IT? ... OR NOT?

One of the *Healthy People 2000* goals is to increase the amount of time that physical education classes in schools spend being physically active. Most students are active during less than 30 percent of their physical education classes. The *Healthy People 2000* goal is to increase the active time to at least 50 percent.

See page 183 for answer.

• *These students are engaging in interval training. What clues tell you that they are working aerobically rather than anaerobically?*

---

interval training

alternating higher-intensity physical activities or exercises with lower-intensity recovery bouts for several minutes at a time.

---

did several laps over a period of several minutes, the activity would also be aerobic.

Alternating higher-intensity physical activities or exercises with lower-intensity recovery bouts for several minutes at a time is called **interval training**. (A slower version of this kind of conditioning was presented to you in Figure 3.11 in Chapter 3.) Interval training allows you to work at higher intensities for longer periods of time than you could work in a continuous manner.

By engaging in specific aerobic or anaerobic physical activities or exercises, you can improve your ability to perform work in both modes for improved skill- and health-related fitness. Developing cardiovascular fitness by engaging in aerobic activities will be discussed in Section 6, later in this chapter. Examples of other anaerobic activities will be discussed in Chapters 7 and 8.

SECTION 3 REVIEW

Answer the following questions on a separate sheet of paper:

1. List and describe three aerobic activities.
2. Name and describe three anaerobic activities.
3. How can you determine if you are working aerobically or anaerobically?

Factors That Influence Your Cardiovascular Fitness Levels

Factors such as age, gender, genetics, body composition, and level of conditioning all help determine how much cardiovascular fitness you can achieve. In this section you will learn about these factors and the typical cardiovascular benefits that **A**ny **B**ody **C**an achieve.

Age

As you age, you lose cardiovascular fitness. You will lose less cardiovascular fitness, however, if you remain active. Remember, most people can develop and maintain their cardiovascular fitness at levels in the good to better range no matter what their ages.

Gender

After puberty, males (on average) have higher cardiovascular fitness levels than females. The higher levels for males are because males usually have higher hemoglobin levels than females and carry less body fat. A higher level of hemoglobin allows an individual to carry more oxygen in his or her blood, which would improve performance in cardiovascular activities. Carrying lower levels of body fat also improves cardiovascular performance as long as an individual does not get too lean (see Chapter 9 for more details). However, some conditioned females have higher levels of cardiovascular fitness than some unconditioned or even moderately conditioned males.

Genetics

Genetics can determine both your initial levels of cardiovascular fitness and your ability to improve your cardiovascular fitness. Some people have, and can develop, higher levels of cardiovascular fitness because they have higher numbers of slow-twitch muscle fibers (or muscle cells) than do other people. **Slow-twitch muscle fibers** are associated with a high ability to do aerobic work. **Fast-twitch muscle fibers** are better suited to help you perform anaerobic work.

Young adults, on average, have about 50 percent slow-twitch fibers and 50 percent fast-twitch fibers in their skeletal muscles (muscles that move joints and help support your body structure). Young adults who are good at aerobic activity and have high to very high levels of cardiovascular fitness have closer to 70 to 80 percent slow-twitch

slow-twitch muscle fiber

a muscle cell that is associated with a high ability to do aerobic work.

fast-twitch muscle fiber

a muscle cell that is suited to anaerobic work.

fibers. The ratio of fibers you have is determined mainly by genetics. You will learn more about slow- and fast-twitch muscle fibers in Chapter 7.

Body Composition

Your percentage of body fat can also influence your cardiovascular fitness level. Generally, the lower or higher your body fat percentage is compared with normal levels (see the skinfold evaluation in Chapter 9), the worse your cardiovascular fitness. By increasing your percentage of body fat (if it is too low, like in starvation), or decreasing it (if it is too high, like in obesity), you can improve your cardiovascular fitness level. After all, if you have abnormal fat levels, you will not be as efficient at moving about as you would if you had normal levels of body fat.

Level of Conditioning

Your level of conditioning can influence your cardiovascular fitness level. If you are currently doing no aerobic activities, you can certainly improve your cardiovascular fitness level if you begin a personal fitness program that includes aerobic exercises. Your potential for cardiovascular fitness depends not only on your initial fitness level but also on genetics, trainability, your FIT, and your specific goals.

In Chapter 1 you learned about personal fitness and the positive outcomes of living an active lifestyle. The more specific benefits of participation in regular cardiovascular physical activities or exercise for 8 to 30 weeks are summarized in Figure 5.15.

For additional methods of measuring your cardiovascular fitness, see the "Fitness Check" on the next page.

SECTION 4 REVIEW

Answer the following questions on a separate sheet of paper:

1. How does your genetic makeup influence your cardiovascular fitness level?
2. How does your body composition influence your cardiovascular fitness level?
3. List and describe five benefits of cardiovascular physical activity and exercise.

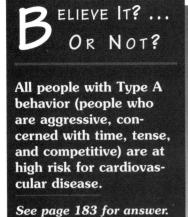

B ELIEVE IT? ...
OR NOT?

All people with Type A behavior (people who are aggressive, concerned with time, tense, and competitive) are at high risk for cardiovascular disease.

See page 183 for answer.

Healthy Heart	• Lower resting heart rate • More blood pumped per beat • Lower blood pressure at moderate physical activity or exercise activities
Healthy Lungs	• Better ability to maintain high breathing rates for longer periods of time
Healthy Blood	• Higher HDL cholesterol • Lower LDL cholesterol and other "bad" blood fats • Higher hemoglobin levels
Healthy Arteries	• Less atherosclerosis • Better blood flow • Lower blood pressure at rest • Improved ability to deliver oxygen to muscles, tissues, and organs
Healthy Cells	• Cells become better at using oxygen that is delivered
Healthy Emotions	• Reduced stress levels
Healthy Image	• Improved self-esteem • Improved personal appearance with weight control
Healthy Lifestyle	• Increased functional health and predicted longevity

• *Figure 5.15* *Typical Benefits Following Cardiovascular Conditioning in a Previously Inactive Young Adult after 8 to 30 Weeks.*

Additional Cardiovascular Fitness Evaluations

In Chapter 4 you performed jumping jacks and one or two cardiovascular "Fitness Checks" to assess your cardiovascular fitness level. In this section you will learn additional ways to evaluate your cardiovascular fitness level now and in the future. You should perform one or more of the evaluations described in this section.

Endurance Walk/Run Evaluations

You can evaluate your cardiovascular fitness level by performing an endurance walk/run assessment for time or for distance. The 1-mile assessment requires you to walk/run as fast as you can to cover the distance. The 12-minute assessment requires you to cover as much distance as possible in the time requirement. The 20-minute assessment requires you to pace yourself steadily as you walk/run for specific distances. If you perform one of these evalua-

(Continued on next page)

• *The endurance walk/run is a great way for beginners to improve their cardiovascular fitness.*

	Male (min:sec)	Female (min:sec)
Age	**Good-Better**	**Good-Better**
13	10:00-7:30*	11:30-9:00
14	9:30-7:00	11:00-8:30
15	9:00-7:00	10:30-8:00
16	8:30-7:00	10:00-8:00
17	8:30-7:00	10:00-8:00
17+	8:30-7:00	10:00-8:00

* Scores below the healthy zone are considered low.

• **Figure 5.16** *1-Mile Walk/Run (healthy fitness zone).*
Source: From The Cooper Institute for Aerobics Research with permission, *The Prudential Fitnessgram Test Administration Manual* (Dallas, TX: 1992), 46–47 for standards in figures.

Additional Cardiovascular Fitness Evaluations *(continued)*

tions, consider the following factors to accurately assess your cardiovascular fitness level:

1. It is recommended that you workout five to eight weeks before the test.

2. Practice walking/running the distance once or twice before the day of the actual test.

3. Learn to pace yourself through the whole distance or for the full amount of time.

4. Evaluate yourself only when the weather conditions are reasonable (not too hot, not too cold, and not too windy).

5. Make sure the distance you walk/run is accurate. It is best to use a regulation track, which is usually about 440 yards or 400 meters in circumference.

Use Figure 5.16 to evaluate your 1-mile cardiovascular performance. For example, if Lisa, a fifteen-year-old girl, can walk/run 1 mile in 10 minutes and 30 seconds, she is at a good level of cardiovascular fitness. A time of 8 minutes would put her in the better or higher range.

Use Figure 5.17 to evaluate your 12-minute walk/run cardiovascular performance. For example, if Lisa completed the 12-minute walk/run and covered 1,900 yards, she would be at a good level of cardiovascular fitness. A distance of 2,100 yards would put her in the better or higher range.

Use Figure 5.18 to evaluate your 20-minute walk/run cardiovascular performance. For example, if Lisa covered 1.5 miles in the 20-minute walk/run, she would be at a good level of cardiovascular fitness. A distance of 1.8 miles for her would be better or higher.

The Walker Evaluation

If you cannot run because of injury, because of poor biomechanics, or because your joints cannot handle the stress, you can assess your cardiovascular fitness by taking a walking test. The walk evaluation is designed to help you assess your cardiovascular fitness while you walk briskly at a steady pace for 30, 35, or 40 minutes. This evaluation is based on the concept that to expend the same amount of energy as you do running, you must walk for a longer period of time, because your intensity of work is lower when you walk.

Use Figure 5.19 to evaluate your walking cardiovascular performance. For example, if Lisa completed the 30-minute walk and covered 1.85 miles, she would be at a good level of cardiovascular fitness. A distance of 2.0 miles for her would be better.

Figure 5.20 on the next page provides you with an example of a six-week walking conditioning program designed to help you walk 2.0 to 2.2 miles (for boys) or 1.85 to 2.0 miles (for girls) in 30 minutes. This program is similar to the 20-minute walk/jog conditioning program you learned about in Chapter 3.

Age	Male distance (yards) Good-Better	Female distance (yards) Good-Better
13	2500-2650*	1800-1900
14	2600-2800	1900-2100
15	2600-2800	1900-2100
16	2600-2800	1900-2100
17	2800-3000	2000-2300
17+	2800-3000	2000-2300

* Scores below the healthy zone are considered low.

• **Figure 5.17** *Twelve-Minute Walk/Run Evaluation (healthy fitness zone).*

Male Distance (miles)

Age	Good–Better
14	1.8–2.0*
15	1.8–2.0
16	1.8–2.0
17	1.8–2.0
17+	1.8–2.0

Female Distance (miles)

Age	Good–Better
14	1.5–1.8
15	1.5–1.8
16	1.5–1.8
17	1.5–1.8
17+	1.5–1.8

• **Figure 5.18** *Twenty-Minute Walk/Run Evaluation (healthy fitness zone).*

Walking Time	Miles—Males		Miles—Females	
	Good	Better	Good	Better
Thirty minutes	2.0–2.2 or farther		1.85–2.0 or farther	
Thirty-five minutes	2.13–2.25 or farther		1.95–2.13 or farther	
Forty minutes	2.23–2.4 or farther		2.0–2.23 or farther	

• **Figure 5.19** *Walk Evaluations (healthy fitness zone, age fourteen and older).*

(Continued on next page)

Believe It? ... Or Not?

The resting heart rates of highly conditioned endurance athletes have been found to be as low as 28 beats per minute. Their hearts can also pump more than twice as much each beat as the hearts of inactive people.

See page 183 for answer.

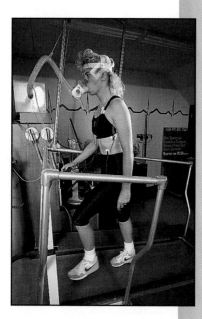

• *If you are at a high risk for cardiovascular disease, your physician may recommend a treadmill stress test.*

continued

30 Minute Walking Conditioning Program	
Week 1	
Day 1	3/1—3/1—3/1
	(3 min. brisk walk/1 min. slow walk—3 min. brisk walk/1 min. slow walk—3 min. brisk walk/1 min. slow walk)
Day 2	3/1—3/1—3/1
Day 3	4/1—3/1—3/1
Week 2	
Day 1	5/1—5/1—4/1
Day 2	5/1—5/1—5/1
Day 3	9/1—9/1 or 15 min. nonstop brisk walk
Week 3	
Day 1	10/1—10/1 or 17 min. nonstop brisk walk
Day 2	11/1—10/1 or 18 min. nonstop brisk walk
Day 3	12/1—11/1 or 19 min. nonstop brisk walk
Week 4	
Day 1	14/1—9/1 or 20 min. nonstop brisk walk
Day 2	15/1—10/1 or 22 min. nonstop brisk walk
Day 3	18/1—9/1 or 24 min. nonstop brisk walk
Week 5	
Day 1	20 min. brisk walk or 30 min. brisk walk — Test (optional)
	(Boys should try to go 2.0 to 2.2 miles; Girls 1.85 to 2.0 miles) Those who completed the goals in 30 minutes on day one can move to a maintenance program. All others should continue on this program for 2 more weeks.
Day 2	22/1—8/1 or 26 min. nonstop brisk walk
Day 3	24/1—8/1 or 25 min. nonstop brisk walk
Week 6	
Day 1	25/1—6/1 or 26 min. nonstop brisk walk
Day 2	26/1—6/1 or 28 min. nonstop brisk walk
Day 3	30 min. brisk walk evaluation

• **Figure 5.20**   *Thirty-Minute Walking Conditioning Program.*

Medical or Laboratory Evaluation

A final way to determine your cardiovascular fitness level is to have it evaluated by trained medical professionals during a treadmill or bicycle exercise stress test. This method would usually be used only if you needed special followup after a medical screening, before you began your personal fitness program. However, adults with serious health risks may require this type of testing before they begin vigorous exercise programs.

SECTION 5   Developing Cardiovascular Fitness

REMEMBER This!

Your FIT is the frequency, intensity, and time/duration of your workout program. Your FIT is based on your goals and individual needs for developing and maintaining personal fitness.

To develop cardiovascular fitness, you need to design your personal fitness plan to include physical activities or exercises that are primarily aerobic. Remember, aerobic activities are rhythmic and continuous, and they force you to use the large muscle groups of your body for several minutes at a time. Aerobic activities include walking, hiking, jogging/running, swimming, cycling, cross-country skiing, dancing, skipping rope, rowing, stair climbing, in-line skating, and endurance games. Always include gradual warm-up and cool-down with your aerobic activities in your personal fitness plan.

In designing your personal fitness plan to develop or maintain cardiovascular fitness, use the scientific principles you learned in Chapter 3. The recommendations that follow are based on these principles.

Overload Principle

To improve your cardiovascular fitness, you need to determine your FIT. Use the results from your cardiovascular fitness evaluations to help you determine your FIT.

CONSUMER CORNER

Misleading Cardiovascular Consumer Claims

Promoters and advertisers make many false or misleading claims, saying that you can develop the benefits of cardiovascular fitness without engaging in moderate to vigorous physical activity or exercise. The truth is, however, that there are no shortcuts to achieving or maintaining good to better levels of cardiovascular fitness. You need to develop a FIT plan, including aerobic activities or exercises, to improve or maintain your cardiovascular fitness levels. Cardiovascular fitness products such as motorized exercise machines that do most of the work for you, vibrators, or massagers, do not overload your heart, lungs, or blood vessels enough to improve your cardiovascular fitness.

Someone who claims you can skip working out and instead simply take a pill or read a book to develop or maintain good cardiovascular fitness levels is guilty of false advertising. Be aware of people who suggest that you will see immediate results (results in less than one or two weeks, for example) from a cardiovascular fitness product or special workout that they want to sell you. Remember, it usually takes 8 to 30 weeks to see significant benefits in your cardiovascular fitness levels, unless you already have good to better levels.

percentage of maximum heart rate

a method of calculating an exercise intensity; 60 to 90 percent of your maximum heart rate.

target heart rate zone

the recommended intensity for aerobic conditioning; estimated to be between 60 and 90 percent of one's predicted maximum heart rate.

• *You can monitor the intensity of your workout by checking your pulse to see if you are in your target heart rate zone.*

Frequency

How frequently should you exercise? A minimum of three days per week is recommended, and four to six days a week is better. If you are just starting out, begin with three days per week. Then, during the improvement stage, add more days per week.

Intensity

You can set the intensity of your aerobic conditioning at a **percentage of maximum heart rate**. This simple method of determining intensity is good to use if you are just starting out or if you need to lose weight before you can do more vigorous physical activity or exercise. With this method you determine your aerobic intensity according to a straight percentage of your maximum heart rate. It is recommended that you work at between 60 and 90 percent of your predicted maximum heart rate, which is called your **target heart rate zone** (Figure 5.21).

In some cases (for example, if you have been very sedentary), you may have to start out at lower intensities (40 to 50 percent of your predicted maximum heart rate) and gradually progress to 60 to 90 percent. To calculate your target heart rate zone for training if you are fifteen years old, first determine your predicted maximum heart rate (220 − age = 205). Then determine 60 percent of 205 (205 × 0.6 = 123). Finally, determine 90 percent of 205 (205 × 0.9 = 184). Thus, your target heart rate zone for training is between 123 and 184 beats per minute using this method.

On days when you feel like doing lighter aerobic activity, you might work at about 123 beats per minute. On days you do more vigorous aerobic activity, you could work at a heart rate of about 184 beats per minute. If you work at levels lower than your target heart rate, your health can still benefit, but you may not see much change in your personal fitness levels. If you work at levels above your target heart rate zone, you may place yourself at higher risk for injury, especially if you work too hard, too often. Remember, you can also use the perceived exertion scale in Figure 3.5 or the talk test to monitor your aerobic intensity.

Time/Duration

At the start of your personal fitness program, your goal should be twenty to thirty minutes of aerobic activity per physical activity or exercise session. If you are deconditioned, however, you may have to accumulate 20 or 30 minutes each day in two or three separate aerobic sessions of 10 to 15 minutes each. You could also do an interval workout at low intensity to accumulate your 20 or 30 minutes. For example, you might jog for two minutes at 60 percent of your maximum heart rate and then walk for a minute to recover.

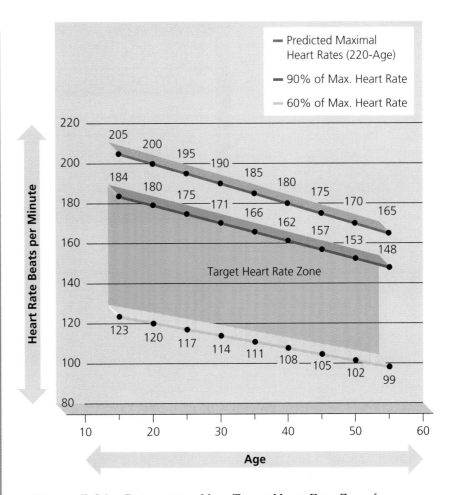

• **Figure 5.21** *Determining Your Target Heart Rate Zone for Training.*

You would repeat this ten times to accumulate your 20 or 30 minutes (review Figure 3.11 in Chapter 3). As your aerobic fitness level improves, or if you have good to better aerobic fitness already, increase your workout time/duration to 40 to 60 minutes.

Progression Principle

The rate at which you modify your FIT should be based on your personal fitness goals and your changing levels of aerobic fitness. Remember, never change your frequency, intensity, or time/duration all at the same time or too quickly. Be patient, and allow for gradual improvements. It is easier on your body to work at a lower intensity and to work longer. However, to achieve higher goals of personal fitness, you will need to work more frequently, harder, or for longer periods of time.

SECTION 5 REVIEW

Answer the following questions on a separate sheet of paper:

1. What is the minimum number of days recommended for improving your cardiovascular fitness?
2. What is the target heart rate zone for a 20-year old?
3. What should your beginning time/duration goal be for personal fitness?

SUMMARY

Cardiovascular fitness refers to your ability to work continuously for extended periods of time. Your level of cardiovascular fitness depends on the ability of your heart to pump large amounts of blood to the muscles and organs of the body. It also is related to how well your lungs function and how well your blood vessels can deliver blood (oxygen) to your body.

Moderate to high levels of cardiovascular fitness or aerobic fitness are associated with increased longevity and reduced risk for cardiovascular disease. Moderate to high levels of cardiovascular fitness can help prevent atherosclerosis, which is the most common disease process causing heart attacks and strokes. Your commitment to regular cardiovascular activity can also reduce your risk for hypertension.

Cardiovascular fitness or aerobic activities might include walking, hiking, jogging, dancing, skipping rope, rowing, swimming, skating, and endurance games or sports. Anaerobic activities are different from aerobic activities because they are done at very high intensities and last only a few seconds or a few minutes.

Your cardiovascular fitness level will be influenced to some extent by factors such as your age, gender, genetics, body composition, and level of conditioning. You can expect to see many specific improvements such as a lower resting heart rate, higher HDL cholesterol, and improved self-esteem levels following 8–30 weeks of cardiovascular conditioning.

You can use a variety of walking and running cardiovascular fitness evaluations to help you determine your cardiovascular fitness. You can then improve or maintain your cardiovascular fitness simply by accumulating 20 to 30 minutes of activity several times a week in play, games, sports, work, getting to school, recreation, or planned exercise.

Chapter 5 Review

True/False

On a separate sheet of paper, mark each question below either T for True or F for False.

1. Muscular fitness is the most important of all the skill-related and health-related fitness components in relation to your functional health.

2. Healthy lungs breathe between 6 (at rest) and 150 (during exercise) liters of air per minute.

3. The resting heart rate usually falls between 50 and 80 beats per minute.

4. A twenty-year-old female has a predicted maximum heart rate of 180 beats per minute, on average.

5. Atherosclerosis is the most common cause of cardiovascular disease.

6. Regular aerobic exercise is associated with increases in HDL cholesterol.

7. Strokes are caused by restriction of blood flow to the heart.

8. Systolic blood pressure is the pressure on the arteries when the heart contracts.

9. Slow-twitch muscle fibers are associated with your ability to do anaerobic work.

10. A male who can complete 2 miles of walking/running in 20 minutes has a good level of cardiovascular fitness.

Multiple Choice

1. Which of the following are not muscles associated with deep breathing?
   a. abdominals
   b. intercostals
   c. tongue
   d. diaphragm

2. Which of the following conditions is associated with asthma for many people?
   a. dust
   b. allergies
   c. exercise
   d. all of the above

3. Which of the following is caused by a blockage of a coronary artery?
   a. atherosclerosis
   b. muscle pump
   c. stroke
   d. myocardial infarction

4. Which of the following is an example of an anaerobic physical activity?
   a. walking 2 miles
   b. swimming 1 mile
   c. sprinting 40 yards
   d. in-line skating for 30 minutes

5. Which of the following will not have a major influence on your cardiovascular fitness?
   a. genetics
   b. conditioning level
   c. strength
   d. gender

6. Following twenty weeks of cardiovascular fitness conditioning, your resting heart rate would most likely do which of the following?
   a. be slower
   b. be faster
   c. stay the same
   d. none of the above

7. Which of the following would not be a benefit you would expect to see after 8 to 30 weeks of cardiovascular conditioning?
   a. decreased resting blood pressure
   b. lower HDL cholesterol levels

c. greater self-esteem
d. decreased stress levels

8. Which of the following is a good time for a fifteen-year-old female who evaluates her cardiovascular fitness by completing the Prudential *Fitnessgram* 1-mile walk/run?

a. 10 minutes, 30 seconds
b. 12 minutes flat
c. 14 minutes, 30 seconds
d. 20 minutes flat

9. Which of the following methods should you use to determine your intensity for cardiovascular physical activity or exercise?

a. target heart rate zone
b. talk test
c. rating of perceived exertion
d. all of the above

10. The target heart rate zone for a sixteen-year-old female should be in what range?

a. 104 and 124 beats per minute
b. 112 and 123 beats per minute
c. 118 and 147 beats per minute
d. 123 and 184 beats per minute

Discussion

1. List and identify five different physical activities or exercises that will help you improve or maintain your cardiovascular fitness level.

2. List and describe five typical benefits of cardiovascular conditioning in a previously inactive young adult after 8 to 30 weeks of training.

3. How can you reduce your own risk of having a heart attack, a stroke, or hypertension by engaging in regular cardiovascular conditioning?

Vocabulary Experience

Match the correct term in Column A to the definition in Column B by writing the appropriate number in each blank.

Column A

_____ hemoglobin

_____ interval training

_____ muscle pump

_____ recovery heart rate

_____ circulatory system

_____ asthma

Column B

1. Restriction of your breathing passages due to dust, allergies, pollution, or even vigorous exercise.

2. Should be less than 120 within 10 minutes of cardiovascular activity or exercise.

3. Arteries, veins, and capillaries.

4. Sprinting the straightaways on a track and walking/jogging the curves for several laps.

5. Helps squeeze the veins to help blood move back to the right side of the heart.

6. An iron-rich compound that carries oxygen in blood.

Critical Thinking

1. How can you help reduce your risk of cardiovascular disease? Explain your answer.

2. What cardiovascular evaluation would you recommend to a friend who was very sedentary and 20 pounds overweight? Explain your answer.

3. How can you use interval training in your personal cardiovascular fitness plan? Give an example.

Case Study — Diane's Fitness Level

Diane is a seventeen-year-old. She was very active when she was fourteen through sixteen years old. However, in the past year she has become very inactive because she took a part-time job after school and does not take physical education in school (it is not required for her to graduate). Diane has noticed that her aerobic fitness level has dropped. She gets tired almost every day and feels she has low levels of energy. Although Diane used to participate regularly in aerobic dance, walking, and swimming, she has never had a class that educated her about personal fitness. Therefore, she needs the help of someone knowledgeable about designing and implementing fitness programs—someone like you!

Here is your assignment:

Assume you are Diane's friend, and she asks you for some help with her plans for returning to an active lifestyle. Organize a list of things Diane should consider and do before beginning a moderate to vigorous personal cardiovascular fitness program. Then list the recommendations you would give to Diane for the first 2 weeks of her conditioning. Use the following keys to help you:

KEYS TO HELP YOU

- Consider Diane's history of personal aerobic activity and exercise.
- Consider how she should evaluate her current cardiovascular fitness level.
- Consider her needs and goals (for example, how she will find time to do physical activity or exercise).
- Determine a reasonable plan to give Diane that covers the concepts of overload, frequency, intensity, time/duration, and progression.

Chapter 6

Your Flexibility

Contents

1. Flexibility and Functional Health
2. Factors That Influence Your Flexibility
3. Types of Stretching and Your Flexibility
4. Developing Your Flexibility Fitness

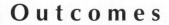

Outcomes

After reading and studying this chapter, you will be able to:

1. Explain why flexibility is important and how it contributes to the development and maintenance of moderate to high levels of personal fitness.
2. Explain how moderate to high levels of flexibility fitness can reduce your risk for functional health problems.
3. Discuss the benefits of developing and maintaining good to better levels of flexibility.
4. Give examples of the types of stretching that can positively influence your flexibility.
5. Explain how you can develop moderate to high levels of flexibility.

Key Terms

After reading and studying this chapter, you will be able to understand and provide practical definitions for the following terms:

range of motion (ROM)
hyperflexibilitiy
muscle imbalance
low back injury

elasticity
static stretching
ballistic stretching
reflex

reflex-assisted stretching
plyometric training
passive stretching

INTRODUCTION

Flexibility *refers to the* range of motion (ROM) *that your joints have during movement. Range of motion is the varying degrees of motion allowed around a joint (see Figure 6.1). Your flexibility levels can influence your functional health.* Poor flexibility of one or more of your body parts could restrict your ability to carry on normal, daily physical activities, which would reduce your quality of life. Many adults lose their normal levels of flexibility due to the aging process and decreased participation in physical activity and exercise. Poor flexibility can contribute to many types of injuries, including low back pain, muscle pulls, muscle strains, and muscle cramps. In this chapter you will learn about the relationship between flexibility and your functional health, different types of stretching and flexibility activities, the specific benefits of flexibility, and how to develop your flexibility fitness.

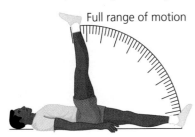

Full range of motion

• **Figure 6.1**   *Full Range of Motion.*

SECTION 1

Flexibility and Functional Health

range of motion (ROM)

varying degrees of motion allowed around a joint.

Your body has many types of joints (places where bones meet and move) that allow for varying **range of motion (ROM)**. Joints like those in your shoulders and hips are ball-and-socket joints, which allow a wide ROM. Joints such as those in your knees are hingelike, and allow you to move forward and backward. Your neck joints allow you to pivot and rotate through a wide ROM. Your wrist and ankle joints allow your bones to glide over one another. (See Figure 6.2.)

Hyperflexibility and Muscle Imbalances

You might think that the more flexibility a person has, the better. This is not necessarily true. A joint with too much flexibility around it (**hyperflexibility**) can become injured easily.

hyperflexibility

the condition of having too much flexibility.

Hyperflexibility can occur when a joint has been stretched beyond its normal ROM, or when weak muscles surround a joint (as can happen following a muscle injury). Hyperflexibility can also occur because of genetic tendencies for "loose joints." A person with a hyperflexible shoulder joint may have stretched ligaments or tendons that cause the shoulder to dislocate easily.

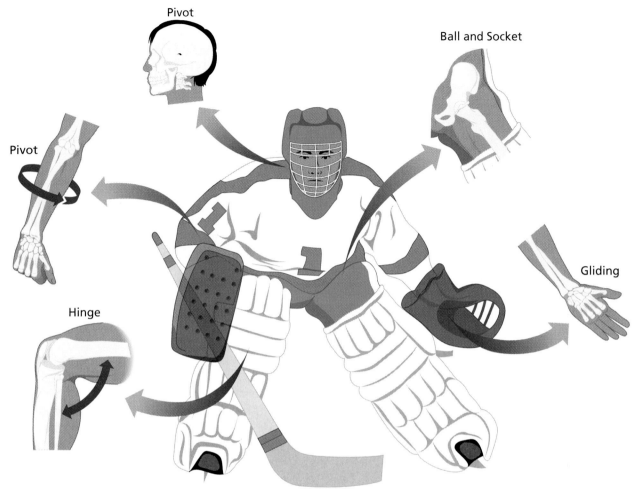

- **Figure 6.2** *Joints of the Human Body.*

muscle imbalance

an imbalance that occurs when one muscle group that controls a joint is too strong in relation to a complementary set of muscles (another set of muscles that helps control the same joint).

By strengthening the muscles that control the movement of the shoulders, you can help improve the stability of your shoulders. These muscles are the rotator cuff (the muscles that surround the shoulder joint) and the biceps (the muscles in the front of your upper arm).

When you strengthen your muscles for improved flexibility, make sure you work the muscles that oppose one another in movements. This will help you avoid a **muscle imbalance**. Muscle imbalances occur when one muscle group, such as the quadriceps (the muscles in the front of your thigh), is too strong in relation to a complementary set of muscles, such as the hamstrings (the muscles in the back of your thigh). Biomechanically it is normal for your quadriceps to be stronger than your hamstrings. However, overdeveloping your quadriceps in relation to your hamstrings puts you at risk for a hamstring injury. An imbalance can also reduce your normal ROM.

• *Improving or maintaining your flexibility can reduce your risk for low back pain.*

low back injury

injury to the muscles, ligaments, tendons, or joints of the lower back.

Low Back Pain

Functional health depends upon good to better levels of flexibility and strength. For example, there is a relationship between **low back injuries** and poor flexibility.

Low back pain is a major health problem in industrial societies like the United States. It has been estimated that 80 percent of all people on Earth will suffer from low back pain at one time or another in their lives. You probably know of at least one or two adults who suffer from low back pain or injuries.

People with low back pain often end up with more chronic problems, such as low back injuries. Figure 6.3 illustrates the major causes of low back injuries in American workers. As the figure shows, the leading cause of low back injuries is lifting. Twisting, bending, and pulling can also cause you to hurt your back if you are not careful.

Low back injuries are associated with inflexible and weak muscles that support the spine and pelvic girdle. Your risk of back injuries can be decreased if you develop and maintain the muscular strength and ROM of your low back.

You can also help prevent low back injuries by learning to lift and carry heavy objects according to biomechanical principles. You probably have lifted a heavy box or other object like the one shown in Figure 6.4. Did you lean over at the waist and lift upward to move the object? If so, you may have hurt your back. Figure 6.4 shows the preferred lifting technique. You should bend your knees, lift mainly with your quadriceps, and keep the weight close to your body.

When you are carrying heavy objects, try to balance the load so that there is an equal amount of weight stressing your joints. For example, when you carry two sacks of groceries, carry one in each hand, not both in one hand. Avoid excessive twisting, pulling, or pushing movements that could strain your low back. Use proper foot movements when you have to turn while lifting a heavy object. Do

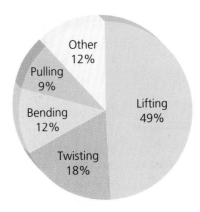

• **Figure 6.3**   *Most Common Reasons for Low Back Injuries.*

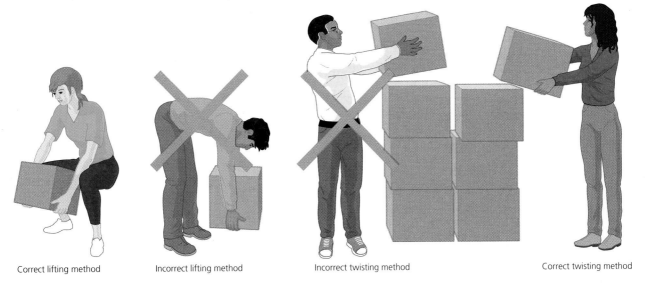

Correct lifting method   Incorrect lifting method   Incorrect twisting method   Correct twisting method

• **Figure 6.4**   *The Right Way and Wrong Way to Lift.*

not twist with the load, as shown in Figure 6.4 unless you move your feet in the direction that you turn. See Figure 6.5 for additional tips on how you can prevent low back injuries and maintain your low back functional health.

REMEMBER This!

If you are in doubt about whether an object is too heavy for you to lift, don't be afraid to ask for help when trying to lift it. There is no reason to risk your functional health to injury because you are too scared or embarrassed to ask for help.

SECTION 1 REVIEW

Answer the following questions on a separate sheet of paper:

1. Define *flexibility.*

2. What are the top three causes of low back injuries in American workers?

SECTION 2 Factors That Influence Your Flexibility

The total ROM that you have around a joint varies from one joint to another and usually differs from one individual to the next. Your muscular flexibility depends on several factors, such as genetics, gender, age, body temperature, injuries, excessive body fat, and lifestyle activity levels.

Don't

Do

Sleeping

Do not lie flat on your back: this arches the spine too much.

Lie on your back and support your knees.

Do not use a high pillow.

Lie on your side with knees bent and pillow just high enough to keep your neck straight.

Do not sleep face down.

Sitting

Do not leave your lower back unsupported when not upright.

Sit straight with back support, knees higher than hips.

Standing

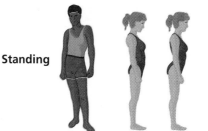

Do not let your back bend out of its natural curve.

Stand upright, hips tucked, knees slightly bent.

Walking

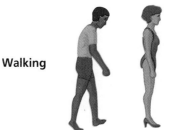

Do not lean forward or wear high heels.

Lead with chest, toes forward.

• **Figure 6.5**   *Care of the Spine. Source:* Reprinted from F. S. Sizer, E. N. Whitney, and L. K. DeBruyne, *Making Life Choices: Health Skills and Concepts* (St. Paul: West Publishing, 1994), 287.

Any Body Can!

John Moreau and Dann Baker

John Moreau and Dann Baker are international competitors who teach physical activity courses that require good to better levels of flexibility at Southwest Texas State University (SWTSU) in San Marcos, TX. John specializes in teaching fencing, weight training, jogging, self-defense, and personal fitness classes, while Dann specializes in teaching wrestling, karate, and jogging classes.

Following his junior year in college, John joined the U.S. Army to train and compete in the modern pentathlon (one-day event including pistol shooting, fencing, swimming 300 meters, horseback riding over barriers, and running 4,000 meters). In 1981, John competed in the World Military Modern Pentathlon Championships where the U.S. team finished third. In 1984 John was on the U.S. Olympic fencing team in the Los Angeles, California games. He repeated this accomplishment in 1988 when he competed in the 1988 Seoul, Korea Olympic games.

John has been teaching at SWTSU since 1984. He continues to live and promote personal fitness to students while staying in good shape himself. In the fall of 1995, he won the first U.S. Olympic trial competition for possible qualification for the 1996 Olympic games in Atlanta, Georgia.

Dann earned a college scholarship to Minot College in Minot, North Dakota for his wrestling and football talents. Following a year at Minot, Dann joined the U.S. Air Force. While in the Air Force, Dann won the interservice wrestling championship and was the Pacific Air Command judo champion. He learned karate (Kenpo style) starting at the age of 10 and later applied his skills in the U.S. Special Forces as a trainer in martial arts. Dann served in Viet Nam in 1968 where he was "missing in action".

In 1973 Dann went to SWTSU to finish his college education, and he has been there ever since. He helped found and has coached the SWT wrestling teams to numerous state championships. Dann also continues to live and promote personal fitness. In 1992, he came out of competition retirement and finished second in the World Black Belt Karate Championships. He repeated his second place finishes in 1993 and 1994. In 1995, Dann became the oldest (48) individual to win the World Black Belt Self-Defense Karate Championship. He was also elected to the Karate Hall of Fame as the Most Outstanding Competitor in the U.S. in 1995.

Not everyone can be as versatile as John and Dann, but **Any Body Can** learn to develop and maintain their own good levels of flexibility. That's right, you can do it!

What Affects Flexibility?

Some people have more flexible joints, tendons, and ligaments than others because of their genetic makeup. In general, females are slightly more flexible than males, at least in some movements (for example, the movements included in the back saver sit and reach evaluation described in Chapter 4). Younger people are usually more flexible than older people, because some elasticity loss occurs with aging and sedentary living. **Elasticity** refers to the rubberband-like flexibility of your muscles, tendons, and other connective tissues. You can maintain your elasticity at higher levels as you age if you stretch regularly.

Flexibility can change by as much as 20 percent with increases or decreases in muscular temperature. If you are properly warmed up, you will have better flexibility than if you are not warmed up. Cold temperatures in your physical activity or exercise environment will probably decrease your flexibility until you warm up.

Injuries to your muscles, skin, or connective tissues may result in the loss of some flexibility. Scar tissue that forms when your body heals itself can limit your ROM. Flexibility exercises can help you regain your normal ROM after an injury.

Excessive body fat can also limit your ROM. The excess fat restricts movement because of extra bulk around your joints. Losing excess body fat (see Chapter 9) can improve your flexibility by allowing joints to move through their full ROM.

The most significant negative influence on your flexibility level is an inactive lifestyle. As you decrease your physical activity or exercise levels, your muscles lose elasticity, and your tendons and ligaments get tighter and shorter. If you remain inactive for long periods of time, you will also probably add body fat, which will limit your flexibility even further.

elasticity

the rubberband-like flexibility of the muscles, tendons, and other connective tissues.

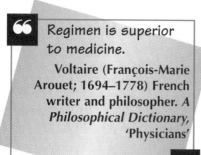

66

Regimen is superior to medicine.

Voltaire (François-Marie Arouet; 1694–1778) French writer and philosopher. *A Philosophical Dictionary,* 'Physicians'

99

Stress Break

Stretching is an effective way to reduce stress. Stretching reduces muscle tension and allows you to feel more relaxed. Stretching also allows you to get in touch with your body and helps you sense which areas are tighter than others. Without regular stretching, your muscles tend to become tighter and feel tense, creating more distress.

Typical Benefits of Flexibility Conditioning

The typical benefits of participating in a regular flexibility stretching program are summarized in Figure 6.6. Flexibility conditioning usually includes a stretching program like the one described for warm-up in Chapter 3. Other flexibility activities and exercises will be illustrated and explained for you later in this chapter.

Participation in some types of physical activities and exercises will help you develop flexibility more than will participation in other types of activities and exercises. Figure 6.7 shows the flexibility benefits of a variety of physical activities and exercises.

Healthy Joints:	• Increases ROM for the joints conditioned • Promotes more flexible muscles and tendons • Decreases risk of joint injury
Healthy Muscles:	• Increases stability for your joints • Increases ROM for strength development
Fewer Health-related Injuries:	• Helps control instability • Reduces risk for various chronic muscle/skeletal pain like low back pain
Reduced Stiffness and Soreness:	• Increases blood flow with warm-up stretching, increases ROM • After physical activities ROM can be regained with stretching resulting in reduced stiffness and muscular soreness the next day • Stretching after physical activity reduces risk for blood pooling and muscle cramping
Healthy Emotions:	• Reduced tension and stress levels
Healthy Image:	• Increased functional health and future opportunities to participate in a variety of physical activity and exercise

Figure 6.6 *Typical Benefits Following Flexibility Conditioning in a Previously Inactive Young Adult after 8 to 30 Weeks.*

Sport or Activity	Flexibility Benefits	Sport or Activity	Flexibility Benefits	Sport or Activity	Flexibility Benefits
Aerobics	***	Dance cont.		Skating; Ice, Roller, or In-line	*
Archery	*	Ballet	****	Skiing	
Backpacking	**	Line	**	Cross-Country	*
Badminton	**	Social	*	Downhill	*
Baseball	*	Fencing	**	Soccer	**
Basketball (half court)	*	Football	*	Softball (fast pitch)	*
(vigorous)	*	Golf (walking)	**	(slow pitch)	*
Bicycling	**	Gymnastics	****	Surfing	**
Bowling	*	Hiking	**	Swimming	**
Calisthenics	****	Horseback Riding	*	Table Tennis	*
Canoeing	*	Jogging	*	Tennis	*
Circuit Training	***	Martial Arts	*	Volleyball	*
Continuous Rhythmical		Mountain Climbing	*	Walking	*
Excercise	***	Racquetball/Handball	*	Water Polo	**
Dance		Rope Jumping	*	Waterskiing	*
Aerobic	***	Rowing	*	Weight Training	*
		Sailing	*		

Better **** Good *** Fair ** Low *

Figure 6.7 *Flexibility Benefits of Various Sports and Activities.*

Fitness Check ✓

Fitness Evaluation

Examine Figure 6.7 on the preceding page to determine whether you engage in activities or sports that help maintain or increase your flexibility levels. If you are not participating in activities or sports that are rated at least fair (**) at positively influencing your flexibility levels, you should add activities or sports to your daily activity routine that are rated fair, good, or excellent.

SECTION 2 REVIEW

Answer the following questions on a separate sheet of paper:

1. List and explain three factors that influence your flexibility.
2. Which two flexibility conditioning benefits are the most important to you, and why?

CONSUMER CORNER

Flexibility and Consumer Issues

Many commercial stretching devices to help increase your flexibility are advertised. Some of these devices are designed to stretch your lower leg and Achilles' tendon (heel cord). Others work your hamstrings and quadriceps. Although these devices may provide a convenient way to stretch, they are not necessary and can be costly.

For example, an exercise bicycle will improve your lower body flexibility, while at the same time building your cardiovascular endurance. Most people can work out on an exercise bike without much difficulty so it is a good choice for people just beginning an exercise program. A wide variety of exercise bikes are available at a wide range of prices so be sure to check sources such as *Consumer Reports* before making a purchase.

Good flexibility levels are important, of course. They help avoid lost time from work, costly medical bills, and needless pain and suffering. By learning a variety of stretches for each of your body parts, you will always be able to practice proper stretching and thus prevent injuries.

SECTION 3   Types of Stretching and Your Flexibility

To improve your flexibility, you must overload your muscles. This is done by stretching them beyond their normal resting length. Four basic stretching techniques can help improve your flexibility level. These include static stretching, ballistic stretching, reflex-assisted stretching, and passive stretching.

Static Stretching

In **static stretching**, you assume a stretch position slowly and then hold it for several seconds (10 to 60), until you feel slight discomfort but no real pain (see Figure 6.8). Variations include slow movements like arm circles or slow neck stretches side-to-side.

Static stretching, when done regularly, is safe and effective at increasing the ROM of the joints you work. Everyone should do some static stretching to help maintain or improve flexibility.

Ballistic Stretching

Ballistic stretching involves quick up-and-down bobbing movements that are held very briefly (Figure 6.9). You may have seen athletes doing ballistic stretches in their warm-ups before a game.

For health-related personal fitness, ballistic stretches are not necessary. In fact, they are not recommended, because they can increase your risk for injury, particularly if you are not warmed up properly before you do them. However, if you are interested in high-performance levels of fitness, you may need to include ballistic stretching in your personal fitness program. Ballistic stretching challenges your reflexes and increases your flexibility, which can help you improve your skill-related fitness.

static stretching

exercises in which you assume a stretch position slowly and then hold it for several seconds (10 to 60 seconds), until you feel slight discomfort but no real pain.

ballistic stretching

exercises that involve quick up-and-down bobbing movements that are held very briefly.

BELIEVE IT? ... OR NOT?

Back problems are the most common reason for decreased work capacity and reduced leisure-time activity in Americans below the age of forty-five. The average American typically experiences his or her first back problems by the age of thirty-two.

See page 203 for answer.

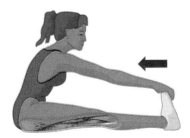

• *Figure 6.8*   Static Stretching.

• *Figure 6.9*   Ballistic Stretching.

Reflex-assisted Stretching

reflex

a response that the nerves and muscles provide to various movements.

reflex-assisted stretching

exercises that challenge the reflexes to adapt so that they allow the joints to move at faster speeds and with more explosive power.

plyometric training

exercises such as bounding and jumping movements that increase your ability to develop force more quickly in explosive movements; a kind of reflex-assisted stretching.

Your **reflexes** are the responses that your nerves and muscles provide to various movements. An example of a reflex is the simple knee jerk, when you involuntarily extend your knee after your doctor taps your knee tendon with a rubber hammer. Your body performs a variety of reflex actions daily, such as reflexes that keep us from falling and help us maintain balance. Reflexes can be very sensitive or dull. Your reflexes can become dull as you age if you have an inactive lifestyle. A regular stretching program can help you maintain or improve many of your normal reflex actions as you age.

Reflex-assisted stretching includes a variety of different stretching movements that will challenge your reflexes to adapt to these movements, allowing your joints to move at faster speeds and with more explosive power. Reflex-assisted stretching is usually not recommended for a general personal fitness program unless you are interested in performance fitness.

An example of reflex-assisted stretching is **plyometric training** (Figure 6.10). Plyometric training includes bounding and jumping exercises. Plyometric training increases your ability to develop force quicker in explosive movements, which is important in sport events that require you to jump at maximal levels. If you are interested in doing plyometric training, seek out a certified strength and conditioning coach to help you develop a safe and effective program for yourself.

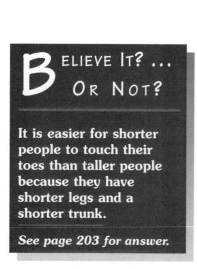

BELIEVE IT? ... OR NOT?

It is easier for shorter people to touch their toes than taller people because they have shorter legs and a shorter trunk.

See page 203 for answer.

Lunge position   Vertical jump   Lunge position with legs switched

• **Figure 6.10** *Plyometric Training (a kind of reflex-assisted stretching).*

Passive Stretching

passive stretching

exercises in which a partner or device provides the force for a stretch.

Passive stretching is a type of stretching in which a partner or device provides the force for your stretch (Figure 6.11). For example, once you have done a static stretch, a partner can push you a bit further to increase your ROM for the joint worked. A device such as a towel can also be used for passive stretching. For example, sit on the floor and place a towel under your heel. Hold the towel with both hands, and pull it toward you. In this way you can passively stretch your hamstring muscles. If you pull too hard you might overstretch your hamstrings, however. Passive stretching can be dangerous if your device or partner pushes you too far and causes muscle pulls or tears. Be careful if you include passive stretching in your personal fitness plan.

All four types of stretching just discussed can help you maintain or improve your flexibility levels. Everyone should do some static stretching regularly. Do some ballistic and reflex-assisted stretching if you want to improve your performance fitness. Finally, passive stretching can improve your ROM but should be done with caution to avoid overstretching your muscles.

The flexibility evaluations discussed in Chapter 4 can help you determine your flexibility levels. Design a plan for maintaining or improving your flexibility according to the results of these evaluations.

If you ever have a serious injury or chronic bone or joint problems, consult an athletic trainer, physical therapist, or physician. These specialists can help evaluate any limitations on your flexibility levels. They may want to conduct more in-depth evaluations to help you improve your flexibility levels or to assist you in returning to your previous level of flexibility.

Stretching Benefits

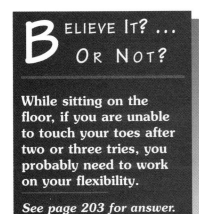

BELIEVE IT? ...
OR NOT?

While sitting on the floor, if you are unable to touch your toes after two or three tries, you probably need to work on your flexibility.

See page 203 for answer.

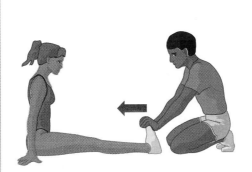

• *Figure 6.11* *Passive Stretching Examples.*

SECTION 4

Developing Your Flexibility Fitness

To develop flexibility fitness, you need to design your personal fitness plan to include physical activities or exercises that will maintain or improve your ROM. An easy way to maintain or develop your flexibility level is to include a stretching program in your warm-up and cool-down routines. Use the scientific principles you learned in Chapter 3 and your personal fitness goals to develop your own flexibility program. The recommendations that follow are based on these principles.

Overload Principle

Determine your FIT by using the results from your flexibility fitness evaluations. If you have good to better levels of flexibility, design a stretching program to help you maintain your flexibility. If you have low levels of flexibility, you need a program of stretching that increases your FIT to help you develop good to better levels of flexibility.

Specificity Principle

To improve the flexibility of a particular joint or body area, do stretches that affect the nerves, muscles, and connective tissues that control movement around that joint or body part. To maintain or improve your overall flexibility levels, do a variety of stretches that influence all your major body parts.

Frequency

How often should you do your stretches? A minimum of three days per week is recommended, but doing some stretching daily is best. If

REMEMBER This!

Never change the frequency, intensity, and time/duration of your exercise all at the same time or too quickly. Be patient, and allow for gradual improvements.

you are just starting out, begin with three days per week. Then, during the improvement stage of progression, add more days per week.

Intensity

The intensity of your stretching is determined by the points where muscles are stretched beyond their normal resting lengths. You have reached that point if you stretch enough to feel slight discomfort but no real pain during the stretch. Be careful to avoid injuries if you do ballistic, reflex-assisted, or passive stretching techniques. Too much bouncing, jerking, or other sudden movements can increase your risk for injuries.

Time/Duration

How do you determine the time/duration of your stretches? For static stretching, begin by holding each stretch for 10 to 15 seconds at a time, repeating this three times for each static stretch you do. As your ROM increases, work toward holding each stretch for 30 to 60 seconds, repeating this three times per stretch.

If you are doing ballistic, reflex-assisted, or passive stretching, do five to fifteen slow and gentle movements, repeating this three times per stretch. You may want to increase the number or sets of stretches over time, based on your own performance fitness needs. Remember, ballistic, reflex-assisted, and passive stretching are more hazardous than static stretching in regard to injury risk and, therefore, should be done with caution.

Progression Principle

The rate at which you modify your FIT should be based on your personal fitness goals and your changing levels of flexibility fitness. In Chapter 3 you learned twelve basic stretches that you could include in the warm-up and cool-down portions of your personal fitness routine. Figure 6.12 shows you several other stretches that you should be able to perform safely and effectively.

Answers to BELIEVE IT? ... OR NOT?

Pg. 194 True.

Pg. 197 False. You will not get muscle-bound or bulky, nor will you develop muscle imbalances that reduce your flexibility unless you overdevelop or overcondition one muscle group (such as your quadriceps) in relation to another muscle group (such as your hamstrings). If you work all sets of muscles surrounding a joint, you will not become muscle-bound. Although ballistic stretching may not be recommended for nonathletes, athletes need to do ballistic stretching to increase their flexibility and ability to develop power. If you are interested in developing high levels of performance fitness, you should include ballistic stretching in your personal conditioning plan.

Pg. 199 True.

Pg. 200 False. This is not normally true because shorter people also have shorter arms than their taller counterparts.

Pg. 201 True.

SECTION 4 REVIEW

Answer the following questions on a separate sheet of paper:

1. What is the minimum frequency recommended for stretching in order to improve flexibility?

2. What time/duration is recommended for the different kinds of stretching to improve flexibility?

Whole-body stretch

Neck stretches

Lower back stretch

Lower back stretches

Calf muscle stretch

Buttocks stretch

Hamstring stretch

Inner thigh stretch

Upper body stretches

Upper back and side stretch

• **Figure 6.12**   *Recommended Stretches to Help You Meet Flexibility Goals Safely. Source:* Adapted from F. S. Sizer, E. N. Whitney, and L. K. DeBruyne, *Making Life Choices: Health Skills and Concepts* (St. Paul: West Publishing, 1994), 251.

Stretches You Can Use in Your Flexibility Plan for Personal Fitness

Choose and safely demonstrate to your instructor one stretch for each of the following parts of your body: your neck, shoulders, abdominals (stomach muscles), low back, quadriceps, hamstrings, groin muscles, and lower leg (calf muscles). Figures 6.13 and 6.14 illustrate and describe more specifically how to perform a variety of stretches for maintaining and developing good to better levels of flexibility. You may need to avoid certain stretching activities because they may increase your risk for injury. Figure 6.14 shows several of the more hazardous stretches, along with suggestions on how you can modify them to make them safer.

• *Figure 6.13* *General Flexibility Routine–Additional Recommended Stretches.*
Source: Adapted from Dintiman et al., *Discovering Lifetime Fitness* (St. Paul: West Publishing, 1989): 113–122.

• *Shoulder shrug*

• *Shoulder blade pull*

(Continued on next page)

• **Figure 6.13**   *(continued)*

• *Shoulder pull*

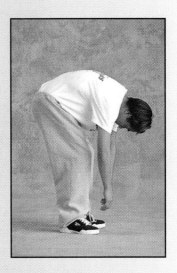

• *Upper torso dangle*

• *Toe touch*

• *Head pull down*

(Continued on next page)

(Continued from previous page)

- *Opposite toe pull*

- *Knee hug*

- *Modified lotus*

- *Side benders*

- *Lower calf stretches*

• **Figure 6.14** *General Flexibility Routine–Hazardous Stretches and Recommended Modifications.* **Do not** *do the exercises shown in the photos on the left. These exercises can cause various strains and sprains, put too much pressure on disks in your back, over stress ligaments and muscles, or in some other way lead to an unnecessary injury. The modifications shown on the right are safe ways to stretch.*

• *Stretch neck roll*

Hazardous   **Modifications**

• *Trunk roll*

(Continued on next page)

• *Toe touch*

Hazardous   **Modifications**

• *Bar stretch*

• *Quadricep stretch*

(Continued on next page)

(Continued from previous page)

Hazardous 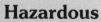   **Modifications**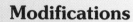

• *Hurdler's stretch*

• *Deep knee bend*

• *Yoga plow*

Hazardous **Modifications**

• *Straight-leg sit-ups*

• *Double leg raise*

• *Prone arch*

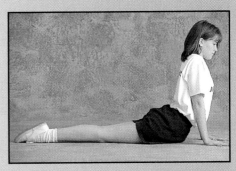

• *Back bend (there is no recommended alternative for the back bend)*

SUMMARY

A moderate to high level of flexibility is important for efficient daily physical movements and to help reduce risks for muscle and bone injuries. Moderate to high levels of flexibility can improve performance fitness and reduce some types of muscle soreness following physical activity or exercise. You can help maintain your good, functional health by maintaining or improving your flexibility. For example, you can help reduce your risk for low back pain and low back injuries by developing flexible and strong muscles that support your spine and pelvic girdle.

Your flexibility levels are influenced by several factors, including your gender, age, genetic makeup, joint structure (connective tissue, such as tendons and ligaments), body temperature, injured joints, excessive body fat, and how active you are. Regular, specific stretching exercises can positively influence your flexibility.

Static stretching, ballistic stretching, reflex-assisted stretching, and passive stretching are all types of stretching that can increase your range of motion (ROM). Static stretching methods are the safest, but the other three types may be important for you to do if you are interested in performance fitness. The easiest strategy for including flexibility exercises in your personal fitness program is to make them part of your regular warm-up and cool-down routines.

Chapter 6 Review

True/False

On a separate sheet of paper, mark each question below either T for True or F for False.

1. When someone tells you that your ROM is within normal limits, it means your flexibility is poor.
2. Hingelike joints allow you to move forward and backward.
3. Your risk of back injuries is increased if you have inflexible and weak muscles that support your spine and pelvic girdle.
4. Lifting movements account for about 50 percent of all low back injuries.
5. The amount of body fat you carry has no effect on how flexible you are.
6. Flexibility can change as much as 80 percent with changes in muscular temperature.
7. Flexibility exercises can reduce the amount of muscle stiffness and soreness you have after exercising.
8. Your flexibility will improve significantly if you go bowling regularly.
9. Ballistic stretching is done very slowly without bouncing up and down.
10. Your reflexes cannot be influenced by a regular stretching program.

Multiple Choice

1. The condition of hyperflexibility is associated with which of the following?
   a. loose joints
   b. tight connective tissue
   c. strong muscles
   d. strong ligaments
2. What percentage of the people on Earth are estimated to have low back pain at one time or another in their lives?
   a. 20 percent
   b. 40 percent
   c. 60 percent
   d. 80 percent
3. Your flexibility is not influenced by which of the following?
   a. genetics
   b. age
   c. height
   d. physical activity level
4. Which of the following factors is the most significant in negatively influencing your flexibility levels?
   a. lack of physical activity
   b. excess body fat
   c. injured joints
   d. your gender
5. Which of the following is not a typical benefit of flexibility conditioning?
   a. increased ROM
   b. increased risk of joint injury
   c. reduced tension and stress levels
   d. increased functional health
6. Plyometric training is a type of _____ stretching.
   a. static
   b. ballistic
   c. reflex-assisted
   d. passive

7. Which of the following types of stretching requires a partner or device to help you complete a stretch?

   a. static
   b. ballistic
   c. reflex-assisted
   d. passive

8. What is the minimum number of days per week that you should do your stretching program to maintain or improve your flexibility levels?

   a. one
   b. two
   c. three
   d. four

9. To improve your flexibility, how must you overload your muscles?

   a. by stretching them beyond their normal resting length
   b. by shortening them below their normal resting length
   c. by lifting, twisting, bending, and pulling
   d. none of the above

10. Which of the following stretches may be hazardous to you and needs to be modified in order for you to do it safely?

   a. knee hug
   b. calf stretch
   c. groin stretch
   d. neck roll

Discussion

1. List and describe five ways you can help reduce your risk for low back pain and low back injuries.

2. Give five benefits that typically follow flexibility conditioning in a previously inactive young adult after 8 to 30 weeks.

3. Identify five stretches that are safe and effective for increasing or maintaining your flexibility levels.

Vocabulary Experience

Match the correct term in Column A to the definition in Column B by writing the appropriate number in each blank.

Column A	**Column B**
____ elasticity	**1.** When one muscle group that controls a joint is too strong in relation to another muscle group that also helps control the joint.
____ plyometrics	**2.** Bounding and jumping exercises.
____ muscle imbalance	**3.** Injury to the muscles, ligaments, tendons, or joints of the lower back.
____ ROM	**4.** The type of stretching that increases the rate at which you develop speed and explosive power.
____ low back injury	**5.** Range of motion or varying degrees of movement.
____ reflex-assisted stretching	**6.** Rubberband-like flexibility.

Critical Thinking

1. Respond to this statement: You can never have enough flexibility.

2. How does maintaining an active lifestyle contribute to the maintenance of the flexibility of your muscles, tendons, and ligaments?

3. Discuss static stretching and why you would recommend this technique to someone just starting a personal fitness program.

Case Study — Bob's Injury

Bob is a fifteen-year-old who is very active and enjoys jogging 3 to 5 miles daily. However, in the past year he has noticed that his muscles feel very tight, his lower back hurts occasionally, and he feels like he has lost some of his flexibility. Bob does not like to stretch and really sees no benefit in it. In fact, he thinks it is a waste of time. However, he is concerned about his loss of flexibility, because he thinks it may increase his risk for injuries during jogging. He would like to improve his flexibility levels back to what is normal for him, but he is not sure how to do so. Therefore, he needs the help of someone knowledgeable about designing and implementing fitness programs—SOMEONE LIKE YOU!

Here is your assignment:

Assume you are Bob's friend, and he asks you for some assistance with his plans for improving his flexibility. Organize a list of things Bob should consider and do before beginning flexibility conditioning. Then list the recommendations you would give Bob for his first two weeks of flexibility conditioning. Use these suggestions as a guide:

KEYS TO HELP YOU

- Consider Bob's history of flexibility conditioning.
- Consider how he should evaluate his current flexibility levels.
- Consider his needs and goals. (For example, how will he find time to do flexibility exercises?)
- Determine a reasonable plan to give Bob that covers the concepts of overload, frequency, intensity, time/duration, and progression.

Chapter 7

Developing Muscular Strength and Endurance through the Science of Weight Training

Contents

Outcomes

After reading and studying this chapter, you will be able to:

1. Discuss the benefits of weight training.
2. Explain how muscular strength and muscular endurance can contribute to good fitness and health.
3. Explain progressive resistance and weight training.
4. Explain how muscles work and grow.
5. Identify the negative effects of steroids.
6. Give examples of weight training myths, and tell why they are incorrect.
7. Describe weight-training equipment and facilities, and discuss how they are used.

Key Terms

After reading and studying this chapter, you will be able to understand and provide practical definitions for the following terms:

relative muscular strength
relative muscular
  endurance
progressive resistance
weight training
cardiac muscle
smooth muscle
skeletal muscle
contract

muscle fiber (muscle cell)
connective tissue
nerve
blood vessel
concentric contraction
eccentric contraction
isotonic progressive
  resistance
isometric contraction

hypertrophy
atrophy
hyperplasia
genetic potential
microtear
testosterone
free weights
weight machines

217

INTRODUCTION

*N*ever before have the benefits of muscular strength and muscular endurance been so accepted and so frequently recommended by experts as being an important part of your physical fitness plan. Experts today have concluded that building muscular strength and endurance, through the use of weight training, is an integral part of good health and fitness for all ages and sexes. Simple, everyday life practices such as climbing a flight of stairs, lifting a backpack full of books, practicing good posture, or any number of running and jumping activities, can become easier and more efficient if weight training is a part of your fitness plan. You should also realize that weight training can have toning, firming, and shaping benefits on our personal appearance.

Years ago lifting weights was thought to be an activity reserved for only a few unusual people, such as the strong man at the circus. It was only a few years ago that professional athletes were not allowed to lift weights for fear it might reduce their speed or limit their abilities to perform. There was even a time when few, if any, exercise and fitness professionals considered lifting weights to be a valuable part of a personal fitness program. In fact, experts considered lifting weights to be potentially harmful to health and fitness.

In the past 15 to 20 years, however, weight training has evolved from the Dark Ages into the Scientific Age—an age that understands its benefits and encourages its use. As a result, students and adults of all ages are going to health clubs, spas, and gyms all across the country to participate in weight training.

This chapter will focus on the benefits of weight training, the different kinds of weight training, and the different kinds of muscles and how they work. You will learn about the many myths that still surround this fitness activity and the equipment associated with weight lifting. Remember, you do not have to be a high-performance athlete to be involved in weight training. *A*ny *B*ody *C*an participate in weight training. All you need is desire.

SECTION 1   How You and Your Muscles Can Benefit from Weight Training

Good levels of physical fitness require adequate levels of both muscular strength and muscular endurance. Even though strength and endurance are closely related, there are some important differences.

Muscular Strength

As you learned in Chapter 4, muscular strength is the amount of force (muscular contraction) a muscle or muscle group can exert against a resistance in one maximum effort. A person who can lift 100 pounds one time during a weight-training exercise is stronger

• *Weight training is a popular physical activity for developing personal fitness.*

relative muscular strength

how much weight you can lift one time in relation to your body weight and gender.

The strongest person may not be the fittest. You do not have to have superhuman strength to be fit and healthy. Although your muscular strength can improve your athletic or performance fitness, your relative muscular strength is more relevant to your functional health. It is important for you to develop and maintain enough strength to carry your body weight efficiently throughout your day-to-day routines. Participation in a regular weight-lifting program can help you achieve this goal.

than a person who can lift 80 pounds one time in the same exercise, regardless of the individual's size, age, or weight.

However, it is important to note that good health and fitness depend more on **relative muscular strength** than on absolute muscular strength. Relative muscular strength is how much weight you can lift in relation to your body weight and gender. For example, Jim weighs 125 pounds and can lift 130 pounds during a weight-training exercise. Wilbur weighs 160 pounds and can lift 150 pounds during the same exercise. Wilbur clearly has the greatest amount of strength, but who is the strongest pound for pound? You can determine this by dividing the amount of weight lifted by the body weight of the individual. The individual with the higher number is exerting more strength per pound of body weight. In this example, Jim has the best *relative* muscular strength:

$$\frac{\text{Bench Press}}{\text{Body Weight}} = \frac{\text{Relative Muscular}}{\text{Strength}}$$

Jim	$\dfrac{\text{Bench Press 130 lbs}}{\text{Body Weight 125 lbs}}$	= 1.04
Wilbur	$\dfrac{\text{Bench Press 150 lbs}}{\text{Body Weight 160 lbs}}$	= .93

Jim's ratio of weight lifted in comparison with his body weight is higher than Wilbur's. In Chapter 8 you will be asked to determine your absolute muscular strength and your relative muscular strength for a variety of weight-lifting exercises.

Muscular Endurance

Muscular endurance, you will recall, is the ability of the same muscle or muscle group to contract for an extended period of time without undue fatigue. The ability to lift 75 pounds on the bench press fifteen times is an example of muscular endurance. Good health and fitness, however, depend more on **relative muscular endurance**. This is measured by how many times you can lift a given weight in relation to your body weight and gender. For example, Jane has a maximum lift of 65 pounds on the shoulder press (an exercise that pushes weight over your head). Susan has a maximum lift of 50 pounds on the shoulder press. If they are asked to do 50 percent of their maximum shoulder press as many times as possible, Susan might do more lifts than Jane. In this case, even though Susan is not the strongest, she has higher relative muscular endurance than does Jane.

If you are interested in improving either your muscular strength or muscular endurance, you might want to experience any of the suggested activities in this chapter. One of the best and most popular ways to improve muscular strength and muscular endurance is to start a weight-training program now!

relative muscular endurance

how many times you can lift a given weight in relation to your body weight and gender.

SECTION 1 REVIEW

Answer the following questions on a separate sheet of paper:

1. Explain the difference between muscular endurance and muscular strength.
2. Why is relative muscular strength more important to physical fitness than just absolute muscular strength?

SECTION 2   Progressive Resistance

To increase a muscle's strength or endurance, you must first overload that muscle. The overload principle is based on putting a greater amount of stress (weight or resistance) on your muscle than the muscle is accustomed to. As your muscle adapts to this stress by becoming stronger, you again increase the amount of stress (more weight or resistance) so that the muscle will continue to grow and become stronger. The continued systematic increase of muscle stress through

progressive resistance

the continued, systematic increase of muscle stress through the use of weights or other forms of resistance.

weight training

the use of such equipment as barbells, dumbbells, and machines to improve fitness, health, and appearance.

the use of weights or other forms of resistance is called **progressive resistance**. **Weight training** (the use of equipment such as barbells, dumbbells, and machines to improve fitness, health, and appearance) has become a very popular and effective way to apply progressive resistance.

The Range of Possibilities

The popularity of weight training has grown tremendously. Weight training is becoming more and more important as science and medicine discover its potential health and fitness benefits. However, the term *weight training* is often misused to describe all forms of progressive resistance. The following is a list of names and descriptions for all forms of progressive resistance training:

- *Weight training.* A general description referring to the use of such equipment as barbells, dumbbells, and machines to improve general fitness, health, and appearance, which **A**ny **B**ody **C**an do.

- *Weight lifting.* Competitive sport lifting performed by athletes who have genetic advantages and who follow very specific programs to build power and strength. For example, an Olympic lifter might perform the clean and jerk or the snatch. A power lifter could do a squat, bench press, and dead lift.

- *Body building.* A competitive sport in which muscle size and shape are more important than muscle strength. Body builders

- *Examples of progressive resistance training: To the Left: Body Building; Center: Olympic Lifting; To the Right: Rehabilitation.*

have genetic advantages and follow very specific programs utilizing many different exercises.

- *Strength training or muscle conditioning.* Training done by competitive sport athletes. The goal is to improve performance in a particular sport and to reduce the chance of injury. The programs of these athletes are specific to their sports.

- *Rehabilitation.* The use of resistance exercises to recover from a muscle or bone injury.

The Many Benefits of Weight Training

There are many reasons why a well-planned weight-training program should be a part of your life. Millions of people are training with weights every day, each for his or her own reasons.

Primary Benefits.   Weight training leads to several primary benefits as listed below, which are directly related to strength gains in both muscles and bones:

Primary Benefits	• Increased size of muscle fibers (bigger muscle) • Increased strength of muscles (stronger muscle) • Increased strength and density of bones (this can prevent a bone disease called osteoporosis) • Increased strength in ligaments and tendons (these connect bones to bones and muscles to bones)

Secondary Benefits	• Increases muscular endurance, which can improve your work capacity (do more work)
	• Helps reduce injury
	  a. serve as shock absorbers for your internal organs when you fall or bump into objects
	  b. protect you from back injuries
	  c. prevent sports injuries
	• Improves personal appearance
	  a. tones, tightens, and shapes muscles
	  b. burns calories, speeds up metabolism, and burns fat (the more muscle you have, the more calories you can burn)
	  c. contributes to good posture
	  d. contributes to good self-esteem and self-concept
	• Improves flexibility if done properly (full range of motion)
	• Enhances sports performance (strength and coordination)
	• Reduces stress in a positive way
	• Can slow down the aging process

As we get older, our bodies shrink in size and strength. Scientists today believe that much of this loss of size and strength is a result of inactivity, not age. Use it or lose it! **A**ny **B**ody **C**an use it!

SECTION 2 REVIEW

Answer the following questions on a separate sheet of paper:

1. Explain the relationship between weight training and progressive resistance.

2. Explain the difference between weight lifting and weight training.

3. In your opinion, which is the most important primary benefit of weight training? Why do you think so?

SECTION 3 The Muscle and How It Works (Physiology)

The muscle is the organ that creates the movement of our bodies. It must contract for movement to occur (Figure 7.1). Understanding how this movement is created can help you better understand and appreciate the many benefits that can be obtained from a weight-training program, now and throughout your life.

BELIEVE IT? ... OR NOT?

Twenty-eight percent of men and 65 percent of women over age seventy-four cannot lift 20 pounds; however, reasonable amounts of weight training can help older adults regain their strength and functional independence, which allows them to care for themselves.

See page 240 for answer.

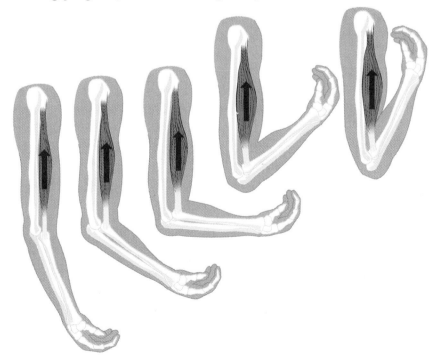

• *Figure 7.1*   *Muscles Become Shorter as They Contract.*

cardiac muscle

muscle in the heart and arteries.

smooth muscle

muscle located around internal organs that automatically controls many functions of the body.

skeletal muscle

muscle located around bones and joints that controls movement.

contract

to shorten.

muscle fibers (muscle cells)

long, thin structures the size of human hairs that contract to create movement. They run the entire length of a muscle.

connective tissue

the "glue" for the body tissue that binds muscles and bones together while still allowing them to move more efficiently.

nerve

in a muscle, the part that delivers the messages from the brain to direct each individual muscle fiber to contract.

blood vessel

in a muscle, the structure that provides oxygen, energy, and a waste removal system for each muscle fiber.

Your body has hundreds of muscles. They are grouped into one of three categories, depending on their function (see Figure 7.2). **Cardiac muscles** are located in the heart. **Smooth muscles** are located around internal organs and arteries, and automatically control many functions of the body. **Skeletal muscles** are located around bones and joints and control movement. Since weight training has little or no effect on cardiac and smooth muscles, the remainder of the chapter will focus mainly on skeletal muscles and how weight training influences them.

Skeletal Muscles: The Movers and Shakers

There are over 430 skeletal muscles in the human body (Figure 7.3). Even though skeletal muscles are usually grouped together, they are also capable of working independently as a highly organized team of movement. Each skeletal muscle has a primary job, which is to **contract** (shorten). When muscles contract, they force bones and joints to move.

Each skeletal muscle contains muscle fibers, connective tissue, nerves, and blood vessels. **Muscle fibers (muscle cells)** are long, thin structures the size of a human hair that contract to produce movement (see Figure 7.4). They run the entire length of the muscle. **Connective tissues** bind the muscles and bones together while still allowing them to move efficiently. Connective tissues include tendons (which connect muscle to bone), ligaments (which connect bone to bone), and cartilage (which is the material located in the joints that serves as a cushion between two bones). (See Figure 7.4.) **Nerves** deliver the messages from the brain that direct each individual muscle fiber to contract. **Blood vessels** provide oxygen, energy, and a waste removal system for each muscle fiber.

The skeletal muscle is capable of three kinds of contraction. Each contraction is unique and is capable of stimulating both muscle growth and muscle strength.

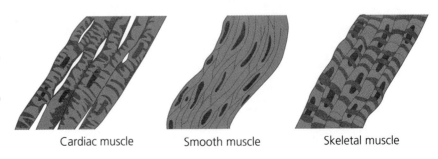

Cardiac muscle   Smooth muscle   Skeletal muscle

• **Figure 7.2**   *Categories of Muscle Tissue.*

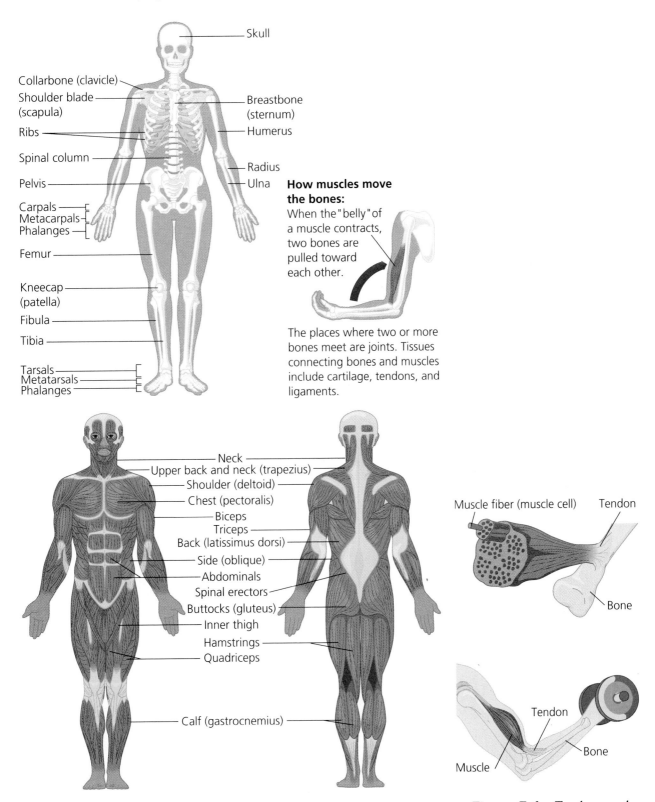

How muscles move the bones:

When the "belly" of a muscle contracts, two bones are pulled toward each other.

The places where two or more bones meet are joints. Tissues connecting bones and muscles include cartilage, tendons, and ligaments.

• **Figure 7.3**   *The Skeletal and Muscular Systems.*

• **Figure 7.4**   *Tendons and How They Attach to the Bone.*

concentric contraction

the contraction and shortening of a muscle, which results in the movement of bones and joints; also called *positive work*.

eccentric contraction

a muscle's slow release of a contraction as it becomes longer; also called *negative work*.

isotonic progressive resistance

a combination of concentric and eccentric muscle contractions.

isometric contraction

a muscle's pushing against an immovable object and having no movement occur as it attempts to contract. The muscle does not become shorter or longer but creates tension.

Concentric Contraction.   When a muscle contracts and becomes shorter, it is undergoing **concentric contraction** (Figure 7.5). The result is a movement of bones and joints. This type of contraction is often referred to as *positive work*.

Eccentric Contraction.   When the muscle slowly releases its contraction and becomes longer, it is undergoing **eccentric contraction** (Figure 7.5). The muscle must control the speed of the lengthening process. The muscle should lengthen slowly and smoothly. Eccentric contraction is often referred to as *negative work*.

If the muscle were to simply relax rather than contract, gravity would quickly pull the arm down. This would not allow for any muscle work to be done during the eccentric contraction. Muscle work during the eccentric contractions is necessary for development of muscle strength and growth. It is believed that eccentric movements cause most of the muscle soreness we experience after weight training sessions.

Most weight-training techniques and equipment combine both concentric and eccentric muscle contractions. This combination of concentric and eccentric muscle contractions is called **isotonic progressive resistance**. It is by far the most popular form of weight training.

Isometric and Static Contractions.   When a muscle pushes against an immovable object, it attempts to contract and create movement, but no movement occurs. This kind of contraction is an **isometric contraction**. The muscle does not become shorter or longer but creates tension (Figure 7.5).

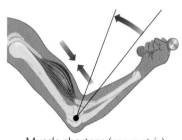

Muscle shortens (concentric)

a

Muscle lengthens (eccentric)

b

Muscle pushes against immovable object (isometric)

c

• *Figure 7.5*   *Different Kinds of Muscle Contraction.*

How and Why Muscles Grow

Even with all of today's scientific technology and equipment, we are still unable to understand exactly how and why muscles grow. However, we do know that weight training, if used over an extended period of time, can and will increase muscle mass.

Hypertrophy—Getting Bigger.   Most experts believe that the number of muscle fibers you have at birth will remain the same throughout your life. These experts believe that muscle growth is due to an enlargement (thickening) of each existing muscle fiber, not to an increase in the number of fibers. This muscle enlargement is called **hypertrophy**.

Most of your muscle growth is caused by the normal growth process that you experience during growth spurts. After your normal growth process stops, however, your muscles are still capable of growth. During weight training, each time you perform a resistance exercise, a chemical is produced that can cause muscle fibers to grow thicker. If each of the thousands of muscle fibers within a muscle slightly increases in size, the entire muscle will become larger.

The exact opposite occurs when you fail to use a muscle. The muscle fibers become smaller, resulting in a smaller muscle. This loss of muscle size is called **atrophy**. For example, the muscles around a broken bone atrophy because the cast around the bone prevents the muscles from being used. They lose some of their size because of lack of use, but this loss is only temporary. The muscles will regain their size after a short time with regular use.

Hyperplasia.   Some experts believe that muscles grow when muscle fibers split and create additional fibers. This process is called **hyperplasia**. The additional fibers, they believe, account for the increase in muscle size. As yet, however, hyperplasia has been seen only in some animals (dogs, cats, and rats).

How and Why Muscles Get Stronger

Increased strength is usually the main goal of individuals who begin a weight-training program. Fortunately, all the primary and secondary benefits listed earlier in this chapter are acquired at the same time. With proper training and good nutrition, weight training can and will improve muscle strength. However, many other factors such as genetic potential, muscle mass, and nerves also affect muscle strength.

Genetic Potential.   Each of us inherits a set number and percentage of different muscle fibers. The individual born with the most muscle fibers has the greatest **genetic potential** for muscle growth.

hypertrophy

muscle enlargement due to the thickening of each existing muscle fiber.

atrophy

a loss of muscle size and strength because of lack of use.

hyperplasia

a theory of muscle enlargement that says muscle growth is due to muscle fibers splitting and creating additional fibers.

genetic potential

inherited muscle characteristics that determine the percentage, type, and number of our muscle fibers.

Hard work in the weight room can help you reach your genetic potential for muscle mass and strength. This does not mean that all individuals can or will obtain the profile of someone like Arnold Schwarzenegger. Very few people are born with the genetic potential to develop muscles with a mass like Schwarzenegger's muscles, no matter how hard they train.

Another genetic factor that influences skeletal muscle growth is the percentage of different types of muscle fibers. As described in an earlier chapter, there are two main types of muscle fibers: fast-twitch and slow-twitch muscle fibers. Fast-twitch fibers are also called *white fibers,* because they are not supplied with much blood. They have a greater capacity to increase in size. They also fatigue very rapidly because they are used more for anaerobic work. Athletic events such as shot put, javelin throw, and football require the use of fast-twitch fibers because these are anaerobic events that require little oxygen.

Slow-twitch fibers are also called *red fibers* because they are richly supplied with blood. These fibers do not grow fast, and they do not have the same capacity for size as the fast-twitch fibers. The slow-twitch fibers do not fatigue as rapidly as fast-twitch fibers and are used more for aerobic work. Activities like cycling, swimming, and running require slow-twitch fibers. Figure 7.6 summarizes the involvement of fast- and slow-twitch fibers in different sports events.

Each of us has both fast-twitch and slow-twitch fibers. The amounts of fast-twitch and slow-twitch fibers we have are determined largely by genetics. However, each of us can realize some degree of muscle growth regardless of our dominant muscle fiber type.

Muscle Mass. The larger the muscle, the greater its potential for strength. As you train, each muscle fiber continues to grow (get

Event	Involvement of Fast-Twitch Fibers	Involvement of Slow-Twitch Fibers
100-yard dash	High	Low
Marathon	Low	High
Olympic weight lifting	High	Low
Barbell squat	High	High
Soccer	High	High
Basketball	High	Low
Distance cycling	Low	High

• **Figure 7.6** *Relative Involvement of Fast-Twitch and Slow-Twitch Skeletal Muscles in Sport Events.*

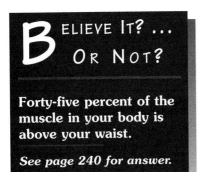

Believe It? ... Or Not?

Forty-five percent of the muscle in your body is above your waist.

See page 240 for answer.

thicker). As the size of the muscle increases, so does its ability to exert force (strength).

Nerves and Muscles (Messages from the Brain). Before a muscle can contract, it must receive a message from the brain. That message is carried by specialized nerves (Figure 7.7). Regular weight-training sessions can improve the ability of nerves to carry messages to a muscle. The messages will then arrive faster and cause more muscle fibers to contract. The result is improved strength.

The beginning weight trainer can attribute most early gains in strength (that is, in the first one to two months) to the nerves' ability to get a better response from the muscle fibers. Continued strength gains will then come from muscle hypertrophy (muscle mass increase).

Other Factors Associated with Muscle Strength. Several other factors can influence the development of muscular strength. Consistent training habits (working out regularly) are important. Your current level of strength is another factor in how fast you'll gain muscular strength. Beginning lifters will see a more rapid strength improvement than experienced weight trainers. Strength will also improve at a rate based on your training intensity. Intensity includes how hard you work and the kind of program (strength versus endurance) you follow. Intensity is also based on the number of sets and repetitions, as well as which muscles are being worked. Finally, strength gain depends on the length of the training program (weeks, months, or years). The longer you work, the more you can improve your strength.

> **66** A feeble body weakens the mind.
> **Jean Jacques Rousseau** **99**

Messages to and from brain

Nerve

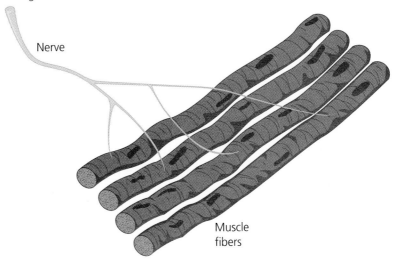

Muscle fibers

• **Figure 7.7**   *Nerves–Connecting Muscles to the Brain.*

The Dangers of Steroids

Steroids are drugs that are illegal and very hazardous to your health. However, many people still use these drugs. Why? People use steroids because they think steroids will give them a performance advantage.

There is no place for the use of steroids in the world of health and fitness. Steroids, health, and fitness simply do not go together. The following is a list of both the long-term and short-term effects of steroids.

Long-term effects	• Increased risk of developing coronary heart disease. • Higher levels of cholesterol. • Elevated blood pressure. • Kidney and liver damage. • Sexual dysfunction. • Increased risk of cancer.
Short-term effects	• Acne. • Loss of hair in males, and facial hair growth in females. • Nausea, diarrhea, fever, and nosebleeds. • Increased appetite. • Psychological symptoms, including aggressive behavior (Roid Rage). • Reduction of hormone secretion.

Why Are My Muscles Sore?

We have all experienced some muscle soreness at one time or another, usually after an active or vigorous session of muscle use. The beginning stages of weight training will also produce a certain amount of muscle soreness. This soreness is usually delayed twenty-four to forty-eight hours after the workout. Don't let this discourage you. It is normal. Everyone has it. With proper training technique and time, the soreness will go away.

There are two main theories about why muscles get sore. The first theory is that **microtears**, or small tears, occur when parts of the muscle fibers and connective tissue actually tear due to the greater-than-usual resistance. These tears are not a serious problem, however. With rest and good nutrition, muscles quickly repair themselves, and you are ready for the next workout.

The second theory of muscle soreness suggests that during intense exercise, a muscle may not receive all the oxygen it needs (anaerobic exercise). Even though this oxygen deficiency is temporary, it may still contribute to soreness. As mentioned earlier, it is during the eccentric (lengthening) movement that most muscle soreness is acquired.

microtear

a small tear in a part of a muscle fiber or connective tissue because of greater-than-usual resistance; causes muscle soreness.

Treatments for Muscle Soreness

There are several strategies for helping alleviate muscle soreness. First, let time heal the muscles. After three days most soreness is usually gone. Be sure to stretch before and after workouts. Reduce the amount of weight you lift, and do a light workout. Finally, drink plenty of water, and eat a sensible diet.

SECTION 3 REVIEW

Answer the following questions on a separate sheet of paper:

1. List and explain the three kinds of muscular contraction.
2. Explain the difference between hypertrophy and atrophy, and discuss how each occurs.
3. How is muscular strength influenced by genetic potential?
4. Explain the theory of muscle soreness associated with microtears.

SECTION 4   Weight Training and Its Many Myths

For years people did not include weight-training sessions in their personal fitness programs. Their decisions to avoid weight training were based on misinformation and the belief that weight training was not healthy. Today, however, people all over the world are participating in and enjoying the many benefits of weight training. This section will explain the differences between the muscles of males and females, identify many of the myths associated with women and weight training, and discuss other myths surrounding weight training.

Myths Associated with Women and Weight Training

Myth 1: Females Who Lift Weights Will Develop Big, Bulky Muscles Like Those of Males.   The average female compared with the average male has a smaller and lighter skeleton, has narrower shoulders, has about 8 percent more body fat, and is 30 to 40 pounds lighter. She also has less muscle mass. The quality of her muscles is the same as the male's. The woman, however, possesses fewer muscle fibers, and those muscle fibers are thinner. (This is determined by genetic potential.) Males, in contrast, generally have considerably more muscle mass and therefore are able to develop bigger and stronger muscles. These differences become much more obvious during the adolescent years and the onset of puberty.

A major reason for the strength and size differences between males and females is the male hormone **testosterone**. Testosterone plays an important role in building muscles. Women do possess testosterone, but at much lower levels than do men.

In summary, females have fewer muscle fibers than males, their muscle fibers are thinner in size, and their levels of testosterone are lower. Some hypertrophy will occur in females, but it is very unlikely that their muscles will become as large as men's muscles.

Myth 2: Female Muscles Will Not Develop Strength.
The average female has less strength than the average male, especially upper body strength. This does not mean females are incapable of obtaining strength, however. When males and females are placed in similar weight-training programs, their strength improvements are similar. In fact, females may improve more because of the lower level at which they started.

In summary, females can develop very beneficial levels of strength in all parts of their bodies. Often females and males have equal relative muscle strength (strength in relation to their body weight).

Myth 3: Weight Training Has Few Benefits for Women and Will Only Detract from Their Personal Appearance ("Defeminize" Them).
Thousands of females concerned about their health and fitness are utilizing weight-training rooms. They now realize the muscle toning, muscle shaping, and weight-control benefits of weight training. In addition, females who follow weight-training programs have stronger muscles and a greater capacity to handle daily tasks, as well as unexpected emergencies. Properly designed programs can help females reach their personal appearance goals and improve their self-esteem. Tight, firm muscles have nothing to do with looking less feminine.

In summary, females can obtain the same weight-training benefits as males. A well-designed program can help females look feminine, but with better-toned muscles and less fat.

Other Weight-training Myths

Myth 4: With Enough Time and Effort, Anyone Can Be a World-Class Bodybuilder or Power Weight Lifter.
You can expect strength and mass improvements as a result of weight training, but you are always limited to your genetic potential. Not everyone can obtain the same results.

---

testosterone

a male hormone that plays an important role in building muscles.

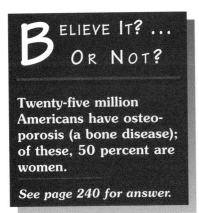

BELIEVE IT? ...
OR NOT?

Twenty-five million Americans have osteoporosis (a bone disease); of these, 50 percent are women.

See page 240 for answer.

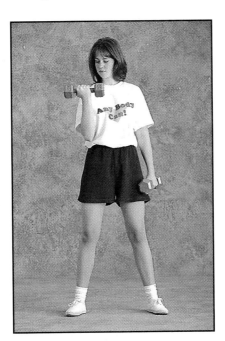

• *More and more women are finding out first hand about the benefits of weight training.*

Myth 5: Muscle Can Turn to Fat if a Person Stops Lifting Weights. Muscle and fat are actually separate kinds of tissue and do not change from one to the other. If you stop lifting, however, you will see a decrease in your muscle size (atrophy). If you continue to eat the same amount and do not exercise, you will gain weight in the form of fat.

Myth 6: Weight Training Reduces Flexibility. Most people who lift properly will actually increase their flexibility. The key is

• *Weight training is just as popular and beneficial for women as men.*

to lift weights through a full range of motion, which keeps the muscles stretched.

Myth 7: Weight Training Will Make You Slower and Less Coordinated.   Weight training can actually improve your strength. That means you can better coordinate your body movements and slightly increase your speed.

> " Exercise and temperance can preserve something of our early strength even in old age.
>
> Cicero
> (106 BC–43 BC) Roman orator and statesman. *An Old Age, X* "

Myth 8: Elderly People Should Avoid Weight Training.   Today doctors are actually encouraging older people to use weight training to improve or maintain their ability to walk, lift things, climb stairs, and stay active and healthy.

Myth 9: Weight Training Is a Good Way to Improve Cardiovascular Fitness.   Weight training is an anaerobic activity that will do little to improve cardiovascular fitness. Other activities such as jogging, cycling, and swimming, must be used to improve cardiovascular fitness.

Myth 10: Weight Training Is Harmful to the Growth and Development of Adolescents.   Most adolescents are able to participate in safe, well-organized, and supervised weight-lifting programs. Weight training can help adolescents obtain many of the same weight-training benefits adults get from this training. In fact, as you go through your adolescent growth spurt, weight training can be very beneficial to you because it can help you maximize the development of your bones.

Any Body Can!

Kevin Saunders

Kevin Saunders is a world-class wheelchair Paralympic champion. He is the first person with a disability to serve on the President's Council on Physical Fitness.

Kevin Saunders was born on December 8, 1955 in Downs, Kansas and grew up on a farm where he learned to work hard from dawn to dusk. In high school he played football and participated in track. As a senior he played quarterback in football and participated in the state tournament in the discus. Following high school, Kevin attended two different community colleges where he played soccer and football. He later transferred to Kansas State University and participated in the club sport of rugby.

Kevin graduated from Kansas State in 1978 and began a job as a federal inspector for the United States Department of Agriculture. His first assignment was in Corpus Christi, Texas. On April 7, 1981, Kevin was at the Port of Corpus Christi Public Elevator to check on grain dust collection, which is highly flammable. At 3:10 P.M. that day an explosion ripped through the area of the elevator where Kevin was working. The explosion threw Kevin 300 feet into the air and over a two-story building into a parking lot, fracturing his skull, collapsing one lung, breaking his shoulder blade, and paralyzing him from the chest down. Doctors said he would not survive, but he did.

After two weeks in intensive care and living in a coma-like state, Kevin accepted what he'd suspected—he would never walk again. His doctor told him, "you'll be confined to a wheelchair the rest of your life." Kevin screamed, "No way! That can't be right!"

Kevin was mad about the accident and his condition (which is understandable). When he was released from the hospital, it took him several months of frustrating rehabilitation to regain his work ethic and motivation to get on with his life.

In 1983 Kevin became motivated to train to rehabilitate his body, because he was very weak. He read and learned how to train scientifically, and began lifting weights and "running" (in his wheelchair). In 1984 he won a bronze medal (3rd place) in the pentathlon (a one-day muscular strength and endurance competition that includes the shot put, the javelin, the 200 meters, the discus, and the 1500 meters) at the National Wheelchair Track and Field Championships.

In 1988 he competed in the Olympic Games in Seoul, Korea where he earned a bronze medal in the pentathlon. In 1992, Kevin competed in the Olympic Games again in Barcelona, Spain. He was able to bring home another bronze medal in the pentathlon event. Later in 1992, Kevin was appointed to the President's Council on Physical Fitness, which was a dream come true for him.

Kevin spends his time now training and lecturing to groups about physical fitness all over the U.S. He has become a hero to young and old, abled and disabled. His autobiography, "There's Always A Way," written with Bob Darden is highly motivating.

Fortunately not everyone has to overcome the personal challenges that Kevin Saunders did to become a champion athlete, but Any Body Can learn to develop and maintain muscular strength and endurance. That's right, you can do it!

SECTION 5   Preparing to Lift

Before you ever push up a barbell or curl a dumbbell, you need to know some important facts. You need to consider such things as proper clothing, footwear, equipment, and facilities—all of which are important to your continued success. How you prepare now can determine your future success and safety.

Clothing and Equipment

The following are some tips for choosing proper clothing and equipment.

Clothes.   A variety of styles, colors, and sizes of clothing can be worn in the weight room. Weight-training clothing is designed to enhance your comfort, performance, and safety in the weight room. Your clothes should be nonbinding to allow full range of motion. They should also keep you warm or cool, depending on the temperature of your workout facility. Wearing layers can help you control your body temperature. Be careful not to wear pieces of clothing that can easily get tangled or caught on the equipment.

Footwear.   You should always wear properly fitted shoes. They should be designed to give you good arch support and to provide a nonslip surface. A cross-training shoe is probably the best style, because it provides better ankle support. Wearing a pair of absorbent socks can help prevent blisters.

Gloves.   You may need a pair of weight-training gloves, which have no fingers. They cover your palms, where most of the blisters and calluses form on your hands. If you have sensitive skin on your hands or you want to avoid rough hands, wear gloves. Gloves will

BELIEVE IT? ... OR NOT?

A pound of fat is 18 percent bigger than a pound of muscle, which means more inches for you to carry.

See page 240 for answer.

• *Examples of weight training equipment: Straps, gloves, belts, weight plates, collars, and dumbbells.*

also improve your grip, should the bars or handles on the exercise machines become slippery.

Weight-training Belts.   The primary purpose of a weight-training belt is to protect your lower back and stomach when you lift heavy weights. The belt gives the stomach muscles something to push against and, as a result, causes pressure to build up in the abdomen. This pressure pushes against and stabilizes the lower spine, which protects the lower back.

Be aware that wearing belts causes an increase in blood pressure. For this reason, belts should be worn only during lifting exercises. Loosen or remove your belt when you rest between lifting exercises. Belts come in all sizes and are made of leather or synthetic fabrics.

Straps and Wraps.   Straps are 1-½ inch wide strips of canvaslike material that are wrapped around your wrist and then twisted around a bar. They are used for very heavy lifts when your grip cannot support the weight. Wraps or elastic bandages are used to give additional support to joints. They are most often used during heavy leg exercises. They can provide support, but they also restrict your range of motion.

Free Weights or Weight Machines?

Weight training can be performed using a variety of equipment. Most weight-training facilities have a variety of both free weights and weight machines.

Equipment such as dumbbells, barbells, plates, and clips is called **free weights**. The name *free weight* describes the unlimited direction and movement capacity of this equipment. This freedom of movement also creates a greater potential for accidents, however, because more balance and coordination is needed than is required when using machines. Thus, you may need a partner or spotter for your safety when you use free weights. Free weights do provide the

free weights

objects of varied weights that can be moved without restriction and used for weight lifting; examples are barbells and dumbbells.

CONSUMER CORNER

Buying Weight-Training Equipment

If you are interested in starting a weight-lifting program, you have a number of options. You could join a health club and use its equipment. This can become expensive, however, because you are usually required to pay monthly fees.

You may be able to use the weight room facilities at your school, but you may run into conflicts caused by time and supervision schedules. If you can find a time to work out at your school, this will probably be your best choice because of convenience and lack of expense.

One other option is to purchase your own equipment to use at home. Free weights (dumbbells, barbells, plates, clips, and so on), are often a consumer's first choice for use at home, because they are less expensive and take up less room than other equipment. If you purchase free weights, be aware that the cheapest product may not be the wisest consumer choice. For example, plastic weights filled with sand do not last as long as metal weights.

Exercising at home with weight machines has become popular. Many different models are available. If you choose to purchase a weight machine for home use, you first need to consider how much you can afford to spend, your space limitations, how durable the machine is, and if it is appropriate for your personal needs and goals.

Active Mind! Active Body!

What Is in Your Weight Room?

Use the equipment checklist in Figure 7.8 to identify all the equipment in your school's weight-training facility. You may also want to use this checklist at the local health club or YMCA facility. Include specific details when you describe equipment.

Free weight	Description
Type of bar:	
Olympic	_____
standard	_____
cambered	_____
Dumbbells:	
type and weight	_____
Benches and weight racks:	_____
Weight plates:	
type and weight	_____

Machines	
Name of machine and specific muscle to be used:	
1. _____	
2. _____	
3. _____	
4. _____	
5. _____	
6. _____	
Other Equipment:	
weight belts	_____
mats	_____
jump ropes	_____
scales	_____
Other Concerns:	
temperature	_____
sound system	_____
lighting	_____

• **Figure 7.8**   *What Is in Your School's Weight Room?*

advantage of being more versatile and less expensive than other weight-training equipment.

Weight-training equipment designed to move weights up and down using a system of cables and pulleys is called **weight machines**. Most machines are designed to work only one muscle area and require little or no balance. They do not require spotters because the weights are connected to the machine and have a predetermined path of movement. With weight machines it is easy to vary the resistance. You simply move a pin to the new weight selection. Weight

weight machines

a system of cables and pulleys designed for the movement of weights as used in weight-training exercises.

machines are much more expensive, however, than free weights and take up large amounts of space. Do the Active Mind/Active Body activity on the preceding page to identify the types of weights in your school's weight room.

Both free weights and weight machines are capable of producing strength and mass improvements through isotonic progressive resistance training. Understanding the advantages and disadvantages of each type of equipment can help you decide which is best for you. Figure 7.9 compares the advantages and disadvantages of free weights and weight machines.

Factor	Free Weights	Machines	Advantage
Cost	Much less expensive, $200 can acquire all you need, one size fits all	Very costly to purchase, maintenance cost, need a variety of machines or pay membership to a club	Free weights
Space	Takes minimal space and may be moved easily	Big, bulky, and heavy; difficult to move	Free weights
Safety	Spotters are required, balance is required, greater chance of injury, weights get left laying around which can cause accidents	Weights cannot fall on you, requires no balance or spotters to lift	Machine
Variety	Allows for many different exercises with the same equipment, helps prevent boredom, works all parts of the body	Usually only one exercise can be done on a machine, need many machines to provide variety, can be boring	Free weights
Technique/Balance	Harder to learn, much more complicated technique, balance is a necessity	Much easier to learn, no balance required	Machine
Time	Requires partner, takes more time to change weight plates	Less total time, can do alone, easier to change amount of resistance	Machine
Beginning lifter	Need a partner, harder technique to learn, balance	Safer, quicker, no need for spotter, easier to learn technique	Machine
Athletic Power and Coordination	Requires coordination and balance of many muscles at same time—more like actual sport activity	Isolates single muscle and reduces need for balance	Free weights
Motivation	Easier to determine and see strength improvement	Harder to understand strength improvement	Free weights

• **Figure 7.9** *Comparison of Free Weights and Weight Machines.*

SECTION 5 REVIEW

Answer the following questions on a separate sheet of paper:

1. Explain how weight-training gloves, weight-training belts, and straps can be of use in the weight room.

2. List what you feel are the three most important advantages of free weights and the three most important advantages of weight machines.

SUMMARY

Muscular strength and endurance are health-related fitness components that everyone should consider vital to good health and fitness. The benefits of muscular strength and endurance are important to you now and throughout your adult life. The sooner you get started, the more protection you will give your body against future problems associated with poor strength and endurance. Weight training is a safe and popular way to incorporate strength and endurance into your life. Understanding how and why your muscles become bigger and stronger can help you consistently participate in progressive resistance activities.

For years, weight training was surrounded by myths that led people to believe that it should be avoided. Fortunately, medical and fitness experts today see weight training as a needed and valued part of a total fitness program.

The existence of many different kinds of weight-training machines and free weights makes it necessary for you to understand the advantages and disadvantages of each so you can be a wise consumer. Weight training can be an enjoyable and beneficial activity that **A**ny **B**ody **C**an do.

Chapter 7 Review

True/False

On a separate sheet of paper, mark each question below either T for True or F for False.

1. The maximum amount of force a muscle can exert against a resistance is muscular strength.
2. Relative muscular strength takes into consideration your body weight and your strength.
3. Putting greater stress on a muscle than it is accustomed to is the principle of specificity.
4. Body builders, athletes, and power lifters use the same kind of weight-training programs.
5. A primary benefit of weight training is the prevention of a bone disease called osteoporosis.
6. Tendons and ligaments are forms of connective tissue.
7. Eccentric muscle contractions are called *positive work.*
8. Isometric contractions start by lengthening and then get shorter.
9. The term *hypertrophy* is used to describe how muscle fibers get thicker and cause muscles to grow.
10. Most experts believe that heavy weight training and good nutrition will increase the number of muscle fibers a person was born with.
11. Slow-twitch muscle fibers contribute more to muscle endurance, while fast-twitch muscle fibers contribute more to muscle mass and strength.

Multiple Choice

1. Which of the following is an example of muscular endurance?
   a. five arm curl reps with 20 pounds
   b. fifteen bench press reps with 75 pounds
   c. ten sit-ups
   d. a fifteen-second isometric contraction

2. When Bob started weight lifting six months ago, he was able to shoulder press 50 pounds, eight times. Later, he was able to press the same weight twelve times. He then increased the weight to 60 pounds and pressed it eight times. Which of the following exercise principles is Bob using?
   a. overload
   b. specificity
   b. intensity
   d. progressive resistance

3. What term describes the use of barbells, dumbbells, and machines to improve fitness, health, and appearance?
   a. body building
   b. strength and conditioning
   c. weight training
   d. weight lifting

4. Which of the following is not a benefit of weight training?
   a. significant increase in cardiovascular efficiency
   b. increased bone strength and density
   c. slowing of the aging process and reduction in stress
   d. faster metabolism and better self-esteem

5. Skeletal muscle does which of the following?
   a. moves bones and joints
   b. protects against injury
   c. burns up calories
   d. all of the above
   e. a and b only

6. Which of the following is *not* a part of each skeletal muscle?
   a. nerves
   b. blood vessels
   c. muscle fibers
   d. cartilage

7. When the muscle becomes shorter, what kind of a contraction is it?

    a. eccentric
    b. concentric
    c. isometric
    d. isotonic

8. Which of the following is not a result of steroid use?

    a. coronary heart disease
    b. kidney damage
    c. decreased appetite
    d. loss of hair in men

9. What is the main reason that females do not grow muscles as large as males do?

    a. Females do not lift hard enough.
    b. Females do not have as much testosterone as men.
    c. The female body is not capable of lifting heavy weights.
    d. Females do not spend enough time in the weight room.

10. Free weights are common in most weight rooms. Which one of the following is *not* an advantage of free weights?

    a. They cost less.
    b. They take up less space.
    c. They are less dangerous.
    d. They require more balance.

Discussion

1. Define and give an example of relative muscular endurance.

2. Discuss the ways in which weight training can improve your personal appearance.

3. Define and give examples of isotonic progressive resistance.

4. Identify and explain five myths associated with weight training.

Vocabulary Experience

Match the correct term in Column A to the definition in Column B by writing the appropriate number in each blank.

Column A

____ relative muscular strength

____ overload principle

____ hypertrophy

____ genetic potential

____ muscular strength

Column B

1. The amount of force a muscle or muscle group can exert in one maximum effort.

2. Applying greater stress to a muscle than it is normally accustomed to.

3. Your strength in relation to your weight.

4. An increase in the size of a muscle.

5. An inherited limitation.

Critical Thinking

1. Explain the differences between weight training and body building.

2. Respond to the following statement: I'm an athlete, and if steroids can make me be the best I can be, I'm going to use them.

3. List and explain reasons why females can benefit from weight training.

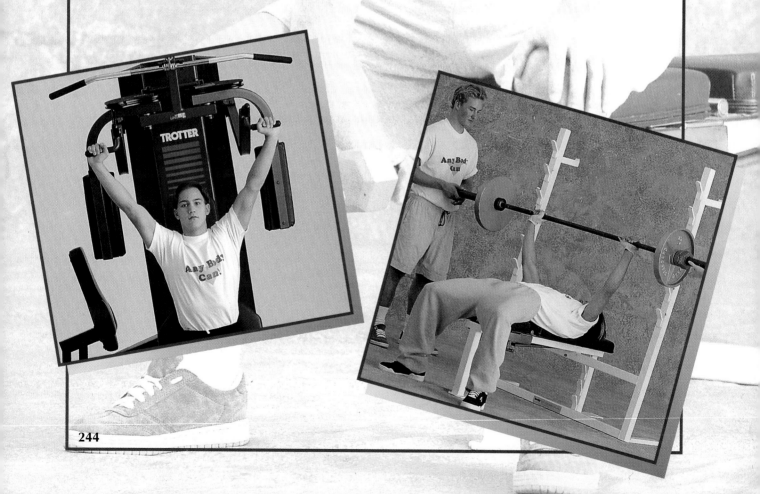

Start Lifting—Safely and Correctly

Contents

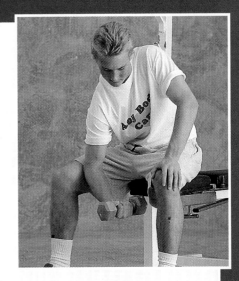

1. Setting Obtainable Goals
2. Weight-lifting Safety
3. Considerations for Your First Workout
4. Developing and Maintaining Muscular Fitness
5. Programs for Strength and Hypertrophy
6. Exercises, Muscles, and Proper Technique

Outcomes

After reading and studying this chapter, you will be able to:

1. Identify and explain obtainable goals for weight training.
2. Demonstrate and explain correct safety practices for a weight lifter.
3. Demonstrate and discuss safety practices for a spotter.
4. List and discuss all the components of a weight-training workout and how they are interrelated.
5. Discuss how frequency, intensity, and time/duration are used in developing weight-training programs.
6. Explain the purposes of strength testing and how you can evaluate your own strength.
7. Explain the differences among a variety of weight-training programs.
8. Demonstrate and explain the correct lifting technique for a variety of weight-training exercises.
9. Design a suitable weight-training program to meet your personal goals, and explain it.

Key Terms

After reading and studying this chapter, you will be able to understand and provide practical definitions for the following terms:

spotters
wraparound thumb grip
  (closed grip)
repetition (rep)
set
weight-training circuit
large muscle group

small muscle group
muscle intensity
training load
recovery time
weight-training cycle
split workout
pyramid training

multiple set method
negative workout method
superset method
antagonistic muscles
compound set method

INTRODUCTION

*H*aving completed Chapter 7, you now know the benefits of weight training and how your muscles grow and become stronger. You may have acquired clothing and equipment suitable for weight training. As soon as you have established your goals, you will be ready to "pump some iron."

This chapter will teach you about the safety practices associated with every aspect of weight training. You will also learn how to evaluate your strength and design a personal weight-training program to meet your needs. In addition, you will learn how to perform properly many different weight-training exercises and other strength-building activities.

SECTION 1   Setting Obtainable Goals

Setting realistic and challenging strength goals is closely connected with your continued success in weight training. A properly planned program can help keep you motivated even through difficult times, when progress is not as fast as you would like it to be. If you keep in mind that you are working toward progress and self-improvement, you will have a better chance at being successful.

Why and How to Set Goals

You are more likely to realize the benefits of a weight-training program if you have a desired goal. Having a well-designed personal goal can help you achieve any task. People who set goals tend to accomplish more than those who don't set goals.

Goals also help keep you motivated. Each time you realize a goal, you feel good about yourself. You are then more likely to establish an even more challenging goal.

Before you set any goal, consider each of the following:

- *Your age.* Adolescents may want strength and muscle mass, whereas older adults may want more endurance and less body fat.

- *Your gender.* Males and females may or may not have the same goals.

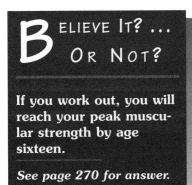

- *Your physical maturation.* How much growth and development you already have can determine reasonable and obtainable goals for you.

- *Your current level of strength.* Beginners can expect rapid gains, whereas advanced and intermediate lifters will have slower progress. Strength pretests can be used to determine strength improvements.

- *Your physical limitations or past injuries.* Your goals may need to be modified if you realize that you are not capable of certain tasks.

- *Your work habits.* How much time you have affects your workout.

Rules for Writing Goals

You should write down your weight-training goals on a sheet of paper, a technique that increases the chances that you will stick to your plan. Here are some important rules to follow as you write your goals:

1. Make the goals reasonable and obtainable, but not too easy.

2. Establish long- and short-term goals. The short-term goals act as motivators to keep you going. For example, suppose you can lift 100 pounds on the bench press now, and you would like to be able to do 135 pounds. Thus, your long-term goal is to lift 135 pounds. Your short-term goals could be to lift 110 pounds, then 120 pounds, then 130 pounds, and finally 135 pounds. Give yourself a reasonable amount of time between each short-term goal.

3. Have a variety of short-term goals, such as controlling your body weight and percentage of body fat, improving your eating habits, and having regular workout attendance. These short-term goals can help you reach your long-term goals.

4. If you have an injury or become ill, it may be necessary to revise your goals.

REMEMBER **This!**

Goals are personal. They represent your desires. If goals are reasonable and obtainable, Any Body Can improve.

SECTION 1 REVIEW

Answer the following questions on a separate sheet of paper:

1. List and explain four things to consider before setting goals for weight training.

2. Why is it important to develop short-term goals?

SECTION 2   Weight-lifting Safety

Safety should always be a foremost consideration when lifting weights. If you don't observe basic safety guidelines at all times, your risk of injury can be great. The following is a list of basic guidelines that can help reduce the possibility of an accident when you lift weights:

BELIEVE IT? ... OR NOT?

Once you get a semester's worth of experience in weight training, you will no longer need to use spotters when you lift.

See page 270 for answer.

1. Have a partner when lifting free weights.

2. Make sure you are familiar with the proper use of all weight equipment prior to using it. Also be familiar with the weight-training area.

3. A brief heart and muscle warm-up combined with specific stretching may be helpful.

4. Never hold your breath. Exhale during the concentric (positive) stage. This can prevent dizziness or fainting.

5. Never sacrifice proper technique to lift extra weight. Cheating can lead to injury.

6. Wear safety belts when doing heavy exercises that require the use of abdominal and back muscles.

7. Use collars for all free weights.

8. Control the speed of the weights at all times.

9. Progress slowly over a period of time.

10. Allow for rest between training days (usually forty-eight hours).

11. Return all equipment to its proper place after using it.

12. Be alert at all times!

13. Act responsibly. The weight-lifting area is no place for irresponsible behavior.

Are Spotters Necessary?

spotters

individuals who assist you with weight-room safety.

Spotters are classmates or friends who assist you with weight room safety. Their responsibilities are very important and should not be taken lightly. How well they perform their duties can make the difference between your having a successful, safe workout or an injury. Spotters should be required for free-weight lifts, such as the bench press, the overhead press, and squats. They may not be necessary for other lifts, but it is always a good idea to have a partner, just in case.

• *Proper spotting techniques should be used at all times in the weight room to maximize safety.*

The spotter has three main jobs:

1. Assist the lifter when help is needed to keep the weight moving in a smooth, steady motion. (The spotter should stay ready at all times.)

2. Observe and point out any improper technique being used by the lifter.

3. Be a motivator. Encourage the partner to maintain an acceptable level of intensity.

In addition to the three primary jobs just described, the spotter should do the following:

• Keep the lifting area free of weights or other equipment that could get in the way.

• Put the proper amount of weight on the bar, and have it evenly spaced.

• Keep body and hands in a ready position at all times.

• Communicate with the lifter. Make sure the commands are understood. Know how many repetitions will be attempted.

• Know how to properly apply enough help without jerking the bar.

• Be ready to assume all the weight, if necessary.

• Be alert at all times!

Lifting—The Right Way

Each weight-training exercise has a specific lifting technique. Later in this chapter, you will learn a variety of weight-training exercises and their proper techniques.

General Lifting Guidelines.

You should follow some guidelines for all weight-training exercises. It is important that you learn and apply these guidelines, especially when using free weights.

(a)

(b)

(c)

• **Figure 8.1** *Bar grips: (a) Overhand, (b) Underhand, and (c) Alternated.*

- Practice all techniques with a very light weight before attempting heavier resistance.
- Know how to use the correct grip for each exercise.
- Communicate with your spotter. Make sure you understand each other's verbal and nonverbal commands.
- Keep your back straight at all times, whether you are lying down or standing.
- When performing standing lifts, be sure to have a wide, stable base with your feet flat on the floor.
- When lifting objects from the floor, use your legs, not your back.
- Keep the weight close to your body.
- All lifts should be done through a full range of motion. This means that muscles should be flexed and extended completely when you lift.
- Concentrate on the muscles that should be doing the work.
- Breathe out (exhale) during the exertion (concentric) phase.
- Breathe in (inhale) during the relaxing (eccentric) phase.
- Never hold your breath, as this can reduce the flow of blood and oxygen to your brain. A lack of oxygen can cause you to pass out while you are lifting.
- Do not hyperventilate (breathe rapidly). Control your breathing at all times.
- Make sure you keep your hands on the bar and maintain pressure until all weights are put safely back on the racks.

---

wraparound thumb grip (closed grip)

a grip used in lifting in which the fingers and thumb go in opposite directions around the bar to help keep the bar from rolling out of the hand.

Proper Grips and Grip Placement.

There are three kinds of grips: the overhand, underhand, and alternated. Their use is determined by the specific exercise to be done. Each of these grips should be done with a **wraparound thumb grip (closed grip)**. In this grip, the fingers and thumb go in opposite directions around the bar, which helps keep the bar from rolling out of the hand (see Figure 8.1).

In the overhand grip, your palms face away from you as you grab the bar. In the underhand grip, your palms face you as you grab the bar. In the alternated grip, one palm faces away from you, and one palm faces you.

There are three widths of grip placement. Their use is determined by the exercise (see Figure 8.2). In the common grip, your hands are evenly spaced, about shoulders' width apart. In the narrow grip, your hands are evenly spaced, but close together. In the wide grip, your hands are evenly spaced, but wider than shoulders' width apart.

• **Figure 8.2**   *Grip Placement. From left to right: Wide, Common, and Narrow.*

SECTION 2 REVIEW

Answer the following questions on a separate sheet of paper:

1. List and explain four reasons why spotters are necessary in the weight room.

2. Why is it important to use proper breathing techniques when lifting weights?

3. Explain the difference between overhand and underhand weight-lifting grips.

SECTION 3 Considerations for Your First Workout

There are several different ways you can vary your weight-training program. Before you design and begin a personal program, make sure you clearly understand each of the following components of weight-training routines: the repetition, the set, the exercises you can choose from, the muscle groups being worked, and the order of exercise (Figure 8.3).

The Repetition

repetition (rep)

the completed execution of an exercise one time.

Each time you lift a weight, do a push-up, or do a chin-up, you have completed a **repetition**, or **rep**. If you do ten push-ups, you have completed ten reps. A person who does a squat twice with 150 pounds has completed two reps with 150 pounds. Reps are the basic unit of any workout plan. The number of reps will vary, depending on your goals.

set

a group of consecutive reps for an exercise.

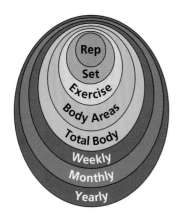

• **Figure 8.3** *The Workout Plan. The Complete Weight-training Program Includes All the Parts of a Workout Shown Here.*

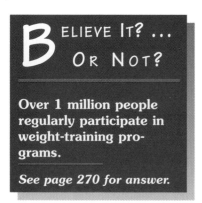

BELIEVE IT? ... OR NOT?

Over 1 million people regularly participate in weight-training programs.

See page 270 for answer.

The Set

Each time you complete a group of consecutive reps for any exercise, you have completed a **set**. If you do ten reps of push-ups consecutively, you have done one set of ten reps. If you repeat the process (ten more push-ups) after a short rest, you have completed a total of two sets of ten reps. The number of sets in each workout can vary. The number of sets, like the number of repetitions, will be determined by your goals.

You can describe your workout using numbers to indicate sets and reps. The first number will always indicate sets; the second number, reps. For example, Renée has decided to lift three sets of twelve reps, which she can indicate by writing 3×12 (the $\times$ means "times"). 4×5 will indicate four sets of five reps.

The Exercises

Just as there are special exercises for cardiovascular endurance and flexibility, there are exercises developed especially for weight-

• *Keeping a log of your weight training goals and workout information can help you keep track of your progress.*

training. All of the weight-training exercises involve the use of equipment—either free weights, such as barbells and dumbbells, or weight machines. Some of the more common weight training exercises are *bench press, arm curl,* and *squats.* You'll learn how to do these exercises and many more in this chapter. You will also learn which parts of your body benefit from each type of exercise. This knowledge will enable you to choose the most appropriate exercises for each muscle group that you want to develop.

Muscle Groups

The Six Major Body Areas

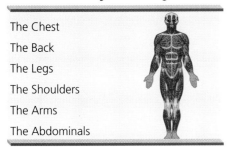

The Chest

The Back

The Legs

The Shoulders

The Arms

The Abdominals

For weight-training purposes, your body has six major areas: chest, back, legs, shoulders, arms, and abdominals. In each of these areas of the body there are different muscle groups, such as the triceps and biceps in the arms.

As a beginning weight trainer you will want to develop a well designed weight-training program for each area of the body. To do this you will need to learn which exercises work which body areas and muscle groups. The "Active Mind/Active Body" activity on the next page will help you match weight-training exercises with specific body areas and muscle groups.

The Order of Exercises— "The Circuit"

Each time you prepare for a weight-training session, you must have a plan that arranges your exercises in an efficient, sensible sequence. The **weight-training circuit** is a plan that organizes weight-training exercises in a specific sequence to best meet the needs of each individual. Weight-training circuits will help you maintain proper intensity for each muscle group, as well as maximize your workout time. You can schedule the order of the exercises in your workout circuit in a variety of ways. The following discussion contains suggestions that will help you develop a circuit to meet your needs and goals.

weight-training circuit

a specific sequence of weight-training exercises.

Large Muscle Groups versus Small Muscle Groups. One way to order the exercises in your workout is by size of muscle groups (large versus small). The term **large muscle group** refers both to groups of muscles of large size and to a large number of muscles being used at one time. Examples of large muscle groups include the legs, chest, and back.

Large muscle group exercises require more strength, energy, and mental concentration than do small muscle group exercises. For any particular area of your body, it is important to do the large muscle group exercises first.

large muscle group

muscles of large size or a large number of muscles being used at one time.

Active Mind! Active Body!

Which Muscle Am I Working?

The purpose of this activity is to help you learn which weight-training exercises you'll need to select to improve strength or endurance in specific areas of your body.

First you need to identify the major muscle groups in the different areas of the body. (See Figures 8.4 and 8.5 on the following pages.)

Next, look at the table below, which lists some of the more common weight-training exercises. For each exercise, on a separate sheet of paper, write the muscle group and body area that is developed by that exercise. You may want to refer to Figures 8.4, 8.5, and 8.6 (on page 258), as you complete the table.

You should actually attempt each of the exercises so you can feel in your own body where the work is being done. The Exercise Technique Checklist at the end of this chapter will guide you and help you prevent injuries. For the purposes of this activity it is not necessary for you to use additional weight—the bar alone will enable you to feel which muscles are working.

Exercise	Muscle group	Body Area
1. bench press	pectoralis	middle chest
2. squat		
3. military press		
4. incline press		
5. shrugs		
6. upright row		
7. dumbbell flys		
8. front, lateral, and back shoulder-raises		
9. lat pull down		
10. bent-over row		
11. good morning		
12. leg curl		
13. leg extension		
14. lunge		
15. heel raises		
16. arm curls		
17. French press		
18. bent knee sit-ups		

Source: Figure 8.6 Adapted with permission from "Exercise Selection" by D. Wathen in *Essentials of Strength Training and Conditioning*, ed. T. R. Baechle (Human Kinetics Publishers, 1994): 419–420.

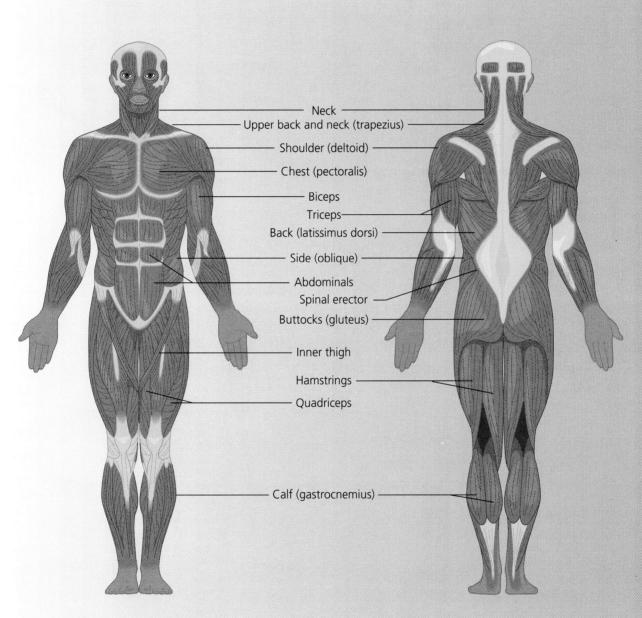

Neck

Upper back and neck (trapezius)

Shoulder (deltoid)

Chest (pectoralis)

Biceps

Triceps

Back (latissimus dorsi)

Side (oblique)

Abdominals

Spinal erector

Buttocks (gluteus)

Inner thigh

Hamstrings

Quadriceps

Calf (gastrocnemius)

• **Figure 8.4**   *The Muscular System.*

(Continued on next page)

Which Muscle Am I Working? *(continued)*

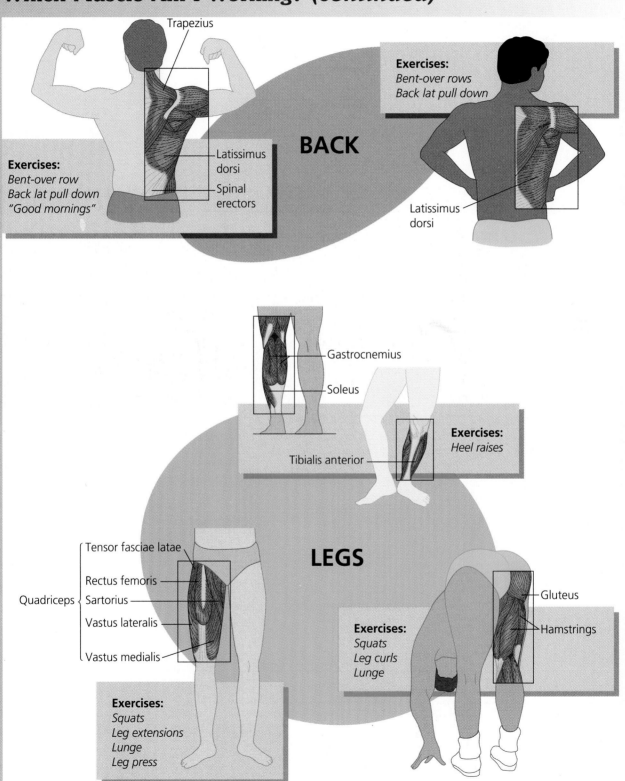

Trapezius

BACK

Exercises:
Bent-over rows
Back lat pull down

Latissimus
dorsi

Spinal
erectors

Latissimus
dorsi

Exercises:
Bent-over row
Back lat pull down
"Good mornings"

LEGS

Gastrocnemius

Soleus

Tibialis anterior

Exercises:
Heel raises

Tensor fasciae latae

Rectus femoris

Quadriceps { Sartorius

Vastus lateralis

Vastus medialis

Gluteus

Hamstrings

Exercises:
Squats
Leg curls
Lunge

Exercises:
Squats
Leg extensions
Lunge
Leg press

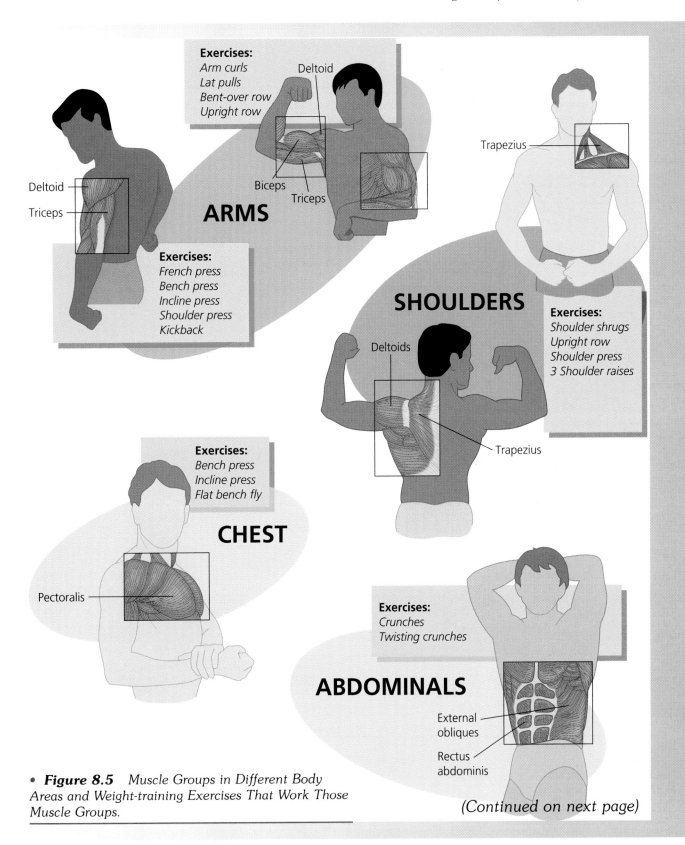

Exercises:
Arm curls
Lat pulls
Bent-over row
Upright row

Deltoid

Deltoid

Triceps

Biceps

Triceps

ARMS

Exercises:
French press
Bench press
Incline press
Shoulder press
Kickback

Trapezius

SHOULDERS

Deltoids

Exercises:
Shoulder shrugs
Upright row
Shoulder press
3 Shoulder raises

Trapezius

Exercises:
Bench press
Incline press
Flat bench fly

CHEST

Pectoralis

Exercises:
Crunches
Twisting crunches

ABDOMINALS

External
obliques

Rectus
abdominis

• **Figure 8.5** *Muscle Groups in Different Body Areas and Weight-training Exercises That Work Those Muscle Groups.*

(Continued on next page)

Exercise	Primary muscle group	Secondary muscle group	Equipment	Sports in which performance is enhanced
Leg extension	Quadriceps	—	Machine	All activities or sports
Leg curl	Hamstrings	Gastrocnemius	Machine	All activities or sports
Heel raise	Gastrocnemius, soleus	—	Machine, barbell	All activities or sports
Leg press	Quadriceps, gluteals	Hamstring	Machine	All activities or sports
Lunge	Quadriceps, gluteals	Hamstring	Barbell, dumbbells	All activities or sports
Squat	Quadriceps, gluteals	Hamstring	Barbell	All activities or sports
Sit-ups	Iiliopsoas	Abdominals	Floor machine	All activities or sports
Bench press	Pectoralis major, anterior triceps, deltoid	Spinal erectors	Barbell, bench, machine, dumbbells	Football, basketball, wrestling, shot put, hockey, rowing, boxing, gymnastics
Dip	Pectoralis major, triceps	Anterior deltoid	Parallel bars	Football, basketball, wrestling, shot put, hockey, rowing, boxing, gymnastics
Incline press	Anterior pectoralis major, deltoid, triceps	—	Barbell, dumbbells, incline bench, machine	Football, basketball, wrestling, shot put, hockey, rowing, boxing, gymnastics
Fly (supine)	Pectoralis major	Deltoid	Dumbbells, machine	Football, tennis, discus throw, baseball, softball, wrestling, backstroke
Overhead press	Deltoid, triceps	Trapezius	Barbell, dumbbells, machine	Gymnastics, shot put
Behind-neck press	Deltoid, triceps	Trapezius	Barbell	Gymnastics, shot put
Bent-over rowing	Latissimus dorsi, rhomboids	Deltoid, biceps	Barbell, dumbbells, pulley machine	Wrestling, rowing, baseball, basketball, bowling
Upright rowing	Trapezius	Deltoid, biceps	Barbell, dumbbells, pulley machine	All activities or sports
Lat pull-down	Latissimus dorsi	Biceps	Pulley machine	Basketball, baseball, swimming, tennis, volleyball, wrestling
Good morning	Spinal erector	—	Barbell	All activities or sports
Internal/external shoulder rotation	Rotator cuff	—	Barbell, dumbbells, machine	All activities or sports
Front shoulder raise	Anterior deltoid	—	Barbell, dumbbells	All activities or sports
Bent-over lateral raise	Posterior deltoid	Rhomboids, Latissimus	Dumbbells, machine	All activities or sports
Lateral shoulder raise	Deltoid	Trapezius	Dumbbells, machine	All activities or sports
Shoulder shrug	Trapezius	—	Barbell, dumbbells, machine	All activities or sports
Arm curl	Bicep	Forearm muscles	Barbell, dumbbells, pulley machine	All activities or sports
French press	Triceps	—	Barbell, dumbbells, pulley machine	All activities or sports

• **Figure 8.6** *Weight-training Exercises, Primary and Secondary Muscles, Equipment, and Their Relationships to Activities and Sports.*

small muscle group

muscles of small size or a small number of muscles being used at one time.

A **small muscle group** refers both to groups of muscles of small size and to a small number of muscles, usually one or two, being used at one time. Examples of small muscle groups include upper arms, forearms, and lower legs.

Small muscle groups are often involved with the movement of larger muscle group exercises. For this reason it is important not to exercise or fatigue small muscle groups before the large muscle exercises for the same body area have been completed. These small muscle groups are best worked individually at the end of the workouts. For example, if you do a bench press (a large muscle group exercise), you use the large pectoralis muscle (chest) and deltoid muscle (shoulder), as well as the small tricep muscle (arm). You will also need to include an individual tricep exercise, such as a tricep extension, but only after you have completed the bench press work. Figure 8.7 shows an example of how to organize the workout of large and small muscle groups in different muscle areas during your workout.

Push Exercises versus Pull Exercises.   Another suggestion for sequencing your exercises is to alternate pulling motions (flexing) with pushing motions (extension). Alternating pushes and pulls gives your muscles more recovery time because the same muscle is not worked two or more times in succession (see Figure 8.8). Figure 8.9 shows an example of how to organize push and pull exercises in your workout.

Upper Body versus Lower Body.   You might choose to alternate an exercise for the upper body (waist and above) with an

Exercise Order	Muscle Type	Muscle Group
1. Squat	Large	Thigh and hips (quadriceps)
2. Heel raise	Small	Calf (gastrocnemius)
3. Bench press	Large	Chest (pectoralis)
4. Tricep extension	Small	Upper arm–back (triceps)
5. Bent-over row	Large	Back (lattissimus dorsi)
6. Arm curl	Small	Upper arm–front (biceps)

• *Figure 8.7*   *Organizing the Work of Large and Small Muscle Groups in a Workout.*

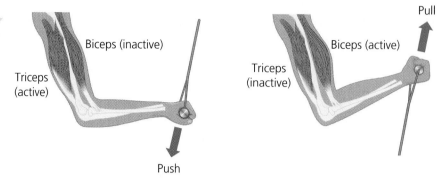

Biceps (inactive)
Triceps (active)
Push

Pull
Biceps (active)
Triceps (inactive)

• **Figure 8.8** *Triceps Create Force by Pushing—Biceps Create Force by Pulling.*

Exercise Order	Exercise Type	Muscle Groups
1. Leg press	Push	Thigh–front (quadriceps)
2. Leg curl	Pull	Thigh–back (hamstring)
3. Bench press	Push	Chest (pectoralis)
4. Bent-over row	Pull	Back (lattissimus dorsi)
5. Military press	Push	Shoulder (deltoid)
6. Arm curl	Pull	Upper arm–front (biceps)

• **Figure 8.9** *Organizing Push Exercises and Pull Exercises in Your Workout to Maximize Recovery Time.*

exercise for the lower body (hips and below). This method allows muscles more recovery time but is more difficult than the two previous ways of ordering workouts.

Workouts alternating upper and lower body muscles require an equal number of upper and lower body exercises. This means you would be doing two to three more leg exercises than you would have done in the two previous types of workouts. These additional leg exercises would require you to use more energy, thus making your workout more difficult. This type of alternating plan is, however, a suitable plan for the individual wanting to perform a higher intensity leg workout. Figure 8.10 shows an example of how to organize upper and lower body exercises in your workout.

Exercise Order	Exercise Type	Muscle Groups
1. Military press	Upper	Shoulder (deltoid)
2. Leg extension	Lower	Thigh (quadriceps)
3. Back lat pull	Upper	Back (lattissimus dorsi)
4. Lunge	Lower	Thigh and hip (quadriceps/gluteals)
5. Arm curl	Upper	Upper arm–front (biceps)
6. Leg press	Lower	Thigh–front (quadriceps)

• *Figure 8.10* *Organizing Upper and Lower Body Exercises in a Workout to Maximize Recovery Time.*

Strongest Muscle versus Weakest Muscle.   A final way to order your exercises is to work the weakest muscle first. For example, if your back muscles are your weakest area, exercise your back muscles first, while you have the most energy and can work at higher intensities.

BELIEVE IT? ... OR NOT?

After their early twenties, most adults lose 0.5 percent of their muscle mass per year.

See page 270 for answer.

SECTION 3 REVIEW

Answer the following questions on a separate piece of paper:

1. Define sets and reps and explain the relationship between them.
2. List and explain three ways to arrange the weight-training exercises in your workout.

SECTION 4   Developing and Maintaining Muscular Fitness

To develop and maintain your muscular fitness, your personal fitness plan must include weight-training exercises. To improve your muscular fitness, you need to determine your FIT (frequency, intensity, and time/duration) by estimating or determining exactly the maximum amount of weight you can lift. Use the scientific principles you learned in Chapter 3 and your personal fitness goals to develop your specific muscular fitness plan.

Determining your FIT for weight training is more complicated than it is for cardiovascular fitness, because frequency, intensity, and time/duration for weight training overlap and are not as easily separated into different components. It is very difficult to determine your intensity without considering your recovery time/duration and the frequency of your workouts at the same time. Therefore, in the following discussion, intensity and recovery time/duration for weight training will be explained before frequency.

Weight-training Intensity

Muscles get stronger and bigger only if you continue to overload them with tension or stress. The amount of tension or stress placed on a muscle is called **muscle intensity**. You can determine the intensity of a workout in a variety of ways.

Your specific weight-training goals will guide your intensity plan. Do you want strength and power, or do you want toning and endurance? Maybe you are only interested in good overall muscle fitness. Knowing how much and the kind of intensity to put into your workout can make a big difference in how successful you will be. When designing the intensity of your workout, consider the amount of weight you will lift, the number of reps and sets, and how many different exercises per body part you will do.

The Amount of Weight. One of the first questions you have to answer in determining your workout intensity is, "How much weight should I lift?" The answer to this question is often determined by a maximum strength test.

A maximum strength test determines the maximum amount of weight a person can lift one time (one rep) for a particular exercise. A simple way of doing this type of test is to keep increasing the amount of weight you try to lift until you cannot lift any more. The maximum amount you can lift one time is often referred to as your *one-rep maximum.*

Beginning weight lifters are advised not to do one-rep maximums to determine their maximum strength. Until they become more experienced, they can estimate their maximum by doing multiple reps with a weight less than their maximum.

As you participate in a regular weight-training program, your maximum strength will increase. You will need to periodically test your maximum so that you can continue to increase your intensity. As you become more experienced, you may choose to do actual one-rep maximums rather than estimating your maximum. The "Fitness Check" activity on the next page will help you determine your personal maximum for a variety of exercises.

muscle intensity

the amount of tension or stress placed on a muscle.

REMEMBER This!

Keep in mind that you are not finding your one-rep maximum so that you can lift that amount. The amount you will lift on a regular basis will be a percentage (from 60% to 95%) of your maximum. You are only determining your maximum so that you can safely train at a lesser weight.

Determining Your Maximum Strength (One-Rep Maximums)

Fitness Check

Determine your estimated one-rep maximum for each of the following exercises: bench press, squat, military press, biceps curl, and bent-over row. As you work to determine these maximums, it is very important that you use the proper technique for each exercise. (See Section 6 later in this chapter.)

Be sure to use the estimated maximum method. To use this method, choose a weight for which you can do 6 to 10 reps. Do the reps, then look at Figure 8.11 to find your one-rep maximum.

For example, Julie can squat 105 pounds seven times. She would find the column for seven reps in Figure 8.11 and then, in that column, find the amount of weight she lifted (105 pounds). She would then read across from 105 to the far-right column to obtain her estimated one-rep maximum (130 pounds).

Pounds Lifted (70% of Max., 9–10 Reps.)	Pounds Lifted (80% of Max., 7–8 Reps.)	Pounds Lifted (85% of Max., 6 Reps.)	Pounds Lifted (100% of Max., 1 Rep.)
40	45	50	60
50	55	60	70
55	65	70	80
65	70	75	90
70	80	85	100
75	90	95	110
85	95	100	120
90	105	110	130
100	115	120	140
105	120	130	150
110	130	135	160
120	135	145	170
125	145	155	180
135	150	160	190
140	160	170	200
150	170	180	210
155	175	185	220
160	185	195	230
170	190	205	240
175	200	210	250

• **Figure 8.11** *Estimate Your Maximum Strength with 6 to 10 Reps (weights rounded off to the nearest 5 pounds).*

(Continued on next page)

Determining Your Maximum Strength (One-Rep Maximums) *(continued)*

Record your results, as described on the preceding page, for each exercise. You can use these results to determine the amount of weight you will use in workouts. You will also use the results to assess your improvement in later tests.

Once you have obtained your estimated one-rep maximum for the five exercises, use Figure 8.12 to determine your pound-for-pound relative strength. Do this for all five exercises, and record how you performed. For example, in Chapter 7, Jim's estimated one-rep maximum for the bench press was 130 pounds, and he weighed 125 pounds. His relative strength was calculated by dividing 130 by 125, which told us that Jim's relative strength was 1.04. To determine Jim's relative performance rates, look at Figure 8.12, and find 1.04 under "bench press." Then read across to the left. Jim's bench press performance would rate as moderate, or average.

Men

Relative Strength Rating	Biceps Curl	Military Press	Bench Press	Squat	Bent-over Row
Outstanding	> .64	> .99	> 1.29	> 1.84	> .94
	.55–.64	.90–.99	1.15–1.29	1.65–1.84	.85–.94
Moderate	.45–.54	.75–.89	1.0–1.14	1.30–1.64	.75–.84
	.35–.44	.60–.74	.85–.99	1.0–1.29	.65–.74
Unacceptable	< .34	< .60	< .85	< 1.0	< .64

Women

Relative Strength Rating	Biceps Curl	Overhead Press	Bench Press	Squat	Bent-over Row
Outstanding	> .45	> .50	> .85	> 1.45	> .55
	.38–.44	.42–.49	.70–.84	1.30–1.44	.45–.54
Moderate	.32–.37	.32–.41	.60–.69	1.0–1.29	.35–.44
	.25–.31	.25–.31	.50–.59	.80–.99	.25–.34
Unacceptable	< .25	< .25	< .50	< .80	< .25

• **Figure 8.12** *One-Rep Maximums Can Be Used to Determine Relative Strength and Strength Range for Specific Exercises.*

training load

the amount of weight a weight trainer lifts during his or her workout.

Once you have determined your maximum for a specific exercise, you can then take a percentage of your maximum to determine how much weight you should lift for each exercise. The amount of weight used during sets and reps is called the **training load**.

See Figure 8.13 to determine your training load. Suppose your maximum lift on the bench press is 100 pounds. Beginners should

1 Rep. Maximum	Training load percentages							
	50%	60%	70%	75%	80%	85%	90%	95%
30	15	18	21	23	24	26	27	29
40	20	24	28	30	32	34	36	38
50	25	30	35	38	40	43	45	48
60	30	36	42	45	48	51	54	57
70	35	42	49	52	56	60	63	67
80	40	48	56	60	64	68	72	76
90	45	54	63	68	72	77	81	86
100	50	60	70	75	80	85	90	95
110	55	66	77	83	88	94	99	105
120	60	72	84	90	96	102	108	114
130	65	78	91	98	104	111	117	124
140	70	84	98	105	112	119	125	133
150	75	90	105	113	120	128	135	143
160	80	96	112	120	128	136	144	152
170	85	102	119	128	136	145	153	162
180	90	108	126	135	144	153	162	171
190	95	114	133	143	152	162	171	181
200	100	120	140	150	160	170	180	190
210	105	126	147	158	168	179	189	200
220	110	132	154	165	176	187	198	209
230	115	138	161	173	184	196	207	219
240	120	144	168	180	192	204	216	228
250	125	150	175	188	200	213	225	238
260	130	156	182	195	208	221	234	247
270	135	162	189	203	216	230	243	257
280	140	168	196	210	224	238	252	266
290	145	174	203	218	232	247	261	276
300	150	180	210	225	240	255	270	285
310	155	186	217	233	248	264	279	295
320	160	192	224	240	256	272	288	304
330	165	198	231	248	264	281	297	314
340	170	204	238	255	272	289	306	323
350	175	210	245	263	280	298	316	333
360	180	216	252	278	288	306	324	342
370	185	222	259	280	296	315	333	352
380	190	228	266	285	304	323	342	361
390	195	234	273	293	312	332	351	371
400	200	240	280	300	320	340	360	380

• **Figure 8.13** *If You are a Beginner, You Should Work at 50 to 60 Percent of Your One-rep Maximum.*

Fitness and Health:
2-3 Sets of 8-12 Reps.
Toning and Endurance:
2-3 Sets of 12-20 Reps.
Strength and Power:
3-5 Sets of 4-6 Reps.
Body Building:
Combination of All Three.

• *Figure 8.15* *Sets and Reps to Meet Your Goals.*

use 50 to 60 percent of their maximums, whereas conditioned weight trainers may want to use 75 to 85 percent of their maximum. Let's suppose you feel you are somewhere between a beginner and a conditioned weight trainer so you decide to work at 70 percent of your maximum. You would use 70 pounds for a prescribed number of reps.

The Number of Reps and Sets. In general, lifting heavy weights with low numbers of reps will build strength and power. Lifting light weights with high numbers of reps will produce muscle tone and endurance (Figure 8.14). Figure 8.15 suggests the numbers of reps and sets you should do for various weight-training goals.

Number of Different Exercises per Body Part. The greater the number of different exercises you use to work a body part, the greater your intensity. One or two different exercises for each of your body parts is sufficient to improve and maintain health and fitness. Athletes, power lifters, and body builders should use three or four different exercises per body part. When you increase the number of exercises, you also increase the number of sets used per body part. This will increase the intensity of your workout, as well as your total workout time.

 Look to your health; and if you have it, praise God, and value it next to a good conscience; for health is the second blessing that we mortals are capable of; a blessing that money cannot buy.

**Izaak Walton
(1593–1683)**
English writer. *The Compleat Angler*, Pt. 1, Ch. 21

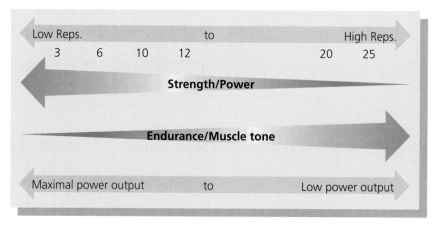

• *Figure 8.14* *Repetition Continuum. Strength/Power versus Endurance/Muscle Tone.*

Recovery Time/Duration

recovery time

time or rest between exercises.

Your **recovery time**—time or rest between exercises—plays a big role in the intensity, and outcome of your workout. Therefore, you must decide how long to rest between sets, between different exercises, and between different workouts. Too much time between sets of different exercises can cause you to cool down, which increases your risk of injury. Too little time prevents your muscles from recovering and does not allow for proper intensity. It takes about thirty seconds for the body to recover one-half of its energy and about three minutes for full recovery. After five minutes the body starts to cool down. Here are some recovery time guidelines.

Between Reps. You should not rest between reps. Reps should be continuous and controlled.

Between Sets. How long you rest between sets depends on your weight-training goals:

- *Fitness and health* . . . . .Rest 1½ to 2 minutes.
- *Strength and body building* . . . .Rest 2 to 2½ minutes.
- *Toning and endurance* . . . . . . .Rest 30 to 60 seconds.
- *Power (very heavy weights)* . . . .Rest 3 to 5 minutes.

Between Exercises. You will determine the amount of rest between exercises when you choose the order of exercises in your workout. The push-pull method and the upper body-lower body method require 1½ to 2 minutes between exercises. The large muscle-small muscle method requires 2 to 2½ minutes between exercises.

weight-training cycle

a change in your weight-training programs over a period of time.

Between Cycles. Athletes or competitive lifters do not train the same way year-round. They must regularly modify their programs to meet the needs of off-season, pre-season, and in-season. Each modified program is called a **weight-training cycle**. Your personal health and fitness weight-training routine will also require modifications (cycles) throughout the year. You should change your exercises, sets, and workout days to prevent boredom. It may even be good to get away from the weights for a few weeks and do some other exercises, such as push-ups, bar dips, chin-ups, or isometrics. See Figures 8.16, 8.17, and 8.18 on the next page. Keep your workouts fresh. Don't be afraid to throw in some variety.

Weight-training Frequency

With weight training there are no shortcuts to success. The frequency and consistency of your workouts is very important. Decide which days of the week are best for you, and then avoid missing sessions.

• **Figure 8.16** *Starting and Finishing Position for Push-ups.*

• **Figure 8.17** *Starting and Finishing Position for Bar Dip.*

• **Figure 8.18** *Starting and Finishing Position for Chin-ups.*

Monday (workout)

Tuesday (off)

Wednesday (workout)

Thursday (off)

Friday (workout)

Sat. & Sun. (off)

• **Figure 8.19** *Sample Workout Week—Three Days, Total Body.*

split workout

a weight-training workout schedule in which you do not work each muscle group at each workout session but, instead, exercise one-half of your body at each session.

A well-designed plan can help you maintain consistency and workout intensity. Each workout should provide enough stress on the muscles to stimulate the muscle growth process. After this stimulation occurs, the muscle must have time to recover and grow. Usually 48 to 72 hours is ample time for muscle recovery. For example, if Jessie completes a chest, shoulder, and tricep workout on Monday afternoon, he should not work the same muscle groups again until Wednesday afternoon (after a total recovery time of 48 hours).

Three-Days-a-Week, Total-Body Workout. You may decide to work all muscle groups (total body) three times a week, with at least one day off between workouts. This is the most popular plan for beginners. It allows for all muscles to receive ample work, while at the same time allowing for ample rest. See Figure 8.19.

Four-Days-a-Week, Split Workout. Those in more advanced weight-training programs may decide to use a split workout schedule, which requires more intensity and frequency (four days a week). In a **split workout**, you do not work every muscle group at every session. Instead, you only exercise one-half of your body at each session. This means that each body part can be worked at a much greater intensity. You do three or four different exercises per body part and three or four sets for each different exercise. Because

• *Testing Your Strength. Top Left: Bench Press; Top Right: Squat; Bottom: Seated Military Press.*

Monday:
Chest, Shoulders, Triceps
Tuesday:
Back, Legs, Biceps, Abs.
Wednesday:
Rest!
Thursday:
Repeat Monday's workout
Friday:
Repeat Tuesday's workout
Saturday/Sunday:
Rest!

• ***Figure 8.20*** *Sample Workout Week—Four Days, Split Workout.*

this workout requires a greater intensity, your muscles need greater recovery time. The split workout requires 72 hours of rest before the same muscle group is again worked. (See Figure 8.20.)

Testing Your Muscular Fitness

Muscular fitness is tested for many reasons. This testing should be done on a regular basis.

Reasons for Testing.   How can you benefit from muscular fitness tests? First, pretests can be used to determine how much weight you should lift in your workouts. Second, muscular fitness tests help identify your weak points, which you can then take into consideration when designing your weight-training program. Finally, these tests will help you keep track of your progress, which becomes a great motivator for your future workouts. Post-tests are used for this purpose.

Answers to

Believe It? ... Or Not?

Pg. 247 False. Most people reach their peak muscular strength between the ages of twenty and thirty. You can also maintain moderate to high levels of strength into your forties and fifties by remaining active.
Pg. 248 False. You can get seriously injured if you lift without spotters, particularly if you are lifting at high intensities with free weights. Exercises like the bench press, squats, and military press are some of the most potentially dangerous lifts for you if you don't use spotters.
Pg. 252 True.
Pg. 259 True.
Pg. 260 False. The largest muscle in your body is the gluteus maximus, which is your buttock muscle.
Pg. 261 True.
Pg. 266 False. Although you might get a bit stronger if you wear ankle weights, you will also significantly increase your risk for lower body injuries. Ankle weights increase the forces acting on your ankles, knees, and hips.
Pg. 275 True.

How to Test. Keep the following tips in mind when taking a muscular fitness test:

- Be sure to warm up before any testing. This prevents injury and will help you achieve your best performance.
- Use correct technique at all times.
- Have spotters assist all lifts.
- Do not take more than one strength test on the same day.
- Do not attempt a maximum lift more than three times with the same weight.
- Do not test on days following a hard workout. Allow for proper rest.
- Test any body part you desire.

Record Keeping

Keeping good records is an important part of your weight-training program. Records provide information from the past that can help you make decisions about the future. Figure 8.21 shows parts of your workout routine that you should keep track of. Figure 8.22 shows a sample record-keeping chart.

Part of the Workout	Example of Record Keeping
Days of the week/date	Monday the 23rd Split week
Body part and sets, repetitions, and amount of weight lifted	Chest: bench press 3 × 10 at 100 pounds Legs: squats 3 × 12 at 165 pounds
Body weight, body composition	September 10, 1995: 150 pounds 18 percent body fat
Absences, illnesses	Missed Tuesday, October 10, and Wednesday, October 11, due to a cold.
Personal best	Maximum on bench press = 135 pounds Maximum on squats = 210 pounds
Eating habits	Started eating better breakfast on Monday; missed lunch on Thursday
Total workout time	Workouts lasted 40 minutes

• ***Figure 8.21*** *Elements of Record Keeping for Weight-training Programs.*

S = Sets
R = Reps.
WT = Weight

Date:																		
Record:	S	R	WT	S	R	WT	S	R	WT	S	R	WT	S	R	WT	S	R	WT
Exercises for the Chest Area (Pectoralis)																		
1 **Bench Press**																		
2 Dumbbell Press																		
3 Flys																		
4 Close Grip Press																		
5 **Incline Press**																		
6 Dumbbell Press																		
7 Flys																		
8 Close Grip																		
9 **Decline Press**																		
10 Dumbbell Press																		
11 Flys																		
12 Close Grip Press																		
13 **Dips**																		
14																		

• **Figure 8.22**   *Sample Record-keeping Chart.*

SECTION 4 REVIEW

Answer the following questions on a separate sheet of paper:

1. Identify three factors that can help you determine the intensity of your weight-training workouts.

2. List three ways to adjust the intensity of your weight-training workout.

3. Why should your total recovery time between workouts of the same body parts be at least forty-eight hours?

4. Identify three reasons for testing your muscular fitness.

SECTION 5   Programs for Strength and Hypertrophy

You can choose from several different methods to increase your strength and hypertrophy. This section will look at ways to improve strength first. It then will examine methods for building muscle mass.

Strength Programs (Strength Is the Primary Goal)

If your primary goal in weight training is to gain strength, you might want to consider the following strength programs. These programs can help you optimize intensity and time as you try to reach your strength potential.

All three of the strength programs require the use of higher percentages of your maximum lifts than is recommended for beginners. Make sure you have been lifting for several (six to eight) weeks before attempting workouts that require you to exceed 80 percent of your maximum. This can help prevent muscle damage or injury.

pyramid training

a weight-training strength program for the large muscle groups that starts by using light weights during the first set and then increases the amount of weight and decreases the number of reps with each following set.

Pyramid Training. **Pyramid training** starts by using light weights during the first set. It then increases the amount of weight and decreases the number of reps with each following set. The amount of weight increase can be determined by increasing the percentage of your own rep maximum. (See Figure 8.23.) No other exercise is done until all pyramid sets are completed. There should be a two- to three-minute rest between each set. Pyramid training is recommended for larger muscle groups, such as those in the chest, back, legs, and shoulders.

For example, John has a bench press maximum of 130 pounds. He might follow this schedule for a pyramid-training session (weights are rounded to the nearest 5 pounds):

First set: 1×10–12, 90 pounds (70 percent of 130 pounds).
Second set: 1×6–8, 105 pounds (80 percent of 130 pounds).
Third set: 1×4–7, 110 pounds (85 percent of 130 pounds).
Fourth set: 1×2–3, 115 pounds (90 percent of 130 pounds).
Fifth set: 1×1–2, 125 pounds (95 percent of 130 pounds).

The fourth and fifth sets should be used only by more advanced lifters since they involve lifting near-maximum weight.

REMEMBER This!

All methods of weight training will increase your strength and muscle mass to some degree. However, certain programs will produce greater increases in strength than in muscle mass, and other programs will produce greater increases in muscle mass than in strength. These differences are due to the way your muscle cells respond to different types of weight training and to the specificity principle. Your muscles will adapt specifically to the challenges you give them as you lift weights.

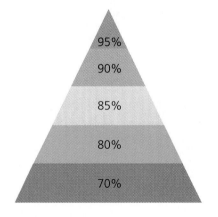

• *Figure 8.23* *Pyramid Training.*

Any Body Can!

Mark Henry

Mark Henry is a 24-year-old African American male, originally from Silsbee, Texas. Mark is one of the strongest people in the world, and he is proud to promote the fact that he is a lifetime drug-free championship weight and power lifter.

Mark began getting serious about weight training and power lifting in high school. He was the three-time power lifting champion (super heavyweight division) in Texas.

Mark is currently 6 feet, 3 inches tall, weighs over 400 pounds, and wears a size 16 E shoe. Yet, he can slam dunk a basketball and earned third place in the 1994 Slamfest sponsored by Footlocker Sporting Goods.

In 1995, Mark became the first individual in decades to earn and hold the simultaneous titles of U.S. national champion in weight and power lifting in the super heavyweight division. His weight lifting and power lifting achievements at the 1995 national meets include the following:

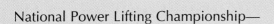

National Weight Lifting Championship—	Snatch Lift	392 pounds
	Clean and Jerk	<u>485</u> pounds
	Total	**977** pounds
National Power Lifting Championship—	Squat Lift	954 pounds
	Dead Lift	903 pounds
	Bench Press	<u>483</u> pounds
	Total	**2,340** pounds

Mark's lift total of 3,317 pounds on the combined five lifts is the most anyone in the U.S. has ever lifted, on or off drugs (for example, anabolic steroids).

Some of Mark's other outstanding weight lifting honors include being a member of the 1992 and 1996 Olympic weight lifting teams. He also won a gold medal in the super heavyweight division at the 1995 Pan American Games in Argentina.

Mark is often asked why he doesn't use anabolic steroids or other drugs to enhance his performance. His standard answer to this question is, "To be honest, I never have thought about using drugs to improve my performances, but I have thought a lot about what others might be able to lift without taking drugs."

Mark has drug tested negative over 30 times for national and international competitions and is an excellent role model for those who want to achieve high levels of personal fitness naturally, without drug influences.

Not everyone can be a weight and power lifting champion like Mark Henry, but Any Body Can learn to lift weights for personal fitness and have success while remaining drug free. That's right, you can do it!

multiple set method

a weight-training strength program that uses the same amount of weight (a percentage of your maximum) for each set until you are fatigued.

negative workout method

a weight-training strength program that uses very heavy weights at the end of a prescribed number of sets and repetitions.

superset method

a weight-training hypertrophy program that uses two different exercises that train opposing muscles, without allowing for rest between sets.

Multiple Sets.   In the **multiple set method**, you use the same amount of weight for each set. You decide which percentage of your maximum to use (85, 90, or 95 percent) and then do reps until you are fatigued. The number of reps should range from three to seven. Rest two to three minutes between each set. As with the pyramid program, the fourth and fifth sets are for more advanced lifters.

For example, Joe has a bench press maximum of 130 pounds. Here is a suggested multiple set program for his training:

First set: 1×4–7, 110 pounds (85 percent of 130 pounds).

Second set: 1×4–7, 110 pounds (same as above).

Third set: 1×4–7, 110 pounds (same as above).

Note that unless you have been lifting for several weeks (six to eight), you should not use these higher maximum percentages.

Negative Method.   In the **negative workout method** you use very heavy weights. You usually use this method at the end of a prescribed number of sets and reps, adding 10 to 15 percent more weight than you usually use. Your spotters, who are required for safety, help place the bar into position. You then slowly control the bar as it comes down. When it gets to your chest (in the bench press), your spotters help raise the bar back to the starting position for another negative (eccentric) rep. Because this method can cause excessive soreness, don't use it often.

Say Fred uses 110 pounds during his normal bench press sets of four to five reps. His negative set would be 1×3, 125 pounds (about a 15 percent increase from 110 pounds). Note that three to four reps per set is the maximum recommended.

Hypertrophy Programs (Muscle Mass Is the Primary Goal)

If your primary goal is hypertrophy (muscle enlargement), you might want to consider some programs that can help you optimize intensity and time as you pursue your hypertrophy potential. Two of the three programs (supersets and compound sets) require high intensities with short rest periods. The third program (multiple sets) requires a greater percentage of your maximum. To prevent possible muscle damage or injury, make sure you have been lifting for several weeks (six to eight weeks) before attempting these workouts.

Supersets.   The **superset method** requires you to use two different exercises that train opposing muscles, without allowing for rest between the sets. For example, do a set of ten biceps curls immediately followed by a set of ten triceps extensions. (These exercises are illustrated in the next section). This is a good way to keep opposite

• An example of the superset weight training method is illustrated above: To the left, leg extensions; to the right, leg curls.

CONSUMER CORNER

Are Supplements Necessary?

With the increased popularity of weight training, many fitness enthusiasts are looking for ways to obtain the "hard body" look that many professional bodybuilders have. Many people are attracted to television, magazine, and book ads that claim supplements can guarantee significant gains in muscle strength and mass. According to the advertisers, these protein powders, amino acids, vitamins, and minerals can enhance the results you can gain from a regular weight-training program.

The truth is that few, if any, of these supplements are beneficial to most fitness enthusiasts. A physician might prescribe a supplement to treat a specific medical problem. However, a healthy diet will provide all the protein, vitamins, and minerals you need for muscle strength and mass gains. Supplements taken above your daily needs are costly and are excreted from your body as waste materials. Some can even be harmful to your health.

antagonistic muscles

opposing muscles.

compound set method

a weight-training hypertrophy program that requires you to do two different exercises that use the same muscle group, without allowing for rest between the sets.

muscles balanced in strength. Another name for these opposing muscles is **antagonistic muscles**.

Compound Sets.   The **compound set method** requires you to do two different exercises that use the same muscle group, without allowing for rest between the sets. For example, do a set of ten reps of bench press, immediately followed by a set of ten reps of flat bench fly.

Multiple Sets.   With the multiple set method, you use the same amount of weight for each set. The amount of weight should be 70 to 80 percent of your maximum. Do three to five sets of eight to ten reps. Rest thirty to ninety seconds between sets. This is the recommended progression for beginners after they've done six weeks of weight training with 50 to 60 percent of their maximum.

REMEMBER This!

A muscle actually grows and becomes stronger between workouts, not during workouts. Never work the same muscle group two days in a row.

SECTION 5 REVIEW

Answer the following questions on a separate sheet of paper:

1. Explain the difference between muscular strength programs and muscular hypertrophy programs.
2. Define and explain pyramid training.
3. Explain the difference between supersets and compound sets.

SECTION 6   Exercises, Muscles, and Proper Technique

Knowing how to lift a weight properly is important, especially when using free weights. Correct lifting technique reduces the possibility of injury, and produces the desired results more quickly. This section provides a detailed checklist to help you learn a variety of weight-training exercises. Go through each part of the exercise checklist to develop good lifting techniques. Practice these lifts with spotters and light weights until you are certain you can correctly execute the lift. To get started, use the "Active Mind/Active Body" activity beginning on the next page.

Active Mind! Active Body!

Lifting Technique Checklist

Study the correct lifting technique for each of the following weight-training exercises. Demonstrate the bench press, military press, bent-over row, squat, arm curl, and French press. Use only an empty bar or broomstick, not weights, for demonstration. Have your instructor or partners use the Exercise Technique Checklist to evaluate you.

The following weight-training exercises are grouped together according to the areas of the body (chest, shoulders, back, legs, arms, abdominals) that they work.

Chest

Bench Press Body area: middle chest.
Muscles: pectoralis, deltoid, triceps.
Variations: Dumbbells.
Caution: Spotters recommended.

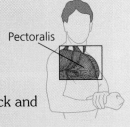
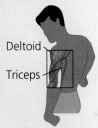

Pectoralis

Deltoid

Triceps

- Lie face up on a bench. Position your back and buttocks flat on the bench.

- Position your eyes directly under the bar. Keep your head down.

- Position your feet flat on the floor. If the bench is too high, use a chair or the end of the bench to lift your feet. (This prevents your back from arching.) Your legs should remain relaxed.

- Grasp the bar with hands slightly farther apart than shoulders' width.

- Your hands should be evenly spaced on each side from the center of the bar; use a wrap-around thumb grip, and lock your wrists.

- Move the bar off the rack, and position it over your chest. (Spotters can assist.)

- *Figure 8.24* *Bench Press.*

(Continued on next page)

Lifting Technique Checklist *(continued)*

- Keep your elbows out, parallel to the bar.
- Stabilize the bar before lowering it. (Spotters should release the bar.)
- Lower the bar slowly to the middle of your chest. Maintain control and speed; touch, do not bounce the bar off your chest.
- Push upward to the starting position. Go through the full range of motion. (Spotters hands should be in the ready position.)
- Breathe out (exhale) during the push stage. Do not hold your breath.
- Keep your back, head, and buttocks in contact with the bench at all times.
- At the completion of the reps, replace the bar on the rack. Never release your grip until the bar is safely in the rack. (Spotters should assist to replace the bar.)

  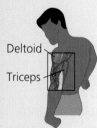

Variation of Bench Press—Flat bench dumbbell press.

Incline Bench Press Body area: upper chest.
Muscles: upper pectoralis, deltoid, triceps.
Variations: dumbbells.
Caution: Spotters recommended.

Pectoralis

Deltoid

Triceps

- Lie face up on an incline bench. Position your back and buttocks flat on the bench.
- Position your feet flat on the floor. If the bench is too high, use a chair or the end of the bench to lift your feet. Do not use your feet to lift your body. Your legs should remain relaxed.
- Grasp the bar with hands slightly farther apart than shoulders' width.
- Your grip should be evenly spaced. Use a wraparound thumb grip, and lock your wrists.
- Move the bar off the rack, and position it over your chest. (Spotters can assist.)
- Keep your elbows out and parallel to the bar.

- Lower the bar slowly to the top of your chest, near your chin. Maintain control and speed. Touch the bar to your chest. Do not bounce it off your chest.

- Push the bar upward to the starting position. Go through the full range of motion. (Spotters hands should be in a ready position.)

- Breathe out (exhale) during the push stage. Do not hold your breath.

- Your back, head, and buttocks must remain in contact with the bench at all times.

- At the completion of the reps, replace the bar on the rack. Never release your grip until the bar is safely in the rack. (Spotters should assist to replace the bar in the rack.)

• **Figure 8.25**   *Incline Bench Press.*

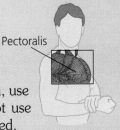

Variation of Incline Bench Press (dumbbells).

Flat Bench Fly   Body area: chest.
Muscles: pectoralis.
Variations: incline or decline bench.

Pectoralis

- Lie face up on a bench. Position your back and buttocks flat on the bench.

- Position your feet flat on the floor. If the bench is too high, use a chair or the end of the bench to lift your feet. Do not use your feet to lift your body. Your legs should remain relaxed.

- Grasp a dumbbell in each hand. Use a wraparound thumb grip.

- Raise your arms and hands to position the dumbbells together over your chest. Your arms should be extended, and your palms should face each other.

(Continued on next page)

Lifting Technique Checklist *(continued)*

- Before you lower the dumbbells, slightly bend both elbows.
- Lower the dumbbells in a wide arc.
- Your elbows should remain slightly bent. Keep your arms in line with your shoulders and chest.
- Lower the dumbbells slowly, controlling their speed until they are level with your shoulders.
- Return the dumbbells to the starting position. Keep your elbows slightly bent until you reach the top of the lift. Continue the reps.
- Breathe out (exhale) during the push stage; do not hold your breath.

- **Figure 8.26**　*Flat Bench Fly.*

Shoulders

Seated "Back" Shoulder (military) Press

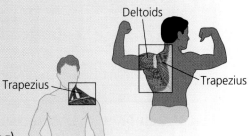

Body area: shoulders.
Muscles: deltoid, triceps, trapezius.
Variation: front of the neck, dumbbell press (standing or sitting), machine.
Caution: Spotters and weight belts recommended.

- Sit on a bench or chair. Place your feet flat on the floor.
- Grasp the bar with hands slightly farther apart than shoulders' width.
- Your grip should be evenly spaced. Use a wraparound thumb grip, and lock your wrists.
- Your elbows should be under the bar and parallel to the bar.
- Your back should be straight (not arched) and your head up.
- The starting position for the bar is at shoulder height and close to the body. (Spotters can assist.)

- The bar is pushed upward to full arm extension.
- Breathe out (exhale) during the push stage; do not hold your breath.
- Your elbows should remain under, and parallel to, the bar at all times, with your back flat.
- Lower the bar slowly to the back of the neck. Maintain control and speed. Do not let the bar bounce off of your neck or shoulder.
- At the completion of the reps, replace the bar on the rack. (Spotters can assist.)

- **Figure 8.27** Seated "Back" Shoulder (military) Press.

Variation "A"—Standing Dumbbell Overhead (military) Press.

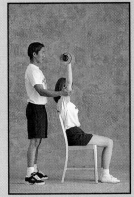

Variation "B"—Seated Military Dumbbell Press.

Variation "C"—Seated Shoulder Press (machine).

Variation "D" Incline Shoulder Press (machine).

(Continued on next page)

Lifting Technique Checklist *(continued)*

Shoulder Shrug Body area: shoulders.
Muscles: trapezius.
Variations: dumbbell.

- To pick up the bar from the floor, assume shoulders'-width stance, with your feet flat.
- Bend your knees, not your waist. To place your hands on the bar, fully extend your arms.
- Your grip should be slightly wider than your shoulders and outside your knees.
- Your grip should be evenly spaced. Use a wraparound thumb grip.
- The bar should be close to your shins.
- Position your shoulders over the bar.
- Your back must stay flat. Keep your head up. Pull your shoulder blades together. Do not bend at the waist.
- Begin lifting by extending your legs, not your back.
- Move your hips forward, and raise your shoulders.
- Keep the bar close to your body, with your back and feet flat.
- Raise the bar until your knees are slightly bent and your arms are fully extended.
- Breathe out (exhale) during the lifting stage.
- Lift the bar by raising your shoulders toward your ears. Do not bend or pull with your arms.
- Hold this "shrug" position for 2 counts.
- Breathe out (exhale) during the lifting stage.
- Lower the bar slowly to your waist. Maintain control and speed. Keep your feet flat and your knees slightly bent.
- At the completion of the reps, return the bar to the floor. To protect your back, be sure that you use the same technique you used to pick up the bar to return the bar to the floor.

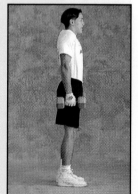

- **Figure 8.28** *Shoulder Shrug (barbell).*

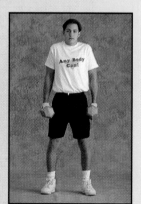

Variation of Shoulder Shrug (dumbbell).

Upright Row Body area: shoulders.
Muscles: deltoids, trapezius, biceps.
Variations: dumbbells.

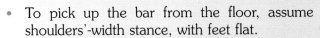

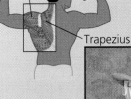

- To pick up the bar from the floor, assume shoulders'-width stance, with feet flat.

- Bend your knees, not your waist. To place your hands on the bar, fully extend your arms.

- Your hands will grip 8 to 10 inches apart and be placed inside your legs.

- Your hands should be evenly spaced in the grip. Use a wraparound thumb grip.

- The bar should be close to your shins.

- Position your shoulders over the bar.

- Your back must stay flat. Keep your head up. Pull your shoulder blades together. Do not bend at the waist.

- Begin lifting by extending your legs, not your back.

- Move your hips forward, and raise your shoulders.

- Keep the bar close to your body, with your back and feet flat.

- Raise the bar until your knees are slightly bent and your arms are fully extended.

- Breathe out (exhale) during the lifting stage.

- Pull the bar upward along your stomach and chest toward your chin. Keep the bar close to your body.

- Continue to raise the bar until it is under your chin.

- Your elbows should be higher than your wrist and shoulders.

- Breathe out (exhale) during the lifting stage.

- Lower the bar slowly to your waist. Maintain control and speed. Keep your feet flat, with knees slightly bent.

- • *Figure 8.29*
  Upright Row (barbell).

- At the completion of the reps, return the bar to the floor. To protect your back, be sure to use the same technique you used to pick up the bar to return the bar to the floor.

- *Variation—Upright Row (dumbbells).*

(Continued on next page)

Lifting Technique Checklist *(continued)*

Front Dumbbell Shoulder Raise Body area: shoulders.
Muscles: front part of deltoids.
Variations: standing or sitting.

- Start in a standing position with feet shoulders'-width apart and head up.
- Hold a dumbbell in each hand, with arms hanging on each side of your body and elbows slightly bent.
- Slowly raise your arms in front of your body. Continue to raise your arms until your hands are level with your shoulders. Your arms must stay in front. (The exercise can be done by alternating arms or raising both arms at the same time.)
- Breathe out (exhale) during the lifting stage.
- Hold this position for 2 counts.
- Lower your arms slowly to the starting position. Maintain control and speed. Continue the reps.

- **Figure 8.30** *Front Dumbbell Shoulder Raise.*

Side (lateral) Dumbbell Shoulder Raise Body area: shoulders.
Muscles: middle part of deltoids.
Variations: standing or sitting.

- Start in a standing position, with feet shoulders'-width apart and head up.
- Hold a dumbbell in each hand, with arms hanging on each side of your body and elbows slightly bent.
- Slowly raise your arms to the side of your body. Continue to raise your arms until your hands are level with your shoulders. Keep your elbows level with your hands.
- As you raise your arms, rotate your wrists down and elbows up, as if you were pouring water out of a glass. (This exercise may be done by alternating arms or raising both at the same time.)

- **Figure 8.31** *Side (lateral) Dumbbell Shoulder Raise.*

- Breathe out (exhale) during the lifting stage.
- Hold the position for 2 counts.
- Lower your arms slowly to the starting position. Maintain control and speed. Continue the reps.

Bent-over Dumbbell Shoulder Raise

Body area: shoulders.
Muscle: back part of deltoid.
Variations: standing or sitting.

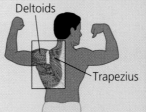

- Start in a standing position with feet shoulders'-width apart, knees slightly bent and head up.
- Hold a dumbbell in each hand with arms hanging on each side of your body.
- Bend your torso at the waist. Your arms should be hanging straight down.
- Slowly raise your arms upward, continue to raise your arms until your hands are almost level with your shoulders.
- Breathe out (exhale) during the lifting stage.
- Hold this position for 2 counts.
- Lower your arms slowly to a starting position. Maintain control and speed. Continue the reps.

• **Figure 8.32**   *Bent-over Dumbbell Shoulder Raise.*

Back

Bent-over Row Body area: upper back.
Muscles: latissimus dorsi, trapezius, biceps.
Caution: Weight belts may be necessary during maximum lifts.

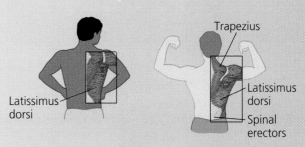

- To pick up the bar from the floor, assume shoulders'-width stance, with feet flat.
- Bend your knees and waist to place your hands on the bar. Fully extend your arms.
- Your grip should be slightly wider than your shoulders and outside your knees.

(Continued on next page)

Lifting Technique Checklist *(continued)*

- Your hands should be evenly spaced in the grip. Use a wrap-around thumb grip.
- The bar should be close to your shins.
- Position your shoulders over the bar.
- Your back must stay flat. Keep your head up, and pull your shoulder blades together.
- Begin lifting by extending your legs until your back is slightly above a parallel position in relation to the floor. Keep your knees flexed and your back flat. Hold this position.
- With arms fully extended, pull the bar up and touch your lower chest or upper abdomen. Keep your elbows out.
- Breathe out (exhale) during the lifting stage.
- Keep your upper body and legs in a set position.
- Lower the bar slowly to the starting position. Maintain control and speed.
- At the completion of the reps, return the bar to the floor. Be sure to use the same technique you used to pick up the bar.

• **Figure 8.33**   *Bent-over Row (free weight).*

Back Lat Pulldown Body area: midback.
Muscles: latissimus dorsi, trapezius, biceps.
Variations: Pull bar to front of chest (this exercise requires special apparatus).

- Grasp the bar with hands 7 to 8 inches wider apart than shoulders' width.
- Your hands should be evenly spaced in the grip. Use the wraparound thumb grip, with arms fully extended.
- Pull the bar straight down until you reach a kneeling position or sit in a chair.
- Your head and torso should remain in an upright position.
- Begin to pull the bar downward toward the back of the neck. Your back muscles, not your arms, should start the motion.

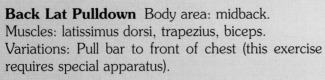
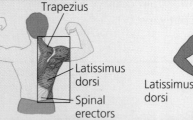

• **Figure 8.34**   *Back Lat Pulldown (machine).*

- Continue to pull the bar downward until it touches the base of your neck. Keep your head and torso up. (In a variation, the bar would go to the front.)
- Breathe out (exhale) during the lifting stage.
- Allow the bar to return slowly to the starting position. Maintain control and speed. Continue the reps.

Straight-back Good Morning Body area: lower back.
Muscles: spinal erectors.
Caution: Spotters and light weights recommended.

- Assume shoulders'-width stance, with feet flat and head and shoulders up.
- Spotters will lift and place the bar across the back of your shoulders, not your neck. (The lifter could use a weight rack to position the bar.)
- Grasp the bar with hands slightly wider apart than shoulders' width.
- Your hands should be evenly spaced in the grip. Use a wraparound thumb grip.
- Slightly bend your knees. Lean forward by bending at the waist.
- Continue downward. Bend until your back is parallel to the floor. Keep your back and feet flat.
- Slowly return to the starting position. Maintain control and speed.
- Continue the reps. Have spotters remove the bar at the completion of the reps.

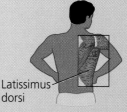
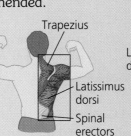

• **Figure 8.35** *Straight-Back Good Morning.*

Legs

Back Squat
Body area: front upper leg.
Muscles: quadriceps, gluteals, hamstrings.
Variations: Machine leg press.
Caution: Spotters and squat rack recommended; weight belt required.

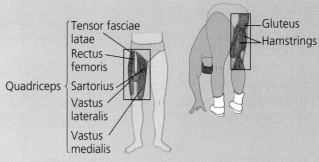

(Continued on next page)

Lifting Technique Checklist *(continued)*

- The bar should be positioned on the rack about shoulder high.
- Your hands should be slightly wider apart than your shoulders.
- Your hands should be evenly spaced. Use a wraparound thumb grip.
- Position your shoulders, hips, and feet under the bar.
- Place the bar across your shoulders (not on your neck).
- Pull your shoulders back. Straighten up your back and raise your chest, with your head up.
- Begin the lift by straightening your legs. (Spotters assist in removing the weight.)
- Take one step away from the rack, and assume shoulders'-width stance.
- Your feet should be lined up evenly and your toes slightly turned out. Your weight should be evenly distributed on your feet.
- Stabilize the bar before starting the downward motion. (Spotters should release the bar.)
- Slowly bend your knees and lower your hips. Keep your back flat. Do not lean forward.
- Continue to lower the bar until your thighs (quadriceps) are parallel to the floor. Do not bounce or hesitate at the bottom.
- Your knees must stay lined up with your feet. Do not let them point in or out.
- Your heels must stay on the floor. Do not lean forward on your toes.
- The bar is lifted by straightening your legs and hips.
- Your head and eyes are up, and your knees are aligned with your toes, and back is flat.
- Your feet are flat, with weight slightly more on the heels.
- Breathe out (exhale) during the lifting stage near the top of the lift.
- Slowly return to the starting position. Maintain control and speed.
- Continue the reps. Replace the bar on the rack. Never release your grip until the bar is safely in the rack. (Spotters should assist in replacing the bar.)

- **Figure 8.36** *Back Squat.*

Leg Press (machine)—Works Quadriceps.

Lunge Body area: leg.
Muscles: quadriceps, gluteals, hamstrings.
Variations: straight bar.
Caution: Spotters recommended.

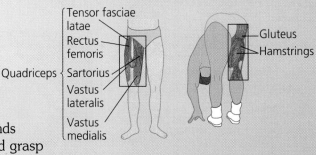

- Assume shoulders'-width stance, with feet flat on the floor and back straight.
- Bend your knees and waist to place your hands on the dumbbells. Fully extend your arms and grasp the dumbbells with a wraparound grip.
- Your hands should be slightly wider apart than your shoulders.
- Return to a standing position.
- Take one big step directly forward with your left leg.
- Your left foot should hit heel first and go to a flat position.
- Bend your left knee slowly to a parallel position. Your left knee should not go beyond your toes.
- Your right knee should slightly bend, but not touch the floor.
- Your back should remain straight. Do not lean forward at the waist.
- Return to the starting position by pushing back with your left leg.
- Breathe out (exhale) during the push stage. Do not hold your breath.
- Hesitate at the starting position. Then repeat the same task with your right leg.
- At the completion of the reps, return the dumbbells to the floor or rack.

- ***Figure 8.37***   *Lunge (free weight).*

Leg Curl (machine) Body area: upper back leg.
Muscles: hamstring.

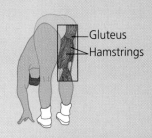

- Lie face down on the bench (machine).
- Keep your hips, legs, and chest flat on the bench.
- Your kneecaps should be past the end of the bench.
- Your hands should grasp the bench handles.

(Continued on next page)

Lifting Technique Checklist *(continued)*

- Position the back of your ankle on the roller pads.
- Begin the lift by flexing your knees. Raise the pads to your buttocks.
- Your hips must remain in contact with the bench.
- Breathe out (exhale) during the pull stage. Do not hold your breath.
- Slowly lower the roller pad to the starting position and continue the reps.

• **Figure 8.38**   *Leg Curl (machine).*

Leg Extension (machine) Body area: front upper leg. Muscles: quadriceps.

- Sit in an upright position on the bench with your head up.
- Your back is flat, and your grip is on the handles.
- Place your upper ankle under the roller pad.
- Raise the roller pad by extending your legs at the knee.
- Extend your legs completely, and hold for 2 counts.
- Breathe out (exhale) during the push stage. Do not hold your breath.
- Slowly lower the pad to the starting position.
- Your back and buttocks must stay in contact with the bench.
- Continue the reps.

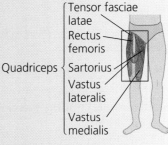

Tensor fasciae latae
Rectus femoris
Quadriceps
Sartorius
Vastus lateralis
Vastus medialis

• **Figure 8.39**   *Leg Extension (machine).*

Standing Heel Raise Body area: lower leg.
Muscle: gastrocnemius.

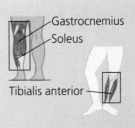

- The bar should be positioned on the rack about shoulder high.
- Your grip width should be slightly wider than your shoulders' width.
- Your hands should be evenly spaced in the grip. Use a wraparound thumb grip.
- Place the bar across your shoulders (not on your neck).
- Your feet should be 8 to 10 inches apart. Place the balls of your feet on a raised surface 1½ to 2 inches high.
- Lock out your knees (straight not flexed).
- Push up on your toes to raise your heels to their highest position.
- Breathe out (exhale) during the push stage. Do not hold your breath.
- Slowly lower your heels until they touch the floor, and continue the reps.
- Replace the bar in the rack.

• **Figure 8.40** *Standing Heel Raise (free weight).*

Arms

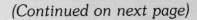

Arm Curl Body area: front of upper arm.
Muscles: biceps.
Variation: dumbbells.

- Assume shoulders'-width stance, with feet flat on the floor.
- Bend your knees, not your waist, to place your hands on the bar.
- Your grip should be the width of your hips.
- Your grip should be evenly spaced. Use a wraparound thumb grip, with palms up.
- Keep your back flat, and straighten your legs to stand up.
- In your starting position, your knees should be slightly bent and your arms fully extended in front.
- Keep your elbows in a stationary position at your side.
- Raise the bar by flexing your arm at the elbow. Raise the bar until your upper and lower arms are squeezed together.

(Continued on next page)

Lifting Technique Checklist *(continued)*

- Keep your back flat and straight. Do not swing your body.
- Breathe out (exhale) during the lifting stage. Do not hold your breath.
- Slowly lower the bar to the starting position. Continue the reps.

• **Figure 8.41**   *Arm Curl.*

French Press Body area: back of upper arm.
Muscle: triceps.
Variation: dumbbells.

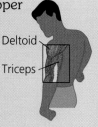

Deltoid

Triceps

- Assume shoulders'-width stance, with feet flat on the floor.
- Bend your knees, not your waist, to place your hands on the bar.
- Your grip should be 6 inches apart in the middle of the bar. Use a wraparound thumb grip.
- Keep your back flat, and straighten your legs to stand up.
- Raise the bar over your head, with arms fully extended and knees slightly bent.
- The area from the shoulder to the elbow should stay in this position throughout the exercise.
- Slowly lower the bar to the back of your neck by bending your arm at the elbow.
- Keep your elbows close to your head and near your ears.
- When the bar touches the back of your neck, return the bar to the overhead position by straightening your arms.
- Do not allow your elbows to move away from your ears.
- Breathe out (exhale) during the pushing stage; do not hold your breath.
- Continue the reps.

• **Figure 8.42**   *French Press.*

• *Variation of French Press (dumbbells).*

Dumbbell Kickback Body area: back of upper arm.
Muscle: triceps.

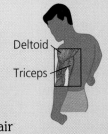

- Assume shoulders'-width stance, with feet flat on the floor and knees slightly bent.
- Bend over at the waist until your upper body is parallel to the floor.
- Extend one arm, and place your hand on a bench or chair for balance.
- Place the dumbbell in your other hand. Use a wraparound thumb grip, with your palm facing your leg.
- Raise the dumbbell to your waist. Bend your arm at the elbow so that your upper arm is parallel to the floor and your lower arm is perpendicular to the floor.
- Straighten your elbow until your arm is straight. Do not move the position of your elbow in relation to your waist.
- Breathe out (exhale) during the lifting stage; do not hold your breath.
- Slowly lower the dumbbell to the starting position. Do not swing your arm.
- Continue the reps, and then switch arms.

- **Figure 8.43**
Dumbbell Kickback.

Abdominals

Abdominal Crunch Body area: stomach.
Muscles: abdominals.
Variations: incline bench, raised feet, machines.

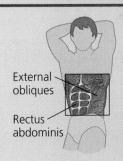

- Lie face up on a mat or carpet floor. Your back and buttocks should be flat on the surface.
- Your knees should be bent. Position your feet flat on the floor with your heels twelve to eighteen inches from your buttocks.
- Place your hands and arms across your chest. Your hands should be placed near the opposite shoulders.
- Position your chin in a tucked position which allows your chin to touch your chest.
- Contract your abdominal muscles and raise your torso until your elbows contact your upper thigh.

(Continued on next page)

Lifting Technique Checklist *(continued)*

- Breathe out (exhale) when your elbows contact your thighs.
- Slowly return to the starting position. Do not let your chin lose contact with your chest. Your head should not touch the floor.
- Repeat the process until the reps are completed.

• **Figure 8.44** *Abdominal Crunch.*

Twisting Abdominal Crunch Body area: stomach.
Muscles: abdominals, obliques.
Variations: incline bench, raised feet.

- Lie face up on a mat or carpet floor. Your back and buttocks should be flat on the surface.
- Your knees should be bent. Position your feet flat on the floor with your heels twelve to eighteen inches from your buttocks.
- Place your hands and arms across your chest. Your hands should be placed near the opposite shoulders.
- Keep your chin in a tucked position, which allows your chin to touch your chest.
- Contract your abdominal muscles and raise your torso from the floor. Continue to raise your torso until your elbows are near your thighs.
- Twist your torso to the left and touch your right elbow to your left thigh. If possible, extend your right elbow past the left thigh.
- Breathe out (exhale) when your elbow contacts your thigh.
- Slowly return to the starting position. Do not let your chin lose contact with your chest. Your head should not touch the floor.
- Start the process again, but twist the torso to the right side touching your left elbow to your right thigh.
- Slowly return to the starting position.
- Repeat the process until the reps are completed.

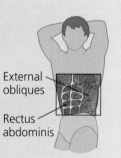

External obliques

Rectus abdominis

• **Figure 8.45** *Twisting Abdominal Crunch.*

Designing Your Personal Weight-training Program

This activity will guide you in designing a program geared to your own needs and goals. Using the following list of program components and the record keeping chart in Figure 8.46, create a three-week workout schedule that will meet your weight-training goals.

Program Components:

1. Your goals (hypertrophy, strength, endurance, and so on).
2. Which days of the week (three days or four days).
3. Which exercises (upper or lower body; big or small muscles).
4. The order of exercises (push-pull or big-small).
5. The weight arrangement (pyramid or same load).
6. Number of reps (based on intensity, such as 60, 75, or 85 percent of maximum).
7. Number of sets (1 to 3 or 4 to 5).
8. Length of rest periods between sets (20 to 30 seconds, 30 to 90 seconds, or 2 to 3 minutes).
9. How to vary the program from week to week.

Weight Training: Daily Workout Design Chart		
Day of the Week		Week #
Body Part	Set x Rep. x Weight	Exercise
Chest		
Shoulder		
Triceps		
Legs		
Back		
Biceps		
Abdominals		

• **Figure 8.46** *Weight Training: Daily Workout Design Chart.*

SECTION 6 REVIEW

Answer the following questions on a separate sheet of paper:

1. List seven upper body weight-training exercises.
2. List six lower body weight-training exercises.

SUMMARY

Weight training is a great way to improve and maintain your muscular strength and endurance. Once you have learned how to design reasonable and obtainable goals you can begin your workouts. Properly designed long- and short-term goals can also help you stick to your workout plans.

Your choice of a weight-training partner is an important consideration. This person should be a friend, a motivator, and a spotter. Your partner's interest and attitude can have an effect on your success. You and your partner need to know safety and correct technique in the weight room.

Because weight training is directed at the muscles of your body, you should be able to identify and explain which muscles are being exercised during your workouts. How the exercises are organized is an important consideration for your muscle development. Organizing your exercises in a variety of ways can keep your workouts intense and prevent workout boredom. Properly designed workouts will allow adequate recovery time between sets, exercises, and workouts.

You should occasionally conduct strength evaluations on a variety of your muscles.

These evaluations should be conducted safely and correctly. Your strength evaluations can both motivate you and help you determine your workout training loads.

As you become more experienced with weight training, you may want to try more advanced programs. Specific programs like supersets, pyramids, and compound sets are designed for specific results. Your goals and desires will help you determine which program to use and how often you should use each one.

Which program you use is subject to change, but correct lifting technique is not. There is only one correct way to lift weights. Never sacrifice correct form while attempting to lift heavy weights. Not everyone has the same type of equipment; therefore, it is necessary that you clearly understand how to conduct a variety of exercises with a variety of equipment.

Weight training is an activity that you can do the rest of your life. The skills and knowledge that you have gained in this chapter and Chapter 7 should provide you with the confidence and ability to establish and revise your own program to fit your changing needs and goals.

Chapter 8 Review

True/False

On a separate sheet of paper, mark each question below either T for True or F for False.

1. Setting realistic goals can determine the success of your weight-training workouts.
2. Safety is always the most important factor in the weight room.
3. It is not necessary to use a wraparound thumb grip on all lifts.
4. Reps are the basic unit of any workout plan.
5. It is usually a good idea to work your smaller muscles first so that you will be warmed up when you go to the large muscles.
6. Pretesting your maximum strength can help you plan your goals and workouts.
7. Muscle strength can best be developed with heavy weights and low numbers of repetitions.
8. Muscles should recover during twenty-four hours of rest before they are worked again in the weight room.
9. Negative workouts are for strength development, but they should not be used often.
10. Supersets should work antagonistic muscles.

Multiple Choice

1. Christen is considering a weight-training program. Which of the following should she consider before developing her goals?
   a. her current level of strength
   b. her daily schedule
   c. past injuries
   d. all of the above
   e. a and c only

2. Which of the following muscle combinations are not considered main muscle areas of the body?
   a. neck and back
   b. chest and shoulder
   c. legs and arms
   d. abdominals and arms

3. Pat has designed a workout with the following order of exercises: bench press, lunge, shoulder press, squat, bent-over row, leg extension. Which of the following best describes this order of exercises?
   a. push versus pull
   b. strongest muscles versus weakest muscles
   c. upper body versus lower body
   d. large muscles versus small muscles

4. Weight room safety includes which of the following rules?
   a. do not hold your breath
   b. control the speed of weights at all times
   c. use proper technique at all times
   d. all of the above
   e. a and c only

5. Which of the following is *not* a responsibility of the spotter?
   a. stay in a ready position at all times
   b. motivate your partner
   c. correct improper technique
   d. determine how much weight your partner should use

6. Paige is interested in improving her muscle tone and endurance. Which of the following plans should she put in her program?
   a. 2 to 3 sets of 12 to 20 reps
   b. 2 to 3 sets of 8 to 12 reps
   c. 3 to 5 sets of 4 to 6 reps
   d. 1 to 2 sets of 7 to 10 reps

7. Recovery time for muscles is important at which of the following times?

   a. between sets
   b. between exercises
   c. between workouts
   d. all of the above
   e. a and c only

8. A split-week workout would use which of the following routines?

   a. Monday, Tuesday, Thursday, Friday (off Wednesday, Saturday, and Sunday)
   b. Monday, Wednesday, and Friday (off Tuesday, Thursday, Saturday, and Sunday)
   c. Sunday, Tuesday, and Thursday (off Monday, Wednesday, Saturday, and Sunday)
   d. Monday, Wednesday, Friday, and Sunday (off Tuesday, Thursday, and Saturday)

9. Tony wants to use the compound set program for more muscle mass. Which routine would he choose?

   a. bench press, no rest, bench press
   b. arm curls, no rest, french press
   c. squats, no rest, arm curls
   d. any of the above

10. Which of the following exercises does not work the chest?

    a. bench press
    b. french press
    c. incline press
    d. flat bench fly

Discussion

1. Design and explain a five-set pyramid workout for the bench press. Choose your own weight. Then design and explain a three-set superset workout for the arms. Choose your own weight.

2. Identify three weight-training exercises that require the use of the common grip and three that require the use of the narrow grip.

3. Identify and explain six techniques used by spotters. Why are these techniques necessary in the weight room?

Vocabulary Experience

Match the correct term in Column A to the definition in Column B by writing the appropriate number in each blank.

Column A

_____ repetition

_____ split workout

_____ superset method

_____ recovery time

_____ negative workout method

_____ set

Column B

1. Using very heavy weights at the end of a prescribed number of sets and repetitions.

2. A group of consecutive repetitions for any exercise.

3. Time or rest between exercises.

4. Workout requiring you to use two different exercises that train opposing muscles without rest between sets.

5. Completed execution of an exercise one time.

6. High intensity workout that exercises one half of your body at each workout session.

Critical Thinking

1. Identify five components of record keeping, and explain why keeping records is important to your weight-training program.

2. Explain how you can determine your estimated one-repetition maximum.

3. Explain how you can apply each of the following plans when arranging the order of exercises in your workout:

a. Large muscles versus small muscles.
b. Push versus pull.
c. Upper body versus lower body.
d. Strong muscles versus weak muscles.

Chapter 9

Your Body Composition

Contents

Outcomes

After reading and studying this chapter, you will be able to:

1. Explain how body composition is important and contributes to the development and maintenance of moderate to high levels of personal fitness.
2. Discuss how developing and maintaining acceptable levels of lean and fat body tissue can reduce your risk for functional health problems.
3. List and describe body composition evaluations that you could use to assess your body composition now and in the future.
4. Identify and explain strategies you can use to influence your body composition in a positive way.
5. Identify and explain how to control your body weight and body composition safely.

Key Terms

After reading and studying this chapter, you will be able to understand and provide practical definitions for the following terms:

somatotype	lean body weight	metabolic rate
ectomorph	underfat	resting metabolic rate
mesomorph	overfat	(RMR)
endomorph	ideal body weight	eating disorders
essential fat	energy balance	anorexia nervosa
excessive leanness	caloric input	bulimia
diabetes mellitus	caloric expenditure	

INTRODUCTION

*I*n Chapter 1 you learned that body composition is determined by the ratio of water, bone, muscle, and fat in your body. When you look around your personal world, you have probably noticed that "thin is in." The images we see in media advertisements emphasize lean, attractive people. Have you noticed that thin people, not overweight people, are the ones typically trying to sell us all types of products, from toothpaste to exercise equipment?

Physical appearance is important to us all, but it is important that you learn about factors that can influence your own body composition and how you can have an impact on it as you age. It is very difficult, and sometimes unhealthy, for you to try to look as lean and attractive as many of the celebrities that you might idolize. Therefore, it is important for you to learn how participation in regular physical activity or exercise, along with the development of proper nutrition behaviors, can help you make significant changes in your body composition. By learning more about body composition, you will be able to develop realistic mental and physical images of what your body composition can and should be.

In this chapter you will learn about the basics of body composition and the factors that influence body composition. You will study examples of body composition self-evaluations, learn how to develop and maintain healthy body composition levels, and understand the facts about controlling your weight and your body composition safely.

SECTION 1   The Basics of Body Composition

somatotype

the type of body you have in terms of your body composition related to heredity.

ectomorph

a slender, lean somatotype.

mesomorph

a muscular somatotype.

If you look around your school, you will notice students and teachers of all sizes and shapes, or body types. Everybody's body type is based, at least in part, on genetics. When you grow to adulthood, you will probably look very similar to your parents. However, you will still have some ability to control your body composition as you age.

Your Body Type

Your body type is determined by the mixture of your bones, muscles, connective tissues, and the amount of body fat you carry. Your **somatotype** is the type of body you have in terms of your body composition related to heredity. You are either small, medium, or large in size. You are also slender and lean (**ectomorph**), muscular (**mesomorph**), or heavier and rounder (**endomorph**). See Figure 9.1. Your somatotype provides a general description of your body composition, although most people are a combination of body types.

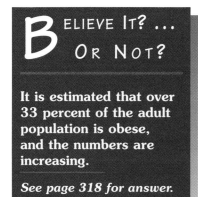

endomorph

a heavier, rounder somatotype.

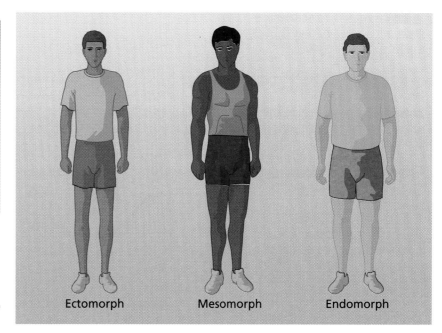

Ectomorph Mesomorph Endomorph

• **Figure 9.1** *General Body Types: Ectomorph, Mesomorph, and Endomorph.*

essential fat

the minimum amount of body fat necessary for good health.

excessive leanness

a percentage of body fat that is too low for good health.

diabetes mellitus

a chronic disease affecting the blood sugar.

It is important that you have an essential amount of fat without having too much fat. **Essential fat** is the minimum amount of body fat necessary for good health. Adolescent males need at least 7 percent body fat. Adolescent females need about 12 percent.

Essential fat helps insulate your body against cold weather and helps cushion your internal organs to protect them from injury. Essential fat also provides you with a valuable source of stored energy so that you can meet your body's need for fuel. Having a percentage of body fat that is too low (**excessive leanness**) or too high (obesity), can be unhealthy.

Body Composition and Your Functional Health

Figure 9.2 illustrates the relationship between carrying too little or too much body weight (and fat) and the risk for developing chronic diseases for adults. The *J* shape of the curve means that those who weigh the least and are excessively lean (those with low essential body fat), as well as those who weigh the most and who are obese (those with excessive body fat) have the greatest risks for developing chronic diseases such as hypertension, heart disease, colon cancer, and **diabetes mellitus**.

Although your weight can influence your functional health, too many people are overly concerned about how much they weigh.

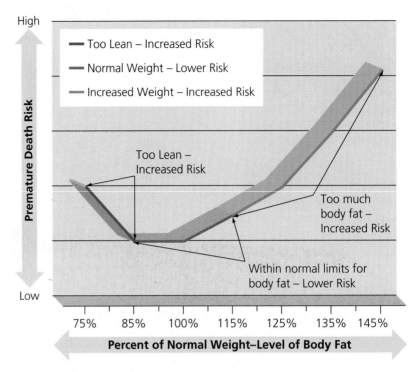

• **Figure 9.2**   *Body Composition and Risk for Chronic Diseases.*

Weight is a poor indicator of your total body composition and really tells you nothing about how lean or fat you are. In reality, when you compare two people of the same size, one may simply weigh more because he or she has more bone, muscle, and connective tissue weight (**lean body weight**) than the other person.

It is more important for you to be concerned about your body composition—particularly the ratio of your lean body weight to your percentage of body fat—than about how much you weigh. Your percentage of body fat can be calculated by using the following equations:

Your body fat weight = Your total body weight − Your lean body weight.

$$\text{Your percentage of body fat} = \frac{\text{Your body fat weight}}{\text{Your total body weight}}.$$

By monitoring your body composition on a regular basis (every 3 to 6 months), you can determine whether your body composition is *within normal limits* (WNL) for good health. For example, adolescent males should carry between 7 and 19 percent body fat, and adolescent females should carry between 12 and 24 percent body fat to be WNL for healthy body composition. If you carry too little body fat, you are **underfat**. If you carry too much body fat, you are **overfat**.

Excessive leanness is associated with being too underfat. Obesity is associated with being too overfat. Adolescent males are considered

lean body weight

the weight of the bones, muscles, and connective tissue.

underfat

carrying too little body fat.

overfat

carrying too much body fat.

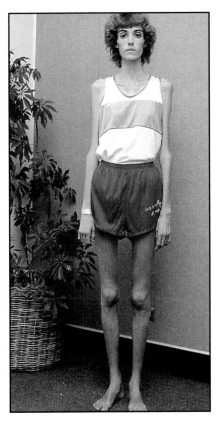 

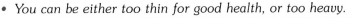

• *You can be either too thin for good health, or too heavy.*

ideal body weight

the perfect weight for good health.

Not everyone can be as lean and glamrous as the media often portrays people.

to be overfat when their body fat is greater than 20 percent and obese when their body fat exceeds 25 percent. Adolescent females are considered to be overfat when their body fat is greater than 25 percent and obese when their body fat exceeds 32 percent.

There is no single **ideal body weight** or ideal percentage of body fat for you. Ideal body weight can be calculated for adults. However, the methods used to do so do not apply as effectively for young adults, whose bodies are still growing and developing.

SECTION 1 REVIEW

Answer the following questions on a separate sheet of paper:

1. Define *somatotype*.
2. What is the *J*-shaped relationship between body composition and the risk for developing chronic diseases?
3. How can you calculate your percentage of body fat?

SECTION 2 | Factors That Influence Your Body Composition

• *Your body composition is influenced by genetics, growth and development, diet, and your physical activity level.*

---

energy balance

the balance between calories consumed in the diet and the amount of calories burned in daily physical activity.

---

caloric input

the number of calories consumed in the diet.

---

caloric expenditure

the number of calories expended or burned in daily physical activity.

Other factors besides genetics can influence your body composition. These factors include your growth and development, diet (the food you consume), and activity level. As you grow, your body increases both the number and size of your fat cells. If you are fatter when you are younger, you tend to develop more fat cells than if you are leaner. Extra fat cells can make it more difficult for you to control your weight and percentage of body fat as you age. The number of fat cells that you will eventually have will be established when you reach your early twenties. However, the size of your fat cells can continue to increase unless you control your diet and adopt an active lifestyle. Fortunately, even individuals with extra fat cells have some control over their body composition and can maintain their body fat levels within normal limits.

Your diet and activity level can also significantly affect your energy balance and body composition. In fact, eating a healthy diet and maintaining an active lifestyle are the two most important steps you can take to help control your body composition now and as you get older.

Energy Balance

Energy balance is the balance between how many calories you *consume* in your diet (**caloric input**) and the amount of calories you *expend* or *burn* in daily physical activity (**caloric expenditure**). If you eat fewer calories in your diet than you expend (or burn) daily, you will lower your percentage of body fat. A simple energy balance equation that illustrates this example might look like the following:

$$\text{Caloric Input} - \text{Caloric Expenditure} = \text{Change in Fat}$$

Caloric Input

Your caloric input is determined by the types and amounts of food you consume. The foods that provide you with calories in your diet are carbohydrates, fats, and proteins. Each of these foods supplies different amounts of calories. For example, 1 gram of carbohydrate provides 4 calories of energy; 1 gram of fat provides 9 calories of energy; and 1 gram of protein provides 4 calories of energy (Figure 9.3). If you know these equivalents and the number of grams of these nutri-

• *It is important for you to be aware of the number of calories that you are consuming each day in order to control your body composition.*

---

1 gram carbohydrates = 4 calories

1 gram fat = 9 calories

1 gram protein = 4 calories

• **Figure 9.3** *Calories per Gram of Nutrient.*

metabolic rate

the number of calories that is burned or expended as heat.

resting metabolic rate (RMR)

the amount of calories you need and expend while sitting comfortably at rest.

ents in the food you consume, you can calculate the amount of calories you consume at each meal and for each day. You can then use this information to determine if your daily caloric intake is appropriate for your energy needs. (Chapter 10 will tell you more about this.)

It is recommended that adolescent males consume between 2,500 and 3,000 calories per day. Adolescent females should consume 2,000 to 2,500 calories per day. These recommendations are based on the average energy needs for adolescents. Females typically need fewer calories than males because males, on average, are larger than females and carry more muscle mass.

The recommended amounts of calories for adolescents are higher than for adults. The reason is that adolescents, who are growing and developing rapidly, need more energy than adults, who are fully grown. If you are a very active person, you will need to consume even more calories than is recommended to meet your energy needs.

Caloric Expenditure

Your **metabolic rate** is the number of calories that you burn or expend as heat. For example you burn calories at rest and during physical activity. Your caloric expenditure is determined by your resting metabolic rate and how physically active you are daily. Your **resting metabolic rate (RMR)** is the amount of calories you need and expend while sitting comfortably at rest.

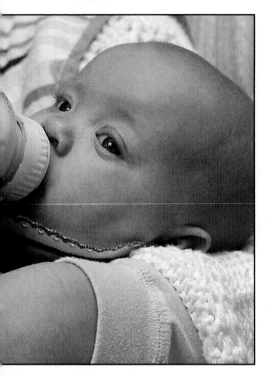

• *Your resting metabolic rate is at its highest during infancy; it slows as you age.*

Resting Metabolic Rate (RMR). Your RMR represents the energy needed for your heart to beat, for blood to be delivered to the tissues, for your muscles to contract, and so on. For most young adults, this amounts to about 1 to 1.5 calories per minute. In other words, even if all you did was sit perfectly still twenty-four hours a day, you would still need to consume between 1,440 and 2,160 calories just to keep your body functioning.

Your RMR can be affected by several factors, including genetics, age, gender, diet, and activity level. Some people have much higher RMRs than others because of genetic differences. This fact explains why some people tend to be able to eat just about anything and everything they want and not gain weight, whereas others eat in a similar way and gain lots of weight. It may also help explain, at least in part, why some people have a much easier time losing weight and body fat than others.

Figure 9.4 illustrates the relationship between RMR, gender, and age. The figure shows that males, on average, have higher RMRs than females, and also that RMR decreases as you age. This decrease with age is very important, because it suggests that as you age, you will not need to consume as many calories to meet your daily energy needs. If you do not reduce your caloric intake or increase your energy expenditure levels as you age, you will typically see a weight and fat gain.

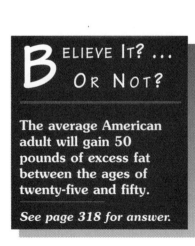

BELIEVE IT? ... OR NOT?

The average American adult will gain 50 pounds of excess fat between the ages of twenty-five and fifty.

See page 318 for answer.

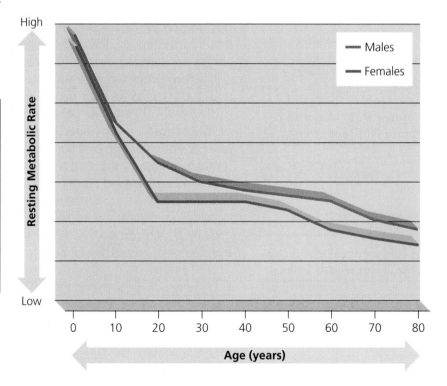

• **Figure 9.4** *Your Metabolic Rate as You Age.*

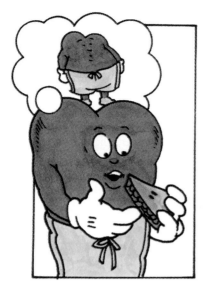

The decrease in RMR helps explain the "creeping" effect of weight and fat gains as people age. Even by consuming just a few more calories than needed, aging adults tend to slowly gain weight and fat over time. Thus, the excess weight and fat that many middle-aged people have "creeps" up on them. For example, a woman might be expected to gain 10 pounds in a year if she consumed about 100 calories (a 2-inch wedge of angel food cake) a day more than she burned.

The number of calories you consume in your diet and the way you eat can stimulate or slow your RMR. For example, if you eat regularly (three to six times) throughout the day, you tend to stimulate your RMR, because digesting your food requires extra energy. However, if you eat only one meal per day (as many busy people do), you actually slow your RMR. This can cause you to gain weight and increase your body fat.

Restricting the number of calories in your daily diet can also significantly slow your RMR. For example, if you went on a diet of 500 calories per day (well below daily recommendations) for several days, you could cause your RMR to drop as much as 75 percent. This would only produce negative results for you. For example, you would always be hungry. You would be tired, because you would have low levels of energy. Finally, you would not see as much weight loss as you had hoped for because your RMR would be lower than normal.

It is thought that by participating in regular physical activity or exercise, you can stimulate your metabolic rate, not only during work but also to some degree following your workout. Because technology (remote controls, dishwashers, garage door openers, and so on) has made it so easy for all of us to remain fairly inactive and comfortable, it only makes sense that we all need to develop and maintain more active lifestyles to achieve energy balance.

Burning Calories with Physical Activity and Exercise. In addition to your RMR, the number of calories you burn in voluntary activities daily also helps determine your total caloric expenditure. You probably have noticed that people have lifestyles that are either very active, very inactive, or somewhere in between. People who are always on the go burn lots of calories, whereas people who just sit around burn few calories.

The number of calories you burn in voluntary activities depends on the number and size of muscles that you work, the weight of the body parts you move, the intensity of your work, and the time/duration of your activities. If you work with your legs (walking) versus your arms (lifting), you will burn more calories, because the larger the active muscle mass (legs versus arms), the more energy needed.

If you weighed 200 pounds and your friend weighed 150 pounds, you would use more energy than your friend if you both did the same

• *You will burn more calories if you are physically active than if you are sedentary.*

Stress Break

It's not enough that your life is full of all kinds of stressors. Now you have pressure to compete with Madison Avenue's or Hollywood's idea of what is thin. Don't get caught up in their unrealistic expectation for thin bodies. In fact, many models are practicing unhealthy behaviors (such as fad diets, diet pills, and so on) to maintain their weight and appearance.

Know what are healthy and reasonable goals for your body composition, and do not allow yourself to fall prey to these unrealistic expectations. After all, working toward a healthy, fit body should make you feel better about yourself, not create undue stress.

activity with equal effort. Moving the heavier body parts requires more energy than moving the smaller body parts.

The longer you engage in physical activity or exercise, the more calories you will burn. You will also burn more calories if you work at a higher intensity, because harder work requires more fuel.

If you engage in daily voluntary activities, you will burn more calories than someone else who lives a sedentary lifestyle. For example, say two individuals have the same resting metabolic rate. One is moderately active, and the other is sedentary. The more active person will burn more calories than the sedentary person. Figure 9.5 shows a typical breakdown of the total energy that these two individuals would spend in one day. The active person burns 500 calories more than the sedentary person. In one week's time, the active person would burn 3,500 calories (7 days × 500 calories) more than the sedentary person.

A pound of fat contains 3,500 calories. If you consume 3,500 calories more than you burn, you will gain a pound of fat. If you want to lose a pound of fat, you need to eat 3,500 fewer calories than you burn. For example, if you wanted to lose a pound of fat in a week, you might use several different strategies. If you were to try to lose the 3,500 calories by just controlling your diet, and you were not active, you would have to reduce your daily caloric intake by 500 calories per day (3,500 calories/7 days = 500 calories/day), which might be difficult. If you tried to lose the 3,500 calories by keeping your diet the same but getting more exercise, you would have to burn an additional 500 calories per day. This would be equivalent to walking an additional 5 miles daily. (Walking 1 mile burns about 100 calories.)

You may have guessed by now that the smartest approach to losing a pound of fat in a week might be to combine the two approaches just described. For example, you could reduce your daily caloric intake by 250 calories and burn an additional 250 calories per day. With this method, you would lose a pound of fat in one week without needing to become too extreme with your diet or activity plan. By combining a proper diet and activity level, you can con-

Energy Needs	Sedentary Person	Active Person
Energy for resting metabolic rate	1,600 calories	1,600 calories
Energy for voluntary activities	100 calories	600 calories
Total energy needs	1,700 calories	2,200 calories

• **Figure 9.5** *Energy Expenditure of Sedentary versus Active Persons.*

trol your lean muscle mass and percentage of body fat much more efficiently than if you work on only one side of the energy balance equation.

Figure 9.6 lists selected physical activities and exercises. The list can give you ideas on how to increase your caloric expenditure. You can then use the "Active Mind/Active Body" activity on the next page to analyze your own caloric expenditure through exercise.

This figure shows how many calories per minute are spent in activities for people at five different body weights. The calories per pound per minute (Cal/Lb/Min) number makes it possible for you to calculate the number of calories for your own body weight, if it is not exactly one of the five weights listed here.

Activity	Cal/Lb/Min[a]	Calories Spent per Minute (for 5 body weights, in pounds)				
		110	**125**	**150**	**175**	**200**
Aerobic dance (vigorous)	0.062	6.8	7.8	9.3	10.9	12.4
Basketball (vigorous, full court)	0.097	10.7	12.1	14.6	17.0	19.4
Bicycling						
13 miles per hour	0.045	5.0	5.6	6.8	7.9	9.0
19 miles per hour	0.076	8.4	9.5	11.4	13.3	15.2
Canoeing (flat water, moderate pace)	0.045	5.0	5.6	6.8	7.9	9.0
Cross-country skiing (8 miles per hour)	0.104	11.4	13.0	15.6	18.2	20.8
Golf (carrying clubs)	0.045	5.0	5.6	6.8	7.9	9.0
Handball	0.078	8.6	9.8	11.7	13.7	15.6
Horseback riding (trot)	0.052	5.7	6.5	7.8	9.1	10.4
Rowing (vigorous)	0.097	10.7	12.1	14.6	17.0	19.4
Running						
5 miles per hour	0.061	6.7	7.6	9.2	10.7	12.2
7.5 miles per hour	0.094	10.3	11.8	14.1	16.4	18.8
10 miles per hour	0.114	12.5	14.3	17.1	20.0	22.9
Soccer (vigorous)	0.097	10.7	12.1	14.6	17.0	19.4
Studying	0.011	1.2	1.4	1.7	1.9	2.2
Swimming						
20 yards per minute	0.032	3.5	4.0	4.8	5.6	6.4
45 yards per minute	0.058	6.4	7.3	8.7	10.2	11.6
Tennis (beginner)	0.032	3.5	4.0	4.8	5.6	6.4
Walking (brisk pace)						
3.5 miles per hour	0.035	3.9	4.4	5.2	6.1	7.0

[a]*Cal/Lb/Min* is an abbreviation for *calories* (Cal) per *pound* (Lb) of body weight per *minute* (Min). You can use it to calculate the number of calories you use at *your* body weight for a minute of activity. To calculate the total number of calories you spend for a longer time, multiply the Cal/Lb/Min factor by your exact weight and then multiply your answer by the number of minutes you spend on the activity. For example, if you weight 142 pounds, and you want to know how many calories you spend doing 30 minutes of vigorous aerobic dance: 0.062 Cal/Lb/Min × 142 lb = 8.8 calories per minute. 8.8 Cal/Min × 30 Minutes = 264 Total Calories Spent.

Source: Values for swimming, bicycling, and running have been adapted with permission of Ross Laboratories, Columbus, Ohio 43216, from G.P. Town and K.B. Wheeler, Nutrition Concerns for the Endurance Athlete, *Dietetic Currents* 13(1986):7-12. Copyright 1986 Ross Laboratories. Values for all other activities: Copyright 1983 by Consumers Union of the United States, Inc., Yonkers, N.Y. 10703-1057. Adapted with permission from CONSUMER REPORTS BOOKS,1983.

• *Figure 9.6* *Energy Demands of Activities.*

Active Mind! Active Body!

Calculating Caloric Expenditure

Review Figure 9.6, and pick two activities or exercises that you do somewhat regularly. Calculate how many calories you would expend for one week if you did each exercise or activity three times a week for twenty minutes, forty minutes, or one hour.

SECTION 2 REVIEW

Answer the following questions on a separate sheet of paper:

1. Give a simple energy balance equation.
2. What is RMR, and what factors influence it?
3. How can voluntary activities increase the number of calories you burn?

SECTION 3 Body Composition Evaluations

In Chapter 4, you performed a simple body composition evaluation by pinching your thigh. You also performed the *Prudential Fitnessgram* Body Mass Index (BMI) Fitness Check in that chapter. In this section you will learn some additional ways to evaluate your body composition. You should perform one or more of the self-evaluations described here.

Height/Weight Chart Fitness Check

Height and weight charts provide average weight ranges based on your height, age, and gender. These charts provide only a very rough measure of body composition. You can use Figure 9.7 to compare your weight with that of others of your same height, age, and gender.

Height (in inches)	Females Weight Range (in pounds)					
	12	13	14	15	16	17
53 – 54.9	58 – 78	—	—	—	—	—
55 – 56.9	76 – 101	74 – 98	—	—	—	—
57 – 58.9	79 – 106	84 – 112	84 – 112	95 – 127	104 – 139	86 – 115
59 – 60.9	87 – 116	88 – 118	95 – 127	99 – 132	103 – 137	99 – 132
61 – 62.9	96 – 128	99 – 132	102 – 136	103 – 137	105 – 140	109 – 145
63 – 64.9	105 – 140	105 – 140	108 – 144	113 – 151	114 – 152	114 – 152
65 – 66.9	109 – 145	115 – 154	116 – 155	121 – 161	122 – 163	121 – 161
67 – 68.9	126 – 168	115 – 154	128 – 170	130 – 173	126 – 168	123 – 164
69 – 70.9	—	—	121 – 162	126 – 168	144 – 192	130 – 174

Height (in inches)	Males Weight Range (in pounds)					
	12	13	14	15	16	17
53 – 54.9	65 – 86	65 – 86	—	—	—	—
55 – 56.9	68 – 91	73 – 97	—	—	—	—
57 – 58.9	78 – 104	77 – 103	80 – 107	—	—	—
59 – 60.9	85 – 114	85 – 113	91 – 121	—	—	—
61 – 62.9	94 – 125	94 – 125	94 – 126	104 – 139	99 – 132	108 – 144
63 – 64.9	101 – 134	105 – 140	103 – 138	105 – 140	105 – 140	114 – 152
65 – 66.9	111 – 148	111 – 148	115 – 154	114 – 152	118 – 157	124 – 166
67 – 68.9	124 – 166	123 – 164	124 – 166	125 – 167	124 – 166	133 – 178
69 – 70.9	—	135 – 180	130 – 173	130 – 174	133 – 178	136 – 181
71 – 72.9	—	—	144 – 192	143 – 191	144 – 192	146 – 194
73 – 74.9	—	—	—	148 – 197	161 – 215	151 – 202
75 – 76.9	—	—	—	166 – 221	—	162 – 216

The numbers in these columns may surprise you. Some older teens weigh less than some younger teens the same height, because gains in weight often don't keep up with gains in height.

Note: The lower number in each weight range was derived by calculating 10 percent below, and the higher number was derived by calculating 20 percent above, the expected weight for height and age of youths 12 to 17 years old.

• **Figure 9.7** *Expected Weight Ranges for Teenagers (based on height and age).*

Remember, however, that your weight in comparison with that of others does not really provide you with information about how lean or fat you are. You should use height and weight charts only in a general way to get an idea about your weight in relation to that of others.

Body Circumference Fitness Check

Another way to evaluate your body composition is to take body circumference measurements to help you estimate your percentage of body fat. When you measure circumferences or girths (measurements around a body), you need to use a tape measure (Figure 9.8).

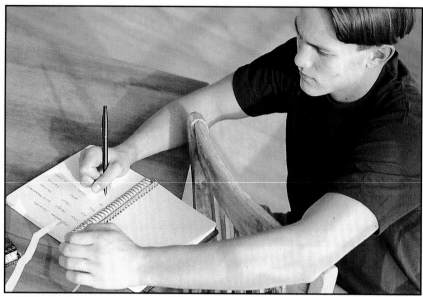

• *Record your body circumference measures and use either your weight (males) or height (females) to determine your body composition as described in the text.*

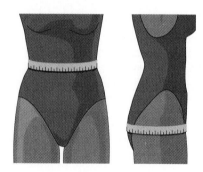

• **Figure 9.8** *Anatomic Landmarks for Measuring Various Girths.*

Two different methods are used for males and females to estimate percentage of body fat from body circumference measurements.

For Males. Males can estimate their percentage of body fat by measuring weight in pounds and then measuring the circumference of the waist at the navel level. To do this estimate, weigh yourself without your shoes on, but dressed in your exercise clothing. Measure your waist circumference with the tape measure pulled snugly, but not too tight. Measure to the nearest half-inch. Once you have obtained your measurements, Figure 9.9 will help you determine your percentage of body fat. Using a ruler, connect the points from your body weight to your waist circumference. The point where the line intersects the middle scale tells you your approximate percentage of body fat.

For Females. Females can estimate their percentage of body fat by measuring their height and the circumference at the widest point of their hips. To do this, measure your height, without your shoes on, to the nearest half-inch. The hip circumference measurement should be taken with the tape measure pulled snugly, but not too tight, and to the nearest half-inch. Once you have obtained your measurements, you can use Figure 9.10 to determine your percentage of body fat. Using a ruler, connect the points from your body height to your hip circumference. The point where the line intersects the middle scale tells you your approximate percentage of body fat.

For Both Males and Females. Whether you are male or female, once you have determined your percentage of body fat, you

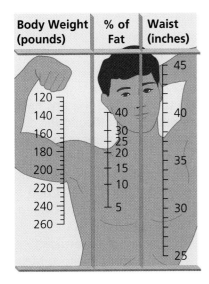

• **Figure 9.9** *Percentage of Body Fat for Males from Weight and Waist Circumference Measurements.*

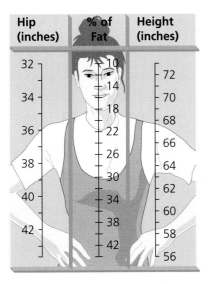

• **Figure 9.10** *Percentage of Body Fat for Females from Hip Circumference and Height Measurements. Source:* Figures 9.9 and 9.10 adapted with permission from J. H. Wilmore, *Sensible Fitness* (Champaign, IL: Human Kinetics, 1986).

can use Figure 9.11 to evaluate your body fat score. For good to better health, males should carry 7 to 19 percent body fat. Females should carry 12 to 24 percent body fat. If you do not score in the *good* to *better* healthy zones, you should try to improve your body composition.

Skinfold Evaluation Fitness Check

The most commonly used method to evaluate body composition is skinfold measurements. Skinfold measurements are good indicators of body composition because 50 percent of all body fat is between the muscles and skin, and the other 50 percent is inside the body. Skinfold measurements are taken with skinfold calipers, which are devices used to pinch the fat between the muscles and skin to measure skinfold thickness in millimeters. For adolescents, two skinfold measurements are typically taken: the back of the upper arm (triceps) and the inside of the calf at its widest part. You can use the "Fitness Check" activity on the next page to determine your skinfold measurements.

Medical or Laboratory Evaluations

Other methods to evaluate body composition are used by medical professionals or laboratory technicians. These methods include underwater weighing, bioelectrical impedance, and magnetic resonance imaging (MRI) scans. The techniques are usually used only in research or for special follow-up after medical screening.

Underwater weighing is based on the concept that people who have lower levels of body fat sink when they try to float in water,

Fitness Rating	% Fat (Males)	Fitness Rating	% Fat (Females)
Too Lean	6 or less	Too Lean	11 or less
Healthy Lean	7–9	Healthy Lean	12–14
Healthy	10–19	Healthy	15–24
Borderline High	20–24	Borderline High	25–29
Overfat	25 or more	Overfat	30 or more

• **Figure 9.11** *Rating Body Fatness.*

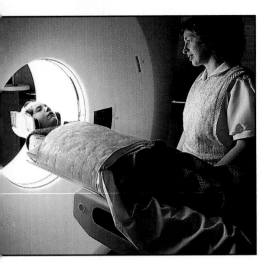

• *MRI scans are the most accurate way to determine body composition levels but cost at least $1,000 a scan.*

whereas people with excess fat float easily in water. This body composition measurement technique involves weighing a person in a submerged chair, which is attached to a scale.

Bioelectrical impedance is a body composition measurement procedure during which harmless electrical current is transmitted between two electrodes attached to your body while you are lying down. A person who is fatter will have a greater resistance to the current flow than a leaner person. Mathematical equations are then used to determine body composition.

MRI scans use the technology of medical imaging techniques, radio waves, and computers to assess body composition. This method is considered to be the most accurate way to assess body composition. However, it is also the most expensive (about $1,000 a scan).

For your own personal fitness assessments, skinfold evaluations provide the most accurate measure of your body composition. Measures of your body mass index (BMI) are the next best way to determine your body composition (see Chapter 4). Body circumference measurements are less accurate, but they are better than just measuring your height and weight.

Fitness Check ✔

Body Fat Measurements

Use the following guidelines to determine skinfold measurements accurately. To measure your skinfolds you should work with a partner and take each other's measurements with a set of calipers.

1. Use your left hand to grasp each skinfold. Avoid grasping the muscle or pinching too tight.

2. For the triceps, use your thumb and index finger to pick up a skinfold in the middle of your partner's right arm exactly half way between the shoulder and the elbow (Figure 9.12). Have your partner keep his or her arm relaxed at the side of the body.

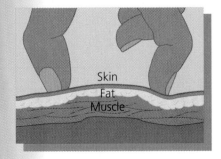
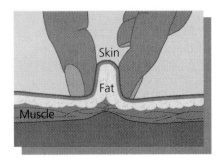

• *Figure 9.12*   *Under-the-Skin View of Skinfold Test.*

3. For the calf, have your partner stand up and place his or her right foot on a bench or chair. Use your thumb and index finger to pick up a skinfold in the middle of the inside part of the lower leg at its widest part (Figure 9.13).

4. With your right hand, place the opened caliper one half inch below the skinfold grasp and directly below the pinch, with the scale of the caliper visible.

5. Close the calipers on the skinfold and hold it for two to three seconds. Read and record the measurement to the nearest millimeter. Repeat this two more times.

6. Use the middle of the three readings as your skinfold score. For example, if the three readings are 18, 16, and 15 mm, use 16 as your score.

7. Add up your tricep and calf skinfold scores and use Figure 9.14 to determine your percentage of body fat. Read straight down from your sum of skinfolds to the "% of Fat" reading. Keep track of your findings as follows:

Triceps skinfold   ____ mm

Calf skinfold   + ____ mm   % body fat ____ %

Sum of skinfolds   = ____ mm

(Continued on next page)

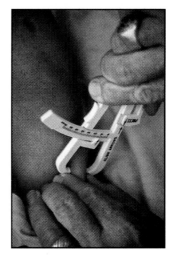

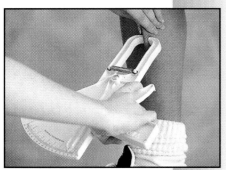

• ***Figure 9.13***   *Skinfold Test for Calf and Tricep.*

Body Fat Measurements *(continued)*

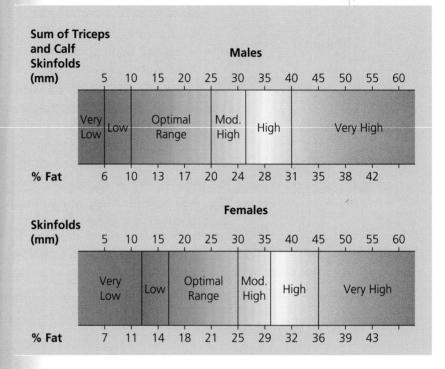

• **Figure 9.14** *Skinfold Measurements (sum of triceps and calf skinfolds) and Body Fat Percentages. Source*: Adapted with permission from: T. G. Lohman, *Measuring Body Fat Using Skinfolds* (videotape) Champaign, IL: Human Kinetics, 1982.

8. Calculate your body fat weight by multiplying your weight by your percentage of body fat:

Weight _____ pounds

% Body fat × _____

Body fat weight = _____ pounds

9. Calculate your lean body weight by subtracting your fat weight from your weight:

Weight _____ pounds

Body fat weight − _____ pounds

Lean body weight = _____ pounds

10. Determine your range of ideal body weight by dividing 0.76 and 0.88 (for females) or 0.81 and 0.93 (for males) into your lean weight. These numbers represent calculations based on good to better levels for body composition. (Males should carry 7 to 19 percent body fat, and females should carry 12 to 24 percent body fat.)

Females:

    Ideal minimum (12%) = Your lean body weight ÷ 0.88 = _____ lbs.

    Ideal maximum (24%) = Your lean body weight ÷ 0.76 = _____ lbs.

Males:

    Ideal minimum (7%) = Your lean body weight ÷ 0.93 = _____ lbs.

    Ideal maximum (19%) = Your lean body weight ÷ 0.81 = _____ lbs.

11. Refer to Table 9.11 to evaluate your body fat score. For good to better health, males should carry 7 to 19 percent body fat and females should carry 12 to 24 percent body fat. If you did not score in the good to better zones, you should try to improve your body composition by getting closer to your ideal body weight range.

SECTION 3 REVIEW

Answer the following questions on a separate sheet of paper:

1. How do you determine your body composition by using body circumference measures?

2. How do you determine your body composition by using skinfold measures?

3. What are two medical or laboratory techniques of measuring body composition?

SECTION 4   Developing and Maintaining a Healthy Body Composition

To develop and maintain a healthy body composition, you need to design a personal fitness plan to control your caloric intake and caloric expenditure. By adjusting your diet, your physical activity, and your exercise level, you can make positive changes in your body composition. You will also need to determine your FIT by using the results from your body composition evaluations. Apply the scientific principles you learned in Chapter 3 and your personal fitness goals to develop your own body composition improvement plan. The recommendations that follow can help you develop your plan.

Any Body Can!

Christy Henrich

Christy Henrich (1972–1994) was at one time one of America's best gymnasts at 4 feet, 10 inches tall, and 95 pounds. She was a world-class competitor. As competitive as she was, however, she could not beat the eating disorder bulimia. When she died at age 22, she weighed 61 pounds.

Christy grew up just outside Independence, Missouri. She started in gymnastics at the age of four. By the time Christy was in high school she was training seven days a week to become an Olympic gymnast.

In 1986, at the age of 14, Christy finished fifth at the national junior (under 18) championships. In 1988, Christy finished tenth at the senior national championships and set her sights on making the 1988 U.S. Olympic gymnastic team. She missed earning a spot on that Olympic team by 0.118 of a point in a vault performance at the Olympic trials.

Christy regrouped somewhat from her Olympic trials disappointment and continued to train harder than ever. In 1989 she finished second in the all-around gymnastic competition at the U.S. championships. She also finished fourth in the world championships in the uneven parallel bars event. Unfortunately, for Christy, at the same time she was having such great success in competition, she developed a serious eating disorder.

She began eating less and less because she felt that she was "too fat," although she only weighed 90 pounds. She also became bulimic. Christy felt that the leaner she could become the better she would perform. Unfortunately, this is not true. The pressure to be thin is, however, one that athletes (for example gymnasts, dancers, runners, and figure skaters) and models face daily. This pressure is even harder on high performance individuals who strive for perfection in everything they do in life.

Christy entered counseling to control her eating disorder once others helped her recognize her problem. She had some moderate success fighting her addiction in the early 1990s. But she had a relapse in June of 1994, and in late July she went into a coma for three days and died. Her body shut down because it did not have enough fuel. In a sense, Christy died of malnutrition.

Christy Henrich was an outstanding athlete, but she was not perfect. She became obsessed with perfection in her sport. This obsession contributed to the development of a fatal eating disorder, that ironically, she thought would improve her performances.

Not everyone can be a world champion athlete like Christy Henrich, but Any Body Can develop a sound nutrition and personal fitness plan. You can also learn to recognize the early signs of eating disorders and understand how to prevent them (see page 323 for more information).

Specificity Principle

To improve your body composition, you need to control the number of calories in your diet and your caloric expenditure in relation to how active your lifestyle is. Aerobic activities are especially important in your plan, because they cause you to expend several calories per minute in each session. Muscular strength and endurance activities are also important to include, because they will help you improve or maintain your muscle mass while helping you control fat weight.

Frequency

The first component of FIT, of course, is *frequency.* The rule for frequency in your diet should be to eat at regular intervals three times per day, plus one or two planned snacks. In this way you will avoid hunger and impulse eating. Snacks should not be potato chips, cookies, and other fattening foods. Carrot sticks, apples, and other fresh fruits and vegetables make nutritious, good-tasting snacks.

As for frequency of physical activity or exercise, try to achieve the goals of Guidelines 1 and 2 in Chapter 1 (see "Remember This!" below). Be active daily, and include aerobic work as well as muscular strength and endurance work regularly.

Intensity

The second component of FIT, *intensity,* also applies both to diet and physical activity or exercise. To lose a pound of fat, you need to reduce your dietary intake by 3,500 calories below what's normal for you over a set period of time. If you want to gain weight, you need to increase your caloric intake above what's normal for you over a set period of time. If you maintain your caloric intake at the same level and do not vary your physical activity levels, you will maintain your weight and percentage of body fat.

As for physical activity or exercise, to lose a pound of fat, you need to expend 3,500 more calories than what's normal for you over a set period of time. If you want to gain weight, you need to decrease your caloric expenditure below what's normal for you over a set period of time. If you maintain your caloric expenditure at the same level and do not vary your caloric intake, you will maintain your weight and percentage of body fat (Figure 9.15). The following equations summarize the intensity relationships:

Weight maintenance:	Caloric input	=	Caloric expenditure.
Weight loss:	Caloric input	<	Caloric expenditure.
Weight gain:	Caloric input	>	Caloric expenditure.

• *It is very difficult to improve or maintain healthy body composition levels without burning calories.*

REMEMBER This!

Guideline 1. All adolescents should be physically active daily, or nearly every day, as part of play, games, sports, work, transportation, recreation, physical education, or planned exercise, in the context of family, school, or community activities.

Guideline 2. Adolescents should engage in three or more sessions per week of activities that last 20 minutes or more at a time and that require moderate to vigorous levels of exertion.

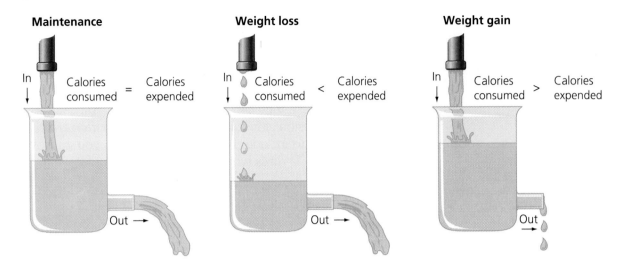

• *Figure 9.15* *Example of Weight Loss, Weight Gain, and Weight Maintenance in Relation to Exercise Intensity.*

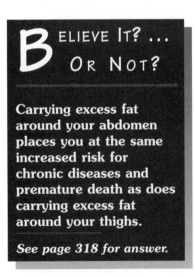

Remember This!

Never change your frequency, intensity, or time/duration all at the same time or too quickly. Be patient, and allow for gradual improvements.

Time/Duration

You have seen that you should work both sides of the energy balance equation to control your body composition. Reduce or increase your caloric intake and caloric expenditure as necessary. In doing so, keep in mind that body composition changes usually occur more slowly than changes in other aspects of personal fitness, such as cardiovascular fitness or muscular strength and endurance.

How can this knowledge be applied to the third component in FIT, *time/duration?* You need to be persistent and patient in working toward your goals. Physical activities or exercises that cause you to work for more than several minutes (45 to 60 minutes) at moderate to vigorous intensity are the most effective at burning fat and excess calories. If you are trying to lose weight and body fat, try to lose no more than 1 to 2 pounds per week for safe, effective results. If you are after weight gain, you should expect slow gains of no more than 1/2 pound per week. By gaining weight slowly and steadily, you add less body fat and more lean muscle. Remember, your ability to change your body composition is related to your genetic potential, so try to develop reasonable and obtainable goals for yourself for the long haul.

Progression Principle

The rate at which you modify your FIT should be based on your personal fitness goals and your changing levels of body composition. Keep in mind that while you are young and growing, your body composition can change fairly quickly. As you get older, however, you wouldn't expect much change for at least 3 to 6 months in most cases.

SECTION 4 REVIEW

Answer the following questions on a separate sheet of paper:

1. What should your frequency of eating be each day to control your body fat percentage?
2. How many calories does a pound of fat have?
3. What equations describe weight maintenance, weight loss, and weight gain?

SECTION 5 # Controlling Your Weight and Body Composition Safely

To control their body composition, young adults sometimes experiment with various quick-fix methods or behaviors such as fad diets, diet pills, and weight-gain powders and pills. These strategies lead to only partial success at best and often lead to dangerous eating disorders.

Eating Disorders

eating disorders

behaviors that cause a person to overeat, undereat, or practice extreme unhealthy actions to control their weight.

anorexia nervosa

an eating disorder in which people abnormally restrict their caloric intake.

Eating disorders are behaviors that cause people to overeat, undereat, or practice extremely unhealthy actions to control their weight. Eating disorders can include a person's eating too much or too little for his or her needs, which is particularly dangerous if the person is still growing and developing. Two eating disorders that are common among young adults are anorexia nervosa and bulimia.

Anorexia nervosa is an eating disorder in which a person abnormally restricts his or her caloric intake. More females than males have anorexia nervosa. People with this disorder believe that they are overweight, even though they appear very lean. People with anorexia nervosa can develop serious malnutrition and have a significant loss of important body fluids. Because they can develop these and other serious health problems, people with this disorder need to seek medical help. In extreme cases, the disease can result in death.

Some common signs or symptoms of a person who is at risk for developing anorexia nervosa are as follows:

- Sudden large weight loss.
- Preoccupation with food, calories, and weight.

bulimia

an eating disorder in which people overeat and then force themselves to vomit afterward or purposely overuse laxatives to eliminate food from their bodies.

• *You should and can develop effective personal strategies for controlling your weight and body composition.*

- Choice of baggy or layered clothing.
- Behaviors of the exercise zealot.
- Mood swings.
- Consumption of minimal amounts of food in front of others.

Bulimia is an eating disorder in which people overeat and then force themselves to vomit afterward (called "bingeing and purging"), or they purposely overuse laxatives to eliminate food from their bodies. Like anorexia nervosa, bulimia is more common among females than males. Bulimics are usually not extremely underweight. In fact, they often have normal body composition. However, they have an addictive behavior that causes them to be obsessed with food and to hide their actions. Bulimia can cause serious negative long-term health effects. Although bulimics need to seek out professional medical help for their problem, they are often reluctant to do so.

Some common signs or symptoms of a person who is at risk for developing bulimia are as follows:

- Noticeable weight loss or gain.
- Excessive concern about weight.
- Habit of visiting the bathroom immediately after meals (to induce vomiting).
- Depressed moods.
- Strict dieting followed by eating binges.
- Very critical attitude toward own body size.

Strategies for Controlling Weight and Body Composition

Poor dietary habits or behaviors and lack of regular physical activity or exercise are the main causes of excessive leanness or obesity. You can use several effective strategies to modify your caloric intake and caloric expenditure habits safely and effectively:

- Eat regularly. Always eat breakfast. Do not starve yourself or fast to lose weight.
- Keep a record of what, where, when, and how much you are eating. (You will learn more about this in Chapter 10.) Cut back on foods that provide empty calories (for example, sodas, candy bars, chips, and cookies). Eat foods that are low in fat.
- Avoid the yo-yo effect of dieting, in which you try to lose weight by dieting without being active (Figure 9.16). If you follow a diet that restricts your caloric intake too much, you tend to lose not only fat but also lean body mass. When you resume normal eating, you also gain back more fat weight than you lost.

"Do you really think five minutes on the skip rope can balance five hours at the trough?"

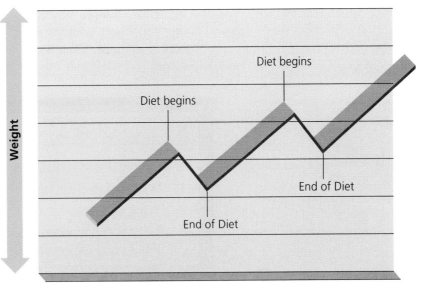

• ***Figure 9.16*** *The Yo-Yo Effect of Dieting.*

• Reward yourself when you accomplish new positive behaviors or habits and achieve your goals. Appropriate rewards should not include food but might be something like some new clothes to fit your new shape.

CONSUMER CORNER Shortcuts Don't Work

Excessive weight loss over a short period of time can be a serious health concern. If you are considering a diet plan that promises huge, fast weight loss, you should follow this plan only under the direction of a physician who specializes in weight-loss medicine. However, choose your health care provider carefully. Many unqualified individuals claim they have a wealth of knowledge about weight-loss procedures when they do not. They only want to charge you for their advice.

Do not accept the opinion of someone who is not professionally trained and certified in nutrition and weight control. Trusting someone who is not professionally trained in nutrition and weight control can be dangerous to your health, as well as a good way to get "ripped off." The best way to control your body weight and body composition is to combine exercise and diet in a sound personal fitness plan.

- Get active. Keep a physical activity and exercise log or journal to help you chart your progress and allow you to reevaluate your goals over time. Chapter 3 has recommendations for keeping a journal.

SECTION 5 REVIEW

Answer the following questions on a separate sheet of paper:

1. What is anorexia nervosa?
2. What is bulimia?
3. List two recommendations for safely modifying your caloric intake and expenditure.

SUMMARY

Physical appearance is important to us all. It is often very difficult and unhealthy, however, to try to be as lean and attractive as many celebrities and models. Many young adults have unrealistic expectations about what their bodies should look like and how much they should weigh.

Each person needs an essential amount of body fat for good health. Excessive leanness and obesity, however, are associated with an increased risk for the development of chronic diseases and premature death. Lean muscle weight includes bone, muscle, and connective tissue weight. Assessing your body composition provides more information than just knowing what you weigh. Your body composition is the ratio of lean body weight to percentage of fat in your body.

Factors that influence your body composition include genetics, growth and development, diet, and activity level. Your resting metabolic rate (RMR) is the amount of calories you need and expend while sitting at rest. Your RMR decreases with age. You can maintain your body composition, however, by balancing your energy input and energy expenditure as you age. You can do this most effectively by monitoring your diet and engaging in voluntary physical activities.

You can evaluate your body composition using a variety of different methods. Skinfold measures are the most accurate, followed in order of accuracy by body mass index (BMI) measures, body circumference measurements, and height/weight charts.

To improve or maintain your good functional health, it is important to develop and maintain an acceptable body composition level. The best way to control your body composition level safely is to modify your diet, if necessary, and adopt an active lifestyle.

Chapter 9 Review

True/False

On a separate sheet of paper, mark each question below either T for True or F for False.

1. Your body type is called your *somatotype*.
2. The graph showing the relationship between body weight and the risk for premature death is *J* shaped.
3. Lean body weight equals body fat weight divided by total body weight.
4. The size of your fat cells will not increase after you reach the age of twenty-five.
5. The energy balance includes energy input and energy expenditure.
6. RMR increases as you age and is higher for females than males.
7. Adopting a diet of less than 1,000 calories is a good way to lose weight.
8. One pound of fat is equivalent to 3,500 calories.
9. Height and weight charts really do not provide information about how lean or fat you are.
10. Anorexia nervosa is associated with disordered eating and excessive exercise disorder.

Multiple Choice

1. What is the minimum recommended amount of essential fat for young adult males?
   a. 1 percent
   b. 7 percent
   c. 12 percent
   d. 18 percent
2. What is the minimum daily recommended caloric intake for young adult females?
   a. 500 calories per day
   b. 1,000 calories per day
   c. 1,500 calories per day
   d. 2,000 calories per day
3. Your body composition is influenced by which of the following?
   a. genetics
   b. age
   c. gender
   d. all of the above
4. Your RMR is not influenced by which of the following?
   a. age
   b. height
   c. gender
   d. physical activity level
5. If you want to lose a pound of fat in a week, how many calories should you lose per day to be successful?
   a. 100
   b. 250
   c. 375
   d. 500
6. What percentage of your body fat is between your muscles and skin?
   a. 25 percent
   b. 50 percent
   c. 75 percent
   d. 100 percent
7. The body composition evaluation method of underwater weighing is based on what concept?
   a. fat floats
   b. fat sinks
   c. fat neither sinks nor floats
   d. none of the above

8. What type of high-calorie burning activity is especially important for you to include in your body composition improvement plan?

  a. flexibility
  b. plyometric
  c. aerobic
  d. anaerobic

9. If you want to gain weight, how many pounds per week would be healthy and effective?

  a. ½
  b. 1
  c. 2
  d. 5

10. Which of the following signs or symptoms is not characteristic of bulimia?

  a. noticeable weight loss or gain
  b. lack of concern about weight
  c. habit of visiting the bathroom immediately after meals
  d. depressed moods

Discussion

1. List and describe five factors that influence your body composition.

2. List and describe five methods to evaluate your body composition.

3. Explain how you can safely reduce your body weight, increase your body weight, or maintain your body weight.

Vocabulary Experience

Match the correct term in Column A to the definition in Column B by writing the appropriate number in each blank.

Column A

_____ caloric input

_____ anorexia nervosa

_____ caloric expenditure

_____ essential fat

_____ lean muscle weight

_____ resting metabolic rate

Column B

1. An eating disorder in which people abnormally restrict their caloric intake.

2. Bone, muscle, and connective tissue weight.

3. Needed to insulate your body against the cold and to help cushion your internal organs and protect them from injury.

4. The number of calories you consume.

5. The amount of calories you expend or burn in daily physical activity.

6. The amount of calories you need and expend while sitting comfortably at rest.

Critical Thinking

1. Why is body weight a poor indicator of total body composition? Explain your answer.

2. What behaviors will slow down or speed up your resting metabolic rate?

3. Respond to this statement: *I don't care if I do look thin in the mirror; I still want to lose more weight.*

Case Study — Jackie's Activity Level

Jackie is a sixteen-year-old inactive female who has 32 percent body fat and would like to lose 20 pounds. However, she is unsure about how to lose the weight safely and effectively, reduce her body fat to 25 percent, and begin a regular physical activity or exercise program. Therefore, Jackie needs the help of someone knowledgeable about designing and implementing fitness programs—someone like you!

Here is your assignment:

Assume you are Jackie's friend. She asks you for some assistance with her plans for improving her body composition. Make a list of things Jackie should consider and do before beginning a program to control her body composition. Then list the recommendations that you would give to Jackie for the first two weeks of her program.

The following will help you guide Jackie:

KEYS TO HELP YOU

- Consider Jackie's current body composition and percentage of body fat.
- Think about how she should evaluate her current body composition.
- Analyze her needs and goals. (For example, how should she go about controlling her body composition?)
- Determine a reasonable plan for Jackie that covers the concepts of specificity, frequency, intensity, time/duration, and progression.

Chapter 10

Nutrition and Your Personal Fitness

Contents

Outcomes

After reading and studying this chapter, you will be able to:

1. Identify the basic food nutrients, and explain how developing and maintaining a healthy diet can positively influence your functional health.

2. Explain how good nutrition contributes to the development and maintenance of moderate to high levels of personal fitness.

3. Give examples of appropriate choices for developing a healthy diet.

4. Discuss ways to evaluate your current and future nutrition.

5. Identify strategies for improving your nutrition choices and making you a smarter food consumer.

6. Identify and explain ways you can make food choices that will improve your performance fitness.

Key Terms

After reading and studying this chapter, you will be able to understand and provide practical definitions for the following terms:

nutrient	fat	water-soluble vitamin
carbohydrate	saturated fat	antioxidant
glucose	unsaturated fat	mineral
hypoglycemic	protein	electrolyte
glycogen	amino acid	Food Guide Pyramid
simple carbohydrate	vegetarian	Recommended Daily
complex carbohydrate	vitamin	Allowance (RDA)
fiber	fat-soluble vitamin	caffeine

INTRODUCTION

Making sure you get proper nutrition involves understanding what nutrients are available in foods and how your body uses them. Nutrients are substances in foods that your body needs for proper growth, development, and functioning. Proper nutrition is closely associated with good health and freedom from disease. You have already learned about the benefits of adopting a physically active lifestyle. You also need to learn about proper nutrition so that you will be able to meet your nutrient needs for regular physical activity and exercise.

The field of nutrition is filled with fallacies, misconceptions, fads, and misinterpretations. It is often difficult, even for experts in the field of nutrition, to determine the difference between fact and fiction in regard to various nutrition claims that we all see in the media. By gaining an understanding about the basic principles of sound nutrition, however, you will become a wiser and better consumer.

A great deal more nutrition information is available to the public today than ever before. This means it is easier than ever to develop and maintain a sound nutrition plan for yourself. In this chapter you will learn about the basic food nutrients, how to balance your dietary needs, how to read food labels, how to evaluate your nutrition, how to develop and maintain healthy nutrition now and in your future, and how to eat to improve your performance fitness.

SECTION 1   The Basic Food Nutrients

nutrient

a substance in foods that the body needs for proper growth, development, and functioning.

carbohydrate

a nutrient that includes sugars and starches (like pasta).

glucose

sugar; the basic form of carbohydrate and a valuable source of energy.

Meeting your dietary requirements involves eating the right proportion of nutrients daily. Adequate intake of all the **nutrients** contributes to your feeling good, looking good, and performing well both mentally and physically. Your body grows and renews itself daily. You develop new tissues every day to build and repair bone, muscle, skin, and blood. What you eat today will influence your growth and development tomorrow.

The best foods for you to consume are those that will meet your daily nutrition needs to maintain and improve your functional health. The nutrients that supply your body with its daily nutrition requirements fall into six classes: carbohydrate, fat, protein, vitamins, minerals, and water.

Carbohydrate

Carbohydrates (which include sugars and starches) is one of the most important nutrients you consume in your diet. **Glucose**, the basic form of carbohydrate, is a valuable source of energy. If your

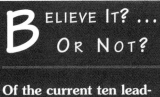

• *You probably first learned about nutrition at an early age. It is now time for you to learn more and put your nutrition knowledge into practice.*

hypoglycemic

having a condition in which the blood glucose level drops and the person feels dizzy, tired, and irritable.

glycogen

the stored form of glucose in the liver and skeletal muscle.

simple carbohydrate

simple sugar; a carbohydrate that is absorbed quickly into the bloodstream and that provides a quick form of energy.

complex carbohydrate

a carbohydrate that is starchy and broken down more slowly in the body than a simple carbohydrate.

blood glucose levels drop significantly, you can become **hypoglycemic** and feel dizzy, tired, and irritable.

Glucose can be stored to a limited extent in your body in the form of **glycogen** in the liver and skeletal muscle. People who engage in ultraendurance training or competition lasting two hours or longer often deplete their glycogen stores. People who are regularly glycogen depleted are at higher risk for overtraining and staleness (poor physical performance). To maintain normal glucose and glycogen levels, you must regularly replenish your carbohydrate stores. Carbohydrates come mainly from plant foods and are classified as either simple or complex.

Simple carbohydrates are called *simple sugars,* and they taste sweet. They are absorbed quickly into your bloodstream and provide a quick form of energy. Examples of simple sugars are milk, fruits, candy, cookies, and soda. **Complex carbohydrates** are starchy—for example, potatoes and corn. They are broken down more slowly by your body than are simple carbohydrates. Other examples of complex carbohydrates are breads, cereals, pasta, and rice.

The total amount of carbohydrates in your diet should be 50 to 60 percent of all the calories that you consume daily. Figure 10.1 provides a list of carbohydrates from various food groups.

Both complex and simple carbohydrates are important for your energy needs, but most of your calories should come from complex carbohydrate sources. Simple carbohydrates supply energy. However, they lack important vitamins (such as B vitamins) and minerals (such as iron) and are associated with producing cavities. Because simple carbohydrates lack essential vitamins and minerals, calories from simple carbohydrates are often called *empty calories.*

Fiber is another type of carbohydrate. It aids in proper digestion. Fiber is not digestible by humans and provides no energy. However, it helps eliminate waste products from the body and provides bulk (volume or size) to the diet. Some foods high in fiber include grains, stems, roots, nuts, seeds, and fruit coverings.

Dietary fiber is associated with reducing your risk for certain cancers, such as colon cancer. Your dietary intake of fiber is important and should be about 30 grams per day. However, you should also avoid too much fiber in your diet. Too much fiber can reduce your absorption of valuable minerals and cause lower digestive tract distress. You can learn to monitor your fiber intake, as well as your intake of other nutrients, by reading the nutrition labels on packaged foods. You will learn more about this in a later section of this chapter.

• *Peas and beans are rich in carbohydrate. They are also good sources of fiber.*

fiber

a type of carbohydrate that is not digestible by humans and provides no energy.

BELIEVE IT? ... **O**R **N**OT?

The best way to get all the vitamins and minerals that you need daily is to take supplements.

See page 359 for answer.

Bread, Cereal, Rice, and Pasta Group	Fruit Group	Vegetable Group	Milk, Yogurt, and Cheese Group
Bagels	Apples	Broccoli	Milk (2% or skim)
Breads	Bananas	Carrots	Pudding
Cereals	Fruit juices	Corn	Sherbet
Crackers	Nectarines	Peppers	Yogurt
English muffins	Oranges	(green, red)	Yogurt, frozen
Graham crackers	Pears	Potatoes	
Pasta (spaghetti, macaroni)		Potatoes, sweet	
Popcorn		Tomatoes	
Pretzels			
Rice			

It is important to choose foods from all the food groups to get the appropriate nutrients your body needs daily.

• **Figure 10.1** *Sources of Carbohydrates. Source:* Adapted with permission from D. S. Jennings and S. N. Steen, *Play Hard, Eat Hard,* American Dietary Association (Minneapolis: Chronimed Publishing, 1995).

BELIEVE IT? ... OR NOT?

Your cholesterol level is within normal limits (WNL) if it is less than 200 milligrams per deciliter. It is considered moderately high if it is between 200 and 239 milligrams per deciliter and high if it is greater than 240 milligrams per deciliter.

See page 359 for answer.

• *Pastas and bread are excellent sources of complex carbohydrates.*

Fat

fat

a type of nutrient that is high in energy; found in animal tissues, nuts, seeds, and oils of some plants.

Fats are nutrients that provide a valuable source of energy for your body. Fats supply twice as much energy per gram as carbohydrates or proteins. Unfortunately, we all can store too much fat, especially if we do not balance our caloric intake and caloric expenditure.

Fats come primarily from animal products, but they also come from the nuts and oils of some plants. Fats help absorb and carry the vitamins A, D, E, and K in your body. Fats can also be stored as triglycerides in your adipose (or fat) tissues. These triglycerides supply energy for exercise, especially as time/durations increase to thirty minutes or longer. Fats also make foods taste good and decrease hunger, because they take longer to digest than the other nutrients.

Saturated Fat.   Fats can be classified as saturated or unsaturated. **Saturated fats** are usually solid at room temperature and come mainly from animal fats. Examples include lard, butter, milk, and meat fats. Some oils, such as palm oil, peanut oil, and coconut oil, are also high in saturated fat.

saturated fat

a fat that is usually solid at room temperature, comes mainly from animal fat, and typically contains high levels of cholesterol.

Saturated fats typically contain high levels of cholesterol. Your body always produces some cholesterol, and cholesterol is important to the normal function of your body's cells. However, consuming a diet high in saturated fats can cause your liver to produce excess cholesterol. Cholesterol levels above normal—especially over time—significantly increase a person's risk for heart disease and atherosclerosis (see Chapter 5). To help you control your cholesterol levels, the

• *French fries may taste good, but they contain high levels of saturated fat when cooked in lard.*

unsaturated fat

a fat that is usually liquid at room temperature, comes mainly from plant sources, and does not contain cholesterol.

protein

a type of nutrient that is the basic building block of the body.

amino acid

a class of compounds that are the basic building blocks for proteins.

National Cholesterol Education Program recommends that you eat no more than 300 milligrams of cholesterol per day.

Unsaturated Fat. **Unsaturated fats** are usually liquid at room temperature, come mainly from plant sources, and do not contain cholesterol. Examples of unsaturated fats include corn oil, soybean oil, olive oil, sunflower oil, and some fish oils.

The total amount of fat in your diet should be no more than 30 percent of the total calories that you consume daily. Your saturated fat intake should be no more than 10 percent of your total daily fat consumption. Individuals who are trying to lose weight may reduce their fat intake to less than 30 percent of their total daily calories. However, excessive fat restriction (less than 20 percent) may be difficult to achieve, take the joy out of eating, and perhaps lead to eating disorders.

Protein

Proteins are nutrients that provide the basic building blocks of your body. They help you repair hair, skin, muscles, hemoglobin, hormones, and other proteins in your blood. Protein is very important for your normal growth and development.

Amino acids are compounds that can combine in different ways to form proteins. Your body can produce some protein (nonessential amino acids), but you must also consume a balanced diet to get the other protein (essential amino acids) that you need. The protein that you consume daily should include low-fat animal foods, as well as a

• *You have a choice when you are eating on the run. Try to make wise nutritional selections.*

wide variety of plant foods. Some foods that are high in protein are meats, fish, poultry, eggs, cheese, and milk.

The total amount of protein in your diet should be 15 to 20 percent of the calories that you consume daily. Figure 10.2 provides a list of foods high in protein and examples of serving sizes.

Protein that comes from animal foods is complete. In other words, it has all the essential amino acids. Protein from plant foods is incomplete, or missing some of the essential amino acids. This fact is important for **vegetarians**, people who eliminate meat, fish, and poultry from their diets. (Some vegetarians also eliminate eggs and milk products from their diets.) Those who adopt a vegetarian diet need to eat a wide variety of plant proteins to get a combination of all the essential amino acids.

Although protein is important for healthy nutrition, eating excessive amounts of protein can do more harm than good. When you consume more protein than your body can use, it is stored as fat. Most people do not need or want to store excess fat. As you have learned throughout this text, excess fat reduces functional health.

Some people think that if they take protein supplements, they can rapidly increase the size of their muscles (hypertrophy). However, you learned in Chapters 7 and 8 that you will only get stronger and develop larger muscles if you lift weights at greater intensities and if your hormone levels (testosterone) increase.

vegetarian

a person who eliminates meat, fish, and poultry (and sometimes eggs and milk products) from their diet.

REMEMBER This!

Although very active people (for example, strength athletes) may need more protein daily because they are expending more calories than normal, they can get all the protein they need by taking in more calories in a balanced diet. Therefore, it is unnecessary and costly to use protein supplements. Advertisements that suggest that their protein supplements will enhance your performance are misleading and often one-sided.

Protein in Various Foods

Food	Protein (grams)	Serving Size
Milk (2% or less)	8	8 ounces (1 cup)
Yogurt	8	8 ounces (1 cup)
Cheese	13	2 ounces (processed)
Fish	21	3 ounces (tuna sandwich)
Poultry	21	3 ounces (grilled chicken)
Meat (beef)	21	3 ounces (hamburger or roast beef sandwich)
Peanut butter	8	2 tablespoons
Nuts	5–7	1 ounce (1 handful)
Eggs	7	1

• **Figure 10.2** *Protein in Various Foods. Source:* Adapted with permission from D. S. Jennings and S. N. Steen, *Play Hard, Eat Hard,* American Dietary Association (Minneapolis: Chronimed Publishing, 1995).

• *Seafood, poultry, and lean red meats are examples of foods that are high in protein content.*

Vitamins

vitamin

a nutrient that helps control growth and helps the body release energy to do work.

fat-soluble vitamin

a vitamin that dissolves in the body's fat tissues and can be stored in the body; the vitamins A, D, E and K.

water-soluble vitamin

a vitamin that is not stored in the body and needs to be replaced regularly; vitamin C and the B vitamins.

antioxidant

a vitamin or mineral that may help protect the body from various types of cell damage.

Vitamins are nutrients that help control growth and help your body release energy to do work. Vitamins do not contain calories and do not provide your body with energy themselves. Vitamins are classified as fat soluble or water soluble.

Fat-soluble vitamins dissolve in your body's fat tissues and can be stored in the body. The fat-soluble vitamins are vitamins A, D, E, and K. **Water-soluble vitamins** are not stored to any real extent in your body and need to be replaced regularly by eating a healthy diet. Vitamin C and the B vitamins (B_1, B_2, B_{12}) are examples of water-soluble vitamins. Figure 10.3 lists the major roles and sources of vitamins.

Many Americans believe that they do not get enough vitamins in their diet because they eat on the run all the time. They respond by taking vitamin supplements. However, supplements are usually not necessary. Although people can develop a vitamin deficiency over time, it is rare. It happens only in extreme situations, such as starvation or certain disease conditions.

Excessive use of vitamin supplements can actually damage your body. Therefore, you should seek medical advice before taking vitamin supplements. A simple multiple vitamin, if needed, is often all that is recommended by physicians or professional dietitians.

Recently, scientists have found that the regular consumption of some vitamins and minerals called **antioxidants** may help protect the body from various types of cell damage. Antioxidants stabilize cells, helping prevent damage to them from cancer, atherosclerosis, overtraining, and premature aging. Vitamin C, vitamin E, and beta-

Fat-soluble

Vitamin	What it Does in the Body	Major Food and Other Sources
A	Maintains normal vision and healthy bones, skin, internal linings, and reproductive system; strengthens resistance to infection	Vitamin A-fortified milk and dairy products; margarine; liver; dark green vegetables (broccoli, spinach, greens); deep orange fruits and vegetables (cantaloupe, apricots, sweet potatoes, carrots)
D	Promotes growth and health of bones	Vitamin D-fortified milk; eggs; liver; sardines; sunlight on the skin
E	Protects the body's cells from attack by oxygen	Vegetable oils and shortening; green, leafy vegetables; whole grains; nuts and seeds
K	Helps with blood clotting and bone growth	Normal bacteria in the digestive tract; liver; dark green, leafy vegetables; milk

Note: The names given here are the official names. Other names still commonly used and seen on labels are *alpha-tocopherol* for vitamin E, *vitamin B₁* for thiamin, *vitamin B₂* for riboflavin, *pyridoxine* for vitamin B$_6$, *folic acid* and *folacin* for folate, and *ascorbic acid* for vitamin C.

Water-soluble

Vitamin	What It Does in the Body	Major Food and Other Sources
C	Acts as the "glue" that holds cells together; strengthens blood vessel walls; helps wounds heal; helps bones grow; strengthens resistance to infection	Citrus fruits; dark green vegetables; cabbage-like vegetables; strawberries; peppers; potatoes
Thiamin	Helps the body use nutrients for energy	Small amounts in all nutritious foods
Riboflavin	Helps the body use nutrients for energy; supports normal vision; helps keep skin healthy	Milk; yogurt; cottage cheese; dark green vegetables; whole-grain products
Niacin	Helps the body use nutrients for energy; supports normal nervous system functions	Milk; eggs; poultry; fish; whole-grain products; all protein-containing foods
B$_6$	Helps the body use protein and form red blood cells	Green, leafy vegetables; meats; fish; poultry; whole-grain products; beans
B$_{12}$	Helps form new cells	Meat; fish; poultry; shellfish; eggs; milk; cheese
Folate	Helps form new cells	Dark green, leafy vegetables; beans; liver
Biotin and pantothenic acid	Helps the body use nutrients for energy	Widespread in foods

• **Figure 10.3** *Major Roles and Sources of the Vitamins. Source:* Reprinted from F. S. Sizer, E. N. Whitney, and L. K. DeBruyne, *Making Life Choices: Health Skills and Concepts* (St. Paul: West Publishing, 1994).

Any Body Can!

Oprah Winfrey

Oprah Winfrey in a well-known television talk-show host and actress. Oprah is also famous for her personal battles with weight gain and loss.

Oprah won a scholarship to Tennessee State University and graduated in 1976. She began her television career during college and became a reporter and news anchor for WTVF-TV in Nashville, Tennessee.

Oprah became the first African American woman to host a successful, nationally syndicated weekday talk show, The Oprah Winfrey Show. She is also the first African American female to own a production company for film and television *(Harpo Studios)* in the U.S.

Although Oprah has had great professional success, she has struggled for the past several years to control her weight. She has often shared her "yo-yoing" weight loss problems with her television audience. She repeatedly went through periods of rapid weight loss as she tried the latest "quick-fix diet," only to see all the weight, and then some, come back.

In March of 1993, Oprah weighed 222 pounds. She decided to contact a nationally known personal trainer to help her achieve and maintain healthy weight loss. Based on her personal goals and desires, Oprah developed a sensible dietary plan and began to exercise regularly. To

achieve her weight loss goals, she would rise at 5:00 AM and run 4 miles on a treadmill. She also added weight lifting into her personal exercise plan.

Oprah progressed steadily in her personal fitness program. After the initial phase (8 weeks), she was able to lose 8 to 10 pounds each month. By July of 1993, she was running 5 to 6 miles per day at a 10 to 11 minute per mile pace. In August of that same year she completed a half-marathon (13.1 miles) in 2 hours and 16 minutes, and on November 10, 1993, she reached her goal weight of 150 pounds. Oprah lost 72 pounds in about 7 months, which is as much as anyone could realistically lose in that time (about 2 pounds per week) and *maintain the weight loss.*

In 1994 Oprah decided to train for a full marathon (26.2 miles). She concentrated on increasing her running mileage, and also intensified her strength and muscular conditioning. In 1994, she successfully completed the Marine Corps Marathon without walking a step. Since the marathon Oprah has cut back on her intensive training, but she is still eating sensibly and exercising regularly, to achieve even better levels of body composition.

Not everyone can be a television talk-show host, actress, and marathon runner like Oprah Winfrey, but **A**ny **B**ody **C**an learn to eat sensibly and live an active lifestyle to control their body composition. That's right, you can do it!

carotene (associated with vitamin A) are examples of antioxidants. You will probably be reading and learning more about antioxidants in the near future.

Minerals

mineral

a chemical element that is important for the body's structure and function and for regulating metabolism.

Minerals are chemical elements that are important for your body's structure and function and for regulating metabolism. Like vitamins, minerals do not contain calories and do not supply your body with energy. Minerals are classified as either major minerals (your body needs more of these) or trace minerals (your body needs less of these). Examples of major minerals include calcium, phosphorus, magnesium, sodium, potassium, chloride, and sulfur. Examples of trace minerals are iron, manganese, copper, iodine, zinc, cobalt, fluoride, and selenium. Figure 10.4 on the next page lists the major roles and sources of minerals.

Four minerals that are particularly important in relation to your personal fitness are calcium, iron, potassium, and sodium. A diet rich in these and other minerals, along with an active lifestyle, can help you reduce your risk for chronic problems and diseases.

If you do not consume enough calcium in your diet or have problems absorbing what you do eat, you may be at a higher risk for

B ELIEVE IT? ... OR NOT?

A person who is lifting weights regularly, and who wants to increase muscle mass, needs to consume four to five times the protein consumed by the average person.

See page 359 for answer.

• *Dairy products are rich in minerals and vitamins.*

Mineral	What It Does in the Body	Major Food Sources
Calcium	Structural material of bones and teeth; helps muscles contract and relax; helps nerves communicate; helps blood to clot	Milk and milk products; small fish with bones; dark green vegetables; beans
Phosphorus	Structural material of bones and teeth; supports energy processes; part of cells' genetic material	All foods that come from animals
Magnesium	Helps build bones and teeth; helps build protein; helps muscles contract and relax; helps nerves communicate	Nuts; beans; dark green vegetables; seafood; whole grains; chocolate
Sodium	Maintains cell fluids; helps nerves communicate	Salt; soy sauce; processed foods; celery; milk
Potassium	Helps build protein; maintains fluid balance; helps nerves communicate; helps muscles contract	All nutritious foods; meats; milk and milk products; fruits; vegetables; whole grains; beans
Iron	Helps red blood cells carry oxygen; helps tissues use oxygen to release energy; supports normal immunity	Red meats; fish; poultry; shellfish; eggs; beans; dried fruits
Zinc	Helps build genetic material and protein; supports normal immunity; supports growth; helps make sperm; helps wounds heal	Protein-rich foods; meats; fish; poultry; whole grains
Iodine	Part of thyroid hormone needed for growth	Iodized salt; seafood
Selenium	Helps vitamin E protect cells from attack by oxygen	Seafood; meats; vegetables
Copper	Helps make red blood cells; helps build protein; helps the body use iron	Organ meats such as liver; seafood; nuts
Chromium	Helps the body use carbohydrates and fats	Liver; nuts; whole grains; cheese
Fluoride	Helps strengthen bones and teeth	Water; seafood
Manganese	Helps with many processes	Whole grains; fruits; vegetables
Molybdenum	Helps with many processes	Milk; beans

• **Figure 10.4**   *Major Roles and Sources of the Minerals. Source:* Reprinted from F. S. Sizer, E. N. Whitney, and L. K. DeBruyne, *Making Life Choices: Health Skills and Concepts* (St. Paul: West Publishing, 1994).

osteoporosis (or brittle bones) as you age. You can significantly reduce your risk for osteoporosis by eating foods rich in calcium (see Figure 10.4) and by doing regular weight-bearing exercises, along with some weight training.

Iron is important for the formation of hemoglobin, which helps the blood carry oxygen (see Chapter 5). If your iron levels drop below normal, you may develop iron-deficiency anemia. This condition reduces your ability to carry oxygen and decreases your aerobic working ability. Vegetarians are at high risk for developing iron deficiencies because they do not eat meats, which are high in iron. However, vegetarians can reduce their risk for iron deficiency by eating a variety of plant foods rich in iron (beets and green leafy vegetables).

Potassium is a mineral that, in combination with sodium and calcium, helps maintain normal heart rhythm and control fluid balance. Sodium (Na^+), calcium (CA^{++}), and potassium (K^+) are often called **electrolytes**, because their electrical charges help control the body's fluid balance. *Fluid balance* refers to the body's ability to balance the amounts of water and electrolytes that are consumed with the amounts that are lost or excreted daily.

Potassium also aids in normal muscle contractions and in the conduction of nerve impulses that control the movement of your muscles. If your potassium levels drop low enough, such as when you exercise and sweat profusely, you may develop muscle cramps or problems with the conduction of nerve impulses. You can help maintain normal potassium levels by drinking plenty of fruit juices (like orange and tomato juices) or commercial sports drinks.

Many foods you eat (especially fast foods) are high in sodium. When you eat high levels of sodium, you tend to retain water. People with hypertension are often placed on low-sodium diets, which can help control their blood pressure by reducing fluid retention. Are you at high risk for developing hypertension? You may be at a higher risk for becoming hypertensive if your mother, father, grandmother, or grandfather has hypertension. If you are at high risk, you probably need to lower your sodium intake. It is a good idea to limit your sodium intake by not adding additional salt to your food. Participation in regular physical activity and exercise can also help control hypertension.

electrolyte

a mineral whose electrical charge helps control the body's fluid balance.

Water

From 60 to 70 percent of your body weight is water. Water is an essential nutrient for life. Without water, death would occur within six to seven days. Water helps regulate your body temperature, carries nutrients to cells, helps with digestion, and is important for chemical reactions in your body. It is recommended that you consume eight 8-ounce glasses of water or other fluids (milk, juices, and so on) daily to maintain your normal fluid balance.

As you learned in Chapter 2, it is especially important to drink adequate fluids when exercising in warm or hot environments. It is often impossible to "catch up" on your fluid balance if you wait until you are actually thirsty before you begin to drink. Thus, it is important to hydrate (drink fluids) before, during, and after moderate to vigorous physical activity or exercise. Figure 10.5 gives some general guidelines for drinking water or other fluids when you are active. Although water is the best and cheapest fluid to rehydrate with, you may pre-

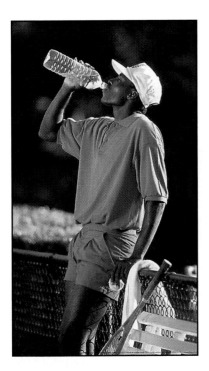

• *Drink plenty of water to maintain your body's fluid balance.*

Before	During	After
Drink 10 to 14 ounces of cold water one to two hours before the activity or exercise.	Drink 3 to 4 ounces of cold water every fifteen minutes.	Drink 2 cups (16 ounces) of cold water for every pound of weight loss.

• ***Figure 10.5***   *Guidelines for Fluid Replacement Before, During, and After Physical Activity or Exercise. Source:* Adapted with permission from D. S. Jennings and S. N. Steen, *Play Hard, Eat Hard,* American Dietary Association (Minneapolis: Chronimed Publishing, 1995).

• *Make sure you drink before, during, and after physical activity or exercise.*

fer a sports drink because of the taste. If you replenish your fluids during physical activity with something other than water, follow the guidelines for these drinks in Chapter 2.

SECTION 1 REVIEW

Answer the following questions on a separate sheet of paper:

1. List and describe the six classes of nutrients.
2. Name three foods that are high in fiber.
3. What is the difference between saturated and unsaturated fat?

SECTION 2

Choosing What You Should Eat: The Food Guide Pyramid

What should you eat? Do you enjoy what you eat? Do you get all the nutrients from your diet that you need to be healthy? These questions are all important for determining or choosing what you should eat.

The U.S. Department of Health and Human Services and the U.S. Department of Agriculture have published the *Dietary Guidelines for Americans,* which provide recommendations for a healthy way to eat. The *Dietary Guidelines* are designed to help you eat sensi-

• *Nutrition professionals, such as these dietitians, analyze foods and counsel people about sensible eating.*

bly and help reduce your risk for heart disease, high blood pressure, stroke, certain cancers, and diabetes mellitus. The recommendations are as follows:

• Eat a variety of foods.
• Maintain a healthy weight.
• Choose a diet low in fat, saturated fat, and cholesterol.
• Choose a diet with plenty of vegetables, fruits, and grain products.
• Use salt and sodium only in moderation.
• Use sugars only in moderation.

Food Guide Pyramid

a visual outline of what people should eat each day.

Recommended Daily Allowance (RDA)

the amount of nutrients recommended daily for individuals by the U.S. Department of Agriculture.

The **Food Guide Pyramid** (see Figure 10.6 on the following page) was also developed by the U.S. Department of Health and Human Services and the U.S. Department of Agriculture to present a visual outline of what to eat each day based on the *Dietary Guidelines*. The Food Guide Pyramid is based on the **Recommended Daily Allowance (RDA)**, the amount of nutrients recommended daily for individuals by the U.S. Department of Agriculture.

Use the Food Guide Pyramid to develop a healthful diet that is right for you. The Food Guide Pyramid emphasizes foods from the five major food groups, which are shown in the lower three sections of the pyramid. Each of the food groups provides some, but not all, of the nutrients you need daily. Foods in one food group can't replace those in another. It is important to choose from all the food groups

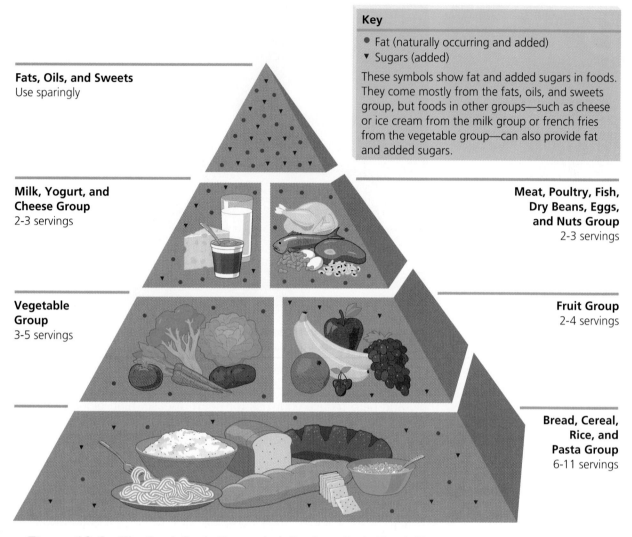

Fats, Oils, and Sweets
Use sparingly

Key
- Fat (naturally occurring and added)
▼ Sugars (added)

These symbols show fat and added sugars in foods. They come mostly from the fats, oils, and sweets group, but foods in other groups—such as cheese or ice cream from the milk group or french fries from the vegetable group—can also provide fat and added sugars.

Milk, Yogurt, and Cheese Group
2-3 servings

Meat, Poultry, Fish, Dry Beans, Eggs, and Nuts Group
2-3 servings

Vegetable Group
3-5 servings

Fruit Group
2-4 servings

Bread, Cereal, Rice, and Pasta Group
6-11 servings

• **Figure 10.6**   *The Food Guide Pyramid: A Guide to Daily Food Choices. Source:* Reprinted from U.S. Department of Agriculture, Human Nutritional Information Service, 6505 Belcrest Rd., Hyattsville, MD 20782.

to get all the nutrients your body needs on a daily basis. Thus, the pyramid illustrates the need to eat a variety of foods to get the proper amounts of all the nutrients you need.

The Food Guide Pyramid shows that you need to eat more servings from foods located at the base of the pyramid than from foods located near the top. For example, the bread, cereal, rice, and pasta group provides you with the high percentage (50 to 60 percent) of carbohydrates your body needs. The fat, oils, and sweets should be consumed sparingly, because you do not need as much of these nutrients.

• *Breads are in the group of foods that forms the base of the Food Pyramid.*

Energy Balance

You can apply the Food Guide Pyramid to what you already know about energy balance. Your goal is to maintain a balance in your diet of energy and nutrients (carbohydrates, fat, protein, vitamins, minerals, and water). You studied energy balance in Chapter 9, primarily with regard to energy expenditure. However, you also need to pay attention to energy input (calories) in order to control the energy balance equation.

The Food Guide Pyramid shows a range of servings for each major food group. The number of servings that you need depends on how many calories you need—which, if you recall, depends on your age, gender, size, and activity level. Almost everyone should have at least the lowest number of servings in the ranges. Figure 10.7 shows how many servings you need each day to help maintain energy balance.

Examples of the amount of food that counts as one serving are listed in Figure 10.8. If you eat a larger portion, count it as more than one serving. For example, a dinner portion of spaghetti would count as two to three servings of pasta. Be sure to eat *at least* the lowest number of servings from each of the five food groups listed in Figure 10.8. You need all these servings for the vitamins, minerals, carbohydrates, and protein they provide. Just try to pick the choices with the lowest fat content. No specific serving size is given for the fats, oils, and sweets group because they are to be consumed sparingly. Figure 10.9 shows how you can cut down on your fat calories.

Stress Break

Have you ever noticed that drinking beverages that contain caffeine, such as tea, cola, or coffee, gives you a quick pick-me-up, energy boost, or jolt? **Caffeine** is a mild stimulant of the central nervous system. The average adolescent drinks at least two to three beverages a day containing caffeine. Caffeine increases your heart rate, can make you feel less tired, increases your alertness, and improves your reaction time. However, caffeine also produces signs of distress. Too much caffeine can cause headaches, upset stomach, nervousness, sleeplessness, irritability, and diarrhea. The side effects of caffeine consumption can make your stressful situations even more stressful. Some people may even have anxiety or panic attacks from consuming too much caffeine.

Is it necessary to eliminate caffeine completely from your diet? Probably not. The equivalent of one or two caffeinated beverages per day is safe. However, you should monitor your caffeine intake. You can consume beverages that have low amounts of caffeine or that are caffeine-free. This will help you deal with or eliminate distress in your daily life.

• *Eating a variety of foods in the proper proportions is the key to sound nutrition.*

Food Group	Servings		
	Many Women and Older Adults (About 1,600 calories)	Children, Teen Girls, Active Women, and Most Men (About 2,200 calories)	Teen Boys and Active Men (About 2,800 calories)
Bread	6	9	11
Vegetable	3	4	5
Fruit	2	3	4
Milk	2–3†	2–3†	2–3†
Meat	2, for a total of 5 ounces	2, for a total of 6 ounces	3, for a total of 7 ounces

• **Figure 10.7** *Examples of Servings (and calories) to Maintain Energy Balance.* * These are the calorie levels if you choose low-fat, lean foods from the five major food groups and use foods from fats, oils, and sweets sparingly. †Women who are pregnant or breastfeeding, teenagers, and young adults to age twenty-four need three servings.

Milk, Yogurt, and Cheese	Meat, Poultry, Fish, Dry Beans, Eggs, and Nuts	Vegetables	Fruit	Bread, Cereal, Rice, and Pasta
I cup of yogurt or milk (2% or less)	2-3 ounces of cooked lean meat, poultry, or fish	1 cup of raw, leafy vegetables	1 medium apple, banana, or orange	1 slice of bread
1-1/2 ounces of natural cheese	1/2 cup of dry beans, 1 egg, or two table-spoons of peanut butter count as 1 ounce of lean meat	1/2 cup of other vegetables, cooked or chopped raw	1/2 cup of chopped, cooked, or canned fruit	1 ounce of ready-to-eat cereal
2 ounces of processed cheese		3/4 cup of vegetable juice	3/4 cup of fruit juice	1/2 cup of cooked cereal, rice, or pasta

• **Figure 10.8** *Examples of Serving Sizes for Each Food Group. Source:* Adapted from U.S. Department of Agriculture, Human Nutritional Information Service, 6505 Belcrest Rd., Hyattsville, MD 20782.

Fat hides calories in food. When you trim fat, you trim calories.

Large pork chop with ½ inch fat (352 calories).

Large potato with 1 table-spoon butter and 1 table-spoon sour cream (350 calories).

Whole milk, 1 cup (150 calories).

Large pork chop with fat trimmed off (265 calories).

Plain large potato (220 calories).

Nonfat milk, 1 cup (90 calories).

• **Figure 10.9** *Fat and Calories. Source:* Adapted with permission from F. S. Sizer, E. N. Whitney, and L. K. DeBruyne, *Making Life Choices* (St. Paul: West Publishing, 1994, page 176).

Reading Food Labels and Evaluating Your Nutrition

Virtually all the food products that you purchase today have a label entitled "Nutrition Facts" on the package or container. Therefore, it is easy for you to determine what and how much you are consuming. If you begin to pay closer attention to food labeling, you will get even better at balancing your caloric intake and caloric expenditure. Figure 10.10 provides a sample food label and highlights factors you should look for to learn about what is in the foods you eat.

Food labels like the one in Figure 10.10 contain nutrition information about the following items:

- Serving size.
- Calories that the food contains per serving.
- Total amount of carbohydrate.
- Total amount of dietary fiber.
- Total amount of protein.
- Vitamins and minerals in each serving.
- Total amount of fat, saturated fat, and cholesterol.
- Total amount of sodium per serving.
- Percentage of calories supplied based on daily needs per serving.

Food labels also have a list of ingredients. The ingredient list contains ingredients by weight, in descending order. The ingredient that is listed first is found in the greatest amount. You can better balance your diet by analyzing what you eat for one to three days or by analyzing sample diets such as the ones in the "Active Mind/Active Body" activities on the next page.

• *You should read the "nutrition facts" on packages and containers of food products before you buy them.*

Serving Size

Is your serving the same serving size as the one on the label? If you eat double the serving size listed, you need to double the nutrient and calorie values. If you eat one-half the serving size shown here, cut the nutrient and calorie values in half.

Calories

Are you overweight? Cut back a little on calories! Look here to see how a serving of the food adds to the daily total. A 5'4", 130-lb. active woman needs about 2,200 calories each day. A 5' 10" 174-lb. active man needs about 2,900. How about you?

Total Carbohydrate

When you cut down on fat, you can eat more carbohydrates. Carbohydrates are in foods like bread, potatoes, fruits, and vegetables. Choose these often! They give you more nutrients than sugars like soda pop and candy.

Dietary Fiber

Grandmother called it "roughage," but her advice to eat more is still up-to-date! That goes for both soluble and insoluble kinds of dietary fiber. Fruits, vegetables, whole-grain foods, beans, and peas are all good sources and can help reduce the risk of heart disease and cancer.

Protein

Most Americans get more protein than they need. Where there is animal protein, there is also fat and cholesterol. Eat small servings of lean meat, fish, and poultry. Use skim or low-fat milk, yogurt, and cheese. Try vegetable proteins like beans, grains, and cereals.

Vitamins and Minerals

Your goal here is 100% of each for the day. Don't count on one food to do it all. Let a combination of foods add up to a winning score.

Nutrition Facts

Serving Size ½ cup (114g)
Servings Per Container 4

Amount Per Serving

Calories 90	Calories from Fat 30

	% Daily Value*
Total Fat 3g	5%
Saturated Fat 0g	0%
Cholesterol 0mg	0%
Sodium 300mg	13%
Total Carbohydrate 13g	4%
Dietary Fiber 3g	12%
Sugars 3g	
Protein 3g	

Vitamin A	80%	•	Vitamin C	60%
Calcium	4%	•	Iron	4%

* Percent Daily Values are based on a 2,000 calorie diet. Your daily values may be higher or lower depending on your calorie needs:

	Calories	2,000	2,500
Total Fat	Less than	65g	80g
Sat Fat	Less than	20g	25g
Cholesterol	Less than	300mg	300mg
Sodium	Less than	2,400mg	2,400mg
Total Carbohydrate		300g	375g
Fiber		25g	30g

Calories per gram:
Fat 9   •   Carbohydrate 4   •   Protein 4

More nutrients may be listed on some labels.

Total Fat

Aim low: most people need to cut back on fat. Too much fat may contribute to heart disease and cancer. Try to limit your calories from fat. For a healthy heart, choose foods with a big difference between the total number of calories and the number of calories from fat.

Saturated Fat

A new kind of fat? No—saturated fat is part of the total fat in food. It is listed separately, because it's the key player in raising blood cholesterol and your risk of heart disease. Eat less!

Cholesterol

Too much cholesterol—a second cousin to fat—can lead to heart disease. Challenge yourself to eat less than 300 mg each day.

Sodium

You call it "salt", the label calls it "sodium". Either way, it may add up to high blood pressure in some people. So, keep your sodium intake low—2,400 to 3,000 mg or less each day. The American Heart Association recommends no more than 3,000 mg sodium per day for healthy adults.

Daily Value

Feel like you're drowning in numbers? Let the Daily Value be your guide. Daily Values are listed for people who eat 2,000 or 2,500 calories each day. If you eat more, your personal daily value may be higher than what's listed on the label. If you eat less, your personal daily value may be lower.

For fat, saturated fat, cholesterol, and sodium, choose foods with a low % Daily Value. For total carbohydrate, dietary fiber, vitamins, and minerals, your daily value goal is to reach 100% of each.

g = grams (about 28 g = 1 ounce).
mg = milligrams (1,000 mg = 1 gram).

• *Figure 10.10 Sample Food Label.*

Active Mind! Active Body!   **Calculating Calories from an Example**

Calculate the number of calories in your meal if you consume the following: 10 grams of carbohydrate, 5 grams of fat, and 4 grams of protein. (Remember from Chapter 9 that 1 gram of carbohydrate = 4 calories; 1 gram of fat = 9 calories; and 1 gram of protein = 4 calories.)

Now calculate what percentage of calories comes from carbohydrate, fat, and protein in the same example. *Hint:* Divide the number of calories for each nutrient by the total number of calories from all the nutrients.

Calculating the Calories in Your Diet and Sample Menus

Perform one or both of the following:

1. Use the West Diet Analysis Computer Software that your teacher will provide you with to analyze either one, two, or three days of your food consumption. The form asks you to list the foods that you have consumed. It is best if you can analyze three days of your diet, particularly for two weekdays and one weekend day. Most people have different eating habits during the week and the weekend. Determine how your diet compares with the dietary guidelines that you have learned so far. For example, how many calories did you consume? What percentages of carbohydrate, fat, and protein did you get? Did you meet the RDAs for various nutrients? How many servings did you have for each food group section in the Food Guide Pyramid? Do you need to adjust your diet to achieve healthier nutrition? If so, how will you do this?

2. Analyze the five menus shown below using the calorie chart provided by your teacher to determine which of the five menus is the most nutritious. You will need to use what you know about the Food Guide Pyramid, serving information, caloric content, and balanced nutrition.

Menu 1

3 ounces baked chicken
1 small baked potato
1/3 cup corn
1 cup broccoli
2 slices pineapple
1 tablespoon margarine

Menu 2

2 ounces link sausage
10 french fries
1/2 cup marinated vegetables
1 slice apple pie
1 cup whole milk

Menu 3

2 slices whole-wheat bread
1 tablespoon mayonnaise
2 ounces deli turkey
1 leaf of lettuce
1 slice tomato
1 slice American cheese
1-ounce pack of corn chips
8 ounces cola

Menu 4

3 ounces baked flounder
1/2 cup zucchini
4 florets of cauliflower
1/4 cantaloupe
8 ounces water

Menu 5

8 ounces yogurt
1 plain bagel
1 teaspoon cream cheese
1 small apple
6 ounces orange juice

• **Figure 10.11** *Sample Menus to Analyze.*

SECTION 2 REVIEW

Answer the following questions on a separate sheet of paper:

1. Give three recommendations to follow in order to eat sensibly and reduce your risk for chronic diseases.
2. List the five major food groups represented in the Food Guide Pyramid, and give the recommended number of servings for each group.
3. Identify three items that are included in nutrition information labeling.

SECTION 3 — Developing and Maintaining Healthy Nutrition

To develop and maintain healthy nutrition, you need to become more aware of your caloric intake and the types of food that you are consuming. Remember, by adjusting your diet and your physical activity and exercise levels, you can make positive changes in your body composition. To improve your nutrition, you need to determine your FIT by using the results from the "Active Mind/Active Body" activity you did on page 352. Use the scientific principles you learned in Chapter 3 and your personal fitness goals to develop your own specific nutrition plan. To do this, use the recommendations that follow.

Specificity Principle

To apply the specificity principle in an attempt to improve your nutrition, keep a record of what, where, when, and how much you are eating. Learn to analyze your diet for unnecessary excess calories, low RDA values, and foods that provide empty calories (such as sodas, candy bars, chips, and cookies). Read the "Nutrition Facts" labels before you consume. If necessary, change your eating habits gradually so that you eat foods that are low in fat and are nutritious.

REMEMBER This!

Caffeinated beverages are often carbonated and contain high amounts of sugar and sodium. These additional ingredients are detrimental to maintaining normal blood sugar levels (they can make you hypoglycemic). They also can interfere with maintaining electrolyte and fluid balances. Therefore, keep your caffeinated drink consumption to a minimum. Make healthier choices, such as fruit juices, water, or sports drinks, whenever possible.

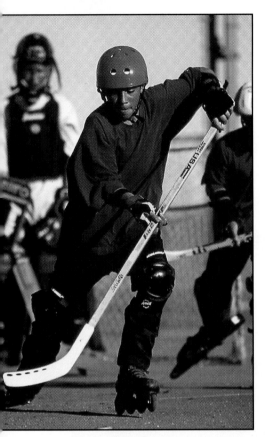

• *Eating sensibly can enhance your physical activity and exercise performance.*

Frequency

The first component of FIT, as you remember, is *frequency.* To apply it to your nutrition plan, eat at regular intervals, three times per day, plus one or two planned snacks to avoid hunger and impulse eating.

Intensity

How does *intensity,* the second component of FIT, apply to your nutrition plan? To lose a pound of fat, you need to reduce your caloric intake by 3,500 calories below what's normal for you over a set period of time (for example, one or two weeks). You also need to include aerobic conditioning and weight training in your plan to maintain your lean body weight while you lose mostly fat weight. If you want to gain weight, you need to increase your caloric intake. You will also want to include weight training as part of your weight-gain plan so that you will mainly increase your lean body weight, not your fat weight. If you maintain your caloric intake at the same level and do not vary your physical activity levels, you will maintain your weight and percentage of body fat.

Time/Duration

As for the *time/duration* component of FIT, you should work both sides of the energy balance equation to control your caloric intake and caloric expenditure as necessary. If you are trying to lose weight and body fat, you should try to lose no more than 1 to 2 pounds per week for safe, effective results. If you are seeking weight gain, you should expect slow gains of no more than ½ pound per week. By gaining weight slowly and steadily, you add less body fat and more lean muscle. Your ability to improve your nutrition will depend on how you use your new knowledge and how you develop reasonable and obtainable goals for yourself over the long haul.

REMEMBER This!

Never change the frequency, intensity, or time/duration of your nutrition plan all at the same time or too quickly. Healthy weight loss should not exceed 2 pounds per week. Weight gain should not exceed ½ pound per week. Be patient, and allow for gradual progress.

Progression Principle

The rate at which you modify your FIT (your progression) should be based on your personal fitness goals and your nutritional goals. Few people eat as well as they can all the time. (Holidays and celebrations are always challenges to good nutrition.) You will undoubtedly experience unwanted weight changes at some time in your life. However, you do have a choice about what and how you eat over time. Therefore, it is important that you establish sound nutritional patterns now that can last you for life.

Examples of Healthy Nutrition

The sample menu in Figure 10.12 provides an example of healthy nutrition for a young adult who wants to consume 2,500 calories. About 55 percent of the calories come from carbohydrate; 25 to 30 percent, from fat; and 15 to 20 percent, from protein.

In Chapter 9 you learned about developing and controlling your body composition at healthy levels. Figures 10.13 and 10.14 provide sample menus that you can either use for effective weight control (loss or maintenance) or for weight gain, depending on your goal.

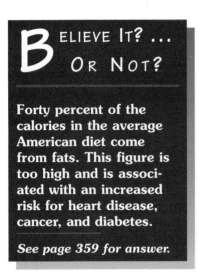

Breakfast	2 pancakes
	Syrup
	1 cup 2% milk
Snack	1 bagel
	Jam or jelly
	6 ounces orange juice
Lunch	1 slice vegetable pizza
	Carrot and celery sticks
	2 graham crackers
	1 cup 2% milk
Snack (Before physical activity or exercise)	2 fig bars
	16 ounces of water
Snack (Afterward)	1 box fruit juice
	1 packet raisins
Dinner	3 ounces roasted chicken breast
	1/2 cup rice
	1 slice bread
	Lettuce and tomato
	1 tablespoon dressing
	1 cup 2% milk
Snack	1 cup frozen yogurt
	1 cup lemonade
	1 sandwich (2 slices multigrain bread, 3 ounces lean turkey, lettuce, tomato, and mustard)

• **Figure 10.12** *Sample Menu for Good Nutrition. Source:* Adapted with permission from D. S. Jennings and S. N. Steen, *Play Hard, Eat Hard,* American Dietary Association (Minneapolis: Chronimed Publishing, 1995).

Figure 10.13 *Sample Menu for Weight Control.*
Source: Adapted with permission from D. S. Jennings and S. N. Steen, *Play Hard, Eat Hard,* American Dietary Association (Minneapolis: Chronimed Publishing, 1995).

Breakfast	3/4 cup orange juice
	3/4 cup raisin bran (1 teaspoon sugar optional)
	1 slice whole-wheat toast
	1 tablespoon jam or jelly
	1 cup low-fat (2%) milk
Lunch	1 turkey sandwich (3 ounces turkey breast, 2 slices whole-wheat bread, mustard, sliced tomato, and lettuce)
Snack	1 banana
Dinner	3 ounces lean beef
	1 medium baked potato
	1 cup plain nonfat yogurt
	1/2 cup green beans
	1 cup low-fat (2%) milk
	1/2 cup ice milk
Snack	3/4 cup tomato juice
	1 ounce pretzels
	1/4 cup raisins

CONSUMER CORNER

Nutrition and Consumer Choices

If you are like most Americans, you are finding that you are eating more meals away from home than ever before. We have all come to depend on fast-food restaurants, cafeterias, and vending machines for our daily nutrition needs.

As a wise consumer, you can make smart choices to guarantee that you get all the nutrients you require when you eat out, while avoiding foods high in calories, fat, and sodium. Most fast-food restaurants and cafeterias provide customers with healthy food choice menus that are low in calories, fat, and sodium. For example, you can choose grilled chicken (less fat) instead of fried chicken (high fat). You can enjoy the salad bar with fruits and vegetables instead of eating french fries (high fat and sodium). You can also choose to avoid overloading on sauces, sour cream, and butter. When making a beverage choice, you can replace high-sugar sodas with low-fat milk or water. Finally, if you learn to read the "Nutrition Facts" labeling on vending machine foods, you can make better consumer choices.

Breakfast	1 cup orange juice
	6 pancakes
	1/4 cup syrup
	2 pats margarine
	1-1/2 cups low-fat (2%) milk
Snack	1 soft pretzel
	1-1/2 cups tomato juice
Lunch	1 turkey sandwich (4-5 ounces turkey breast, 7-inch pita bread pocket, 2 tablespoons light mayonnaise, chopped tomato, and lettuce)
Snack	1 package powdered breakfast mix
	1 cup low-fat (2%) milk
Dinner	1 medium vegetable-cheese pizza
	2 cups low-fat (2%) milk
	1/4 cup raisins
Snack	1 peanut butter and jelly sandwich (3 tablepoons peanut butter, 3 tablespoons jelly, 2 slices whole-grain bread)
	1 cup low-fat (2%) milk

• *Figure 10.14*   *Sample Menu for Weight Gain. Source:* Adapted with permission from D. S. Jennings and S. N. Steen, *Play Hard, Eat Hard,* American Dietary Association (Minneapolis: Chronimed Publishing, 1995).

SECTION 3 REVIEW

Answer the following questions on a separate sheet of paper:

1. How many times per day should you eat?

2. How many calories do you need to cut from your caloric intake to lose a pound of fat?

3. If you are trying to gain weight, how much should you realistically expect to gain each week?

SECTION 4   Eating to Improve Your Performance Fitness

REMEMBER **This!**

Before an athletic event, eat as follows:
- **Complex carbohydrates.**
- **Water.**
- **Moderate portions.**
- **3 to 4 hours before the event.**

Be sure to avoid large amounts of these nutrients:
- **Fat.**
- **Protein.**
- **Fiber.**
- **Last-minute sweets.**

Many young adults are interested in competing in various physical activities or sports, at least occasionally. Others aim for a high-performance personal fitness and are willing to work harder than they would have to just for good health. People in both of these categories need to pay close attention to their diets before and after competition.

If you are one of these people, make sure you have plenty of energy to compete and are well hydrated prior to competition (pre-event). Your last pre-event meal is important, but it's even more important to eat a healthy diet for several weeks before your competition. This is necessary to maintain satisfactory energy levels.

Your last pre-event meal should be eaten at least one to three hours before the practice or competition. You want a relatively empty stomach prior to the practice or competition to avoid nausea or potential stomach cramps. Each person digests food at different rates. Therefore, you may want to be cautious and allow more time (three hours, for example) for digestion of the pre-event meal.

Eat foods high in carbohydrate. Avoid foods high in protein or fat, because they take longer to digest. Also avoid eating foods high in simple sugars (candy bars, honey, and so on) immediately before competition, because they provide only quick energy and may even hamper your performance in the long run. The energy you need for a hard workout or competition comes from foods eaten several hours and days before. You can use the recommendations in Figures 10.15 and 10.16 to help guide your pre-event meal planning.

You may sometimes participate in all-day competitions or a series of physical activities such as track meets, basketball tournaments, tennis tournaments, or wrestling meets. At these times, you need to make wise food choices throughout the day to maintain your energy levels. You also need to prevent dehydration, which would have a negative effect on your performance. Try to consume fluids, particularly water, throughout the day. Avoid foods that take longer to digest (fat, protein, and fiber), especially if you have to perform several times throughout the day. (See Figure 10.17 on page 360.)

Following competition, you must restore your glucose and glycogen stores in order to recover effectively for your next workout or competition. You also need to replace the fluids (as you learned in Chapter 2 and Section 1 earlier in this chapter) that you have lost from sweating during physical activity. Immediately after the competition, you should consume one of the following foods or drinks to

Answers to

B ELIEVE IT? ... OR NOT?

Pg. 333 True.
Pg. 334 False. The only time you need supplements is when you have a medically diagnosed vitamin or mineral deficiency or when you cannot eat a balanced diet for several weeks at a time.
Pg. 335 True.
Pg. 341 False. The average person needs about 1 gram of protein for every 2.2 pounds of body weight. Even an athlete in weight training needs only about 2 grams of protein for every 2.2 pounds of body weight. People who need additional protein can get it by consuming more calories in a balanced diet rather than by taking protein supplements.
Pg. 345 False. Salt tablets can contribute to dehydration and make you nauseous. The best way to maintain fluid balance is to consume a heathy diet and to drink plenty of fluids regularly.
Pg. 347 False. Almost all fast-food restaurants have heathy items on their menus. Fast-food franchises also have brochures or food charts that you can use to select food items that are high in carbohydrates, moderate in protein, and low in fat.
Pg. 355 True.

1 to 2 Hours Before	2 to 3 Hours Before	3 or More Hours Before
Fruit or vegetable juice Fresh fruit (low fiber, such as plums, melon, cherries, or peaches)	Fruit or vegetable juice Fresh fruit Breads, bagels, English muffins (no margarine or cream cheese)	Fruit or vegetable juice Fresh fruit Breads, bagels, English muffins Peanut butter, lean meat, low-fat cheese Low-fat yogurt Baked Potato Cereal with low-fat milk (2%) Pasta with tomato sauce

• **Figure 10.15** *Eating Before the Event. Source:* Adapted with permission from D. S. Jennings and S. N. Steen, *Play Hard, Eat Hard,* American Dietary Association (Minneapolis: Chronimed Publishing, 1995).

A.M.	P.M.
1 cup orange juice Bagel 2 tablespoons peanut butter 2 tablespoons honey **Or** 1 cup orange juice 3/4 cup corn flakes Medium banana Wheat toast and jelly 1 cup low-fat (2%) milk **Or** 1 cup orange juice Pancakes and syrup English muffin and jelly 1 cup low-fat yogurt **Or** 1 cup orange juice Waffles and strawberries 1 cup low-fat yogurt	1 cup vegetable soup 2 ounces skinless chicken 2 slices wheat bread 2 slices tomato 1 cup low-fat frozen yogurt 1 cup apple juice **Or** Large baked potato 1 teaspoon margarine Carrot sticks 1/2 cup fruit salad 1 cup low-fat (2%) milk **Or** Salad: lettuce, 1 ounce ham, 1 ounce turkey, 2 slices tomato, 2 tablespoons dressing 1/2 cup pudding **Or** 2 cups spaghetti 2/3 cup tomato sauce with mushrooms French bread 1 cup lemon sherbet 1 cup low-fat (2%) milk

• **Figure 10.16** *Sample Meals Prior (three to four hours) to Physical Activity or Exercise. Source:* Adapted with permission from D. S. Jennings and S. N. Steen, *Play Hard, Eat Hard,* American Dietary Association (Minneapolis: Chronimed Publishing, 1995).

Good Foods	Foods to Avoid
Bagels	Candy bars
Bananas	Doughnuts
Fruit juice	French fries
Muffins	Hot dogs
Pretzels (hard or soft)	Nachos or potato chips
Sports drinks (6-8% carbohydrate)	Soda

• **Figure 10.17** *Foods for All-Day Competitions. Source:* Adapted with permission from D. S. Jennings and S. N. Steen, *Play Hard, Eat Hard,* American Dietary Association (Minneapolis: Chronimed Publishing, 1995).

help recover your energy stores:

- Medium bagel (50 grams carbohydrate).
- Pretzels (23 grams carbohydrate per ounce).
- Fruit yogurt (40 grams carbohydrate per 8 ounces).
- Large banana (40 grams carbohydrate).
- Cranberry-apple juice (43 grams carbohydrate per 8 ounces).
- Apple juice (30 grams carbohydrate per 8 ounces).
- Orange juice (28 grams carbohydrate per 8 ounces).

Two hours after competition, eat a meal rich in carbohydrates, similar to the meals in Figure 10.16. You can add a bit more protein and fat in the post-event meal for calories and taste.

SECTION 4 REVIEW

Answer the following questions on a separate sheet of paper:

1. For performance fitness, when should you eat your last meal before practice or competition?

2. Why should your pre-event meal be high in carbohydrate and low in fat?

SUMMARY

Proper nutrition is important for good health. If you eat sensibly, you can reduce your risks for developing heart disease, high blood pressure, stroke, certain cancers, and diabetes mellitus. Balancing your diet by paying attention to your personal needs for calories, nutrients, vitamins, minerals, and fluids is the best way to optimize your nutrition. Most Americans eat too much fat and not enough carbohydrates for their nutrition needs. In your diet, 50 to 60 percent of the total calories should come from carbohydrate; 30 percent from fat (with only 10 percent being saturated fat); and 15 to 20 percent from protein. To develop and maintain healthy nutrition habits, use the Food Guide Pyramid to help you meet your daily RDA nutrition needs.

If you learn to read food labels, you can become a better consumer and become skilled at matching your daily caloric intake needs with your daily caloric expenditure. You should regularly evaluate your nutrition habits and your diet to control your body weight and body composition.

If you are involved in high-performance fitness or competitive sports or physical activities, you have special dietary needs. You should develop a nutrition plan that covers the time before the event, during the event, and immediately following the event. By eating right to compete or work out, you can improve your performance and speed your recovery time.

True/False

On a separate sheet of paper, mark each question below either T for True or F for False.

1. When you are hypoglycemic, you are full of energy and pep.
2. Fiber is easily digestible and is high in calories.
3. Of your total calories, 30 percent should come from fat, with no more than 10 percent from saturated fat.
4. Vitamin K is an example of a water-soluble vitamin.
5. Antioxidants may help prevent cancer, atherosclerosis, overtraining, and premature aging.
6. The RDA is the Recommended Daily Allowance for calories, vitamins, minerals, and other nutrients.
7. An example of the size of one serving is one medium apple.
8. Teenage girls should consume two to three servings of milk daily.
9. "Nutrition Facts" are part of the food labeling that you can find on food containers or packages.
10. If you are eating to compete, you should consume simple sugars for quick energy right before the contest.

Multiple Choice

1. What is the basic form of carbohydrate?
   a. fiber
   b. glucose
   c. glycogen
   d. electrolytes

2. What kind of nutrients are candy bars, honey, and fruits?
   a. simple carbohydrates
   b. fiber
   c. complex carbohydrates
   d. fat

3. Cholesterol is found in which of the following?
   a. unsaturated fats
   b. vegetables
   c. saturated fats
   d. corn and olive oil

4. Which of the following vitamins is not fat soluble?
   a. vitamin A
   b. vitamin C
   c. vitamin D
   d. vitamin E

5. Too much sodium in your diet may increase your risk for which of the following medical problems?
   a. hypertension
   b. elevated cholesterol
   c. osteoporosis
   d. none of the above

6. How many 8-ounce glasses of water should you consume every day to maintain a fluid balance (not counting days when you exercise in hot environments)?
   a. two
   b. four
   c. six
   d. eight

7. Which of the following items should be consumed at the highest percentage in your diet?
   a. carbohydrate
   b. fat
   c. protein
   d. saturated fat

8. Which of the following recommendations are part of the U.S. Department of Health and Human Services and the U.S. Department of Agriculture *Dietary Guidelines for Americans?*

   a. eat a variety of foods
   b. maintain a healthy weight
   c. use salt and sodium only in moderation
   d. all of the above

9. Which of the following food groups should be consumed sparingly?

   a. fats, oils, and sweets
   b. fruits
   c. vegetables
   d. milk, yogurt, and cheese

10. How many servings should you eat each day from the bread, cereal, rice, and pasta food group?

    a. one
    b. two to three
    c. four to five
    d. six to eleven

Discussion

1. Discuss how you can make the Food Guide Pyramid work for you in developing a plan for sound nutrition.

2. Explain how you can read and understand food labeling so that you can improve or maintain sound nutrition.

3. If you were to train and compete in a 10-kilometer walk/run in your community, how could you modify your nutrition plan to optimize your performance?

Vocabulary Experience

Match the correct term in Column A to the definition in Column B by writing the appropriate number in each blank.

Column A	Column B
_____ electrolytes	1. A mineral such as Ca^{++} or Na^+ that helps control the body's fluid balance.
_____ vegetarian	2. A nutrient that is the basic building block of the body.
_____ hypoglycemic	3. A substance that is usually liquid at room temperature and that comes mainly from plant sources.
_____ unsaturated fat	4. A chemical element that is important for the body's structure and function and that regulates the body's metabolism.
_____ protein	5. Having low blood glucose (or sugar) levels.
_____ mineral	6. A person who eliminates meat, fish, and poultry from the diet.

Critical Thinking

1. Respond to this statement: Family and culture do not influence what you eat.

2. How is fluid balance influenced by electrolytes and water? How can the maintenance of fluid balance help you prevent heat injuries?

3. Compare your eating habits with those of a family member. Which one of you is making wiser food choices?

Case Study — Gaining Weight

Javier is a fifteen-year-old active male. He lifts weights two times a week. Javier is interested in gaining weight, particularly muscle mass. However, he is unsure about how to gain the weight safely and effectively, get stronger, and not increase his percentage of body fat. Therefore, he needs the help of someone knowledgeable about designing and implementing fitness programs—someone like you!

Here is your assignment:

Assume you are Javier's friend, and he asks you for some assistance with his plans for gaining weight by adjusting his nutrition and physical activity routine. Make a list of things Javier should

consider and do before beginning his program. Then list the recommendations you would give to Javier for the first two weeks of his program.

The following suggestions may help you:

KEYS TO HELP YOU

- Consider Javier's current diet and nutrition habits.
- Decide how he should evaluate his current diet.
- Think about his needs and goals. For example, how should he go about changing his diet?
- Determine a reasonable plan to give Javier that covers the concepts of specificity, frequency, intensity, time/duration, and progression.

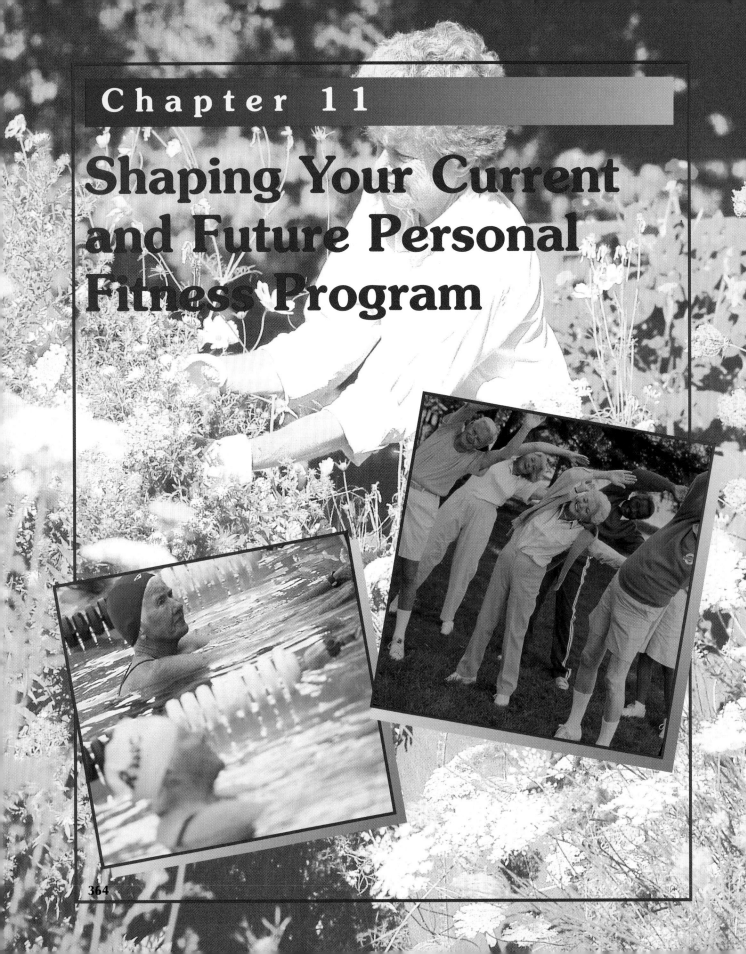

Chapter 11

Shaping Your Current and Future Personal Fitness Program

Contents

1. The Aging Process
2. The Physical Activity, Exercise, and Sports Spectrum
3. Becoming a Better Health and Personal Fitness Consumer

Outcomes

After reading and studying this chapter, you will be able to:

1. Explain how you can use what you have learned about developing personal fitness to help you control the aging process.
2. Discuss why and how you may have to adjust your personal fitness plan as you age.
3. Identify examples of leisure activities from the physical activity spectrum.
4. Explain how to find professional personal fitness advice.
5. Explain strategies for becoming a more informed and wiser personal fitness consumer.
6. Evaluate health and fitness centers to identify those that are reputable.

Key Terms

After reading and studying this chapter, you will be able to understand and provide practical definitions for the following terms:

aging process
leisure
leisure activity
lifetime activity
family physician
physical therapist
athletic trainer
podiatrist
dietitian
exercise physiologist

professional health and
  fitness certification
health educator
physical educator
personal trainer
aerobic dance instructor
fitness specialist
commercial gym
commercial fitness center
commercial dance studio

hospital-based wellness
  center
corporate fitness center
community recreational
  center
college- or university-
  based fitness center
sports medicine clinic
  center

INTRODUCTION

*I*f *you are like most adolescents, you haven't given much thought to how you will look and feel as you age. How healthy and fit will you be by the year 2000? By 2010? By 2050? How old do you think you will live to be?*

Life expectancy has increased dramatically in the United States since 1900. People who live to the age of sixty-five have very good odds of living into their eighties. However, these people won't be satisfied just to be alive. They will want to feel good and be healthy. They will want to be able to take care of themselves and live independently.

As you learned in Chapter 1, a healthy, active lifestyle can add years to your life and help you maintain your physical independence. In previous chapters you explored the many aspects of personal fitness. It is now time for you to use what you have learned to shape your current and future fitness.

You are at a critical age for making decisions about how healthy and active you will be in the future. Research has shown that young adults who do not develop positive attitudes and behaviors toward health and physical activity often become sedentary and inactive adults. You know what happens to sedentary people. Sedentary living and poor health behaviors can expose you to increased risk for chronic disease, disability, and even death. This means that the personal fitness habits you develop and maintain now can help you age more gracefully and reduce your risks for health problems throughout your life.

In this chapter you will learn more about the aging process and how you can control some of the mental and physical factors related to aging. You will learn more about a variety of physical activities, exercises, and sports that can help you stay active throughout your life. You will design your personal fitness program for now and the future. You will also learn more about becoming a better and wiser personal fitness consumer.

SECTION 1 The Aging Process

aging process

how the body changes as a person gets older.

The **aging process** is how your body changes as you get older. Figure 11.1 illustrates four physical functions and how they change with age. Notice that not all of the functions illustrated change at the same rate or to the same amount. For example, the speed at which nerve impulses travel in your body decreases only by about 10 to 15 percent from age 30 to 90, but maximum breathing capacity decreases 50 to 60 percent in the same amount of time. As you might guess, decreases in physical functions depend to a large extent on how healthy and active you remain. That is why it is said that a healthy, active lifestyle can slow the aging process.

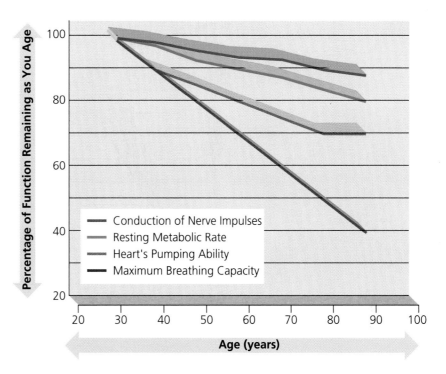

• **Figure 11.1** *Effects of Aging on Selected Physical Functions.*

Preventing or Slowing Aging of Bone Mass

Figure 11.2 shows one strategy to prevent or slow the aging process. Researchers have been studying bone mass and the development of osteoporosis to see if there is a relationship between being physically active and reducing bone mass loss with aging. Typically, as people grow and develop, they reach their peak bone mass between the ages of 27 and 32. After bone mass levels peak, they then decrease with age.

More active people have greater bone mass than inactive people as they age. This means that as active people age, they will be at a lower risk for osteoporosis than inactive people. If you are active now, you can increase your peak bone mass. If you stay active as you age, you may be able to maintain a higher bone mass than if you are inactive. Instead of getting brittle bones by age 65, you may still have strong bones into your eighties.

Controlling the Aging Process

The sum of all your mental and physical functions determines your functional health (see Chapter 1). As you age, you will be able to slow down the rate and the amount of change for many, but not all, men-

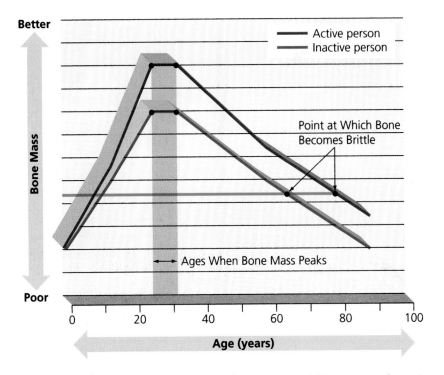

• **Figure 11.2** *Increasing Peak Bone Mass and Preventing Osteoporosis. Source:* Adapted with permission from H. C. G. Kemper and Niemeyer, "The Importance of a Physically Active Lifestyle during Youth for Peak Bone Mass," in *New Horizons in Pediatric Exercise Science,* ed. C. J. R. Blimkie and B. Oded (Champaign, IL.: Human Kinetics, 1995).

• *Participation in regular physical activity and exercise can help you increase your bone mass and maintain it longer than if you remain sedentary.*

BELIEVE IT? ... OR NOT?

You can lose 6 inches around your waist in two weeks; you can lose 10 pounds of fat in a week; you can make your stomach washboard hard and trim in six weeks; you can run a 26-mile marathon after conditioning for only five weeks.

See page 389 for answer.

tal and physical functions. Figure 11.3 indicates whether or not a physically active lifestyle and healthy eating can have a positive impact on various body functions as you age. As you can see, an active lifestyle and healthy eating will not necessarily keep you from getting gray hair or going bald. However, being active and eating well can help you stay mentally and physically young relative to your age. You probably know some people who look and feel much younger than most people their age. You may know people in their fifties, sixties, and seventies who are able to do more physical work than other, much younger people. Staying active and eating right can keep you in the younger-looking, more productive group.

Body Function	You Can Make a Positive Impact	You Cannot Make an Impact
Graying of hair		X
Balding		X
Resting energy metabolism	X	
Increased body fat	X	
Increased blood presssure	X	
Increased resting pulse	X	
Elevated cholesterol levels	X	
Decreased functional health	X	
Inherited diseases		X
Hypokinetic diseases	X	
Loss of elasticity of joints*		X
Loss of flexibility of joints**	X	
Bone loss	X	
Mental confusion	X	
Reduced self-esteem	X	
Depression	X	

 * elasticity = ability to return immediately to its original size, shape, etc.
** flexibility = ability to bend without breaking

• **Figure 11.3** *Controlling the Aging Process by Being Physically Active and Eating a Healthy Diet. Source:* Adapted with permission from F. S. Sizer, E. N. Whitney, and L. K. DeBruyne, *Making Life Choices: Health Skills and Concepts* (St. Paul: West Publishing, 1994).

• *Regular physical activity and exercise are important to people of all ages.*

The aging process also depends on a person's state of mind. Some people think and act much older than they actually are in terms of their health and activity levels. They practice poor health habits and adopt sedentary lifestyles. These habits and lifestyles, in turn, cause them to become depressed, lose self-esteem, and prematurely lose their physical independence. Thus, many older people will tell you, "If you don't use it, you'll lose it!"

Of course, it is normal to lose some mental and physical functioning as you age. You will probably have to adjust your personal fitness program as you age to meet your changing needs. For example, you may have to adjust your FIT for selected activities so that you can recover more completely between workouts. You may find that you need to select different physical activities as you age to keep yourself from getting bored and thus help maintain your adherence. You may find that you can adjust your personal fitness program by cross-training (see Chapter 3). In that way you can recover effectively from day to day and minimize your risk for an overuse injury.

As you age, you will need to pay even closer attention to your body. You will need to understand your mental and physical limitations. You then will be able to meet special situations and needs more effectively and maintain a healthy, active, and productive lifestyle until the end of your years.

Figure 11.4 shows you an activity pyramid that can help you develop and maintain regular physical activity patterns that will help you reduce your risks for chronic diseases as you age. The pyramid illustrates a sensible, step-by-step, daily and weekly plan to help you become and stay active.

Notice that "everyday" physical activities form the base of the pyramid. The next step, or level, of the pyramid includes exercise and recreational activities. The third level promotes leisure activities and the development and maintenance of strength and flexibility. The top step reminds you to cut down on your sedentary habits so that you sit less and move more.

SECTION 1 REVIEW

Answer the following questions on a separate sheet of paper:

1. List and explain three examples of how your body will change as you get older.

2. How can living a physically active lifestyle influence your bone mass?

3. Why is the aging process related to state of mind?

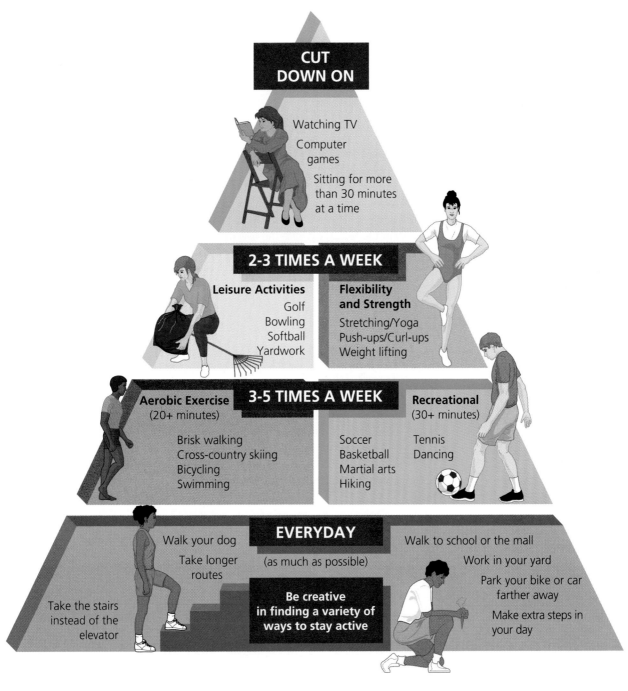

• **Figure 11.4** *Use your "Active Mind" to think of a variety of ways to have an "Active Body." This Activity Pyramid provides a plan for developing a physically active lifestyle.*

Adapted with permission from Park Nicollett Medical Foundation, 1995.

Believe It? ... Or Not?

"Physical activity is a key ingredient to healthy aging"

See page 389 for answer.

Stress Break

....

As you age, you will have to deal with new and different stressors daily. To reduce and deal effectively with stress, you can use various stress-relieving strategies. Some effective stress-relieving strategies are relaxation techniques, breathing exercises, meditation, distraction or imagery, yoga, slowing down, cutting back, physical activity, and exercise. The strategies that last the longest and are most effective in reducing heart rate, blood pressure, and other physical markers of stress are physical activity and exercise.

In addition to using appropriate stress relievers, you should learn to practice common stress management techniques. Some keys to stress-relieving strategies and relaxation techniques that you can practice now and in the future include the following:

- Accept some lack of ability in controlling everything in your life. You can't control everything that happens to you daily.
- Keep in mind that your own perceptions can create stress. Try to have a variety of viewpoints to understand other individuals' perceptions and attitudes.
- Realize that happiness is a by-product of what you do. It isn't something that is given to you.
- Focus on the entire process of your activities, not so much on how you are doing them each second.
- Find a sense of purpose (family, friends, ideas, and so on).
- Learn to forgive others.
- Don't live in the past. You can't undo what happened yesterday or the day before.
- Remember that laziness, procrastination, and sloppiness usually create more stress than they relieve.

SECTION 2   The Physical Activity, Exercise, and Sports Spectrum

Throughout this text you have been encouraged to develop and maintain an active lifestyle. You have learned that some physical activities are aerobic, and others are anaerobic. Some activities will improve your flexibility, whereas others are better designed to improve your cardiovascular fitness. There is a spectrum (a wide variety and range) of physical activities, exercises, and sports that can

- *Whatever physical activities or exercises you decide to do, you should strive to improve or maintain good to better levels of functional health.*

leisure

free (nonwork) time.

leisure activity

an activity, sport, or other experience that people participate in during their free (nonwork) time.

help you improve or maintain your functional health. Some are better suited than others to the development of certain aspects of your healthy, active lifestyle.

Leisure Activities

Figures 4.3 and 4.12 in Chapter 4 rated several different physical activities, exercises, and sports on how well they would help you develop the skill- and health-related components of your personal fitness. Notice that many activities (for example, golf) were rated low in terms of helping develop health-related fitness. However, playing golf recreationally does improve some skill-related fitness components (coordination and power) and is a good way to spend your **leisure** time.

Golf is just one example of a leisure activity. **Leisure activities** are the activities, sports, and other experiences that people participate in during their free (nonwork) time. Leisure activities do not necessarily help develop either your health- or skill-related fitness, but they do provide other benefits. By engaging in leisure activities, you can reduce your stress levels, have fun with others socially, burn calories, develop and maintain self-esteem, and pursue an active lifestyle.

As you continue to develop and refine your personal fitness program, you should experiment and try a wide variety of physical activities, exercises, and sports. You then can select the ones you like to do, as well as choose ones that will help you meet your personal fitness goals.

- *Golf is an example of a popular leisure activity.*

As you create your personal fitness program, you should focus first on developing and maintaining your health-related fitness. If you then want to participate in sports, your moderate to high levels of health-related fitness will make you better prepared physically to compete, reduce your risks for injuries, and improve your overall performance. Having moderate to high levels of health-related fitness will also help you enjoy leisure activities even more than if you had a low level of personal fitness.

Lifetime Activities

Your ultimate goal should be to engage in lifetime activities. **Lifetime activities** include any and all physical activities, exercises, sports, and leisure-time activities that you can participate in for long periods of time (years to decades). It is only natural that your choice of lifetime activities will change as you age. Your interests in personal fitness now are different than they will be in ten, twenty, or thirty years.

The following are descriptions of just a few of the many lifetime activities you may find that you enjoy. Learn to analyze your lifetime activities to make sure they help you meet your personal needs for health-related fitness, skill-related fitness, stress reduction, and worthwhile leisure pursuits. Also, determine which lifetime activities are realistic for you based on the following:

- *Cost.* Can you afford to participate in the activity?
- *Your personality and attitude.* Does the activity fit your style?
- *Availability of equipment and facilities.* Where can you find equipment or facilities for the activity?
- *Your social needs.* Will you do the activity alone or with friends?
- *Environmental hazards.* Can you engage in the activity safely?

Lap Swimming.   Swimming laps is a great way to develop and maintain coordination and agility. If you swim for several minutes, you can also develop or maintain your cardiovascular fitness and help control your body composition. You can use all kinds of strokes in lap swimming and vary your routine to help you with your fitness adherence.

Aqua Activities.   In recent years many people have discovered that they enjoy working out in the pool by doing exercises against the resistance provided by the water. For example, when you stand in a pool with water at chest level and move your arms back and forth through the water, you can feel the resistance of the water. Aqua activities reduce the pounding that your body takes in weight-bearing activities (for example, walking or jogging) and can be modified in intensity by working in the shallow or deep ends of the pool. You can use aqua activities to develop and maintain good to better levels of aerobic fitness, muscular endurance, and body composition.

lifetime activity

a physical activity, exercise, or sport that a person can participate in for long periods of time (years to decades).

- *Volleyball is a lifetime activity that can be played at the recreational or competitive level.*

Cycling (touring, mountain biking, and stationary cycling). Cycling is a very popular form of exercise with all age groups. Tour cycling is usually done on roads with a light-framed bike that has thin tires. Mountain biking is designed to be done on trails with a bike having a heavier frame and wider tires for better traction. For safety, always wear a helmet for tour or mountain bike cycling. Stationary cycling can be done at home or at a health and fitness club. Cycling is excellent for developing and maintaining balance and cardiovascular fitness and for helping you control your body composition.

Skating (in-line skating, rollerskating, and street hockey). In-line skating and street hockey have become extremely popular in the last few years. To be safe in these activities, you need to wear safety gear. In-line skating activities are excellent for developing and maintaining balance and are moderately good for improving cardiovascular endurance and body composition.

Rock Climbing. Rock climbing is a challenging anaerobic activity that requires high levels of muscular strength and endurance, as well as excellent balance and coordination. Rock climbing will also stress you aerobically on longer climbs. You should practice safe

REMEMBER This!

Experiment to find the lifetime activities that will work for you. Seek out new lifetime activities if you get bored with the old ones, but *get active and stay active!* If you become inactive again for a period of time, regroup and *get active again.*

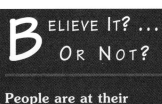

BELIEVE IT? ... OR NOT?

People are at their physical peak for performance at age twenty. From that point on, people go "downhill."

See page 389 for answer.

• *Lap swimming and rock climbing are both popular lifetime activities.*

• *Downhill skiing requires good to better levels of coordination and power.*

• *Ballet dancers usually have high levels of balance, coordination, and agility.*

climbing skills by always climbing with a partner and using your safety gear.

Tennis.   Tennis is a popular lifetime activity. It requires high levels of coordination and can help you develop and maintain your aerobic fitness if you play with partners of ability similar to yours. Many city parks, city recreation departments, and private tennis clubs offer lessons for people of all ages and abilities.

Water or Snow Skiing.   Whether you're on the water or the snow, skiing allows you to enjoy the great outdoors. The safest way to participate in skiing is to take lessons and purchase or rent quality equipment. Skiing of any type requires excellent coordination and power. Cross-country skiing is an excellent way to develop and maintain your cardiovascular fitness and body composition.

Racquetball.   Racquetball requires excellent coordination and agility. It is one of the most popular indoor lifetime activities. It is an excellent sport to help you develop and maintain your cardiovascular fitness and body composition. If you like to compete, racquetball tournaments are regularly held at many fitness clubs and are designed to challenge players of all ages and abilities.

Aerobic Dance (step aerobics).   Aerobic dance and step aerobics classes are held in just about every community in the United States. Aerobic dance develops coordination and is excellent for aerobic conditioning and controlling body composition. Aerobic dance or step aerobics classes are usually designed for people of all levels, from beginners (low impact or lower intensity, less bouncing and jarring movements), to those at intermediate and advanced conditioning levels. If you participate in aerobic dance or step aerobics, make sure you purchase a pair of shoes with good cushioning and support to help prevent overuse injuries.

Aerobic dance was originally developed by Jacki Sorenson in 1969 as a way of combining music and dance movements to achieve physical fitness. Although there are many variations of aerobic dance routines, the basic formula for an aerobics dance routine includes the following: warm-up, cardiovascular work (aerobic exercise), muscular strength, muscular endurance, flexibility components, and a cool-down. Use the instructions in the "Active Mind/Active Body" activity on the next page to design an aerobics dance exercise routine for yourself to present to your classmates (as an option, you can do this as a group project, with three or four other students).

Dance (ballet, line dancing, square dancing, and country-and-western dancing).   Many popular types of dance are easy to do, once you've had a few lessons. Dancing is good for developing your balance, coordination, and agility. Many forms of dance are also good for aerobic conditioning and weight

Designing an Aerobic Dance Exercise Routine

Watch and critique four or five aerobic dance exercise routine videotapes. Examine the videos to determine the types of music used, intensities of the exercises done (low, moderate, and high intensity), the types of warm-up and cool-down done, and the types of dance movements performed. Then, design your own aerobic dance exercise routine by following these guidelines:

1. Develop a routine that lasts 12–15 minutes.
2. Select music that is appropriate for school use and that matches your routine.
3. Vary the routine intensity with low-impact and high-impact exercises.
4. Set the routine cadence to an 8 count.
5. If you use a group to develop the routine, make sure each group member contributes equally to the routine or exercise leadership.
6. Develop smooth transitions from one exercise to the next.
7. Use correct exercise technique at all times.
8. Make sure your routine includes these components: warm-up, activities for arms and shoulders, aerobic activities, abdominal exercises, activities for leg work, and a cool-down.
9. Practice your routine with music several times before your presentation.

control, if you dance regularly and for long enough periods of time. (As you have learned, health-related fitness results depend on your FIT.) Dancing is an excellent way to interact socially with others. In fact, many people would say that dance, in its many forms, is both a social grace and a skill.

Volleyball. Volleyball helps develop your coordination. It is an activity that can be played recreationally or as a competitive sport. Recently, two-person sand volleyball has become very popular. More and more communities are building sand courts to promote participation. If you want to play volleyball at levels above the recreational level, make sure you have developed good to better levels of health- and skill-related fitness to minimize your risks for injuries.

• *Basketball is a lifetime activity you can engage in either by yourself or with friends.*

Basketball.   Basketball is excellent for developing your coordination, reaction time, and power. It can also be fun just to shoot the ball in a game of "HORSE." You can also get an excellent cardiovascular and muscular endurance workout in basketball if you play half-court or full-court games for several minutes. Playing half-court or full-court basketball is not an activity that most people can do for a lifetime, but you probably can participate in it well into middle age if you maintain good to better fitness levels.

Calisthenics.   Doing regular calisthenics (push-ups, curl-ups, jumping jacks, and so on) can help you improve your muscular endurance and flexibility. If you do calisthenics in a continuous, rhythmic manner, you can also develop and maintain your aerobic fitness and control your body composition.

Circuit Weight Training.   Circuit weight training involves lifting weights and doing calisthenics at different stations for several seconds, followed by periods of brief rest while moving to the next station. For example, you might lift 50 percent of your maximum on leg extensions for thirty seconds and then rest fifteen seconds. You then would move to the next station, which might be push-ups, and do as many as you could in thirty seconds. Your circuit should include at least eight to ten different exercise stations. You should gradually increase your workout time in the circuit from twenty to thirty minutes.

Circuit training is excellent for developing a combination of muscular strength, muscular endurance, and cardiovascular endurance, all in one workout. By lifting weights and doing calisthenics for thirty seconds to a minute at several (about eight to ten) stations, for several minutes, you optimize the time you have to develop and maintain your health-related fitness.

Kayaking and Canoeing.   Kayaking and canoeing can be done recreationally or at competitive levels. These activities help develop your power. When done for long periods of time per session, they are good for aerobic fitness, muscular strength, and muscular endurance. These activities are also great ways to get outside, explore new areas, and help control stress levels.

Rowing (crew and stationary).   Rowing in all its different forms is an excellent activity to develop your coordination, power, aerobic fitness, and muscular endurance. It is also a great way to control your body composition. Rowing in a crew can be a great way to meet other people and be part of a team, even if it's just for recreation. Stationary rowing can be lots of fun, particularly if you can get access to a rowing machine with interactive video feedback to enhance your workout.

T´ai Chi.   T´ai chi is a Chinese physical activity that includes various movements, including light calisthenic activities with controlled

• *Circuit weight training is a great way to emphasize aerobic and anaerobic work together.*

• *Canoeing is a good way to get outside, enjoy nature, and reduce your stress levels. Working out regularly on a rowing machine can build your muscular strength, muscular endurance, and cardiovascular endurance.*

• *You can increase your self-confidence and self-esteem by participating in the martial arts.*

breathing. T´ai chi exercises are excellent for improving flexibility and are helpful in stress reduction.

Martial Arts.   You might want to participate in one of the various martial arts. Karate and judo are two popular forms. A good teacher can help you develop martial art skills. All the martial arts are excellent ways to develop skill-related fitness and to control emotional stress. They can also help you develop self-confidence and self-esteem. However, the martial arts are not very effective at helping you develop or maintain health-related fitness levels.

Hiking and Backpacking.   Hiking and backpacking are excellent ways to get outside and enjoy nature while developing your muscular endurance and cardiovascular fitness. You probably won't have to go very far from where you live to find a county, state, or national park in which you can do some hiking. For safety, you should hike on well-marked trails and carry a water supply to prevent dehydration. If you hike in an area you're not familiar with, make sure you carry a map and compass to keep from getting lost.

Backpacking requires more planning than does just a half-day or full day of hiking. Before backpacking, you need to plan what supplies you will carry in your backpack (for example, tents, foods, and fluids), particularly if you will be gone for several days. You also have to decide how much weight you can carry for extended periods of time (perhaps an hour or two).

Hiking and backpacking can help you develop or maintain your personal fitness levels. However, you need to do some muscular endurance and cardiovascular conditioning prior to going on a long hike or backpacking trip. You should also make sure you purchase good hiking shoes or boots and break them in before participating regularly in hiking or backpacking.

Walking and Jogging.   Walking is one of the most popular activities that people of all ages engage in to develop and maintain muscular endurance and cardiovascular fitness. Jogging is not as popular as walking but has the same benefits. Chapters 3 and 5 gave examples of walking and jogging conditioning programs to help you reach good to better levels of cardiovascular fitness. You also know from Chapter 2 that it is important for you to wear proper shoes when you walk or jog.

Triathlons, Biathlons, and Marathons.   Triathlons (for example, the Ironman Triathlon in Hawaii) are endurance competi-tions that include swimming, cycling, and running for various dis-tances. Biathlons are endurance events that usually combine two activities—for example, running and cycling, swimming and running, or cross-country skiing and rifle shooting. Marathons are endurance competitions that usually include running distances of at least 26.2 miles. Triathlons, biathlons, and marathons all require high levels of performance fitness.

Most people will never try to complete a triathlon, biathlon, or marathon. However, you may find that you want to challenge your-self to complete one of these events just for your own self-satisfaction. If you decide to attempt one of these activities, make sure you seek out professional advice from your physical education teacher, school coach, or other expert and also condition yourself properly for several months before the event.

SECTION 2 REVIEW

Answer the following questions on a separate sheet of paper:

1. List three benefits of participating in leisure activities.
2. What five factors should you consider before choosing lifetime activities that are realistic for you?
3. Why is circuit weight training a good way to develop and maintain health-related fitness?

Designing Your Personal Fitness Program

You have learned all about personal fitness in Chapters 1 through 10. Now take some time and write out a plan for your personal fitness program. Use the "Active Mind/Active Body" activities and "Fitness Checks" you have done throughout the text, as well as the exercise science principles and the FIT recommendations you have learned, to write a personal fitness prescription for good health and an active lifestyle. Focus on the health-related components of personal fitness (cardiovascular fitness, flexibility, muscular strength and endurance, body composition, and nutrition). Reviewing the Case Studies you completed will also help you develop an appropriate program.

List your goals and how you expect to accomplish them. Don't forget to describe in detail the healthy nutrition practices you intend to follow. If you are interested in high-performance fitness, you can use some of the activities described in this chapter to develop a program for yourself that focuses on skill-related fitness (agility, balance, coordination, power, speed, and reaction time). After you complete your plan, explain how you might need to modify your program when you are thirty, fifty, and seventy years old.

SECTION 3
Becoming a Better Health and Personal Fitness Consumer

Throughout the text you have read the "Consumer Corner" features. It is important for you to become a better health and personal fitness consumer. Now, more than ever before, a large number of health and fitness products and services are being marketed and sold to the public. Many of these products and services are not effective or produce only partial positive results, leaving consumers frustrated and angry about their purchases and the money that they wasted.

In this section you will learn how to find qualified and knowledgeable health and fitness experts who can help you get accurate, professional, personal fitness advice. You will learn how to identify and

Any Body Can!

Gabrielle Reece

Gabrielle Reece is a 6'3", 172-pound professional four-woman circuit beach volleyball player and a super model. She has become a role model for women's fitness for the 1990s and the future.

Gabrielle (who prefers to be called "Gabby" or "Gab") was born in 1970. In her junior year of high school, she began playing volleyball and was discovered by a modeling scout. She did well at both modeling and volleyball, and by her senior year she had earned a volleyball scholarship to Florida State University.

At Florida State Gabby continued to play volleyball and to model. She spent six months of the year playing middle blocker in volleyball and spent the other six months in New York modeling for magazines like *Elle* and *Italian Vogue*. In 1990, she was named All-Southeastern Conference middle blocker and is still Florida State's all-time leader in blocks.

In 1992, Gabby began playing women's doubles beach volleyball (2 women per team), but struggled due to the differences in the style of play of this kind of volleyball versus the collegiate game (6 women on a team). Later in the same year, she was asked to join a new, professional circuit beach volleyball tour with four women on a team. In 1993, she led the league in kill shots and blocks, and she signed an endorsement contract with a major shoe manufacturer. The next year she was voted the league's best offensive and the most improved player.

Gabby has continued both her successful modeling and volleyball careers. She has been named to *Elle* magazine's "Five Most Beautiful Women in the World" list and is one of *People's* magazine's "50 Most Beautiful People." She has become a national celebrity promoting health and fitness.

Gabby has become a role model for many young men and women. She promotes participation in physical activities and sports as a way for adolescents to learn to control their bodies. Gabby feels that regular participation in physical activities and sports helps build confidence and self-discipline, and adds meaning to life.

Gabby works hard to maintain her own physical skills and good looks. In addition to playing competitive volleyball, she works out regularly at a gym. Her typical workout includes a 50-minute circuit of aerobics with strength and flexibility training. This has helped her develop a physique that has only 15 percent body fat. She also follows a sound nutrition plan to meet her daily energy needs and to control her weight.

Not everyone can be a super model and professional athlete like Gabrielle Reece, but **A**ny **B**ody **C**an learn to develop and maintain personal fitness for a lifetime of active living.

evaluate reputable health and fitness information, including information on practicing sound nutrition or purchasing home exercise equipment. This section will also suggest some questions to ask when choosing a health and fitness club.

Finding Qualified Fitness Experts

At some point you will probably want to learn more about personal fitness or seek more in-depth, professional advice about nutrition, recreational activities, body building, or rehabilitation from injuries. It is important, as a wise consumer, that you seek out qualified and certified health and fitness professionals. Some examples of health and fitness professionals who are available to help you are physicians, physical therapists, athletic trainers, podiatrists, dietitians, exercise physiologists, health and physical educators, personal trainers, aerobic dance instructors, and fitness specialists.

Family physicians usually treat day-to-day health problems or injuries. These physicians train for many years in academic and clinical settings (settings where they are actually practicing medicine) and are licensed by the state. Other kinds of physicians have additional specialized training in specific medical areas, including surgery, cardiology (disorders of the heart), or orthopedics (bone and joint disorders).

Physical therapists are specially trained to work with people in rehabilitation (recovery from injury). They use a variety of treatments and techniques to help manage their patients' health problems.

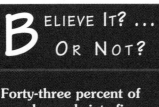

BELIEVE IT? ... OR NOT?

Forty-three percent of people aged sixty-five and older did not engage in any leisure activity in 1985; the *Healthy People 2000* goal is to reduce this number to no more than 22 percent.

See page 389 for answer.

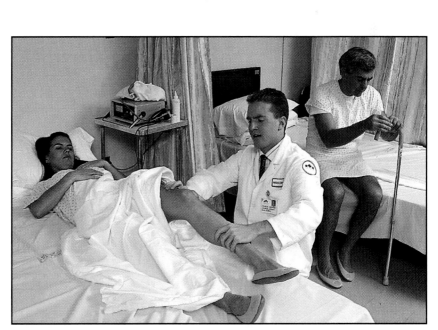

• *Physical therapists are specially trained to work with people who are rehabilitating from injuries.*

Physical therapists undergo four to six years of academic and clinical training and must be licensed by the state. Clients are referred to physical therapists by physicians.

Athletic trainers usually work in the rehabilitation of athletes at the high school, college, or professional levels. Athletic trainers undergo at least four years of academic and clinical training before they can practice. They work under the supervision of physicians and are often licensed by the state.

Podiatrists are professionals trained specifically to treat disorders of the feet. They train at least five to six years in academic and clinical settings and are licensed by the state.

Dietitians specialize in providing nutrition advice and helping people control their weight. They undergo at least four years of academic and clinical training before they can practice. They are registered and licensed by the state.

Exercise physiologists are specially trained to understand the body's physical reactions to exercise. They complete at least four to six years of college and earn a degree with an emphasis in exercise physiology. They are not licensed by the state but usually earn **professional health and fitness certification** as fitness instructors or program directors by a national organization. To do so, individuals must pass written tests and demonstrate their skill as leaders of physical activity to be certified by national fitness and health organizations.

Health educators and **physical educators** have special training in wellness, personal fitness, and often coaching. They attend at

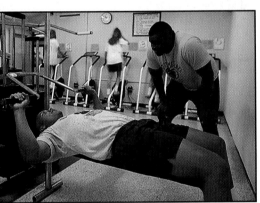

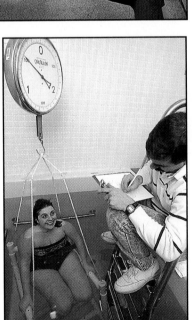

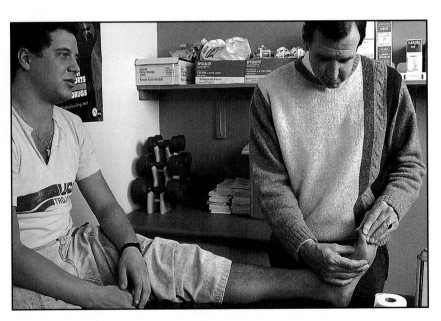

• *Personal trainers, exercise physiologists, and athletic trainers are just a few of the health and fitness specialists who can help you maintain or improve your personal fitness.*

least four to six years of college and earn degrees in health or physical education specialties. The instructor for the class you are now taking is most likely a health or physical educator. This professional is a very valuable first stop when you are seeking professional personal fitness advice. Health educators and physical educators are certified by the state to teach.

Personal trainers, aerobic dance instructors, and **fitness specialists** are individuals who specialize in working with people alone or in groups to help them achieve individual personal fitness goals. They may or may not have any formal academic or clinical training. Many organizations have programs that provide professional health and fitness certification for personal trainers, aerobic dance instructors, or fitness specialists who pass written and practical examinations. Unfortunately, some certification programs are very superficial. In fact, in some cases all an individual needs to do to receive a certification is mail in a fee. This type of certification is unethical, yet it occurs regularly.

Many excellent personal trainers and aerobic dance instructors are practicing their skills. You need to be aware, however, that others have little, if any, professional qualifications. If you choose a trainer or instructor who is not reputable, you probably will get inaccurate advice and may increase your risk for injury.

personal trainer

individual who specializes in working alone with people, instructing exercise sessions, and developing personal fitness programs for a fee.

aerobic dance instructor

individual who specializes in teaching aerobic dance activities to groups of people.

fitness specialist

individual (other than a personal trainer or aerobic dance instructor) who specializes in physical fitness and nutrition promotion.

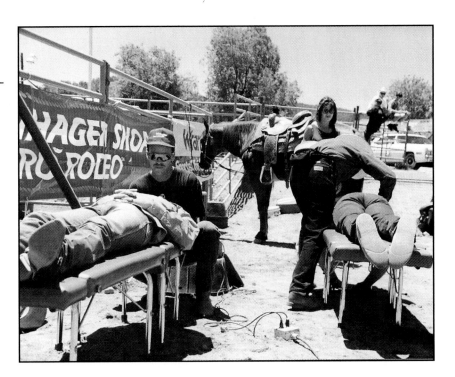

• *Health and fitness professionals are often seen at competitive events where they provide competitors with a variety of important services prior to and following the events.*

Evaluating Health and Fitness Information

Another important consumer issue has to do with health and fitness information claims that require you to be able to distinguish fact from fiction. As a consumer you are bombarded every day by advertisements in print, and on television and radio that promote health and fitness products (diets, fitness equipment, and so on). All these products claim they will make you fitter, look better, or feel better. You will also find many articles and books about health and fitness. Often the claims of these advertisements, books, and articles are false, misleading, unsafe, or ineffective.

You can become a better health and fitness information consumer by using the following guidelines:

- Look at the credentials (a list of a person's professional training and experiences) of the people making health and fitness claims, particularly if they are selling products.
- Be suspicious of claims of quick and simple results associated with health and fitness.

CONSUMER CORNER

Listening to the Experts

Many so-called health and fitness experts who look fit know very little about the whys and hows of developing and maintaining fitness. To find reputable professional personal fitness advice, follow these guidelines:

1. Ask your personal fitness course instructor to refer you to someone he or she respects professionally.
2. Ask your personal physician for advice.
3. Ask to see professional licenses or special training certifications.
4. Make sure a professional's certifications are from reputable organizations, such as the following:
   - American College of Sports Medicine, or ACSM (exercise physiologists and fitness specialists);
   - Young Men's Christian Association, or YMCA (fitness certifications);
   - American Council on Exercise, or ACE (aerobic dance instructors, fitness specialists);
   - Aerobics and Fitness Association of America, or AFAA (aerobic dance instructors, step aerobics instructors—individuals who teach aerobic dance with bench stepping routine, personal trainers);
   - National Strength and Conditioning Association, or NSCA (personal trainers and strength coaches—individuals who specialize in helping people build muscular strength and endurance).
5. Make sure the advice you get includes information that you can understand and use in your life.

BELIEVE IT? ... OR NOT?

One goal of *Healthy People 2000* is to reduce the proportion of people aged sixty-five who have difficulty performing two or more personal care activities from 11 to 9 percent.

See page 389 for answer.

- Beware of miracle breakthroughs that you have not read or heard about elsewhere.

- Beware of individuals testifying that they got great results with a product, particularly if there is a label or disclaimer stating, "Results may vary."

- Check out home exercise equipment before you buy it. Make sure you know how to use it, that it is built to last, and that it is safe and effective. Seek professional advice before you buy if you have any questions.

- Beware of mail-order sales or infomercials that promote products or services that are not endorsed by qualified health and fitness professionals.

- Don't spend your money on a health and fitness product until you've had a chance to evaluate whether or not it is truly effective and practical for you.

Practice your skills at evaluating health and fitness claims by doing the exercise in the "Active Mind/Active Body" activity below.

Health and Fitness Facilities

At some point in your life, you may find it helpful to join a health and fitness club or center in order to restart or maintain your personal fitness program. If you do want to join a club or center, keep in mind that some are more reputable than others. A quality health and fitness facility should be a place where you can pursue your fitness conditioning safely and effectively, get sound professional advice, and achieve your personal goals.

Active Mind! Active Body!

Evaluating Health and Fitness Information

Identify and describe five different examples of misleading or false health and fitness information that you have seen in the last six weeks. If you need help, look for examples in your local newspaper, health and fitness magazines, television commercials, health and fitness club advertisements, and trade shows.

• *If you join a health and fitness center or club, find one that meets your specific needs.*

Kinds of Clubs.   You can choose from many different types of health and fitness clubs or centers. These facilities often specialize in or cater to specific consumer needs or clients. For example, in your community you may find commercial gyms, commercial fitness centers, commercial dance studios, hospital-based wellness centers, corporate fitness centers, community recreational centers, college- or university-based fitness centers, or sports medicine clinic centers.

Commercial gyms are health and fitness facilities that are usually small in size and have relatively few members. These centers usually specialize in providing a few physical activities to the consumer. They cater to the serious weight trainer or high-performance athlete.

Commercial fitness centers are health and fitness facilities that offer a wide variety of resistance and aerobic training equipment and cater to all types of people. These centers are often found in neighborhood shopping centers. YMCAs and YWCAs are considered commercial fitness centers.

Commercial dance studios are health and fitness facilities that usually do not have much exercise equipment and cater to people interested in aerobic dance and jazz forms of exercise. These studios are often found in neighborhood shopping centers.

Hospital-based wellness centers are health and fitness facilities associated with neighborhood hospitals. These centers usually have

Answers to

B ELIEVE IT? ... OR NOT?

Pg. 369 False. If a claim sounds too good to be true or possible, it probably is. Don't fall for fitness claims that sound simplistic. Developing and maintaining personal fitness need not be painful or even uncomfortable, but it does take some discipline and time.

Pg. 372 True.

Pg. 375 False. You can find numerous examples of people in their forties, fifties, and beyond setting personal performance records in such diverse activities as weight lifting, golf, and target shooting.

Pg. 380 True.

Pg. 383 True.

Pg. 384 False. Only about 5 percent of people over sixty-five are in nursing homes. Most older Americans live independently and depend on their mental and physical abilities to function daily.

Pg. 387 True.

a wide variety of exercise and educational programs focusing on personal fitness. Hospital-based wellness centers cater primarily to clients who need medical screening before beginning a fitness program or medical supervision during their physical activity.

Corporate fitness centers are health and fitness facilities that are associated with businesses such as telephone companies or computer companies. These centers often offer a variety of recreational and fitness programs for employees and their families.

Community recreational centers are health and fitness facilities operated by a city park and recreation department. These centers offer a variety of recreational activities and programs to members of the community.

College- or university-based fitness centers are health and fitness facilities operated by state or private colleges or universities. These centers usually provide a variety of recreational and fitness programs for students, faculty, and staff from a particular school.

Sports medicine clinic centers are health and fitness facilities that focus on research promoting health and fitness, as well as on the development and operation of health, fitness, recreation, and educational programs. These centers are usually associated with large hospitals in large cities and cater to clients in the upper-middle socioeconomic class.

Figure 11.5 on the next page gives the advantages and disadvantages of the various types of health and fitness facilities that have been described. Study the figure carefully.

Choosing a Facility.   How can you pick a health and fitness club from the many kinds available? To pick a quality health and fitness club or center for yourself, you need to determine your personal fitness needs and the type of facility that can best meet these needs. Visit several facilities to get an idea of what they offer. Always visit a health and fitness club or center before joining it.

As you visit a facility, ask yourself these questions:

- Is the facility conveniently located for you?
- What time does the facility open and close, and is it open on holidays?
- Is the facility clean and well maintained?
- Does the facility have a locker room? If so, are there towels and laundry service?
- Does the facility have enough showers, hot tubs, saunas, and steam rooms? Are they kept clean?
- What are the prices, and does the club have package deals or season specials?
- Is the facility very crowded when you want to use it?
- Can you fit in and socialize easily with the other members?

Health and Fitness Facility	Advantages	Disadvantages
Commercial gym	Is good for high performance	Has limited facilities; members may be too serious for your needs
Commercial fitness center	Has a large variety of activities	May be expensive or too crowded
Commercial dance studio	Usually has certified instructors	Has a limited number of fitness activities
Hospital-based wellness center	Has medical supervision and highly trained personnel	Has a relatively higher cost
Corporate fitness center	Has a variety of recreational and fitness activities	Is limited to employees and family members
Community recreational center	Has a variety of recreational activities and is economical	May have limited health and fitness activities
College- or university-based fitness center	Has a wide variety of programs and trained personnel	To join, you must be associated with the school (student, faculty, or staff); it may be very expensive for others to join
Sports medicine clinic center	Has comprehensive programs and medical supervision; is research based	Is expensive

• **Figure 11.5** *Comparison of Various Types of Health and Fitness Facilities.*

- Are the instructors or personal trainers certified and well skilled in correct resistance training?
- Are individual exercise programs available?
- Are educational programs available?
- Does the facility have a medical advisor for any special medical needs you have?
- Are the instructors certified in cardiopulmonary resuscitation (CPR) and first aid?
- Is the equipment well cared for and in top working condition?
- Is the exercise area uncluttered and well monitored for safety?
- Does the facility have a variety of both machines and free weights?

- Does the facility have a variety of aerobic conditioning activities (swimming, cycles, treadmills, stair steppers, and so on)?
- Are aerobic exercise classes offered?
- Are racquetball, basketball, or tennis courts available?
- Are there indoor and outdoor hiking and jogging tracks or trails?
- Is there a system for evaluating your progress?
- Does the facility have computers to log or chart your progress?

All these steps should help you choose a health and fitness club or center wisely.

SECTION 3 REVIEW

Answer the following questions on a separate sheet of paper:

1. What is the difference between a physical therapist and a podiatrist?
2. List four ways to become a better health and fitness information consumer.
3. Discuss four factors you should consider before joining a health or fitness club.

SUMMARY

You can have some control over your aging process. You can maintain many of your mental and physical abilities, or even slow down their loss. A regular personal fitness program and sound nutrition can increase your chances for living a longer and more productive life. The maintenance of your functional health depends to a large extent on how active you are now and in the future. You should be prepared to make any necessary adjustments in your personal fitness plan to remain active as you age.

A wide variety or spectrum of physical activities, exercises, and sports can help you improve or maintain your functional health.

You should find the leisure and lifetime activities that work effectively for you in order to maintain your functional health and enjoy life more fully.

If you become a better health and fitness consumer, you will be able to spend your money more wisely on products and services that are available. By knowing how to seek professional health and fitness advice, you can save yourself time and money, as well as reduce your chances of getting poor service. Finally, if you desire to join a health and fitness club or center, choose it wisely. Visit several facilities, and choose one that meets your needs.

Chapter 11 Review

True/False

On a separate sheet of paper, mark each question below either T for True or F for False.

1. You can have a positive impact on your risk for chronic diseases.

2. Leisure activities will not help you reduce your stress levels.

3. Aqua activities can reduce the pounding your body takes in weight-bearing activities.

4. Circuit weight training is an excellent way to develop a combination of health-related fitness components all at the same time.

5. If you live to be sixty-five, you can expect to live five more years at most.

6. Your resting metabolic rate does not decrease with age.

7. You reach your peak bone mass between the ages of twenty-seven and thirty-two.

8. Podiatrists are physicians who specialize in disorders of the feet.

9. Personal trainers are certified and licensed by states.

10. As you age, you will need to join a health and fitness club to continue your personal fitness program.

Multiple Choice

1. Which of the following can help you determine which lifetime activities are realistic for you?
   a. cost
   b. personality and attitude
   c. social needs
   d. all of the above

2. In-line skating will help you develop and maintain all but which one of the following?
   a. reaction time
   b. balance
   c. cardiovascular fitness
   d. body composition

3. By what percentage will your maximum breathing capacity decrease from ages thirty to ninety?
   a. 5 to 10 percent
   b. 15 to 25 percent
   c. 30 to 40 percent
   d. 50 to 60 percent

4. Which of the following changes associated with aging can you control by being physically active and eating a healthy diet?
   a. increased body fat
   b. graying of hair
   c. inherited diseases
   d. balding

5. Which of the following does not usually occur in people who remain sedentary as they age?
   a. They get depressed.
   b. They maintain functional health.
   c. They lose self-esteem.
   d. They lose bone mass.

6. With whom do physical therapists primarily work?
   a. athletes
   b. people with foot problems
   c. people in rehabilitation
   d. people who need to control their weight

Discussion

1. Identify the mental and physical functions that change with the aging process. Describe how you can control to some degree the rate and amount that these functions will change.

2. Describe and explain why some older people can outwork or physically outperform much younger individuals.

3. Describe and explain how you can be a better health and fitness consumer.

Vocabulary Experience

Match the correct term in Column A to the definition in Column B by writing the appropriate number in each blank.

Column A

_____ aging process

_____ dietitian

_____ professional health and fitness certification

_____ leisure

_____ lifetime activities

_____ physical educator

Column B

1. Process where individuals must pass written tests and demonstrate their physical-activity-leading skills in order to be certified by national health and fitness organizations.

2. Free time.

3. How your body changes as you get older.

4. A professional with special training in wellness and personal fitness.

5. A professional who develops nutrition programs and works with people to control their weight.

6. Activities in which participation can last years to decades.

Critical Thinking

1. Develop a list of lifetime activities that you do now or would like to do now or in the future. Then explain why you enjoy them and how they can help you develop and maintain your personal fitness levels.

2. List and explain the changes in physical functioning that your parents and grandparents are facing as they age. How might staying physically active and eating a healthy diet help them cope with these changes?

3. React to this statement: *Education can make you a better health and fitness consumer and can prevent you from being the victim of rip-offs.*

GLOSSARY

A

abdominal a muscle in the lower stomach area that is used in breathing.

acclimatization the process of allowing the body to adapt slowly to new conditions.

active warm-up a warm-up that attempts to raise the body temperature by actively involving the muscular, skeletal, and cardiovascular systems.

acute occurring over a short time.

adherence the ability to continue something, such as your chosen personal fitness program, over a period of time.

aerobic dance instructor individual who specializes in teaching aerobic dance activities to groups of people.

aerobic fitness level cardiovascular fitness level.

aerobic with oxygen.

agility the ability to change and control the direction and position of your body while maintaining a constant, rapid motion.

aging process how the body changes as a person gets older.

amino acid a class of compounds that are the basic building blocks for proteins.

anaerobic without oxygen.

anorexia nervosa an eating disorder in which people abnormally restrict their caloric intake.

antagonistic muscles opposing muscles.

antioxidant a vitamin or mineral that may help protect the body from various types of cell damage.

artery a blood vessel that carries blood away from the heart and branches out to supply oxygen and other nutrients to the muscles, tissues, and organs of the body.

asthma restriction of the breathing passages due to dust, allergies, pollution, or even vigorous exercise.

atherosclerosis a disease process that causes substances to build up inside arteries, reducing or blocking blood flow.

atrophy a loss of muscle size and strength because of lack of use.

B

balance the ability to control or stabilize your equilibrium while moving or staying still.

ballistic stretching exercises that involve quick up-and-down bobbing movements that are held very briefly.

biomechanics the study of the principles of physics applied to human motion.

blood pooling a condition, following exercise, in which blood collects in the large veins of the legs and lower body, especially when the exercise is stopped abruptly.

blood pressure the force by which blood is pushed against the walls of the arteries.

blood vessel in a muscle, the structure that provides oxygen, energy, and a waste removal system for each muscle fiber.

bulimia an eating disorder in which people overeat and then force themselves to vomit afterward or purposely overuse laxatives to eliminate food from their bodies.

C

caloric expenditure the number of calories expended or burned in daily physical activity.

caloric input the number of calories consumed in the diet.

capillary a small blood vessel that delivers oxygen and other nutrients to the individual muscle, tissue, and organ cells.

carbohydrate a nutrient that includes sugars and starches (like pasta).

cardiac muscle muscle in the heart and arteries.

cardiovascular cool-down a period after exercise in which you try to prevent blood pooling by moving about slowly and continuously for about three to five minutes.

cardiovascular disease heart and blood vessel disease.

cardiovascular fitness the ability to work continuously for extended periods of time.

cardiovascular warm-up a warm-up that gradually increases the heart rate and internal body temperature.

cartilage a soft, cushioned material that surrounds the ends of bones at a joint to prevent the bones from rubbing against each other.

center of gravity the area of your body that determines how your weight is distributed.

cholesterol a blood fat.

chronic occurring over an extended time.

circulatory system the heart and the system of blood vessels in the body, including the arteries, capillaries, and veins.

complex carbohydrate a carbohydrate that is starchy and broken down more slowly in the body than a simple carbohydrate.

compound set method a weight-training hypertrophy program that requires you to do two different exercises that use the same muscle group, without allowing for rest between the sets.

concentric contraction the contraction and shortening of a muscle, which results in the movement of bones and joints; also called *positive work*.

conditioning engaging in regular physical activity or exercise that results in an improved state of physical fitness.

connective tissue the "glue" for the body tissue that binds muscles and bones together while still allowing them to move more efficiently.

contract to shorten.

coordination the ability to use your eyes and ears to determine and direct the smooth movement of your body.

cross-train to vary activities and exercises from day to day to prevent detraining, especially after an injury.

D

dehydration excess fluid loss from the body; symptoms include weakness and fatigue.

detraining the loss of health and fitness benefits when a personal fitness program is stopped.

diabetes mellitus a chronic disease affecting the blood sugar.

diaphragm a muscle in the middle chest area that is used in breathing.

diastolic blood pressure the pressure on the arteries when the heart relaxes after contraction.

distress excess negative stress, such as fear, anger, or confusion.

diuretic a substance that promotes water loss through urination.

dose the amount and frequency of an activity or substance.

E

eating disorders behaviors that cause a person to overeat, undereat, or practice extreme unhealthy actions to control their weight.

eccentric contraction a muscle's slow release of a contraction as it becomes longer; also called *negative work*.

ectomorph a slender, lean somatotype.

elasticity the rubberband-like flexibility of the muscles, tendons, and other connective tissues.

electrolyte a mineral whose electrical charge helps control the body's fluid balance.

endomorph a heavier, rounder somatotype.

energy balance the balance between calories consumed in the diet and the amount of calories burned in daily physical activity.

energy cost the amount of energy required for you to perform different physical activities or exercises.

energy expenditure the number of calories you burn each minute.

essential fat the minimum amount of body fat necessary for good health.

eustress positive stress; an enjoyable type of stress.

excessive leanness a percentage of body fat that is too low for good health.

exercise physical activity that is planned, structured, repetitive, and results in the improvement or maintenance of personal fitness.

F

fast-twitch muscle fiber a muscle cell that is suited to anaerobic work.

fat a type of nutrient that is high in energy; found in animal tissues, nuts, seeds, and oils of some plants.

fat-soluble vitamin a vitamin that dissolves in the body's fat tissues and can be stored in the body; the vitamins A, D, E, and K.

fiber a type of carbohydrate that is not digestible by humans and provides no energy.

FIT the three components of the overload principle: Frequency, Intensity, and Time/Duration; a level of physical conditioning that is desirable and obtainable by everyone.

fitness specialist individual (other than a personal trainer or aerobic dance instructor) who specializes in physical fitness and nutrition promotion.

flexibility the range of motion that your joints have during movement.

Food Guide Pyramid a visual outline of what people should eat each day.

free weights objects of varied weights that can be moved without restriction and used for weight lifting; examples are barbells and dumbbells.

frequency in a personal fitness prescription, how often you work.

frostbite damage to the body tissues due to freezing.

functional health a person's physical ability to function independently in life, without assistance.

G

general active warm-up a warm-up tailored to individual physical activities. It is less structured than a specific active warm-up.

genetic potential inherited muscle characteristics that determine the percentage, type, and number of our muscle fibers.

glucose sugar; the basic form of carbohydrate and a valuable source of energy.

glycogen the stored form of glucose in the liver and skeletal muscle.

H

health a state of well-being that includes physical, mental, emotional, spiritual, and social aspects.

health-related fitness physical fitness primarily associated with disease prevention and functional health. Health-related fitness has five components: cardiovascular fitness, body composition, flexibility, muscular strength, and muscular endurance.

heart attack the blockage of vessels feeding the heart, causing the death of heart tissue.

heat cramps painful contractions of the muscles used during physical activity or exercise due, at least in part, to dehydration.

heat exhaustion an overheating condition that includes weakness; headache; rapid pulse, stomach discomfort; dizziness; heavy sweating; muscle cramps; and cool, clammy skin.

heat stress index a number that reflects a combination of high temperatures and high humidity.

heat stroke a life-threatening condition resulting from a buildup of body heat; can be fatal.

hemoglobin an iron-rich compound in the blood that helps carry oxygen from the lungs to the muscles, tissues, and organs.

heart rate the number of times your heart beats per minute.

high-density lipoprotein (HDL) "good cholesterol"; the type of cholesterol that is associated with a lower atherosclerosis risk.

hyperflexibility the condition of having too much flexibility.

hyperplasia a theory of muscle enlargement that says muscle growth is due to muscle fibers splitting and creating additional fibers.

hypertension high blood pressure.

hyperthermia overheating; body temperature above 98.6 degrees Fahrenheit.

hypertrophy muscle enlargement due to the thickening of each existing muscle fiber.

hypoglycemic having a condition in which the blood glucose level drops and the person feels dizzy, tired, and irritable.

hypokinetic physically inactive, or sedentary.

hypothermia a condition in which the body temperature drops below normal (98.6 degrees Fahrenheit).

I

ideal body weight the perfect weight for good health.

intensity in a personal fitness prescription, how hard you work.

intercostal a muscle around the ribs that is used in breathing.

interval training alternating higher-intensity physical activities or exercises with lower-intensity recovery bouts for several minutes at a time.

isometric contraction a muscle's pushing against an immovable object and having no movement occur as it attempts to contract. The muscle does not become shorter or longer but creates tension.

isotonic progressive resistance a combination of concentric and eccentric muscle contractions.

K

kilocalorie a unit used to measure energy; also called a *calorie.*

L

large muscle group muscles of large size or a large number of muscles being used at one time.

lean body weight the weight of the bones, muscles, and connective tissue.

leisure activity an activity, sport, or other experience that people participate in during their free (nonwork) time.

leisure free (nonwork) time.

life expectancy the number of years a person can expect to live.

lifetime activity a physical activity, exercise, or sport that a person can participate in for long periods of time (years to decades).

ligament a band of tissue that connects bone to bone and limits the movement of a joint.

longevity the actual length of a person's life.

low back injury injury to the muscles, ligaments, tendons, or joints of the lower back.

low-density lipoprotein (LDL) "bad cholesterol"; a type of cholesterol that is associated with higher atherosclerosis risk.

M

maximum heart rate the maximum number of times your heart can beat in a minute.

medical examination a more extensive evaluation than is done in a medical screening, assessing any or all of the following: exercise stress test, blood test, urinary analysis, or family health-risk history.

medical screening a basic evaluation of the eyes, ears, nose, throat, blood pressure, height, weight, and a check for possible hernia.

mesomorph a muscular somatotype.

metabolic rate the number of calories that is burned or expended as heat.

microtear a small tear in a part of a muscle fiber or connective tissue because of greater-than-usual resistance; causes muscle soreness.

mineral a chemical element that is important for the body's structure and function and for regulating metabolism.

mode in a personal fitness prescription, the type of activity or exercise you do.

multiple set method a weight-training strength program that uses the same amount of weight (a percentage of your maximum) for each set until you are fatigued.

muscle fibers (muscle cells) long, thin structures the size of human hairs that contract to create movement. They run the entire length of a muscle.

muscle imbalance an imbalance that occurs when one muscle group that controls a joint is too strong in relation to a complementary set of muscles (another set of muscles that helps control the same joint).

muscle intensity the amount of tension or stress placed on a muscle.

muscle pump the contraction of the muscles in the body (especially the legs) as the muscles squeeze the veins to help blood move back to the right side of the heart.

muscle/skeletal warm-up a warm-up that usually involves a series of static body stretches.

muscular endurance the ability to contract your muscles several times without excessive fatigue.

muscular strength the maximal force that you can exert when you contract your muscles.

myocardial infarction (MI) a heart attack; a blockage of a vessel that feeds the heart muscle.

N

negative workout method a weight-training strength program that uses very heavy weights at the end of a prescribed number of sets and repetitions.

nerve in a muscle, the part that delivers the messages from the brain to direct each individual muscle fiber to contract.

nutrient a substance in foods that the body needs for proper growth, development, and functioning.

obesity excessive body fat; excessive weight (20% or more above appropriate weight).

osteoporosis a condition in which the bones are porous and brittle.

overfat carrying too much body fat.

overload principle the principle that says to improve your level of physical fitness, you must increase the amount of activity or exercise that you normally do.

overtraining being too active or exercising too much. Overtraining leads to overuse injuries and addictive behaviors.

overuse injury an injury caused by doing too much,

too soon, too often in an exercise program.

P

passive stretching exercises in which a partner or device provides the force for a stretch.

passive warm-up a warm-up that raises the body temperature using outside heat sources such as blankets, and hot baths.

perceived exertion how hard a person feels he or she is working during physical activity or exercise.

percentage of body fat the percentage of your body weight that is fat.

percentage of maximum heart rate a method of calculating an exercise intensity; 60 to 90 percent of your maximum heart rate.

personal fitness prescription an exercise or physical activity plan that includes frequency, intensity, time/duration, mode, and other factors.

personal fitness the result of a way of life that includes living an active lifestyle, maintaining good or better levels of physical fitness, consuming a healthy diet, and practicing good health behaviors throughout life.

personal trainer individual who specializes in working alone with people, instructing exercise sessions, and developing personal fitness programs for a fee.

physical activity zealot; exercise zealot a person who is addicted to a physical activity or exercise program.

physical fitness a level of individual physical ability that allows a person to perform daily physical tasks effectively with enough energy reserves for recreational activities or unexpected physical challenges.

physically active lifestyle a way of living that regularly includes physical activity such as walking, climbing stairs, or participating in recreational movements.

plateau effect the leveling off of physical fitness improvement in a personal fitness program.

plyometric training exercises such as bounding and jumping movements that increase your ability to develop force more quickly in explosive movements; a kind of reflex-assisted stretching.

power the ability to move your body parts swiftly while at the same time applying the maximum force of your muscles.

predisposition susceptibility to increased health risk due to genetic makeup.

progression principle the rate at which you change the frequency, intensity, and time/duration (FIT) of your personal fitness prescription.

progressive resistance the continued, systematic increase of muscle stress through the use of weights or other forms of resistance.

pronation an inward rolling of the foot in walking or jogging.

protein a type of nutrient that is the basic building block of the body.

pyramid training a weight-training strength program for the large muscle groups that starts by using light weights during the first set and then increases the amount of weight and decreases the number of reps with each following set.

R

range of motion (ROM) varying degrees of motion allowed around a joint.

reaction time the ability to react or respond quickly to what you hear, see, or feel.

Recommended Daily Allowance (RDA) the amount of nutrients recommended daily for individuals by the U.S. Department of Agriculture.

recovery heart rate the gradual return of the heart rate to resting levels within 5 to 10 minutes of a session of normal cardiovascular physical activity or exercise.

recovery time time or rest between exercises.

reflex a response that the nerves and muscles provide to various movements.

reflex-assisted stretching exercises that challenge the reflexes to adapt so that they allow the joints to move at faster speeds and with more explosive power.

rehydration the process of replacing fluids that have been lost or excreted from the body.

relative muscular endurance how many times you can lift a given weight in relation to your body weight and gender.

relative muscular strength how much weight you can lift one time in relation to your body weight and gender.

repetition (rep) the completed execution of an exercise one time.

resting metabolic rate (RMR) the amount of calories you need and expend while sitting comfortably at rest.

risk factor a condition or trait that increases the likelihood that people will develop chronic diseases.

S

saturated fat a fat that is usually solid at room temperature, comes mainly from animal fat, and typically contains high levels of cholesterol.

sedentary lifestyle an inactive lifestyle.

set a group of consecutive reps for an exercise.

simple carbohydrate simple sugar; a carbohydrate that is absorbed quickly into the bloodstream and that provides a quick form of energy.

skeletal muscle muscle located around bones and joints that controls movement.

skill-related fitness the ability to perform successfully during games and sports; also called *performance fitness*. Skill-related fitness has six components: agility, balance, coordination, power, speed, and reaction time.

slow-twitch muscle fiber a muscle cell that is associated with a high ability to do aerobic work.

small muscle group muscles of small size or a small number of muscles being used at one time.

smooth muscle muscle located around internal organs that automatically controls many functions of the body.

somatotype the type of body you have in terms of your body composition related to heredity.

specific active warm-up a warm-up structured primarily for a specific skill or game activity.

specificity principle the principle that says improvements in your personal fitness will occur in the particular muscles that you overload during physical activity or exercise.

speed the ability to move your body or parts of your body swiftly.

split workout a weight-training workout schedule in which you do not work each muscle group at each workout session but, instead, exercise one-half of your body at each session.

spotters individuals who assist you with weight-room safety.

static body stretches stretches that are done slowly, smoothly, and in a sustained fashion.

static stretching exercises in which you assume a stretch position slowly and then hold it for several seconds (10 to 60 seconds), until you feel slight discomfort but no real pain.

stitch a sharp pain on the side or sides of the abdomen; a common form of muscle cramp most commonly caused by improperly conditioned breathing muscles.

strain a pull, tear, or rip in a muscle or tendon.

stress fracture a bone injury caused by overuse; also called *fatigue fracture.*

stress the physical and psychological responses of your body as you try to adapt to stressors.

stressor anything that requires you to adapt and cope with either positive or negative situations.

stretching cool-down a period after cardiovascular cool-down in which you perform stretching exercises for three to five minutes to minimize stiffness and muscle soreness.

stroke blockage of blood flow to the brain.

superset method a weight-training hypertrophy program that uses two different exercises that train opposing muscles, without allowing for rest between sets.

supination a movement of the foot when walking or jogging in which the foot strikes the ground on the outside of the heel.

systolic blood pressure the pressure on the arteries when the heart contracts.

T

talk test a test that uses a person's ease or difficulty in carrying on a conversation while engaged in physical activity or exercise to measure exercise intensity.

target heart rate zone the recommended intensity for aerobic conditioning; estimated to be between 60 and 90 percent of one's predicted maximum heart rate.

tendon a band of tissue that connects muscle to bone.

testosterone a male hormone that plays an important role in building muscles.

time/duration in a personal fitness prescription, the length of time you work.

trainability the rate at which a person improves personal fitness following physical activity or exercise conditioning. Trainability is determined, to a large extent, by genetic makeup.

training load the amount of weight a weight trainer lifts during his or her workout.

triglyceride a blood fat.

U

underfat carrying too little body fat.

unsaturated fat a fat that is usually liquid at room temperature, comes mainly from plant sources, and does not contain cholesterol.

V

vegetarian a person who eliminates meat, fish, and poultry (and sometimes eggs and milk products) from their diet.

vein a blood vessel that collects blood from the capillaries and carries it back to the heart.

very low density lipoprotein (VLDL) "bad cholesterol"; a type of cholesterol that is associated with higher atherosclerosis risk.

vitamin a nutrient that helps control growth and helps the body release energy to do work.

W

warm-up a variety of low-intensity activities that are designed to prepare your body for moderate to vigorous activities.

water-soluble vitamin a vitamin that is not stored in the body and needs to be replaced regularly; vitamin C and the B vitamins.

weight machines a system of cables and pulleys designed for the movement of weights as used in weight-training exercises.

weight training the use of such equipment as barbells, dumbbells, and machines to improve fitness, health, and appearance.

weight-training circuit a specific sequence of weight-training exercises.

weight-training cycle a change in your weight-training programs over a period of time.

wellness the attainment and maintenance of a moderate to high level of physical, mental, emotional, spiritual, and social health.

wraparound thumb grip (closed grip) a grip used in lifting in which the fingers and thumb go in opposite directions around the bar to help keep the bar from rolling out of the hand.

Photo Credits

2a—David Madison 2b—David Madison 2c—David Lissy 3—David Madison 5a—David Madison 5b—David Lissy 10b—David Madison 13—Phyllis Dicardi, The Picture Cube 17—Pacific Rim, Mary Van de Ven 18—Shaffer/Smith, The Picture Cube 20—David Lissy 26—David Madison 27a—Bettmann 27b—Bettmann 30a—David Lissy 30b—David Lissy 36a—David Lissy 36b—David Lissy 36c—David Lissy 37—David Lissy 39—Gaye Hilsenrath, The Picture Cube 44—David Madison 47—David Lissy 50—Frank Siteman, The Picture Cube 54—John Coletti, The Picture Cube 62—David Lissy 73—David Madison 81—David Madison 82a—Spencer Grant, The Picture Cube 82b—David Lissy 95—David Madison 104a—David Lissy 104b—David Lissy 104c—David Lissy 105—David Lissy 107—The Kobal Collection 108a—Focus on Sports 108b—David Madison 108c—David Madison 109a—David Madison 109b—David Madison 110—David Lissy 115a—David Madison 115b—David Madison 116—David Madison 117—David Lissy 120a—David Madison 120b—David Madison 148a—Bettmann 148b—Bettmann 156a—David Madison 156b—David Madison 156c—David Madison 157—David Madison 167a—Focus on Sports 167b—Focus on Sports 169a—Reproduced by permission of ICI Pharmaceuticals Division, Cheshire, England 169b—Reproduced by permission of ICI Pharmaceuticals Division, Cheshire, England 170—W. B. Spunbarg, The Picture Cube 173b—David Madison 178—David Lissy 180—David Madison 182—David Madison 188a—David Madison 188b—David Madison 189—David Madison 192—David Madison 216a—Comstock 216b—David Lissy 216c—David Madison 217—Comstock 219—David Madison 221a—Hal Gage, The Picture Cube 221b—David Madison 221c—Tom McCarthy, The Picture Cube 232—Comstock 234—Comstock 239c—David Madison 273a—U.S. Weight Lifting 273b—U.S. Weight Lifting 300a—R. Michael Stucky, Comstock 300b—David Madison 300c—David Madison 301—R. Michael Stucky, Comstock 305c—Spencor Grant, The Picture Cube 305a—Wm. Thompson, The Picture Cube 305b—Tom Hannon, The Picture Cube 306—Cleo Freelance, The Picture Cube 307—David Lissy 308—Ed Malitsky, The Picture Cube 309—David Madison 316—Kindra Clineff 330a—Cleo Photography, The Picture Cube 330b—Renee Lynn 330c—Jeff Greenberg, The Picture Cube 331—Cleo Photography, The Picture Cube 333—Larry Lawter, The Picture Cube 334—Gaye Hilsenrath, The Picture Cube 335—David Madison 336a—Eric Roth, The Picture Cube 338a—Eric Roth, The Picture Cube 338b—Henry T. Kaiser, The Picture Cube 340a—Bettmann 340b—Bettmann 341—Eric Roth 343—David Madison 344—Nancy Sheean, The Picture Cube 345—Frank Siteman, The Picture Cube 347—Eric Roth 348—Renee Lynn 349a—Ray Stanyard, Photo Edit 349b—Ray Stanyard, Photo Edit 349c—Ray Stanyard, Photo Edit 349d—Ray Stanyard, Photo Edit 349e—Ray Stanyard, Photo Edit 349f—Ray Stanyard, Photo Edit 354—David Madison 364a—Renee Lynn 364b—Shelby Thorner 364c—Comstock 365—Renee Lynn 368a—Shelby Thorner 368b—Kindra Clineff 370—McDonald Photography, The Picture Cube 373a—David Madison 373b—David Lissy 374—Sunstar, The Picture Cube 375a—David Madison 375b—David Madison 376a—David Madison 376b—Fred Scribner, The Picture Cube 378a—David Madison 378b—David Madison 379a—Kindra Clineff 379b—David Madison 379c—David Lissy 382a—Steve Woltmann 382b—Steve Woltmann 383—Tom McCarthy, The Picture Cube 384a—Bob Kraemer, The Picture Cube 384b—Frank Siteman, The Picture Cube 384c—Bob Kraemer, The Picture Cube 385—Courtesy of Terry Weyman, D.C. 388—Tim Davis